YOU & HARUJION

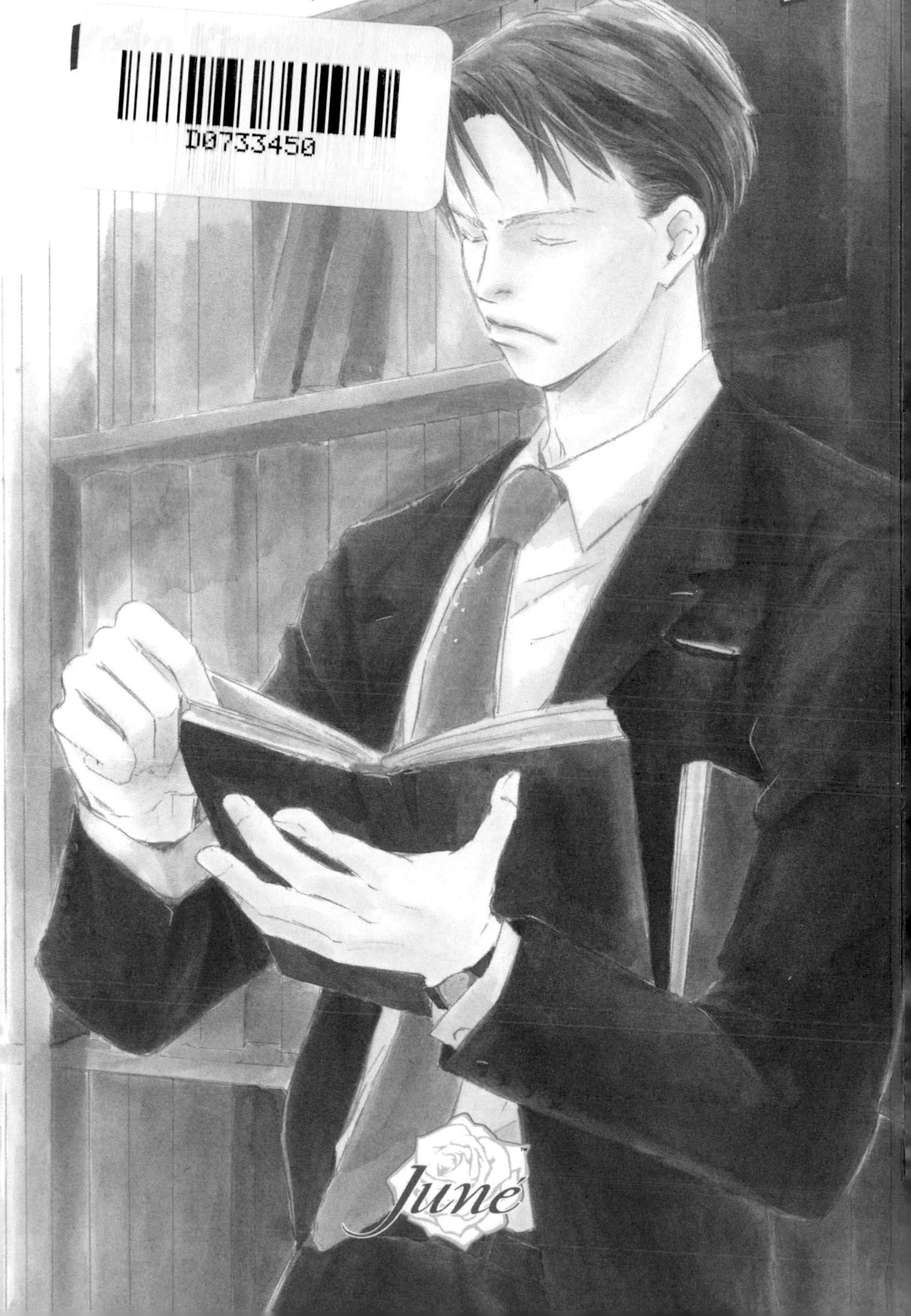
Juné

YOU & HARUJION

Translation	Duane Johnson
Lettering	Replibooks
Editing	Bambi Eloriaga
Editor in Chief	Fred Lui
Publisher	Hikaru Sasahara

English Edition Published by
DIGITAL MANGA PUBLISHING
A division of DIGITAL MANGA, Inc.
1487 W 178th Street, Suite 300
Gardena, CA 90248

www.dmpbooks.com

First Edition: March 2006
ISBN: 1-56970-925-4

1 3 5 7 9 10 8 6 4 2

Printed in China

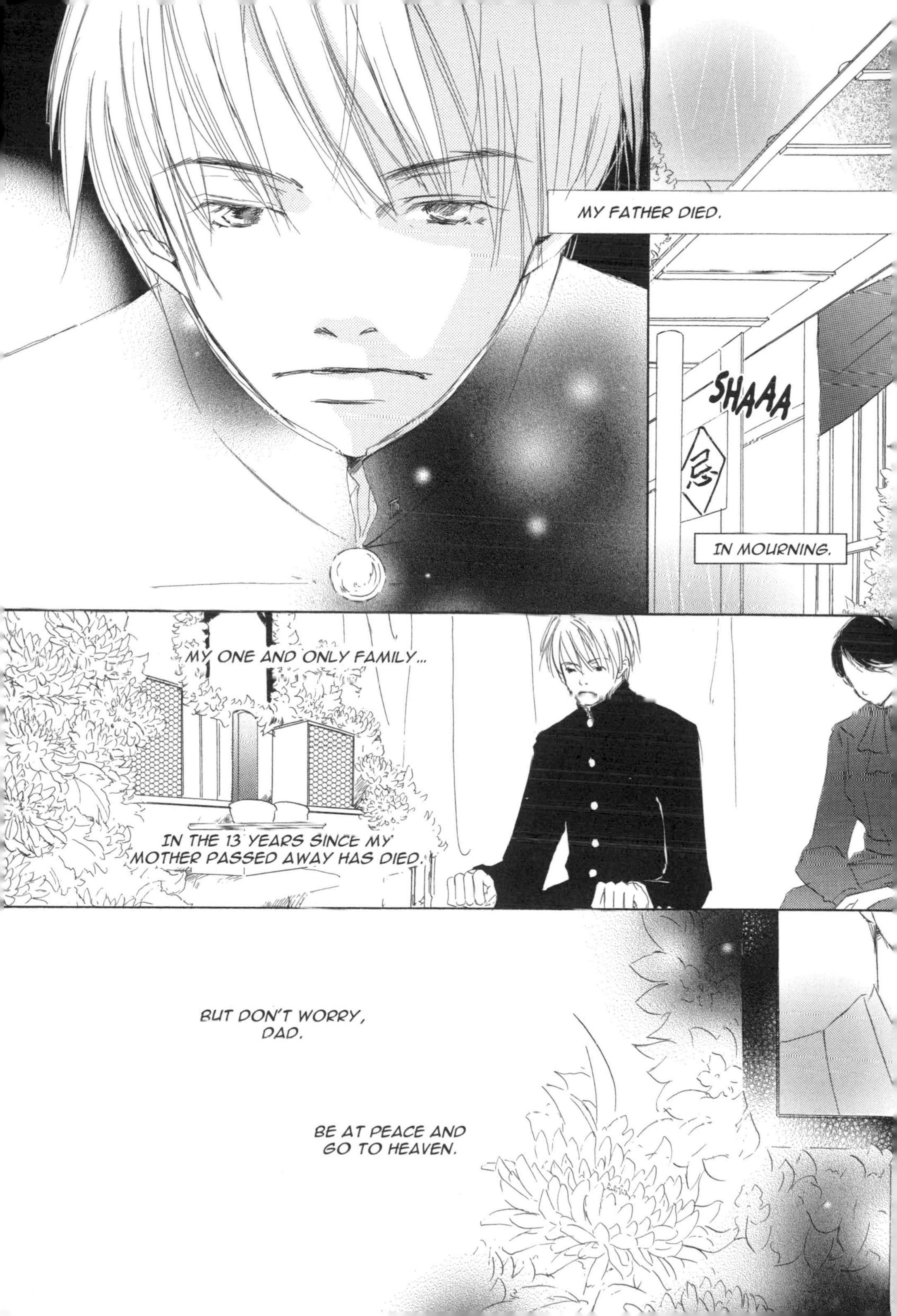
MY FATHER DIED.
SHAAA
忌
IN MOURNING.
MY ONE AND ONLY FAMILY...
IN THE 13 YEARS SINCE MY MOTHER PASSED AWAY HAS DIED.
BUT DON'T WORRY, DAD.
BE AT PEACE AND GO TO HEAVEN.

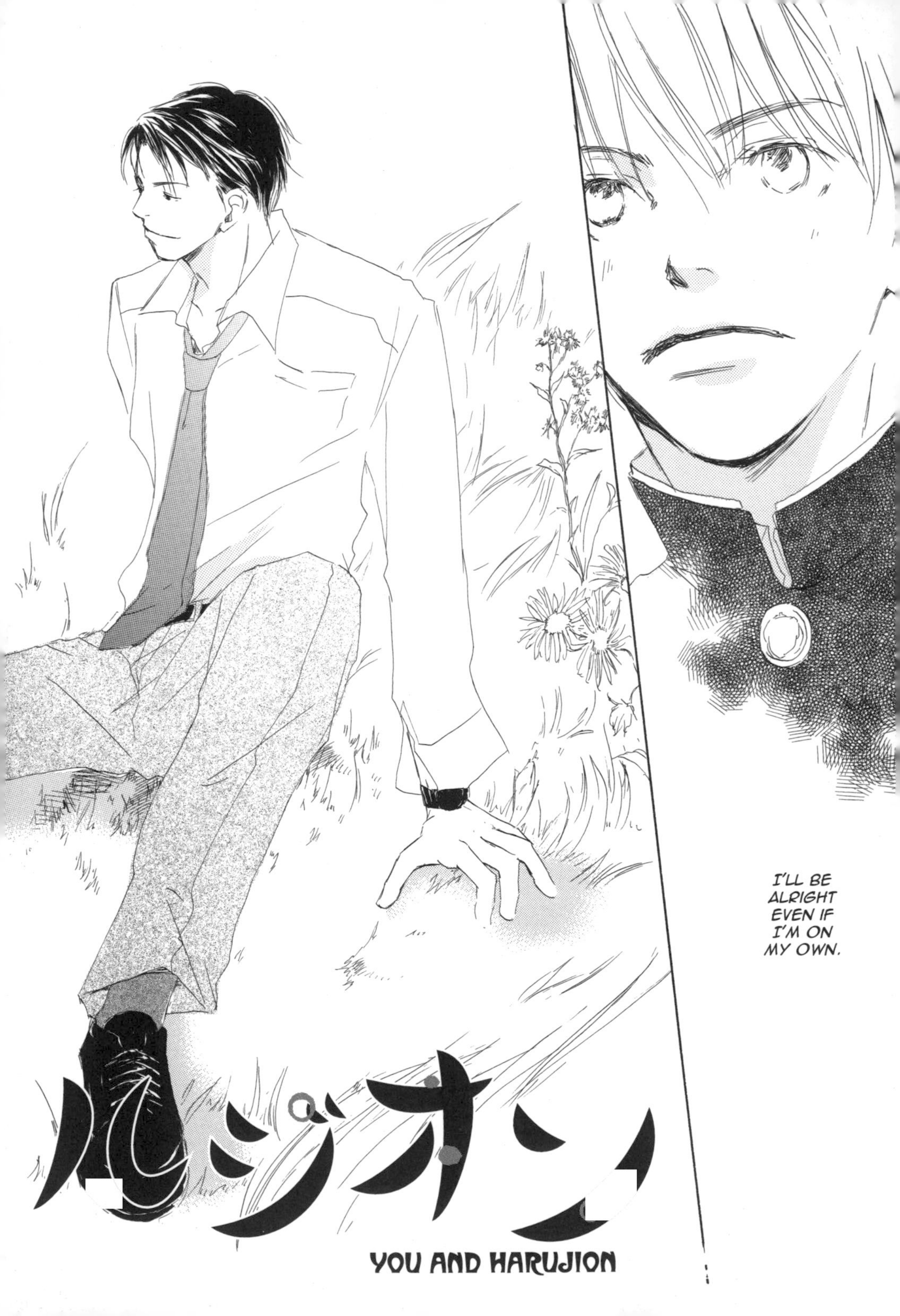
I'LL BE ALRIGHT EVEN IF I'M ON MY OWN.
YOU AND HARUJION

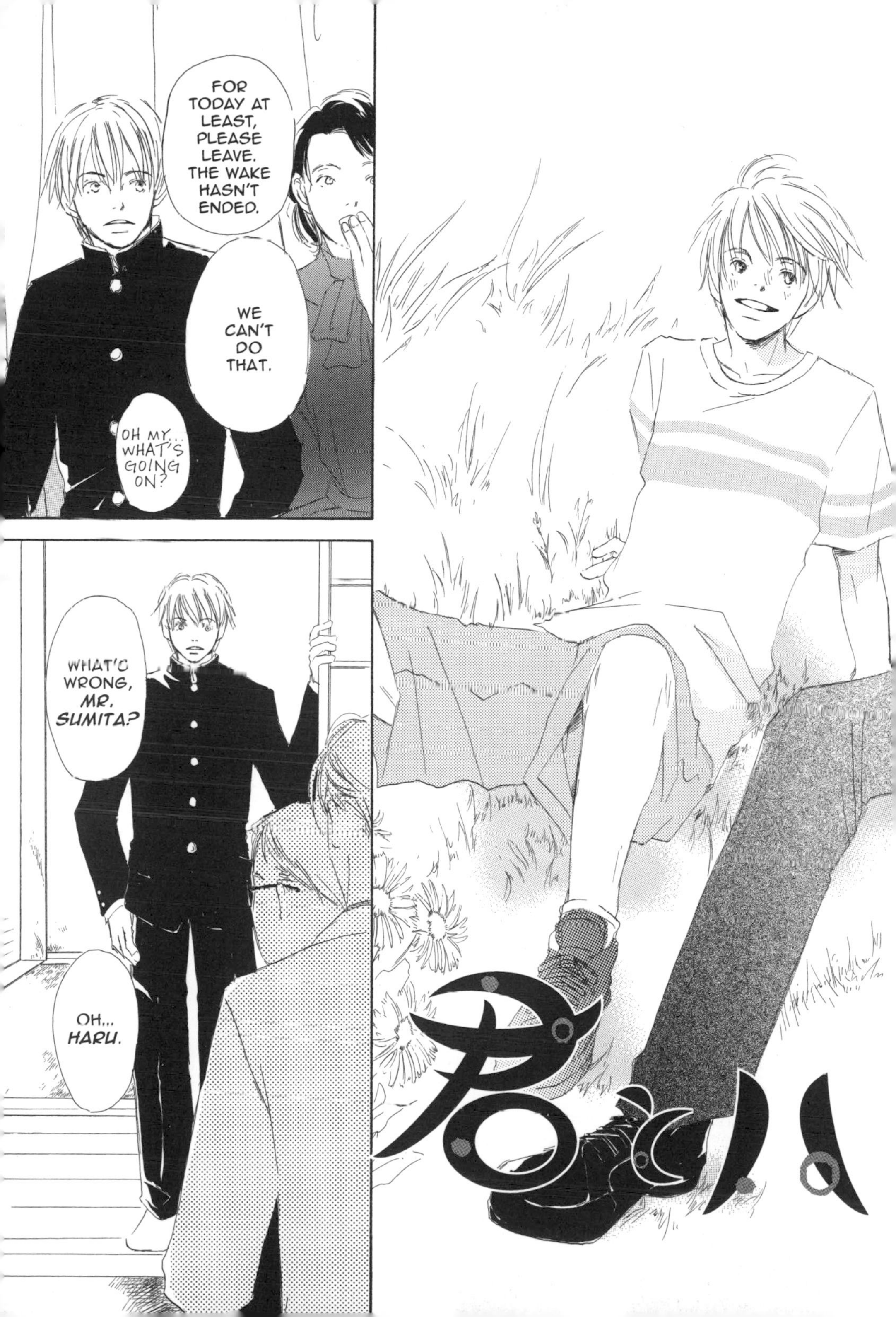
FOR TODAY AT LEAST, PLEASE LEAVE. THE WAKE HASN'T ENDED.
WE CAN'T DO THAT.
OH MY... WHAT'S GOING ON?
WHAT'S WRONG, MR. SUMITA?
OH... HARU.

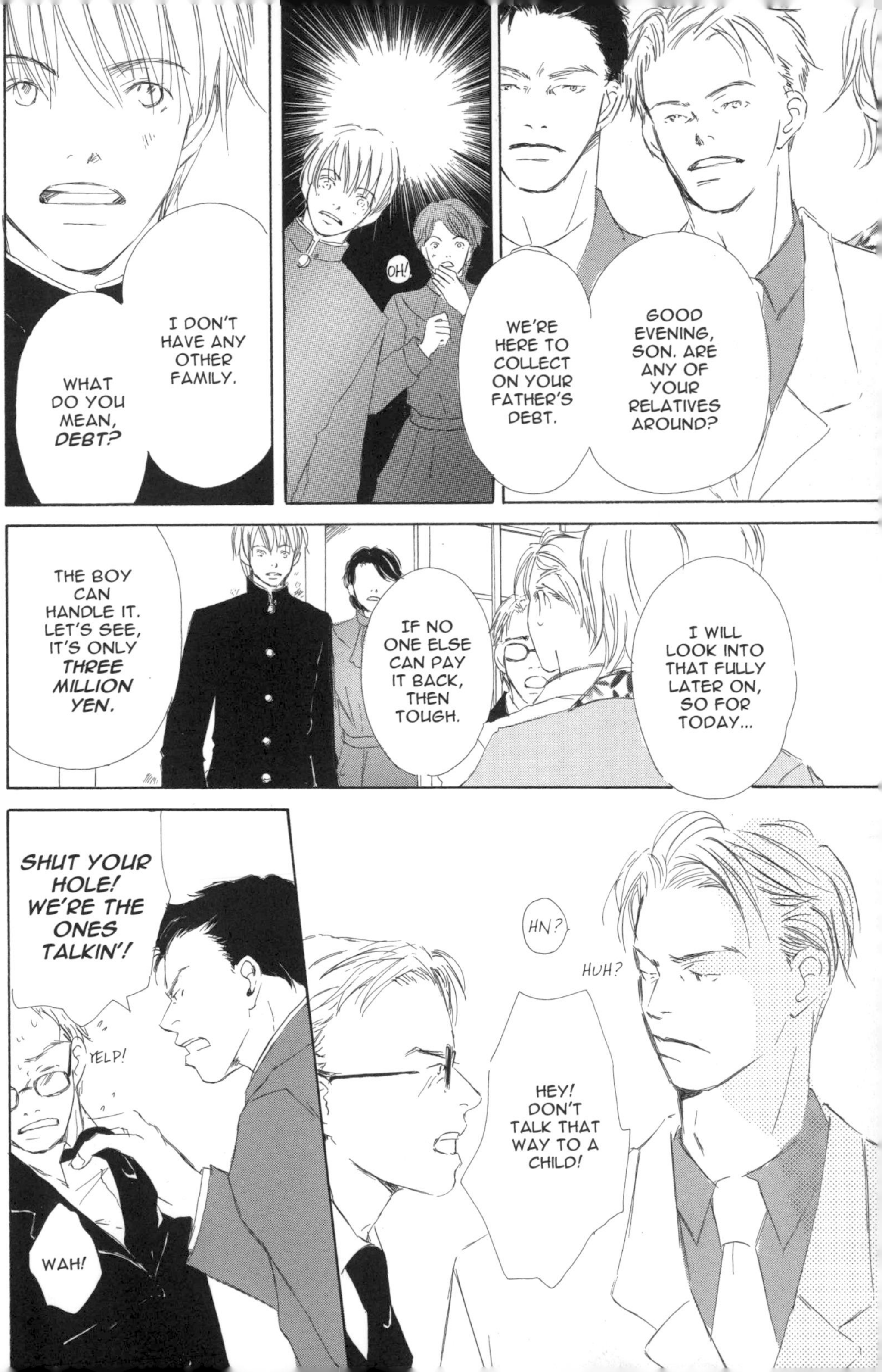
GOOD EVENING, SON. ARE ANY OF YOUR RELATIVES AROUND?
WE'RE HERE TO COLLECT ON YOUR FATHER'S DEBT.
OH!
I DON'T HAVE ANY OTHER FAMILY.
WHAT DO YOU MEAN, *DEBT?*
I WILL LOOK INTO THAT FULLY LATER ON, SO FOR TODAY...
IF NO ONE ELSE CAN PAY IT BACK, THEN TOUGH.
THE BOY CAN HANDLE IT. LET'S SEE, IT'S ONLY *THREE MILLION YEN.*
HN?
HUH?
HEY! DON'T TALK THAT WAY TO A CHILD!
SHUT YOUR HOLE! WE'RE THE ONES TALKIN'!
YELP!
WAH!

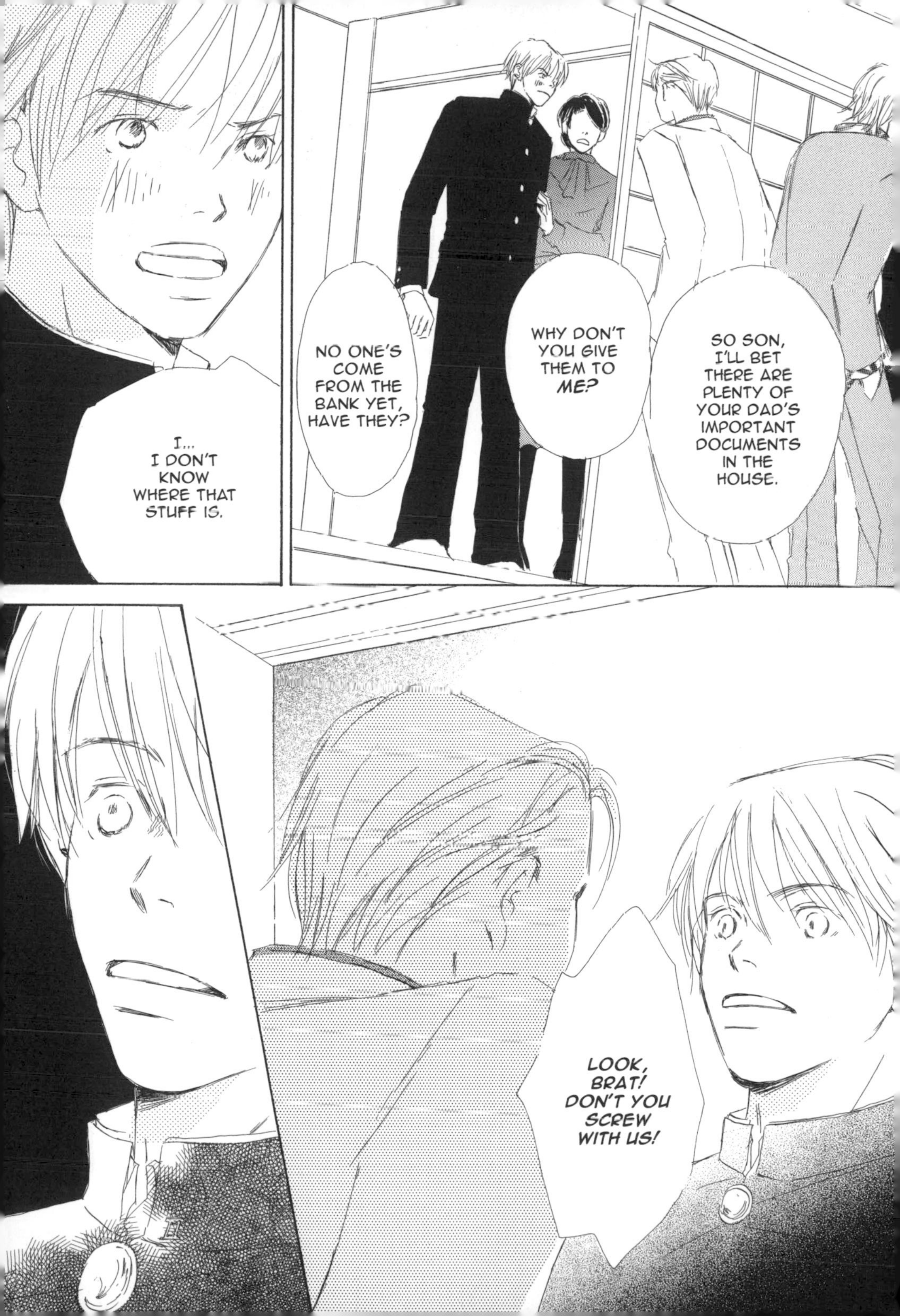
SO SON, I'LL BET THERE ARE PLENTY OF YOUR DAD'S IMPORTANT DOCUMENTS IN THE HOUSE.
WHY DON'T YOU GIVE THEM TO *ME?*
NO ONE'S COME FROM THE BANK YET, HAVE THEY?
I... I DON'T KNOW WHERE THAT STUFF IS.
LOOK, BRAT! DON'T YOU SCREW WITH US!

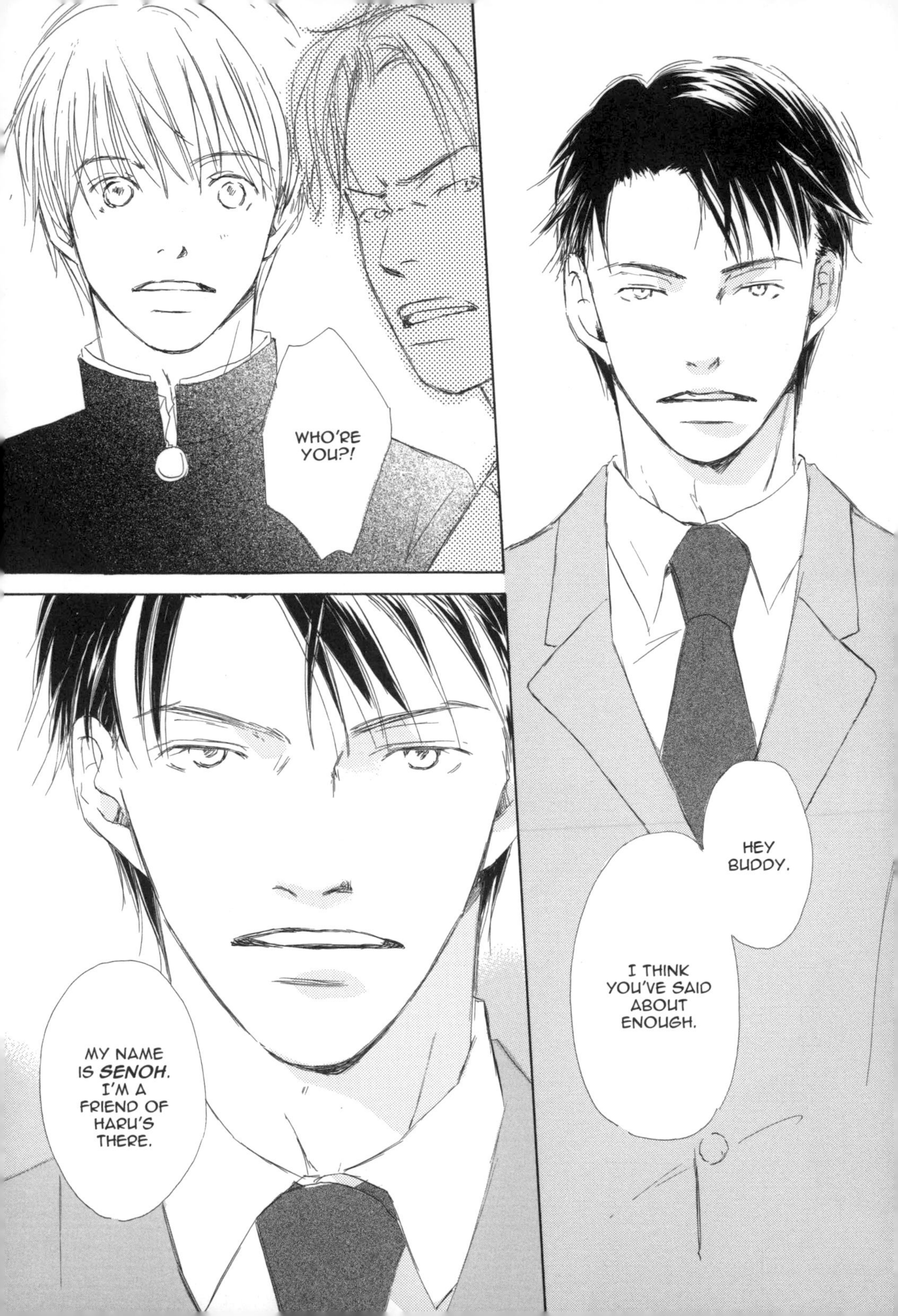
HEY BUDDY.
I THINK YOU'VE SAID ABOUT ENOUGH.
WHO'RE YOU?!
MY NAME IS *SENOH*. I'M A FRIEND OF HARU'S THERE.

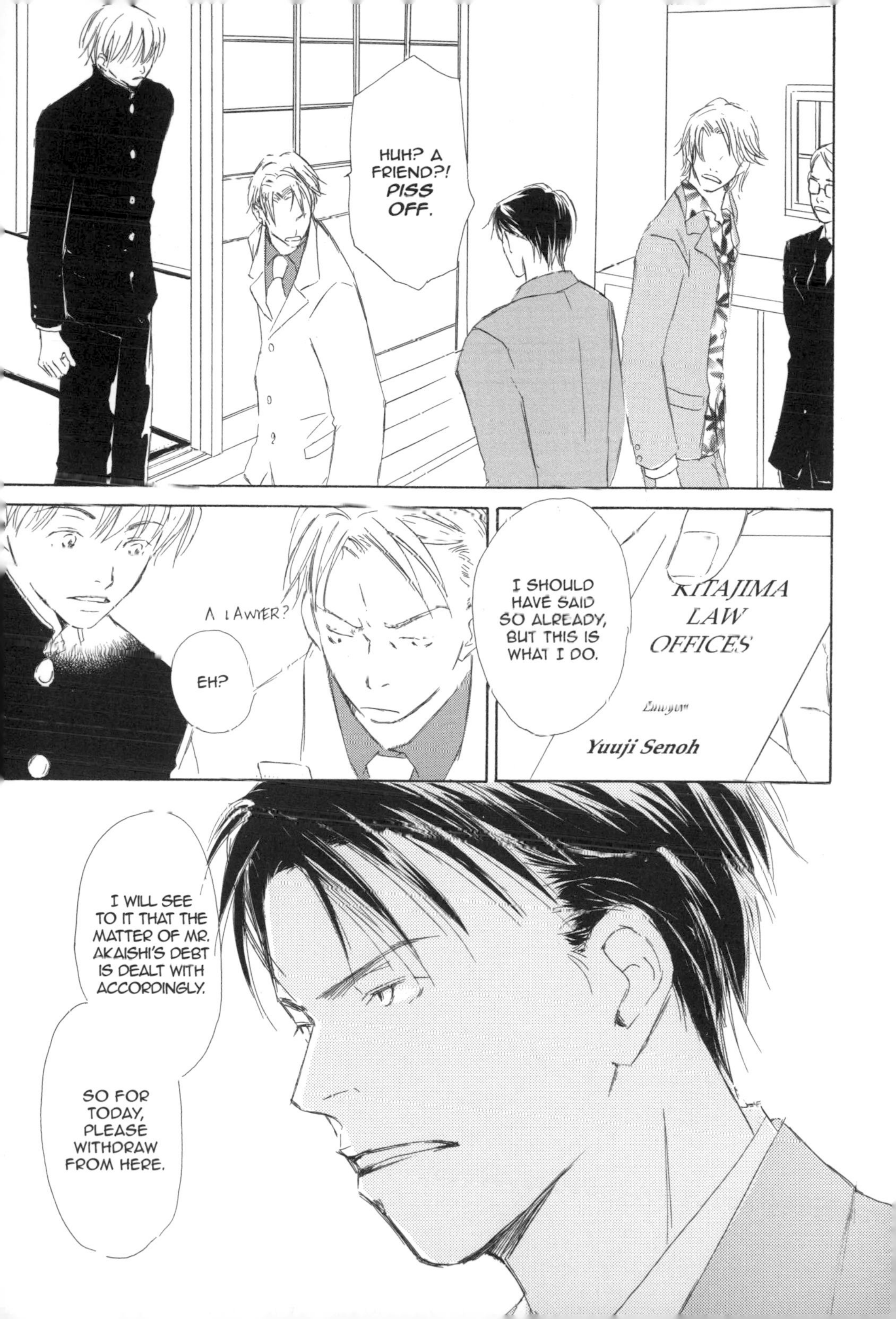
HUH? A FRIEND?! PISS OFF.
I SHOULD HAVE SAID SO ALREADY, BUT THIS IS WHAT I DO.
KITAJIMA LAW OFFICES
Yuuji Senoh
A LAWYER?
EH?
I WILL SEE TO IT THAT THE MATTER OF MR. AKAISHI'S DEBT IS DEALT WITH ACCORDINGLY.
SO FOR TODAY, PLEASE WITHDRAW FROM HERE.

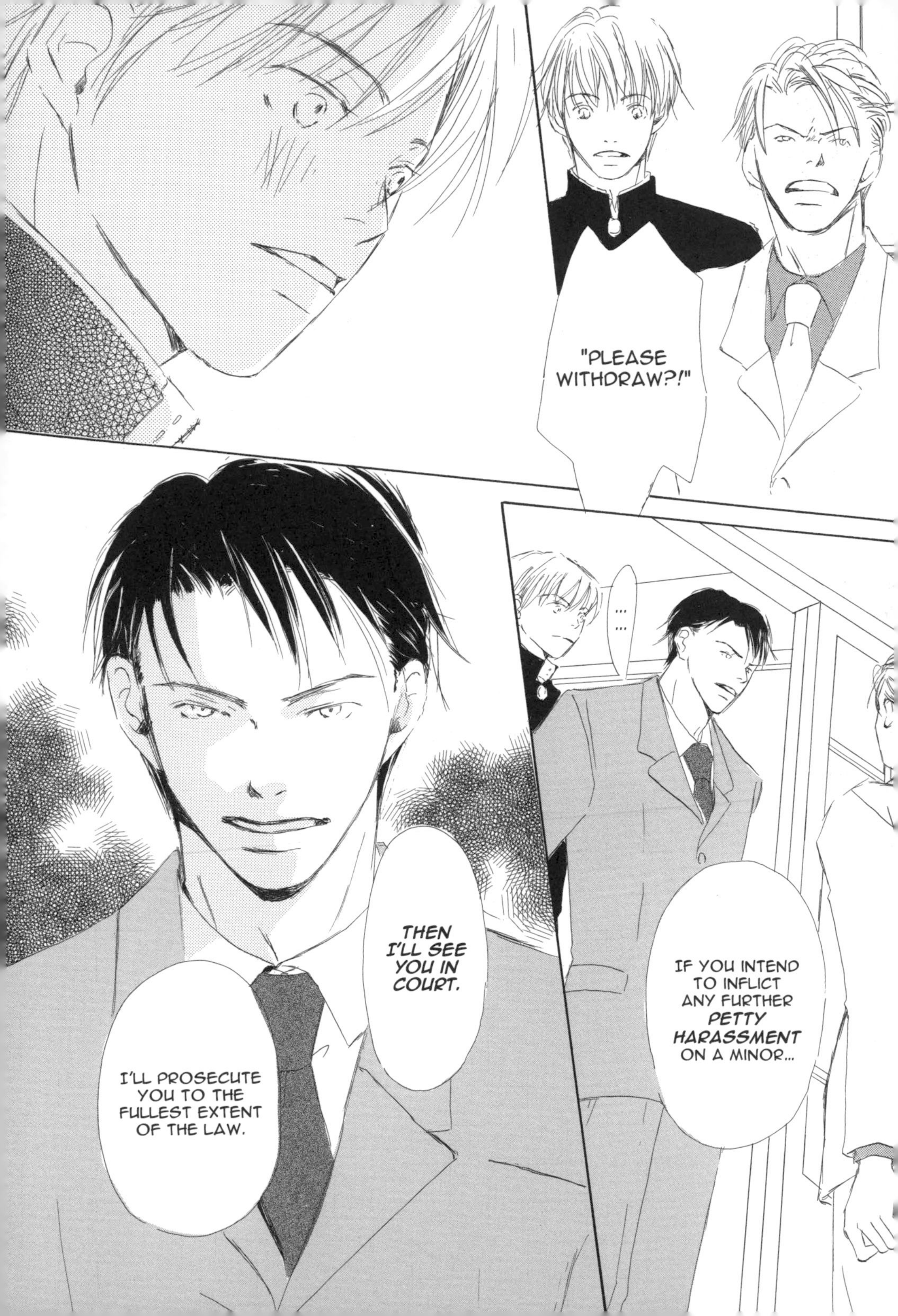
"PLEASE WITHDRAW?!"
...
...
IF YOU INTEND TO INFLICT ANY FURTHER *PETTY HARASSMENT* ON A MINOR...
THEN I'LL SEE YOU IN COURT.
I'LL PROSECUTE YOU TO THE FULLEST EXTENT OF THE LAW.

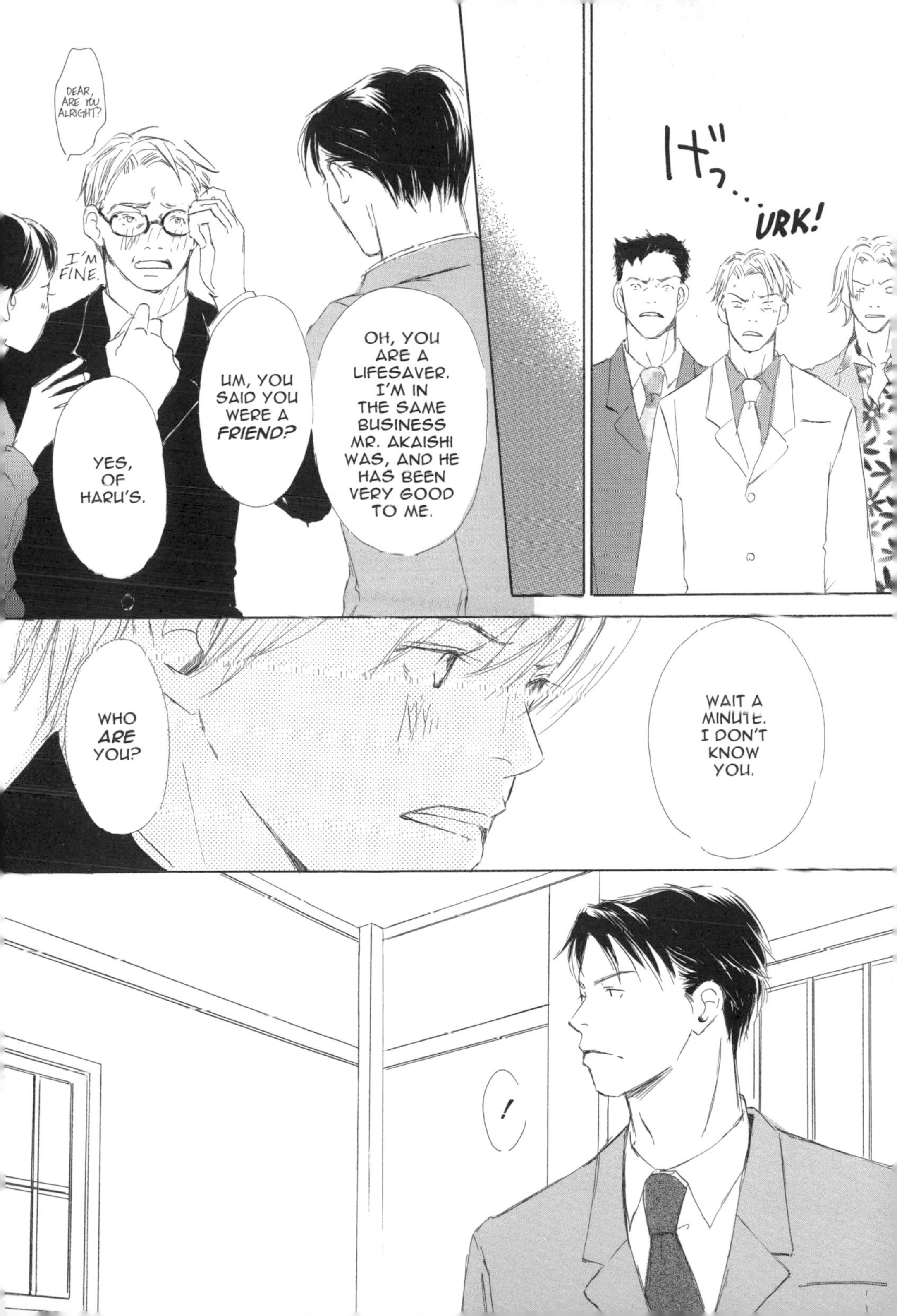
げっ…
URK!
DEAR, ARE YOU ALRIGHT?
I'M FINE.
OH, YOU ARE A LIFESAVER. I'M IN THE SAME BUSINESS MR. AKAISHI WAS, AND HE HAS BEEN VERY GOOD TO ME.
UM, YOU SAID YOU WERE A *FRIEND?*
YES, OF HARU'S.
WAIT A MINUTE. I DON'T KNOW YOU.
WHO *ARE* YOU?
!

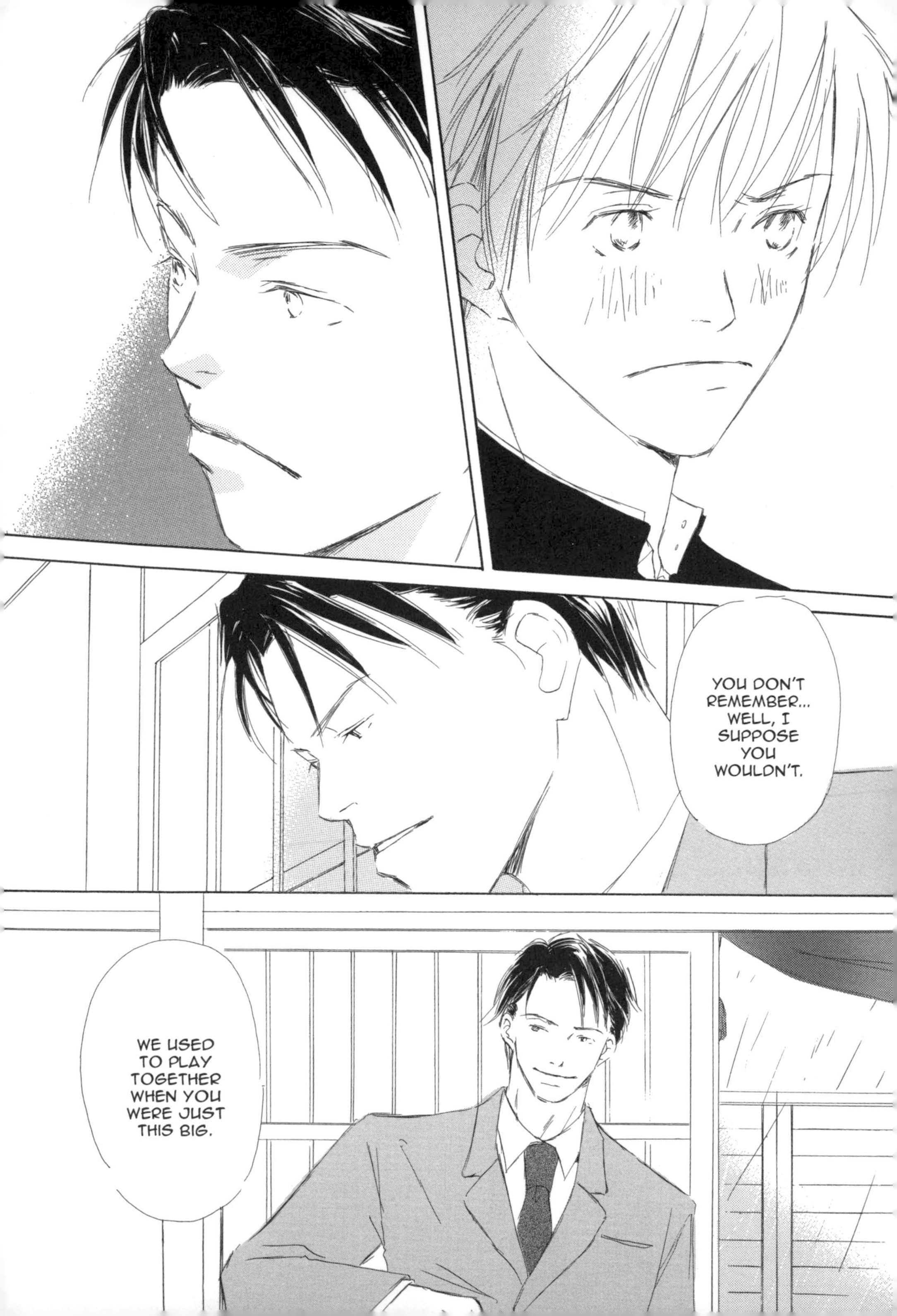
YOU DON'T REMEMBER... WELL, I SUPPOSE YOU WOULDN'T.
WE USED TO PLAY TOGETHER WHEN YOU WERE JUST THIS BIG.

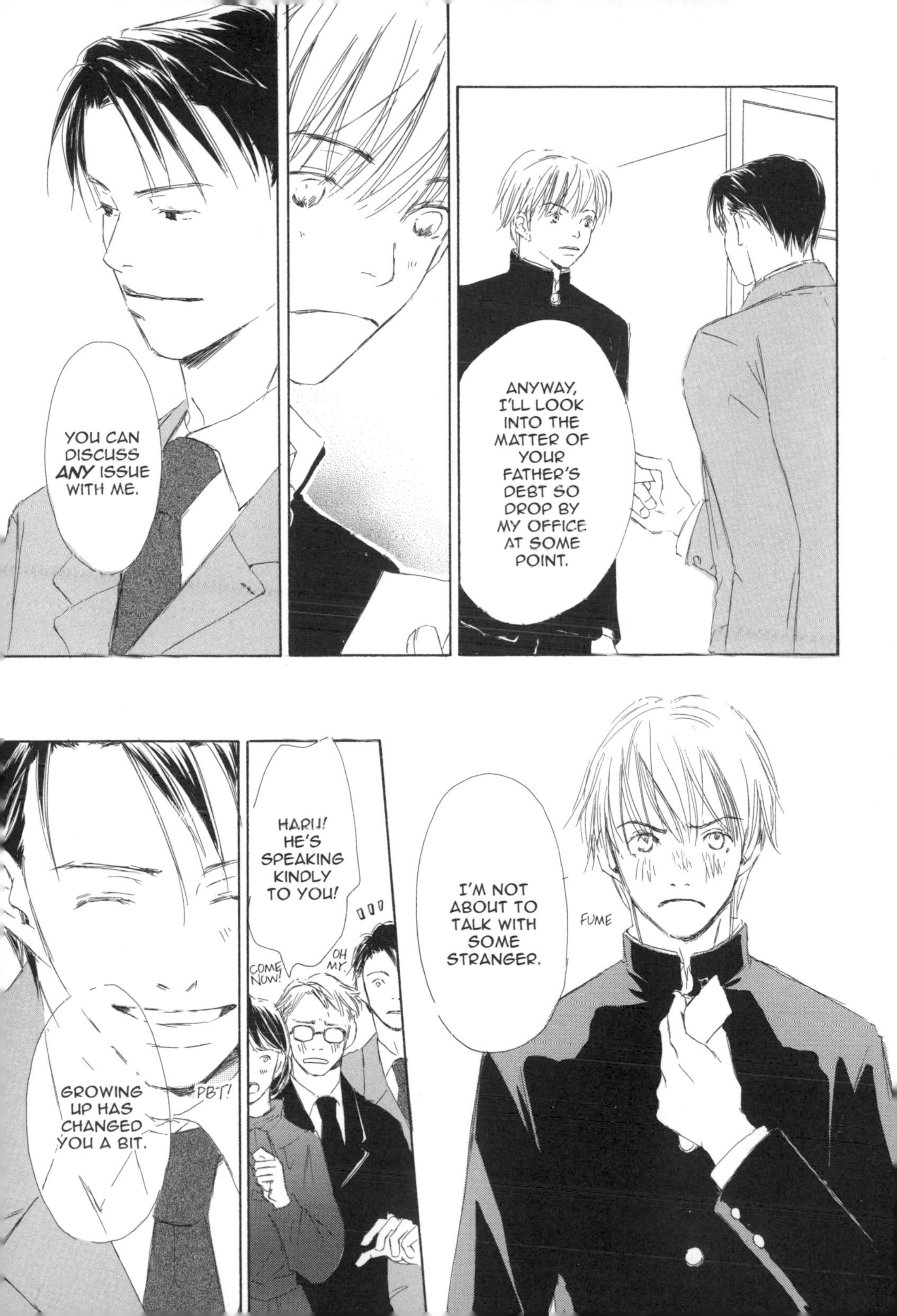
ANYWAY, I'LL LOOK INTO THE MATTER OF YOUR FATHER'S DEBT SO DROP BY MY OFFICE AT SOME POINT.
YOU CAN DISCUSS ANY ISSUE WITH ME.
I'M NOT ABOUT TO TALK WITH SOME STRANGER.
FUME
HARU! HE'S SPEAKING KINDLY TO YOU!
OH MY.
COME NOW!
GROWING UP HAS CHANGED YOU A BIT.
PBT!

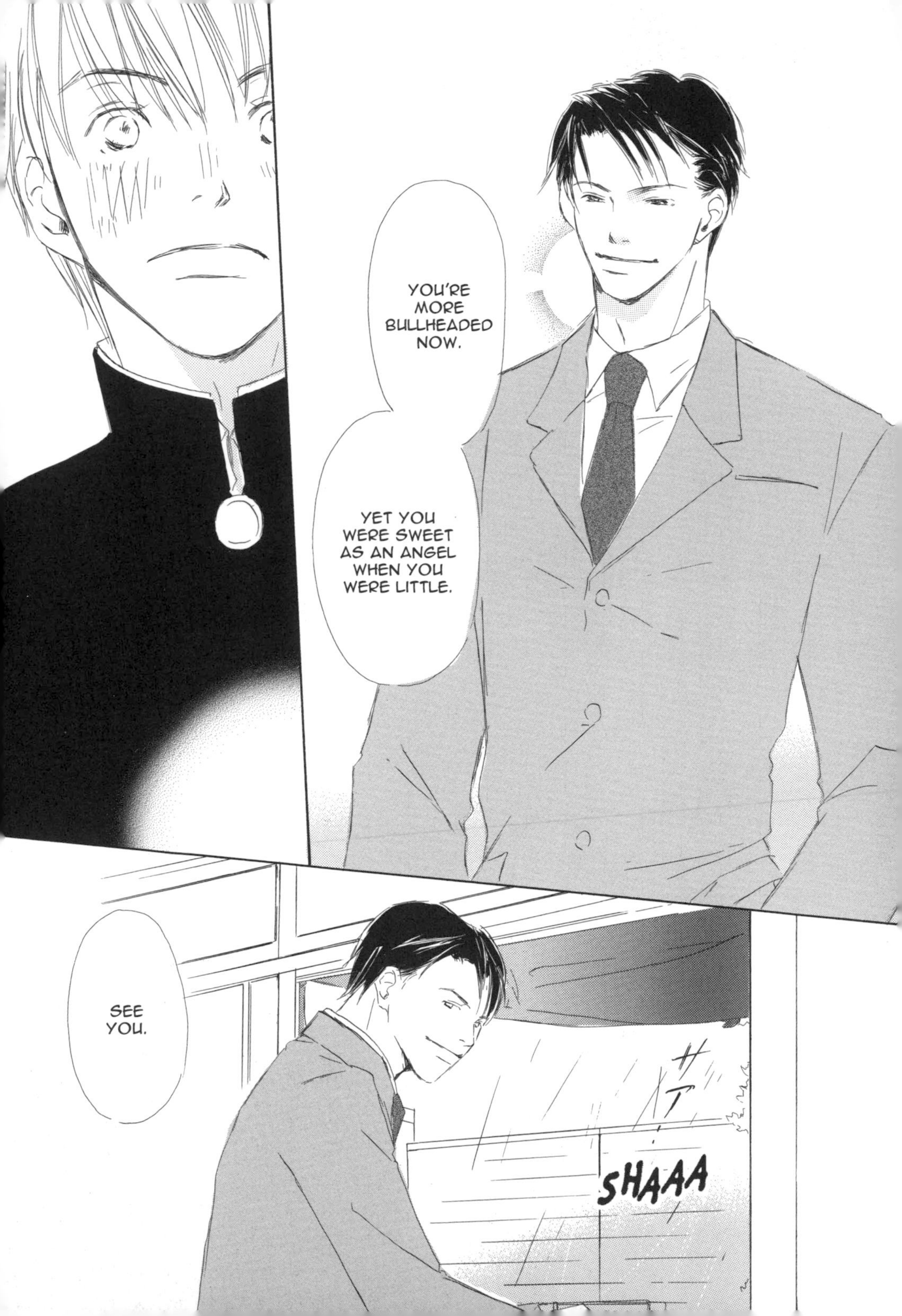
YOU'RE MORE BULLHEADED NOW.
YET YOU WERE SWEET AS AN ANGEL WHEN YOU WERE LITTLE.
SEE YOU.
SHAAA

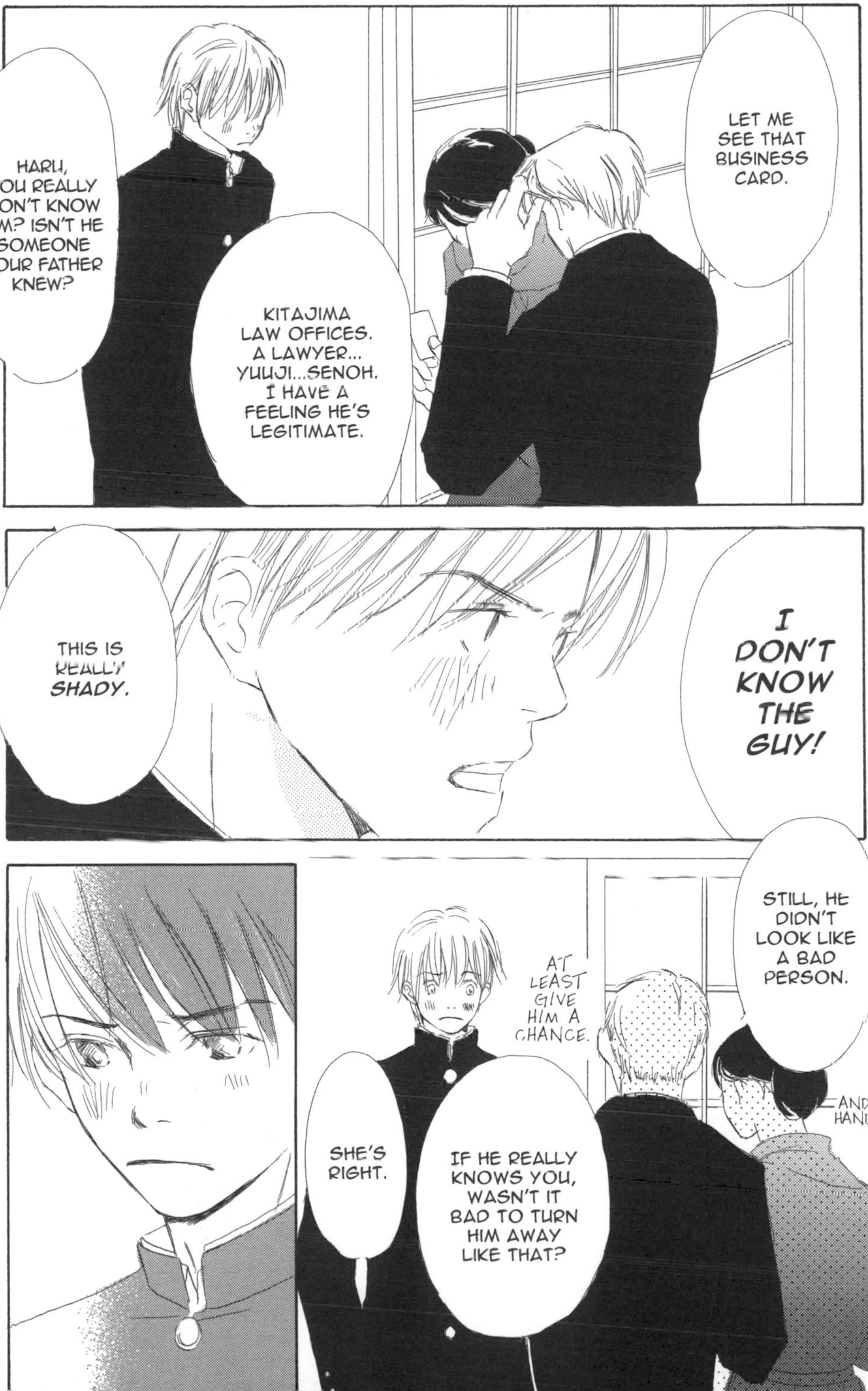
LET ME SEE THAT BUSINESS CARD.
HARU, YOU REALLY DON'T KNOW HIM? ISN'T HE SOMEONE YOUR FATHER KNEW?
KITAJIMA LAW OFFICES. A LAWYER... YUUJI...SENOH. I HAVE A FEELING HE'S LEGITIMATE.
I DON'T KNOW THE GUY!
THIS IS REALLY SHADY.
STILL, HE DIDN'T LOOK LIKE A BAD PERSON.
AT LEAST GIVE HIM A CHANCE.
AND HE'S HANDSOME.
IF HE REALLY KNOWS YOU, WASN'T IT BAD TO TURN HIM AWAY LIKE THAT?
SHE'S RIGHT.

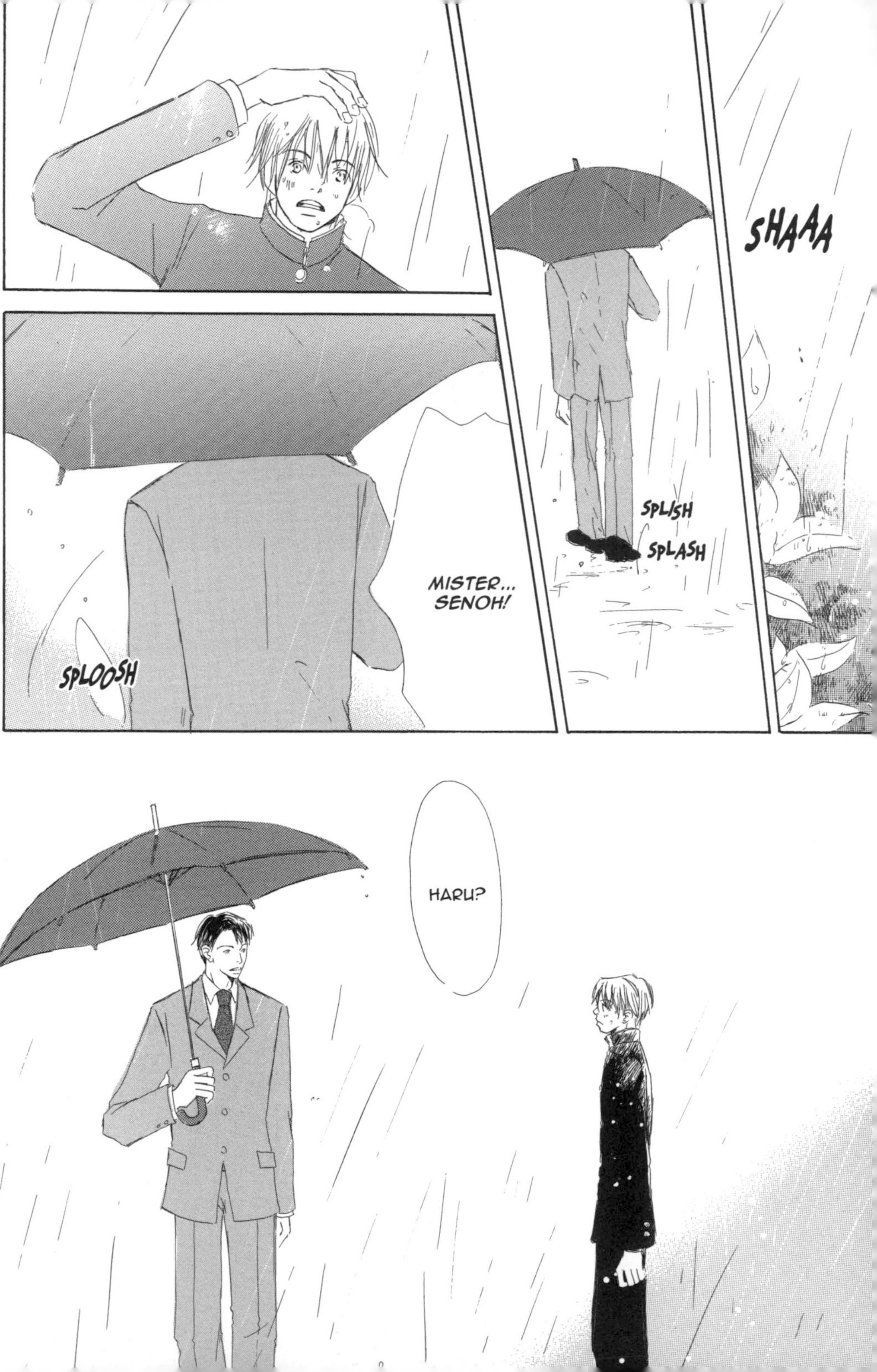
SHAAA
SPLISH
SPLASH
MISTER... SENOH!
SPLOOSH
HARU?

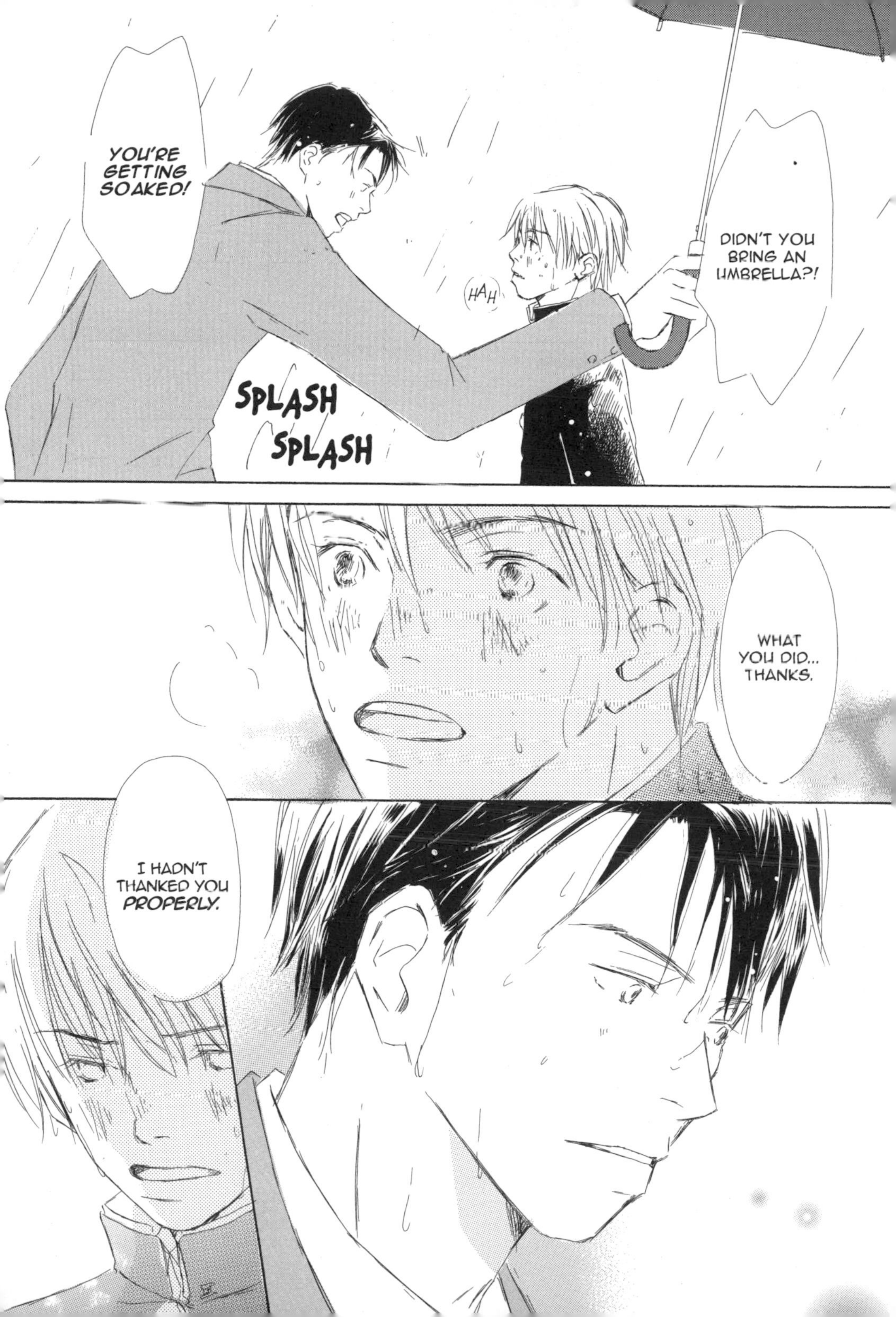
DIDN'T YOU BRING AN UMBRELLA?!
YOU'RE GETTING SOAKED!
HAH
SPLASH
SPLASH
WHAT YOU DID... THANKS.
I HADN'T THANKED YOU PROPERLY.

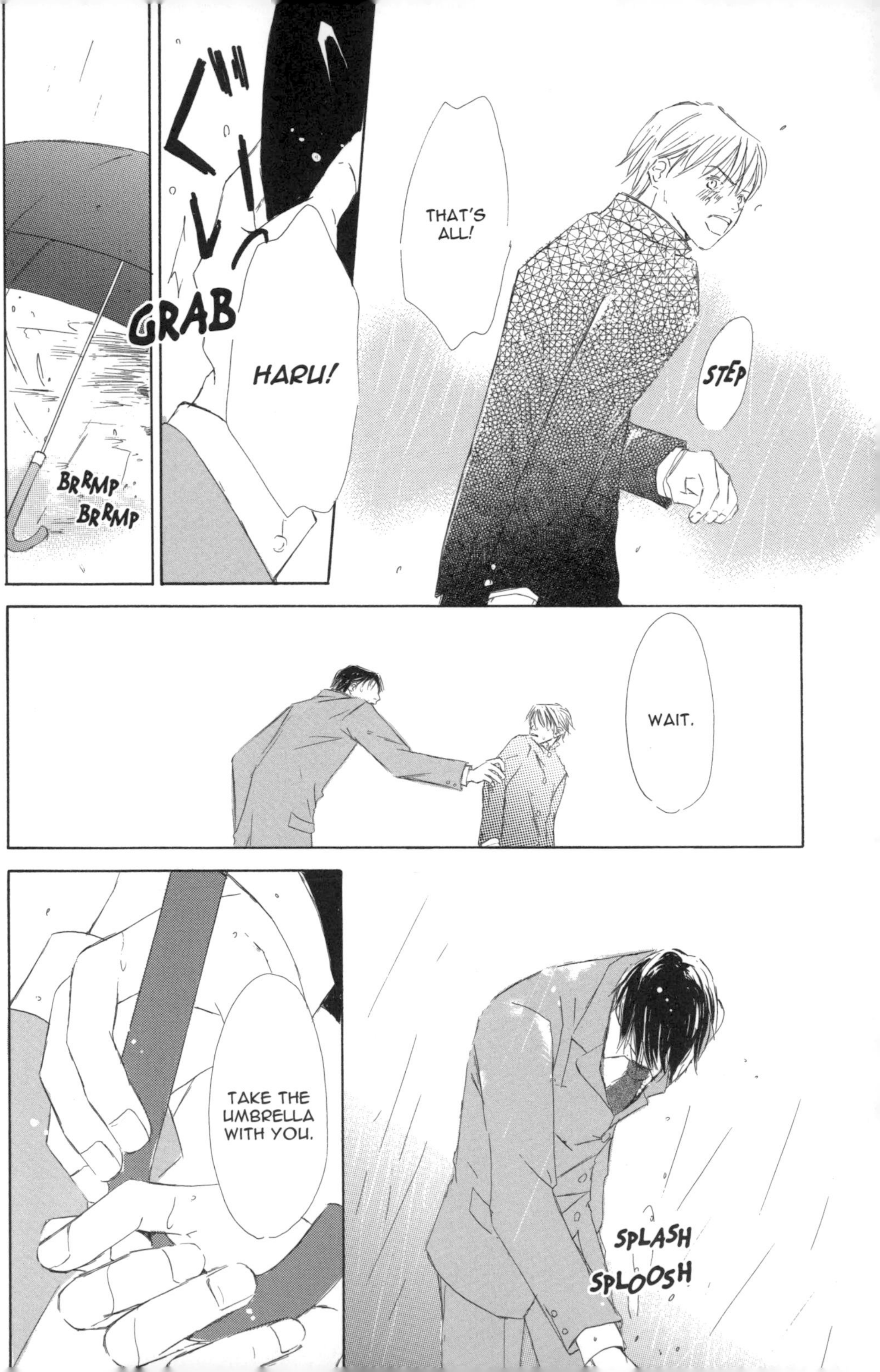
THAT'S ALL!
STEP
GRAB
HARU!
BRRMP
BRRMP
WAIT.
SPLASH
SPLOOSH
TAKE THE UMBRELLA WITH YOU.

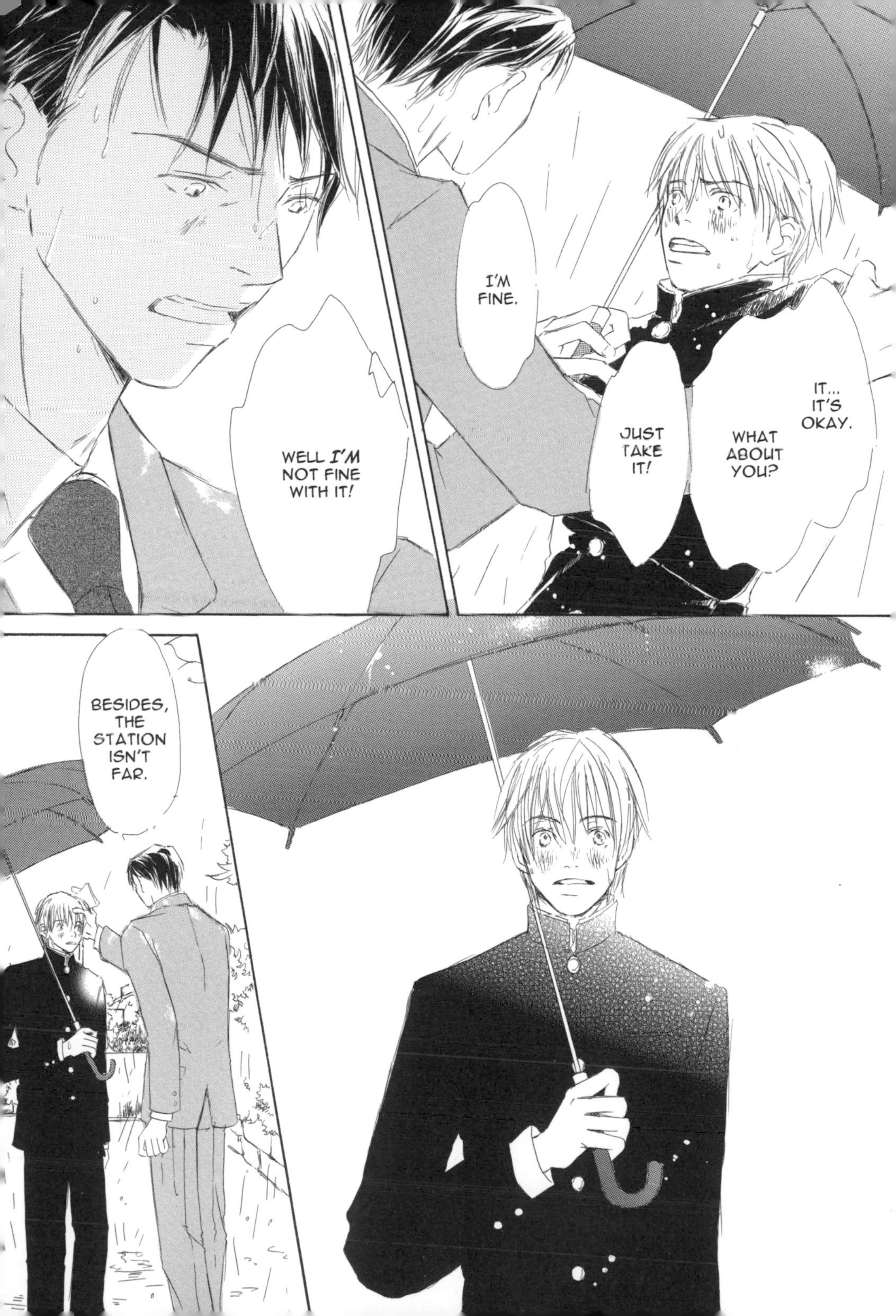
IT... IT'S OKAY.
WHAT ABOUT YOU?
I'M FINE.
JUST TAKE IT!
WELL *I'M* NOT FINE WITH IT!
BESIDES, THE STATION ISN'T FAR.

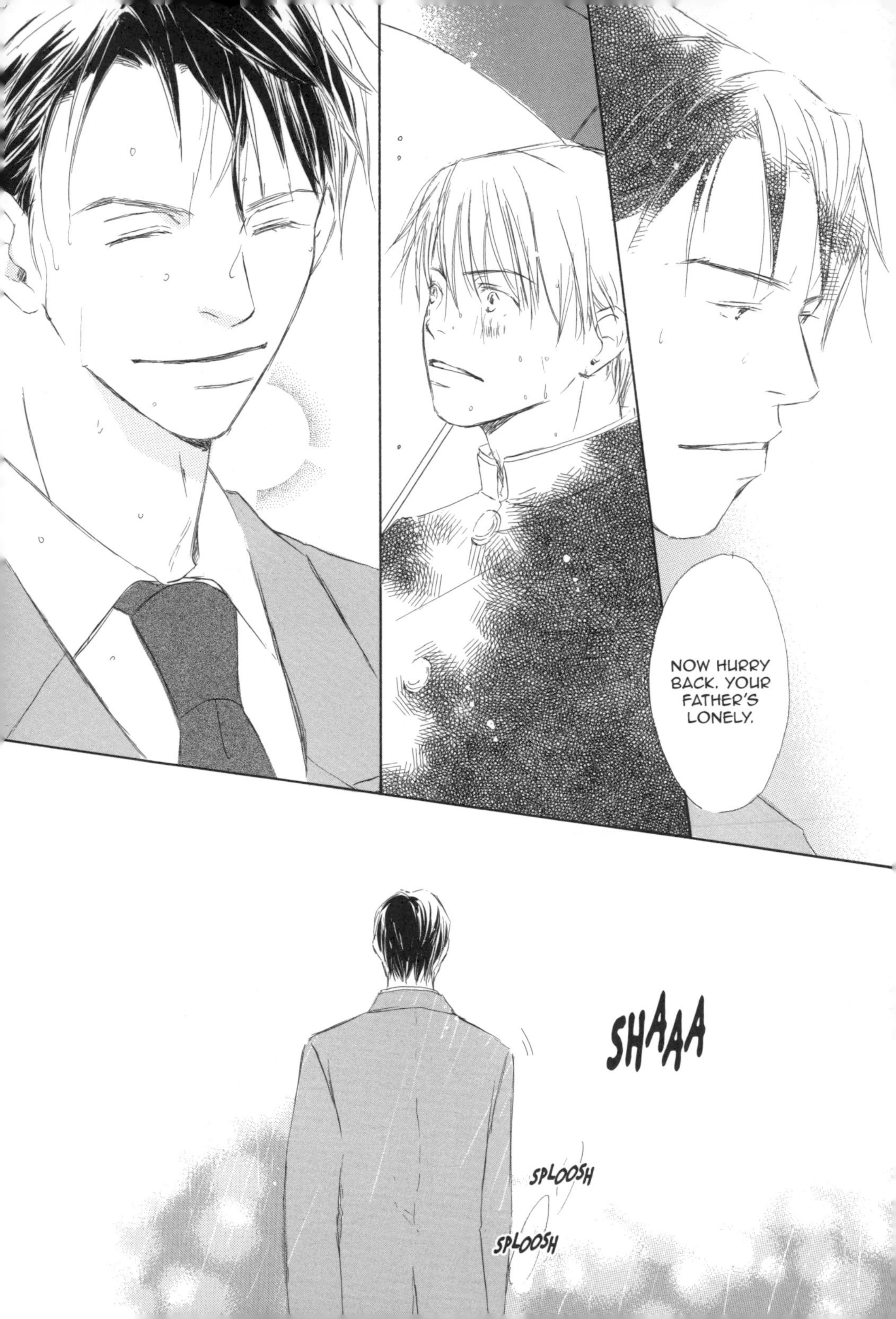
NOW HURRY BACK. YOUR FATHER'S LONELY.
SHAAA
SPLOOSH
SPLOOSH

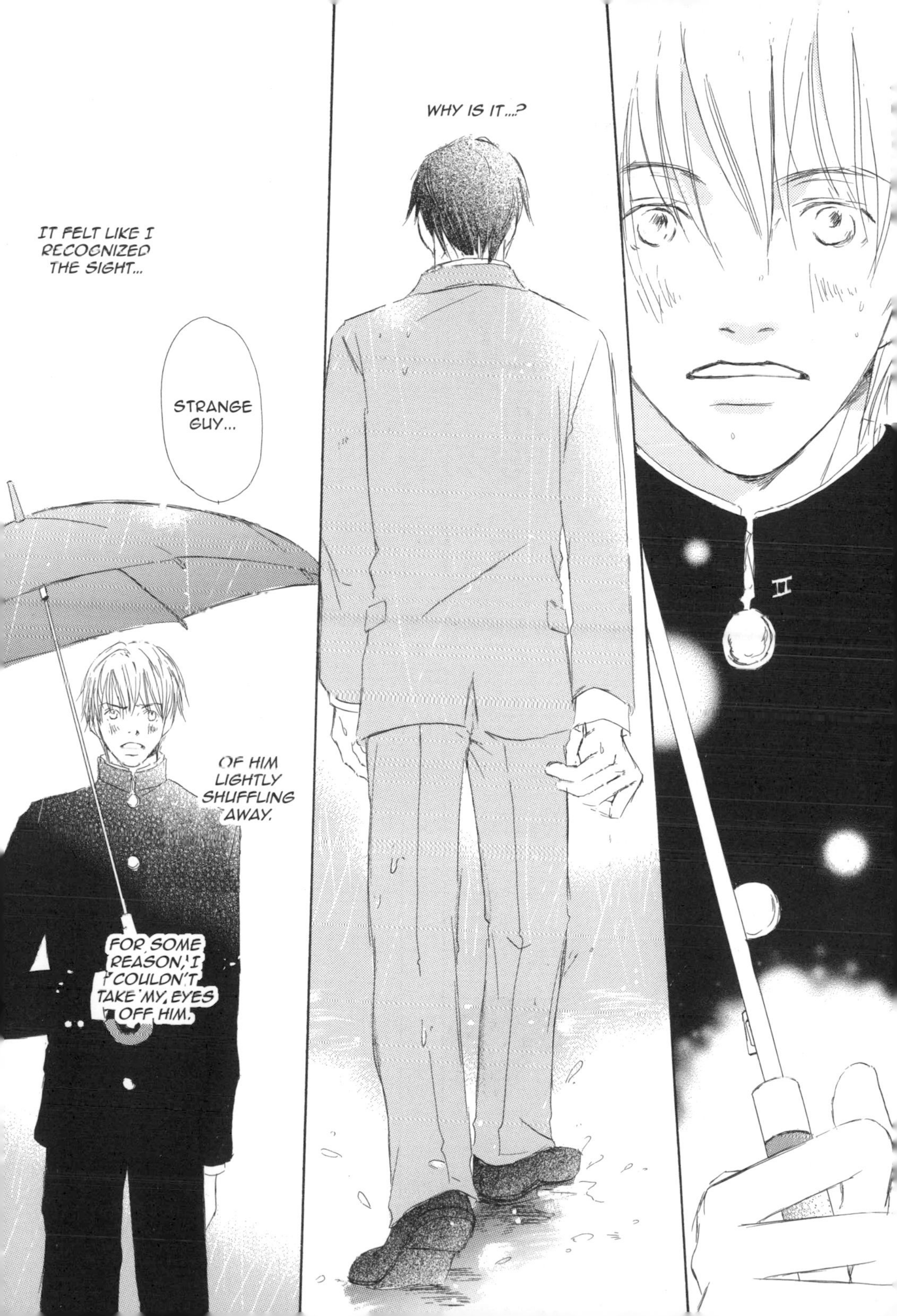
WHY IS IT...?
IT FELT LIKE I RECOGNIZED THE SIGHT...
STRANGE GUY...
OF HIM LIGHTLY SHUFFLING AWAY.
FOR SOME REASON, I COULDN'T TAKE MY EYES OFF HIM.

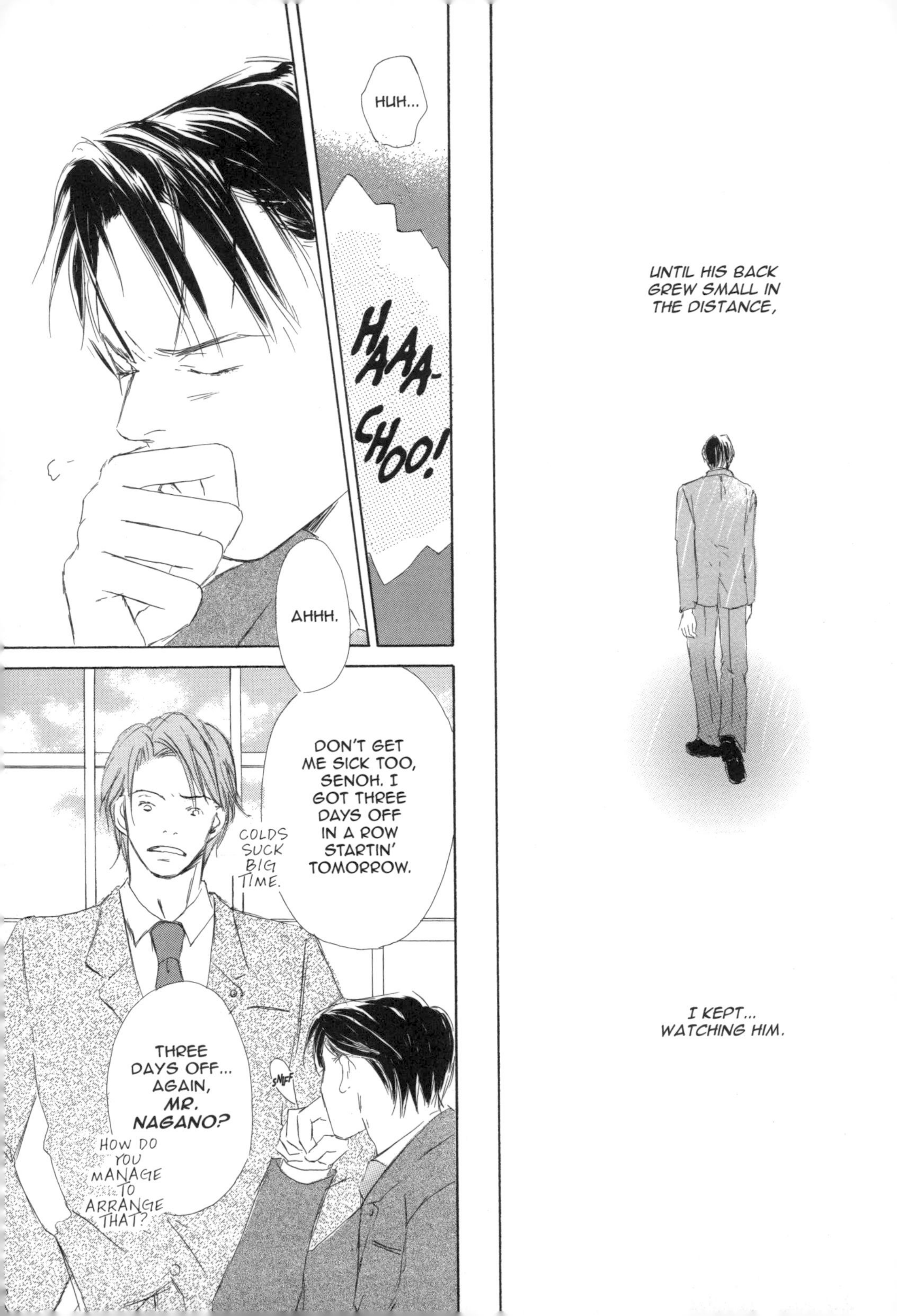
UNTIL HIS BACK GREW SMALL IN THE DISTANCE,
I KEPT... WATCHING HIM.
HUH...
HAAA-CHOO!
AHHH.
DON'T GET ME SICK TOO, SENOH. I GOT THREE DAYS OFF IN A ROW STARTIN' TOMORROW.
COLDS SUCK BIG TIME.
THREE DAYS OFF... AGAIN, MR. NAGANO?
SNIFF
HOW DO YOU MANAGE TO ARRANGE THAT?

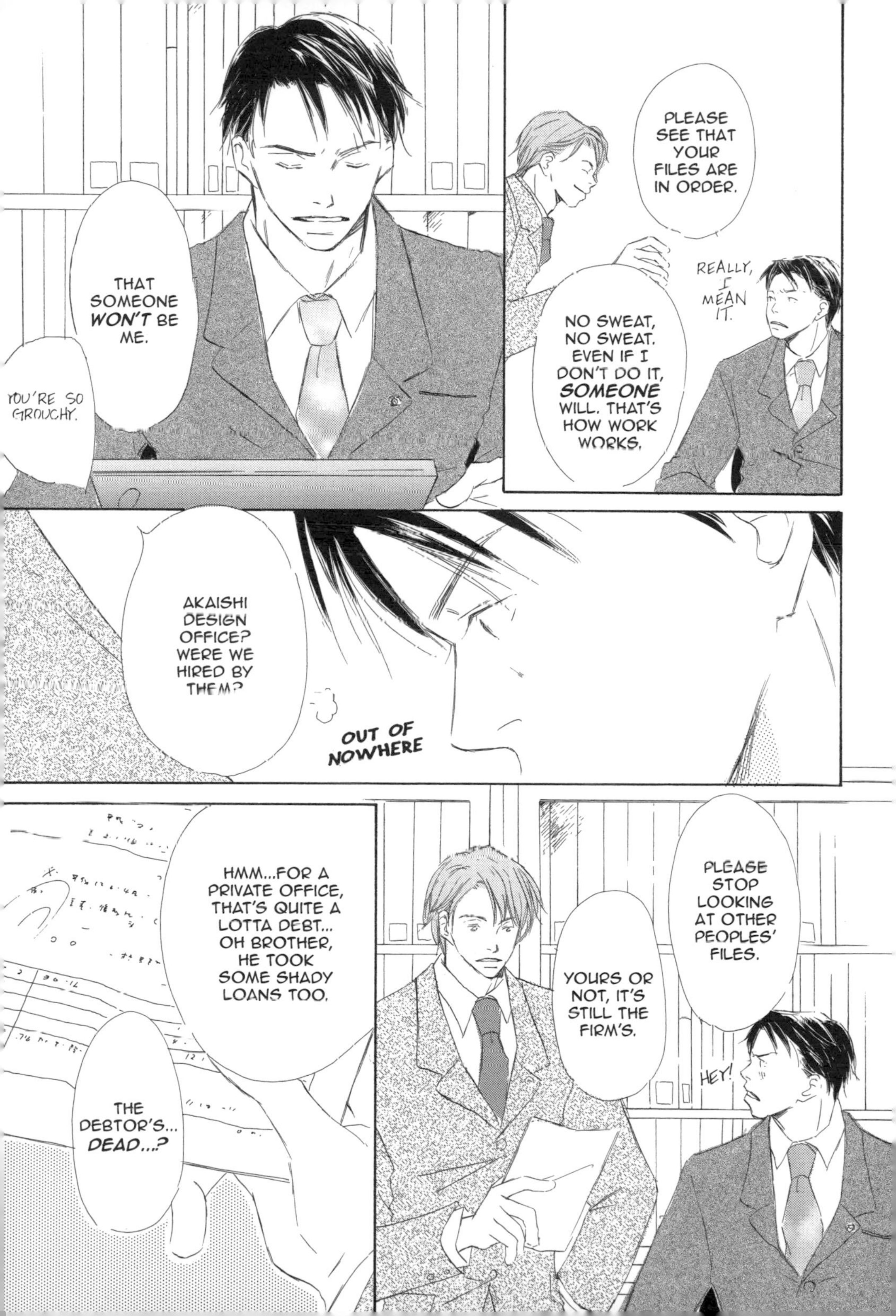
PLEASE SEE THAT YOUR FILES ARE IN ORDER.
NO SWEAT, NO SWEAT. EVEN IF I DON'T DO IT, SOMEONE WILL. THAT'S HOW WORK WORKS.
REALLY, I MEAN IT.
THAT SOMEONE WON'T BE ME.
YOU'RE SO GROUCHY.
AKAISHI DESIGN OFFICE? WERE WE HIRED BY THEM?
OUT OF NOWHERE
PLEASE STOP LOOKING AT OTHER PEOPLES' FILES.
YOURS OR NOT, IT'S STILL THE FIRM'S.
HEY!
HMM...FOR A PRIVATE OFFICE, THAT'S QUITE A LOTTA DEBT... OH BROTHER, HE TOOK SOME SHADY LOANS TOO.
THE DEBTOR'S... DEAD...?

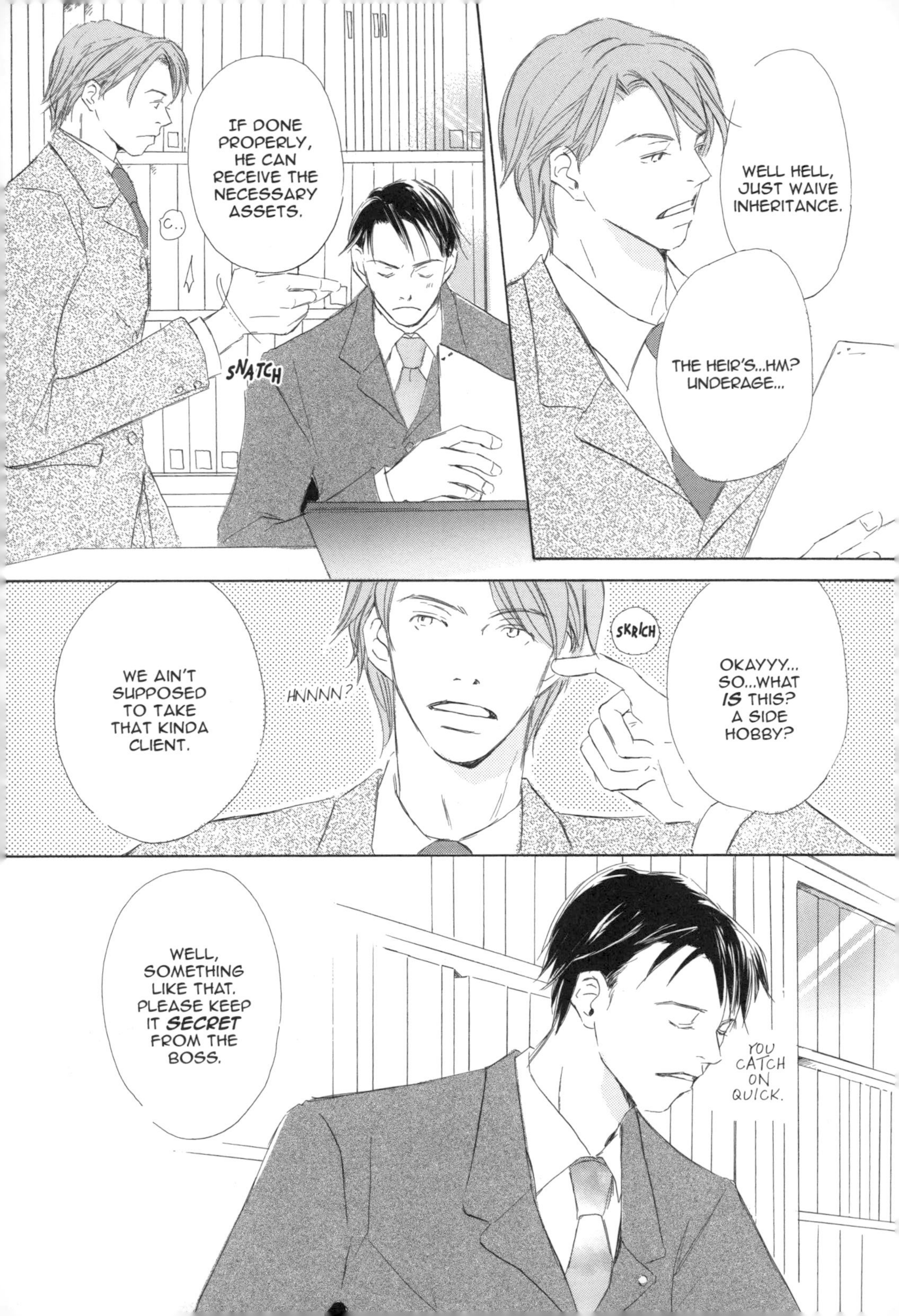
C...
IF DONE PROPERLY, HE CAN RECEIVE THE NECESSARY ASSETS.
SNATCH
...
THE HEIR'S...HM? UNDERAGE...
WELL HELL, JUST WAIVE INHERITANCE.
WE AIN'T SUPPOSED TO TAKE THAT KINDA CLIENT.
HNNNN?
SKRICH
OKAYYY... SO...WHAT IS THIS? A SIDE HOBBY?
WELL, SOMETHING LIKE THAT. PLEASE KEEP IT SECRET FROM THE BOSS.
YOU CATCH ON QUICK.

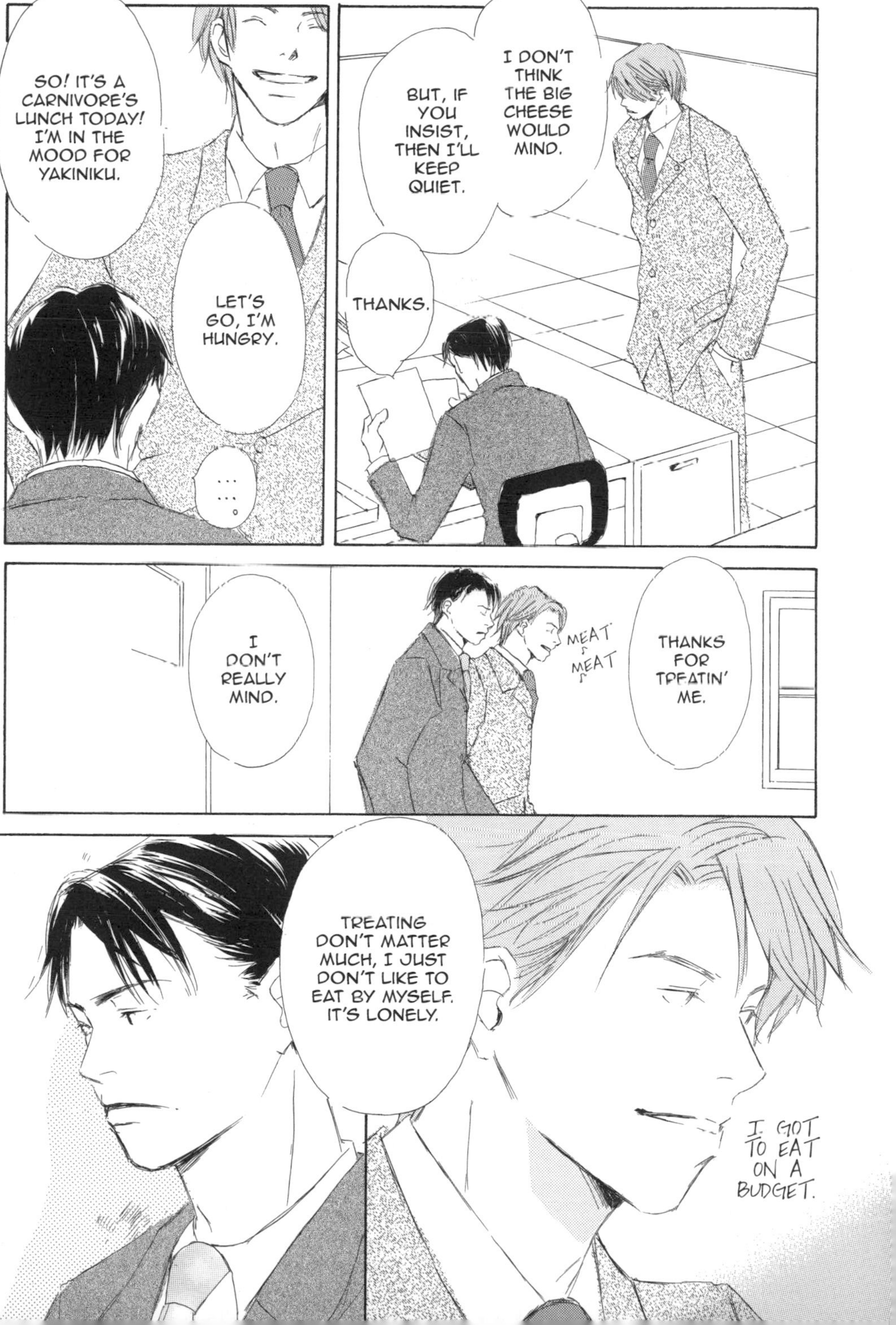
I DON'T THINK THE BIG CHEESE WOULD MIND.
BUT, IF YOU INSIST, THEN I'LL KEEP QUIET.
THANKS.
SO! IT'S A CARNIVORE'S LUNCH TODAY! I'M IN THE MOOD FOR YAKINIKU.
LET'S GO, I'M HUNGRY.
......
THANKS FOR TREATIN' ME.
MEAT MEAT
I DON'T REALLY MIND.
TREATING DON'T MATTER MUCH, I JUST DON'T LIKE TO EAT BY MYSELF. IT'S LONELY.
I GOT TO EAT ON A BUDGET.

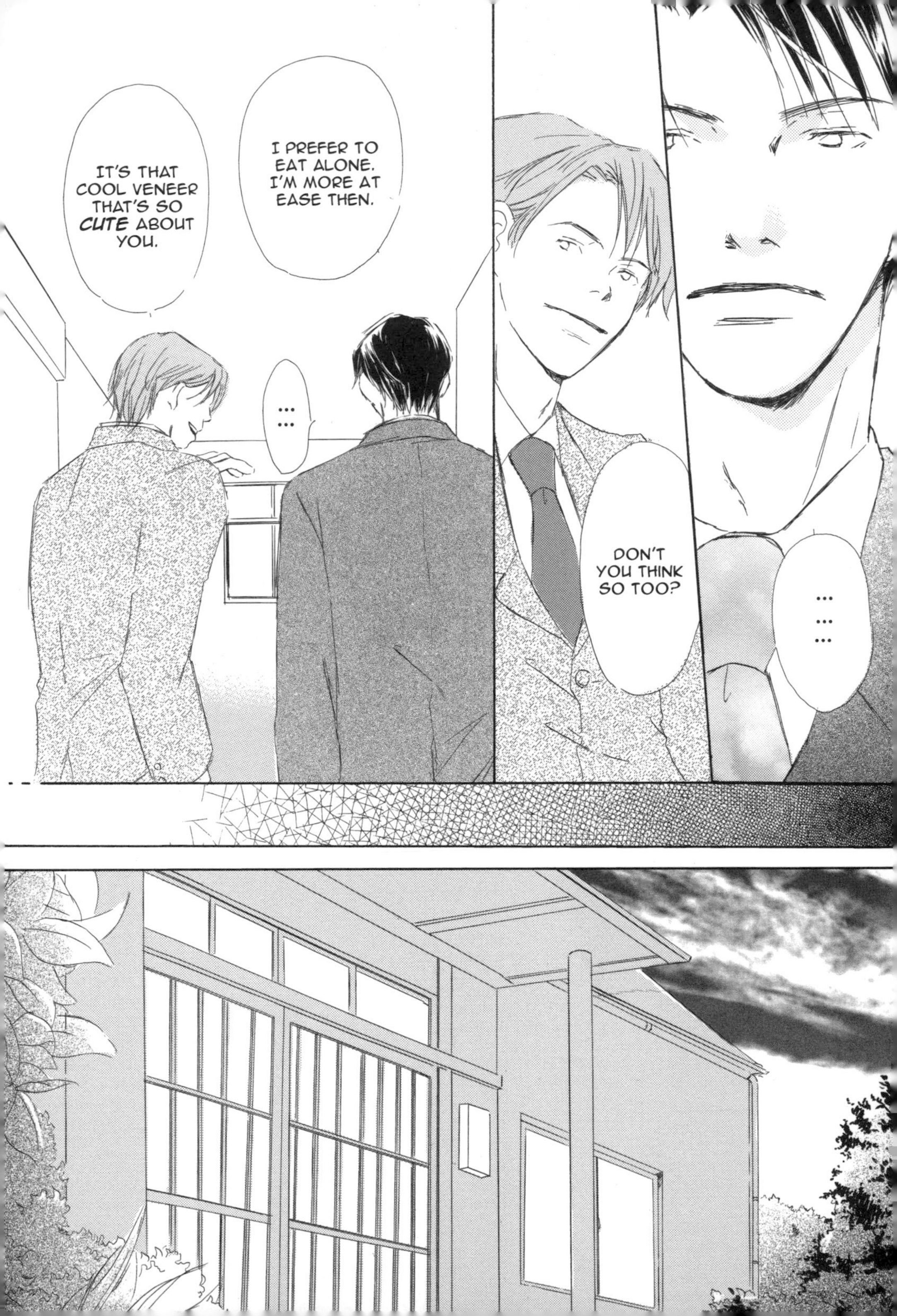
I PREFER TO EAT ALONE. I'M MORE AT EASE THEN.
IT'S THAT COOL VENEER THAT'S SO *CUTE* ABOUT YOU.
......
DON'T YOU THINK SO TOO?
....

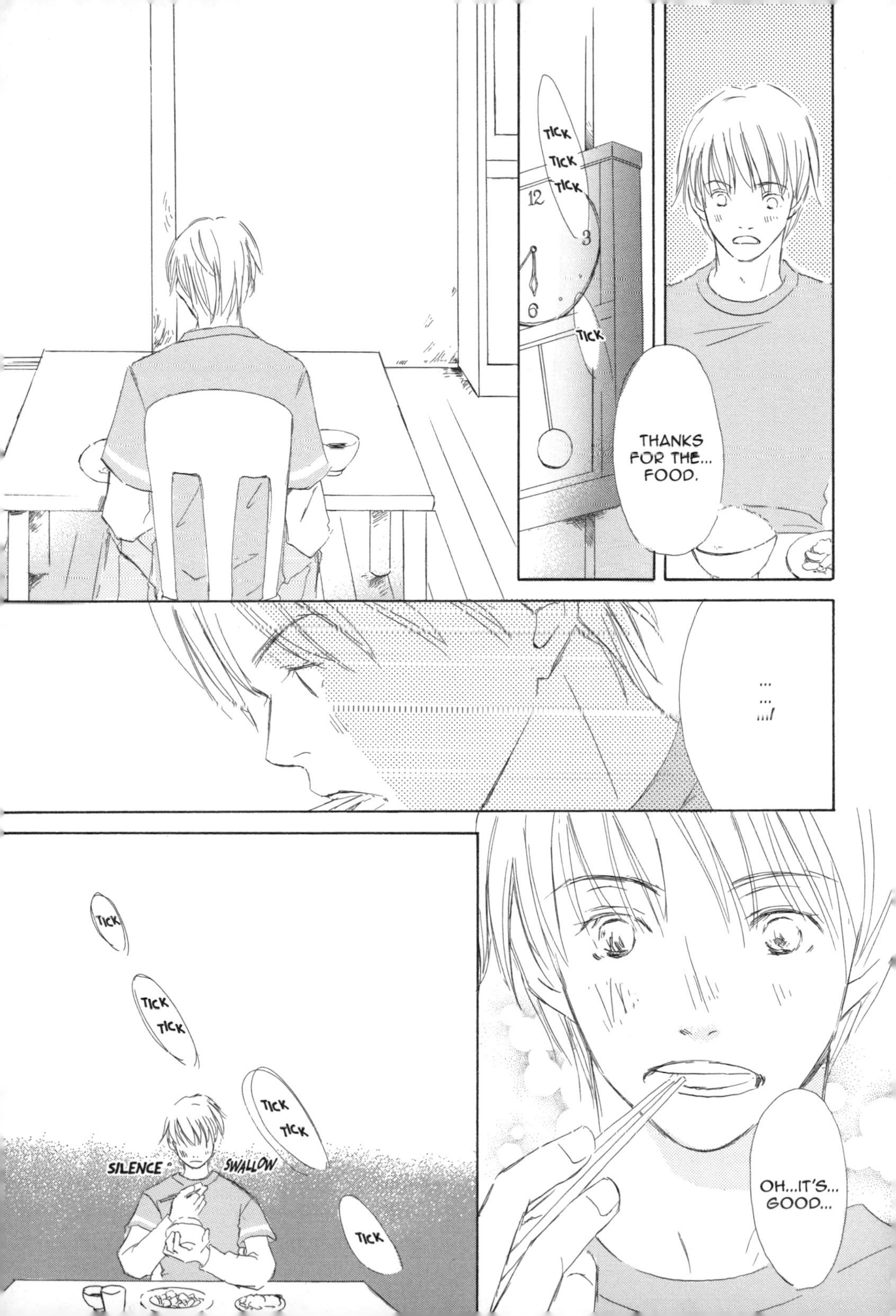
THANKS FOR THE... FOOD.
TICK
TICK
TICK
TICK
...
...
...!
OH...IT'S... GOOD...
TICK
TICK
TICK
TICK
TICK
SILENCE
SWALLOW
TICK

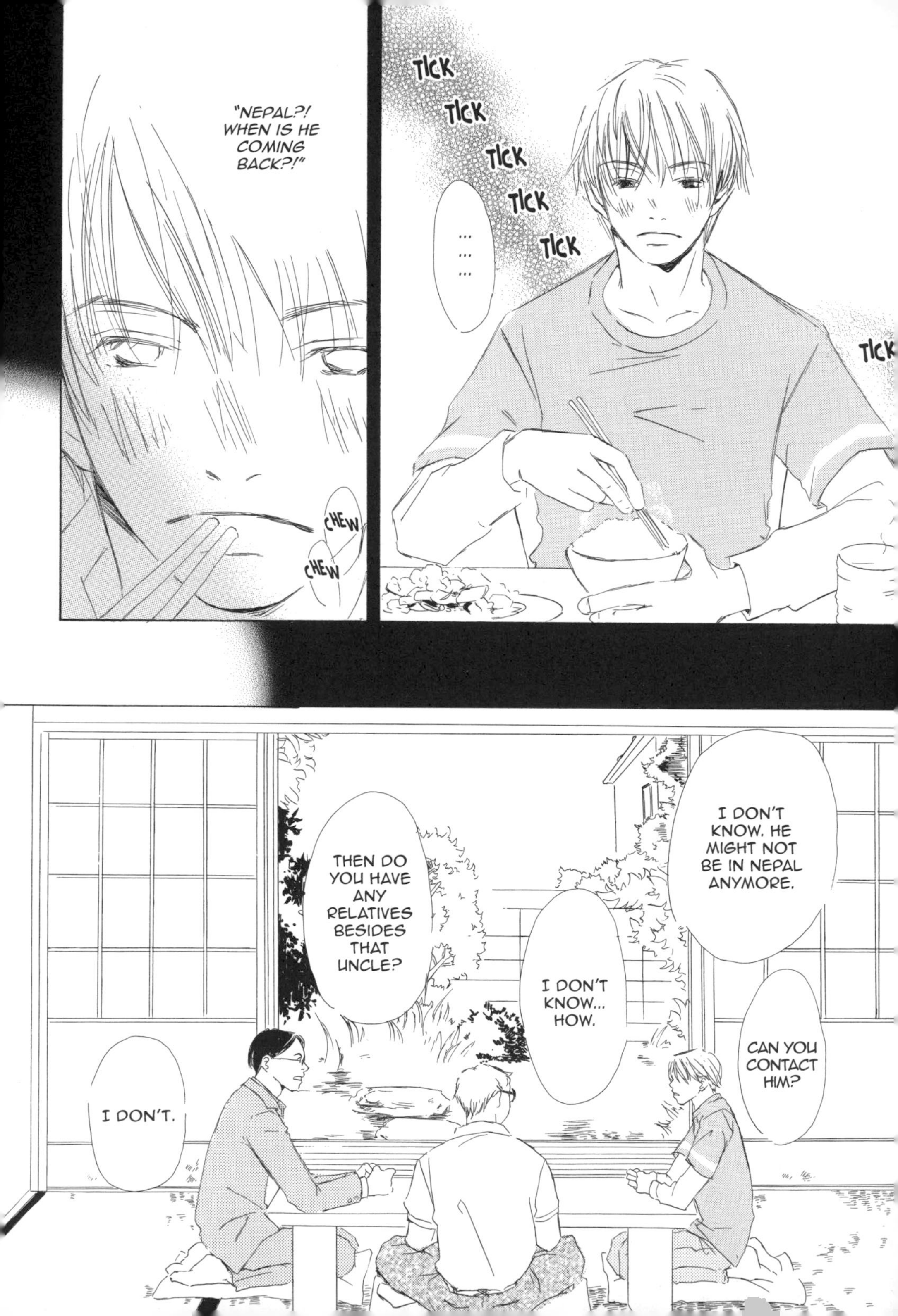
TICK
TICK
TICK
TICK
TICK
TICK
......
"NEPAL?! WHEN IS HE COMING BACK?!"
CHEW
CHEW
I DON'T KNOW. HE MIGHT NOT BE IN NEPAL ANYMORE.
CAN YOU CONTACT HIM?
I DON'T KNOW... HOW.
THEN DO YOU HAVE ANY RELATIVES BESIDES THAT UNCLE?
I DON'T.

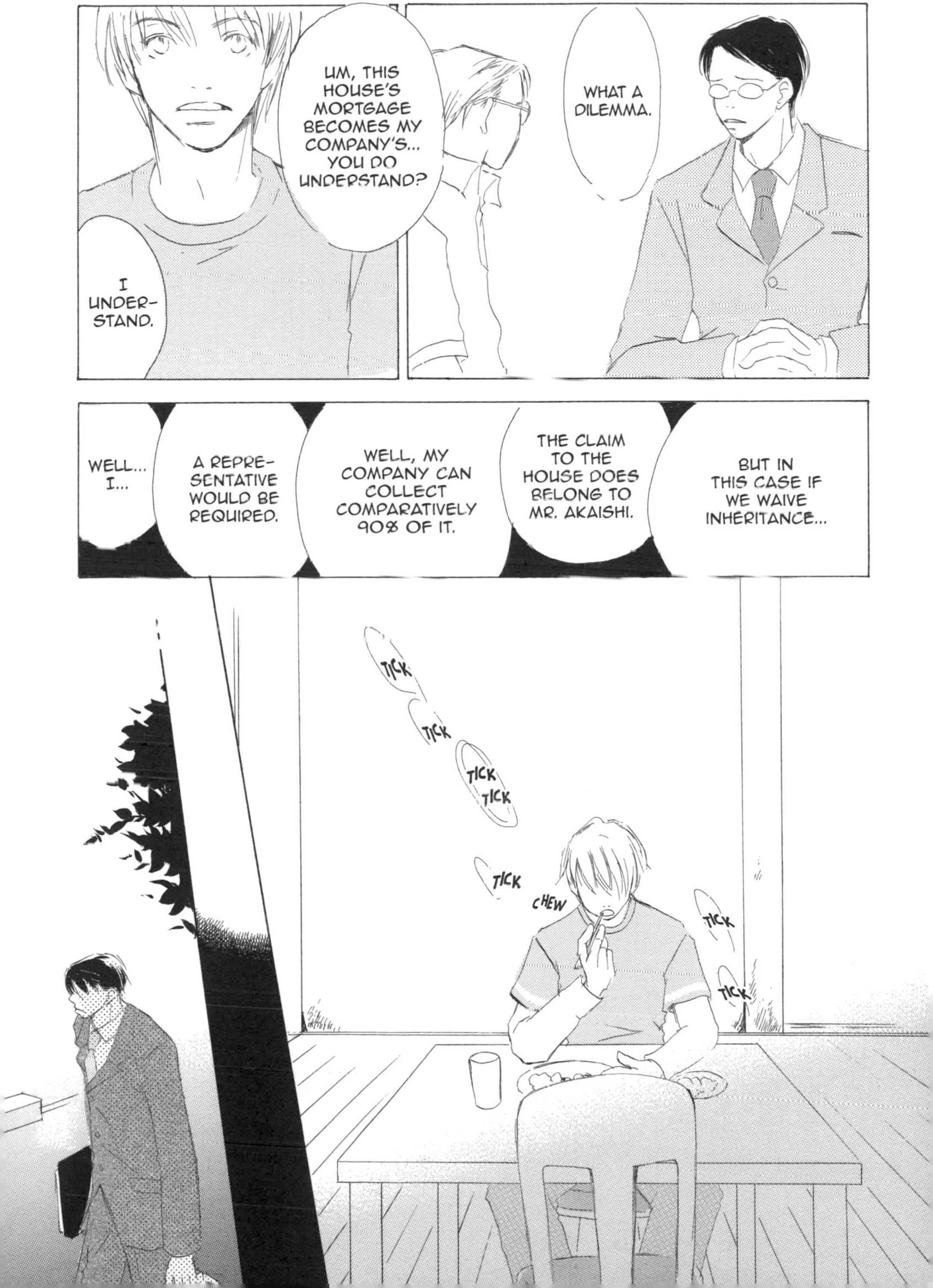
WHAT A DILEMMA.
UM, THIS HOUSE'S MORTGAGE BECOMES MY COMPANY'S... YOU DO UNDERSTAND?
I UNDER-STAND.
BUT IN THIS CASE IF WE WAIVE INHERITANCE...
THE CLAIM TO THE HOUSE DOES BELONG TO MR. AKAISHI.
WELL, MY COMPANY CAN COLLECT COMPARATIVELY 90% OF IT.
A REPRE-SENTATIVE WOULD BE REQUIRED.
WELL... I...
TICK
TICK
TICK
TICK
TICK
CHEW
TICK
TICK

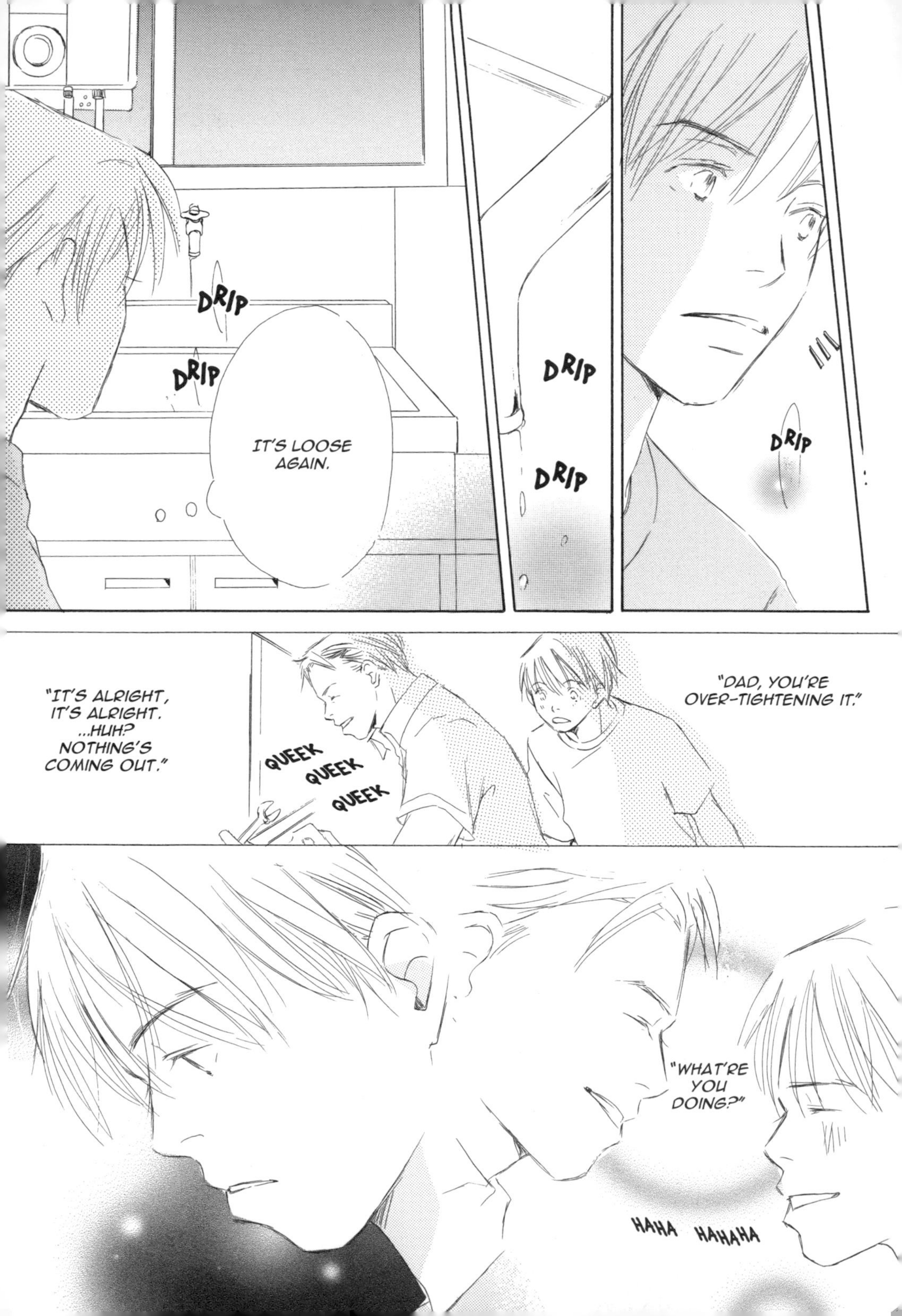
DRIP
DRIP
DRIP
DRIP
DRIP
IT'S LOOSE AGAIN.
"DAD, YOU'RE OVER-TIGHTENING IT."
QUEEK QUEEK QUEEK
"IT'S ALRIGHT, IT'S ALRIGHT. ...HUH? NOTHING'S COMING OUT."
"WHAT'RE YOU DOING?"
HAHA HAHAHA

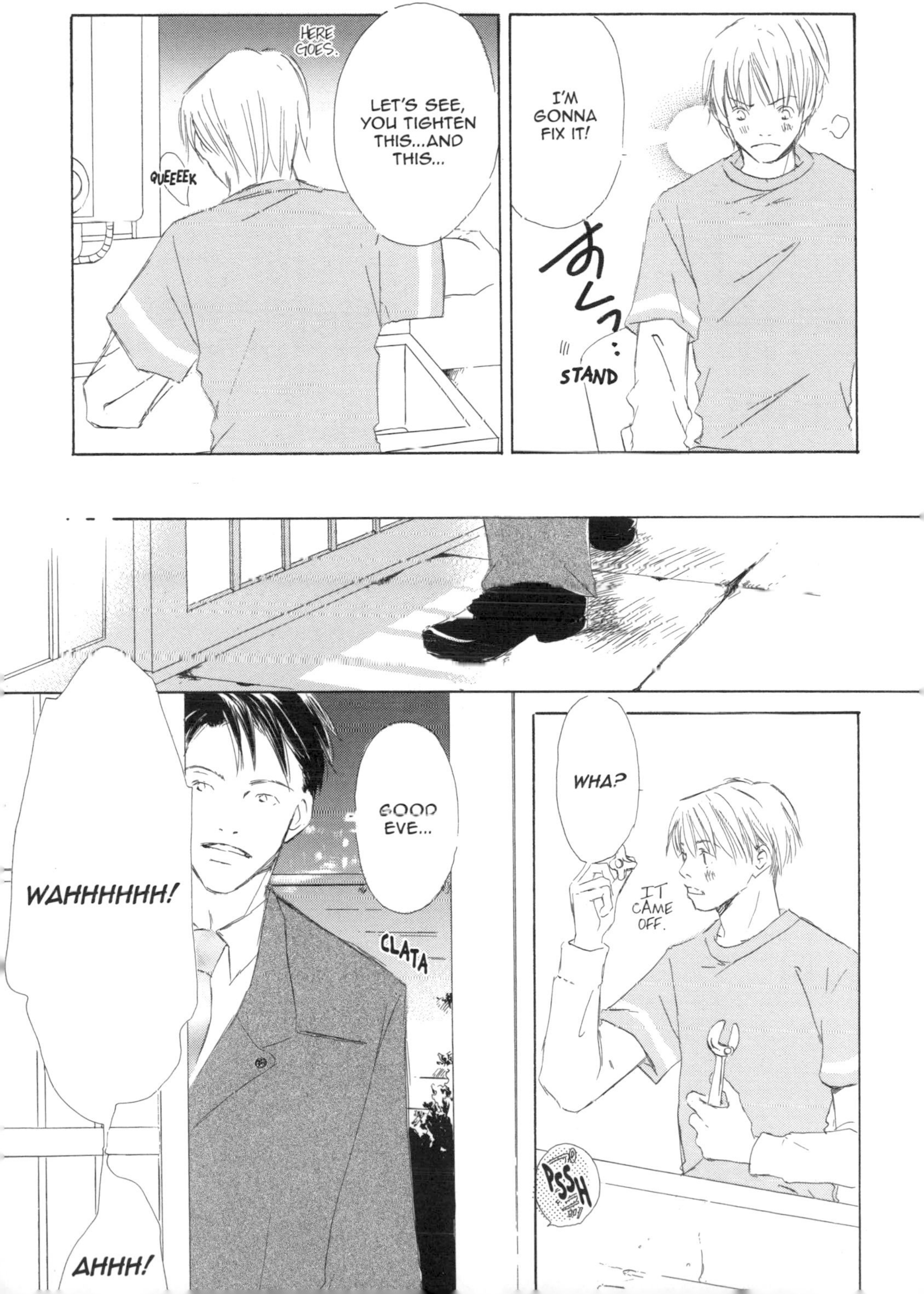
I'M GONNA FIX IT!
STAND
HERE GOES.
LET'S SEE, YOU TIGHTEN THIS...AND THIS...
QUEEEEK
WHA?
IT CAME OFF.
PSSSH
GOOD EVE...
CLATA
WAHHHHHH!
AHHH!

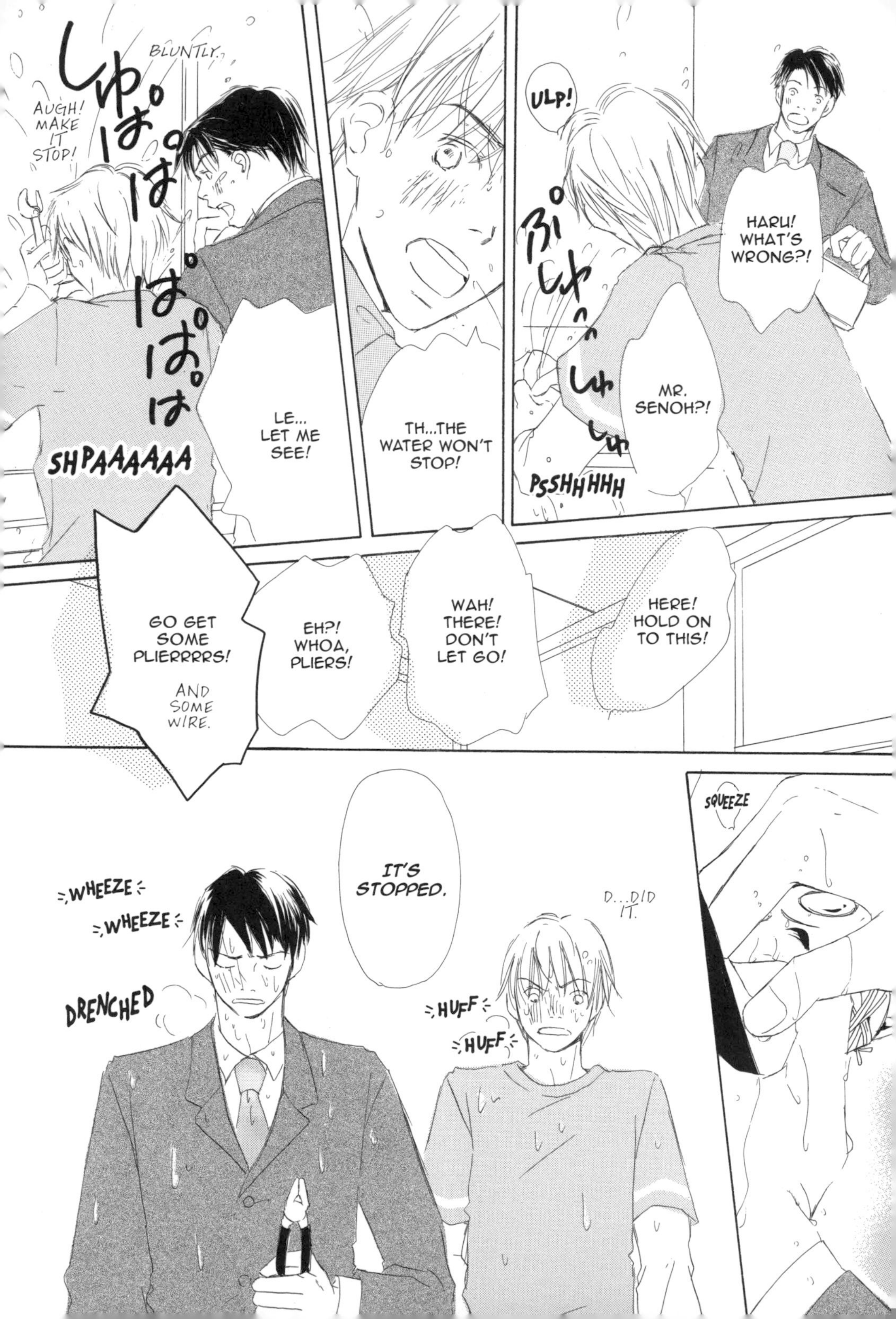
ULP!
HARU! WHAT'S WRONG?!
MR. SENOH?!
PSSHHHHH
TH...THE WATER WON'T STOP!
BLUNTLY.
AUGH! MAKE IT STOP!
LE... LET ME SEE!
SHPAAAAAA
HERE! HOLD ON TO THIS!
WAH! THERE! DON'T LET GO!
EH?! WHOA, PLIERS!
GO GET SOME PLIERRRRS!
AND SOME WIRE.
SQUEEZE
IT'S STOPPED.
D...DID IT.
HUFF
HUFF
WHEEZE
WHEEZE
DRENCHED

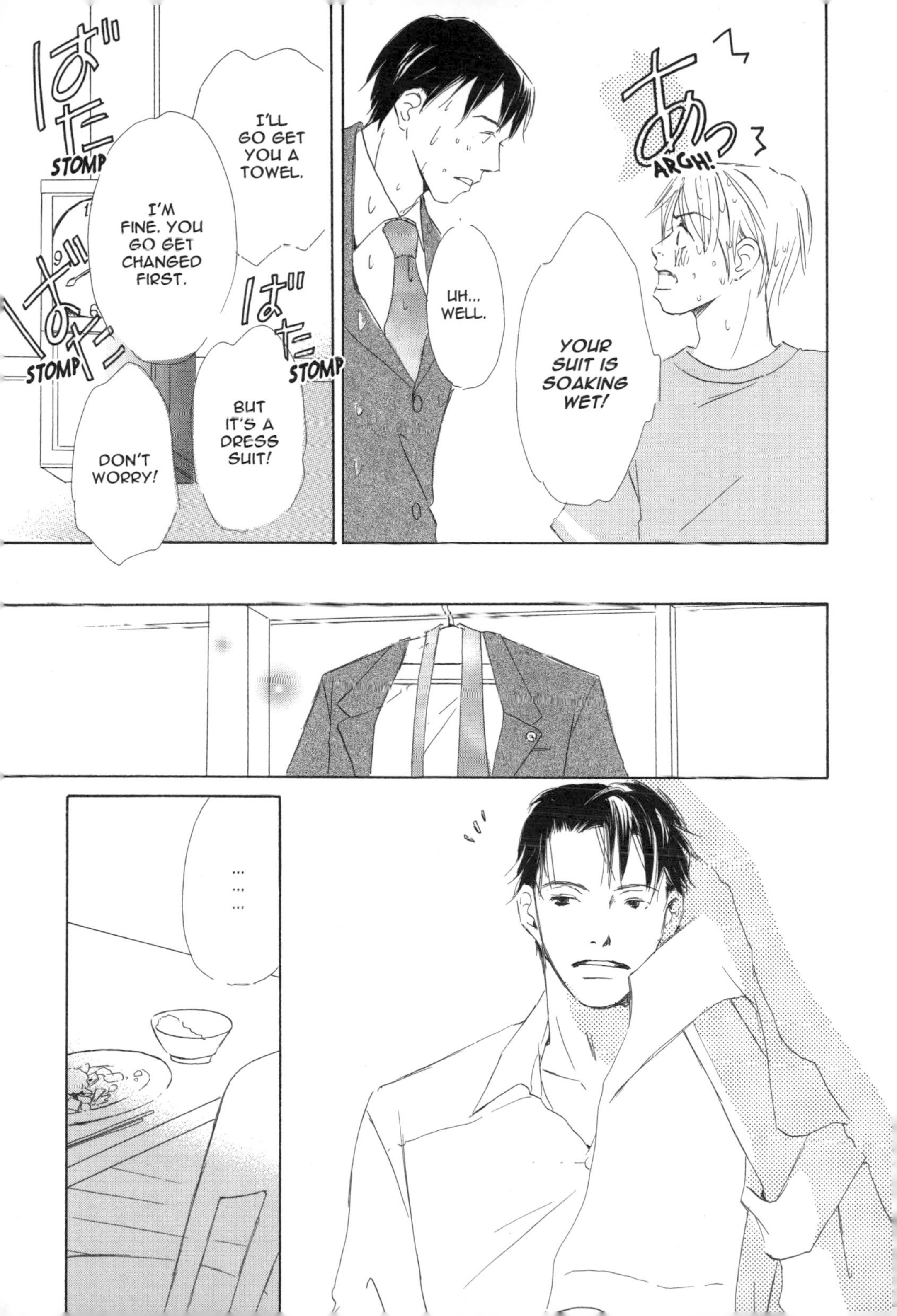
ARGH!
YOUR SUIT IS SOAKING WET!
UH... WELL.
I'LL GO GET YOU A TOWEL.
STOMP
I'M FINE. YOU GO GET CHANGED FIRST.
STOMP
BUT IT'S A DRESS SUIT!
STOMP
DON'T WORRY!
...
...
...

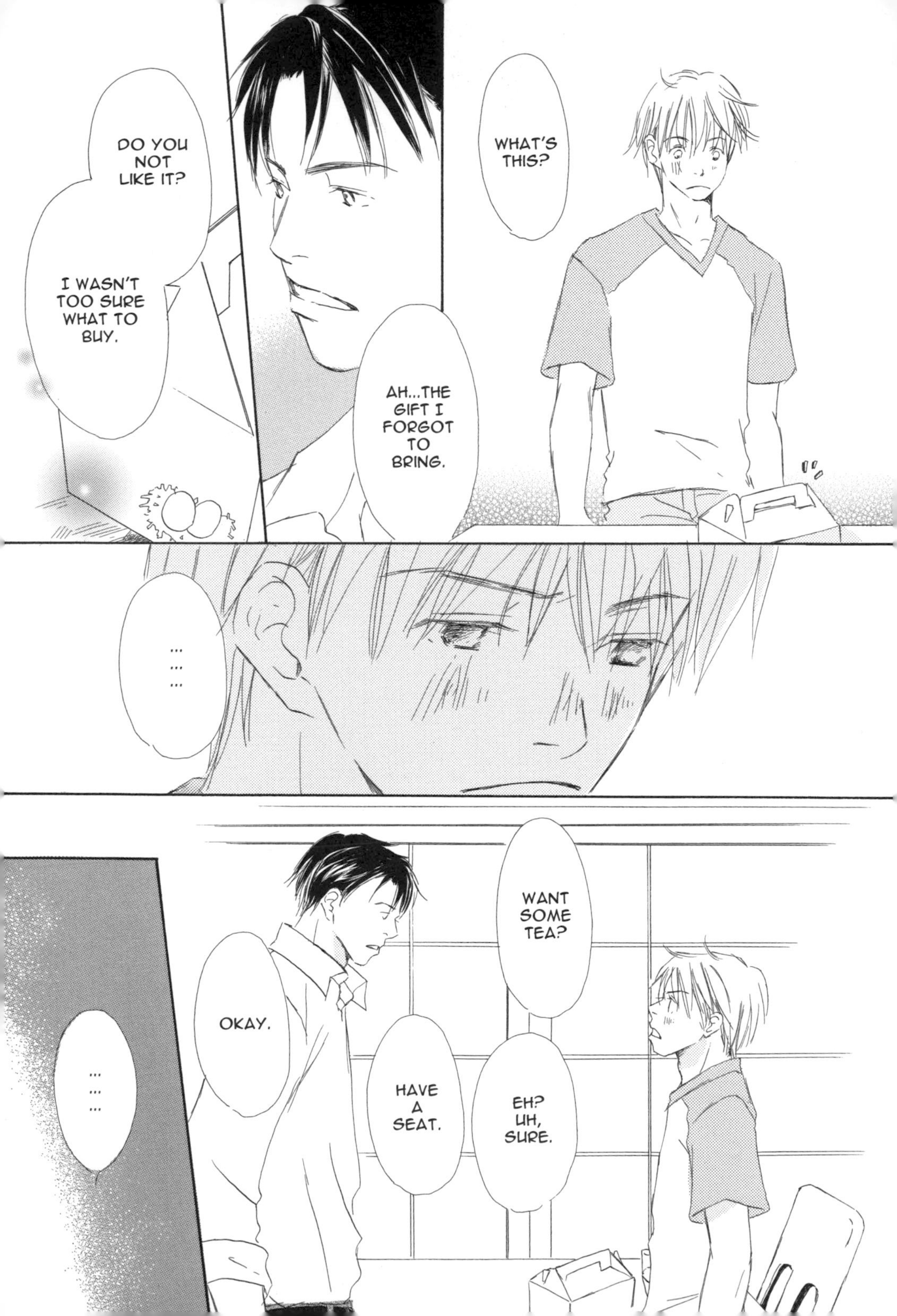
WHAT'S THIS?
AH...THE GIFT I FORGOT TO BRING.
DO YOU NOT LIKE IT?
I WASN'T TOO SURE WHAT TO BUY.
... ...
WANT SOME TEA?
EH? UH, SURE.
HAVE A SEAT.
OKAY.
... ...

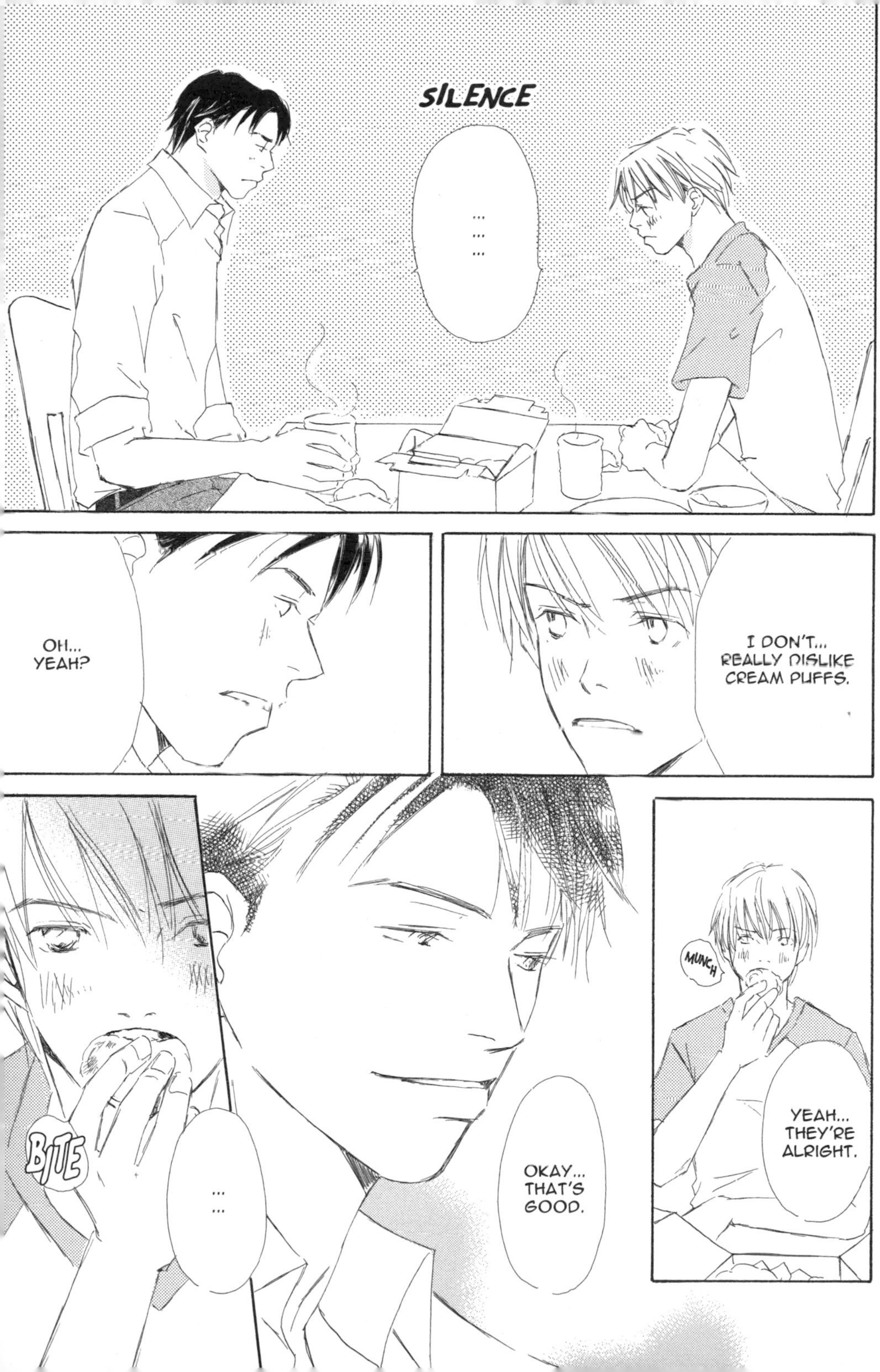
SILENCE
... ...
I DON'T... REALLY DISLIKE CREAM PUFFS.
OH... YEAH?
MUNCH
YEAH... THEY'RE ALRIGHT.
OKAY... THAT'S GOOD.
... ...
BITE

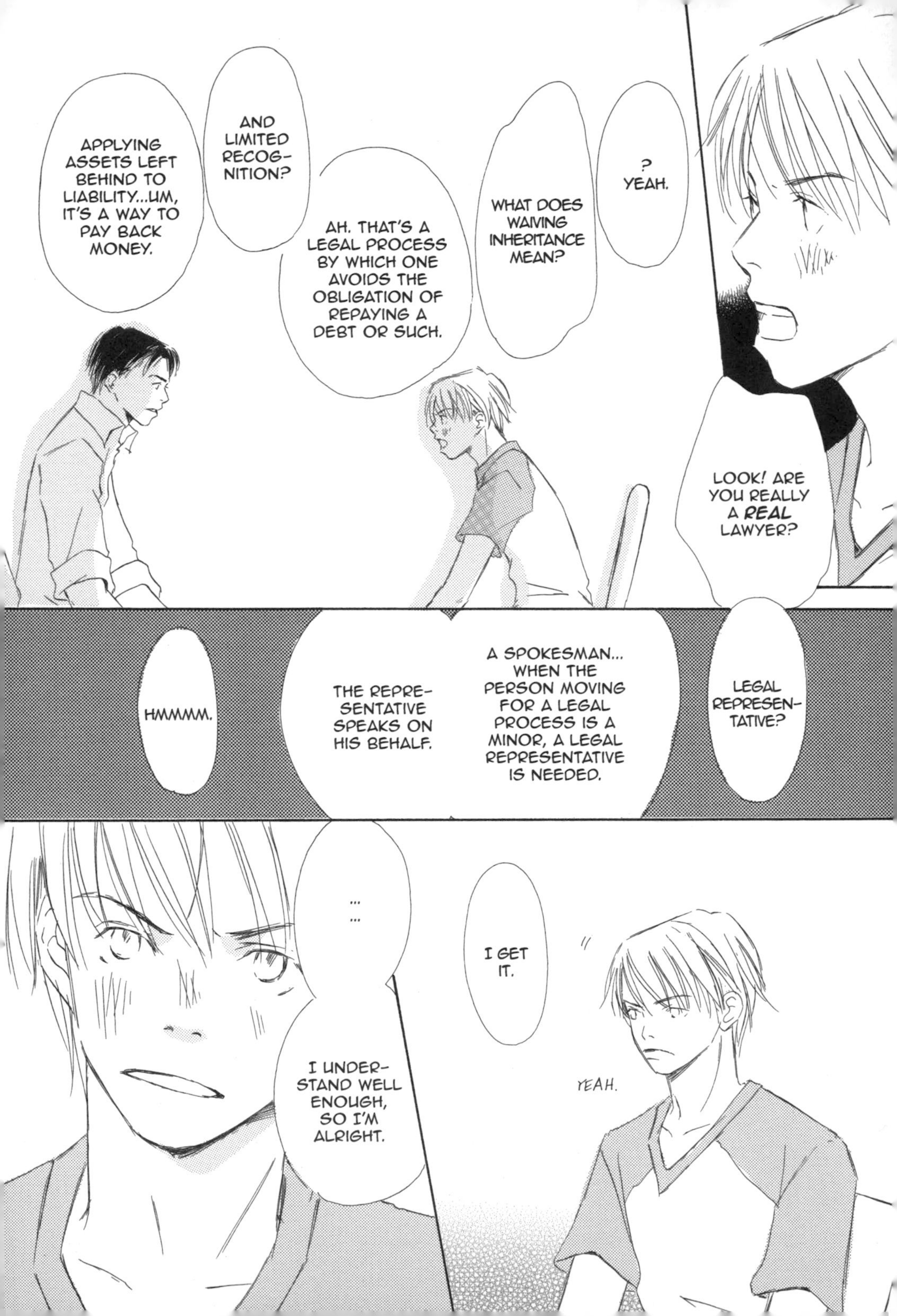
LOOK! ARE YOU REALLY A REAL LAWYER?
? YEAH.
WHAT DOES WAIVING INHERITANCE MEAN?
AH. THAT'S A LEGAL PROCESS BY WHICH ONE AVOIDS THE OBLIGATION OF REPAYING A DEBT OR SUCH.
AND LIMITED RECOGNITION?
APPLYING ASSETS LEFT BEHIND TO LIABILITY...UM, IT'S A WAY TO PAY BACK MONEY.
LEGAL REPRESENTATIVE?
A SPOKESMAN... WHEN THE PERSON MOVING FOR A LEGAL PROCESS IS A MINOR, A LEGAL REPRESENTATIVE IS NEEDED.
THE REPRESENTATIVE SPEAKS ON HIS BEHALF.
HMMMM.
I GET IT.
YEAH.
... ...
I UNDERSTAND WELL ENOUGH, SO I'M ALRIGHT.

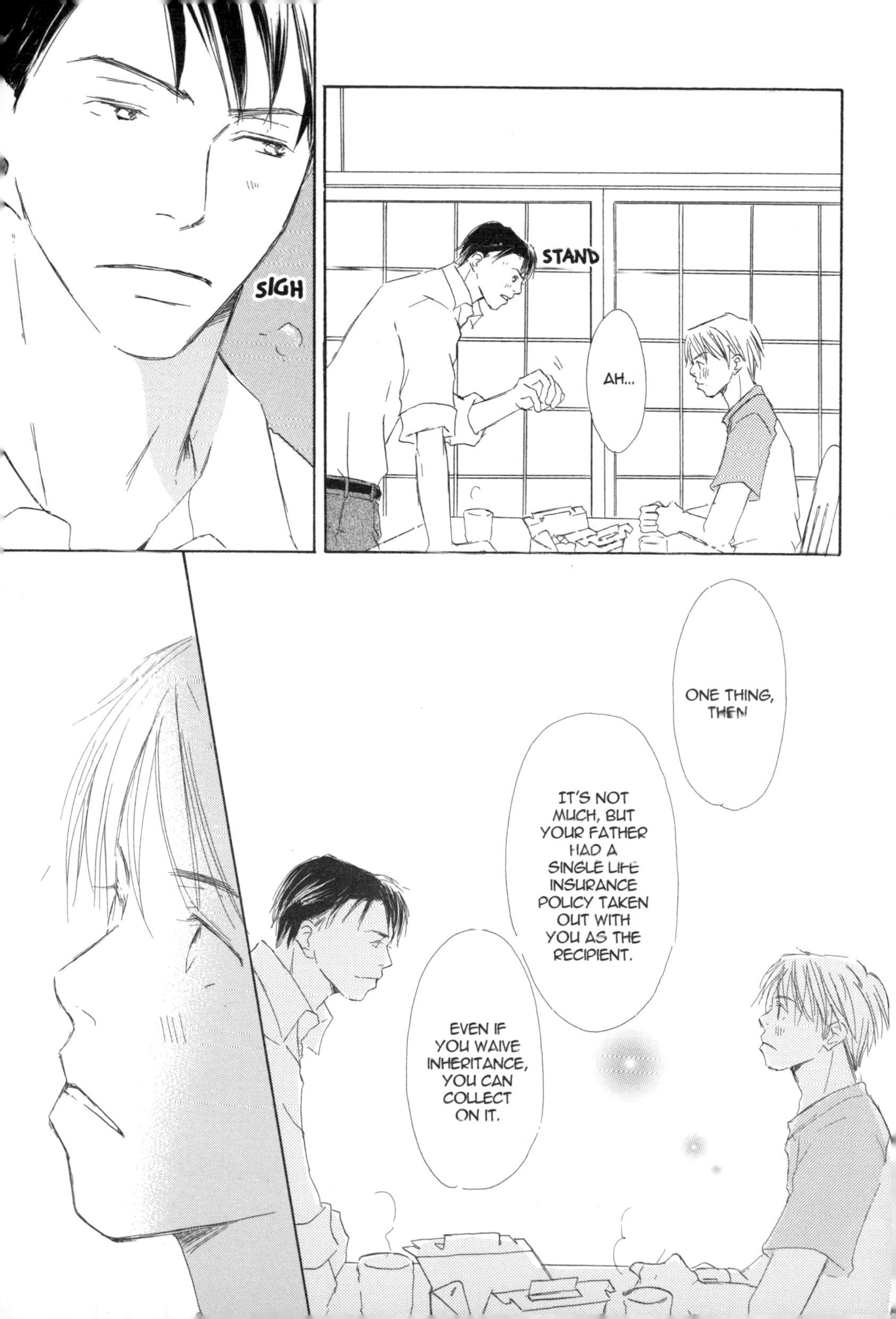
STAND
AH...
SIGH
ONE THING, THEN
IT'S NOT MUCH, BUT YOUR FATHER HAD A SINGLE LIFE INSURANCE POLICY TAKEN OUT WITH YOU AS THE RECIPIENT.
EVEN IF YOU WAIVE INHERITANCE, YOU CAN COLLECT ON IT.

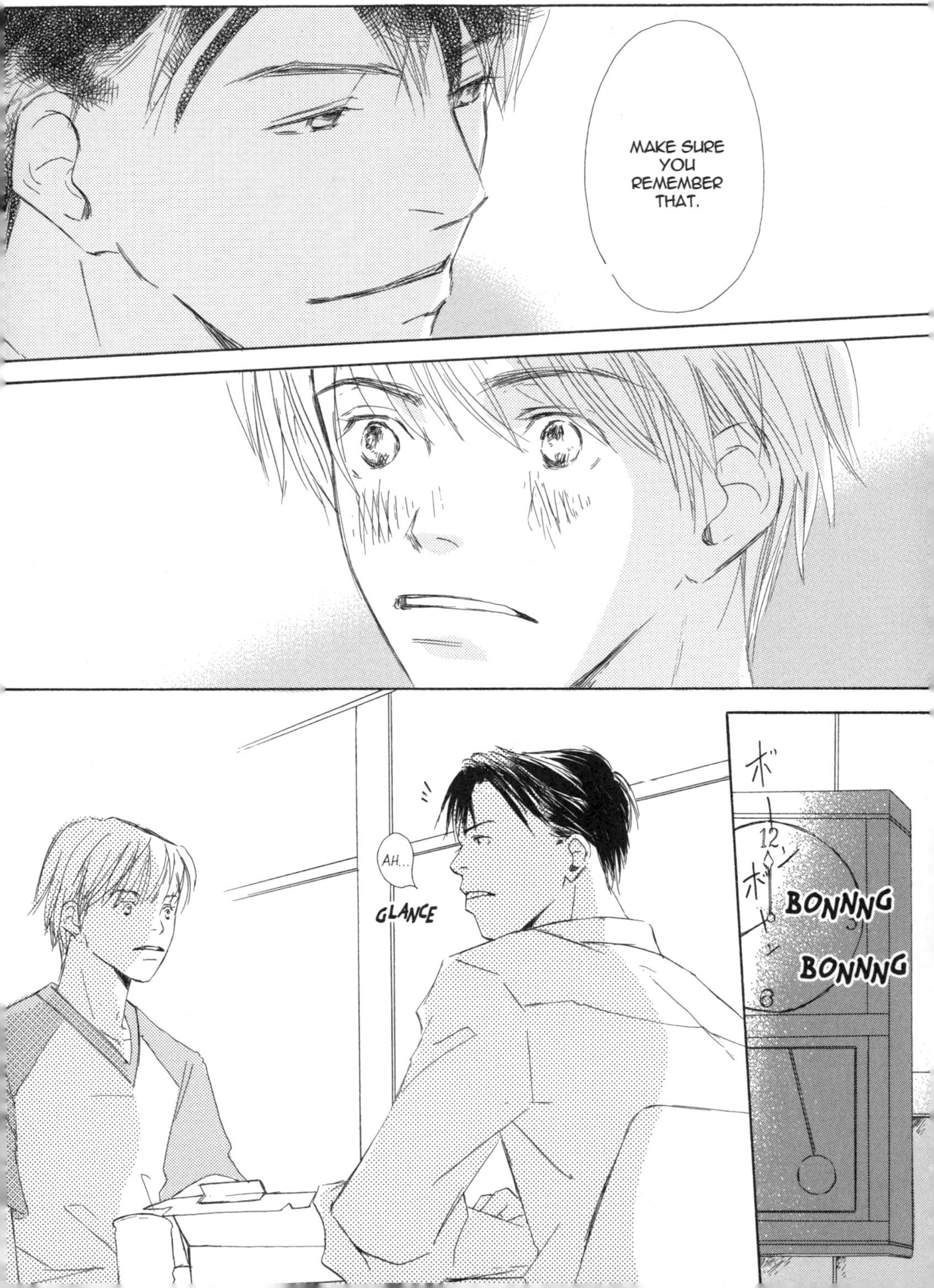
MAKE SURE YOU REMEMBER THAT.
AH...
GLANCE
BONNNG
BONNNG

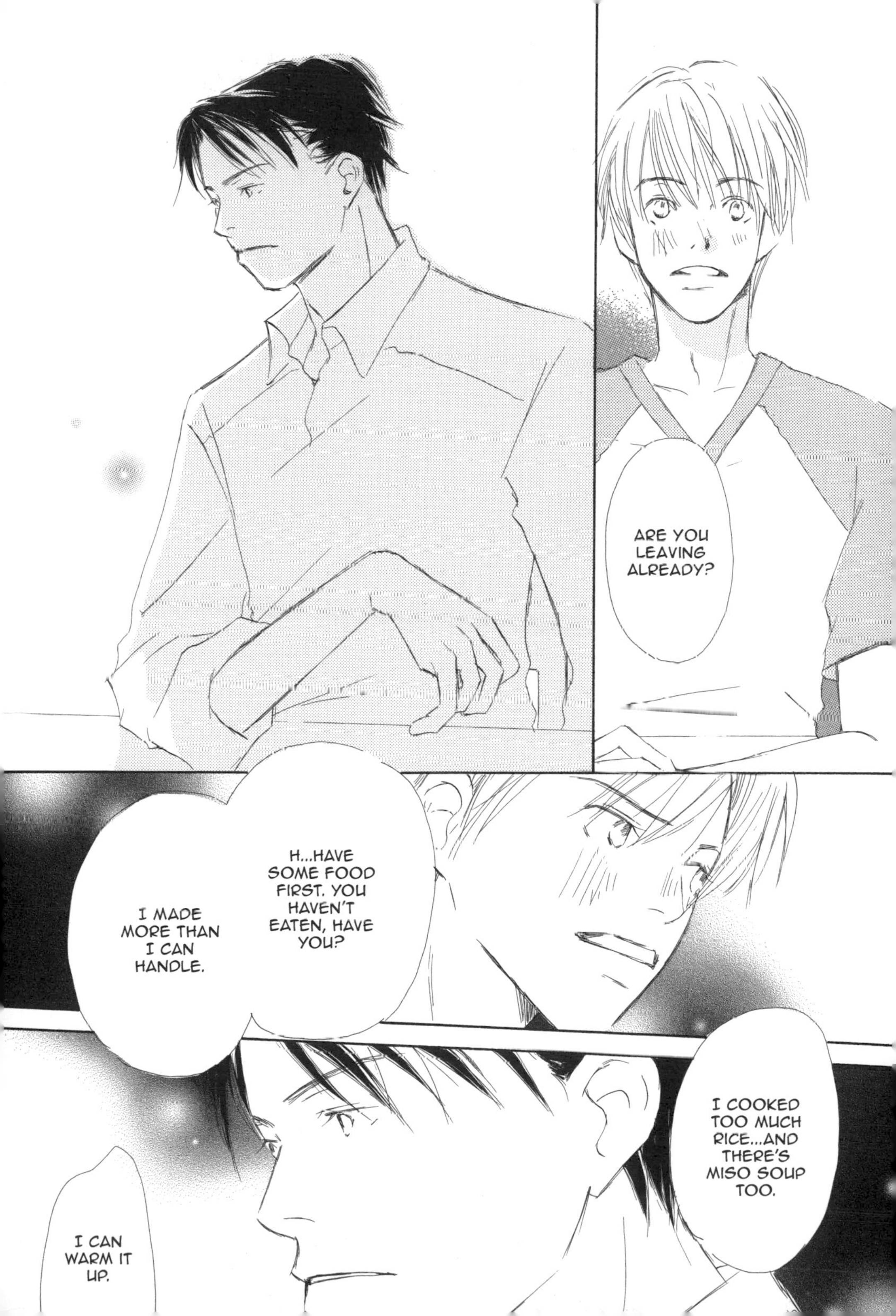
ARE YOU LEAVING ALREADY?
H...HAVE SOME FOOD FIRST. YOU HAVEN'T EATEN, HAVE YOU?
I MADE MORE THAN I CAN HANDLE.
I COOKED TOO MUCH RICE...AND THERE'S MISO SOUP TOO.
I CAN WARM IT UP.

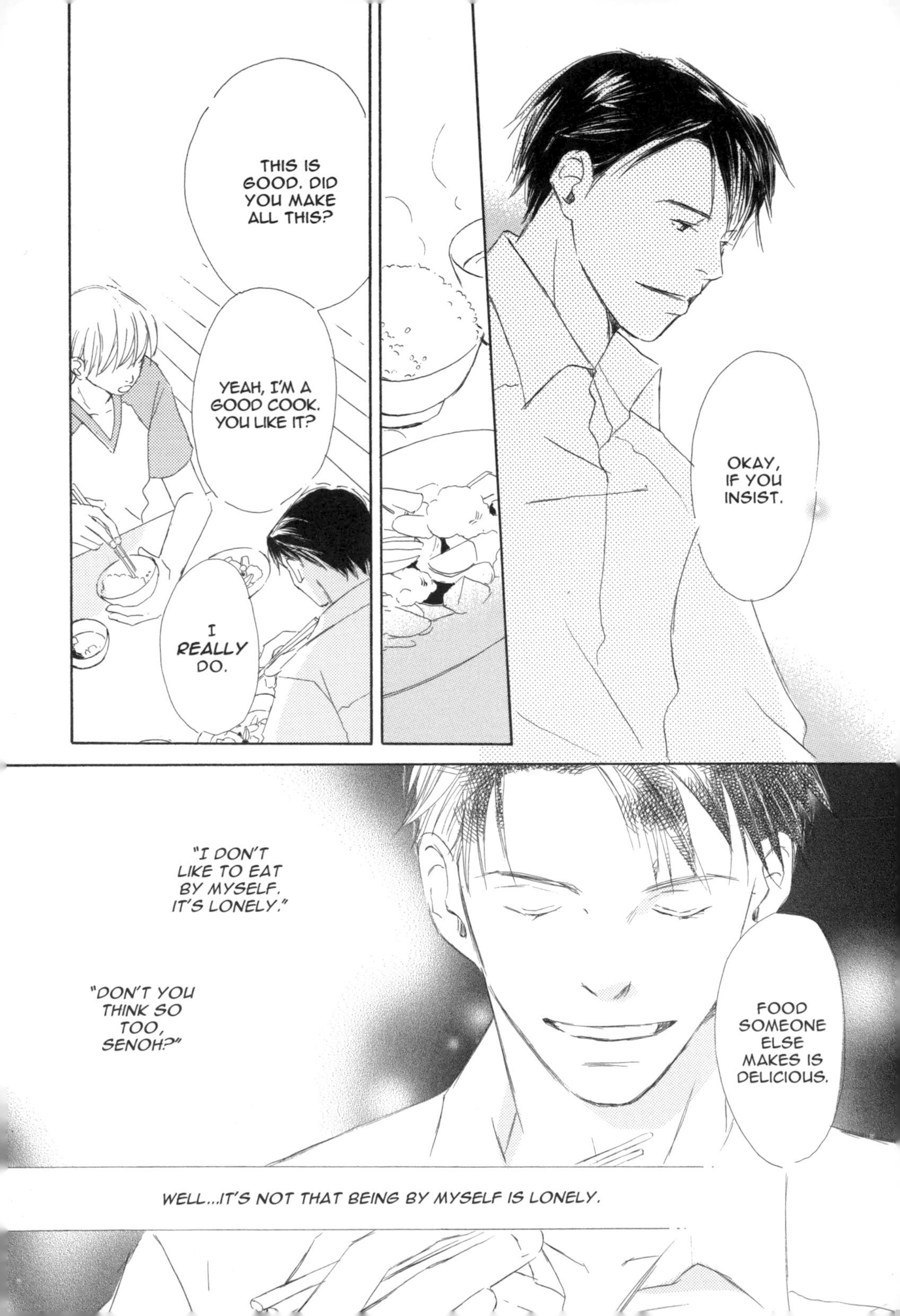
OKAY, IF YOU INSIST.
THIS IS GOOD. DID YOU MAKE ALL THIS?
YEAH, I'M A GOOD COOK. YOU LIKE IT?
I REALLY DO.
FOOD SOMEONE ELSE MAKES IS DELICIOUS.
"I DON'T LIKE TO EAT BY MYSELF. IT'S LONELY."
"DON'T YOU THINK SO TOO, SENOH?"
WELL...IT'S NOT THAT BEING BY MYSELF IS LONELY.

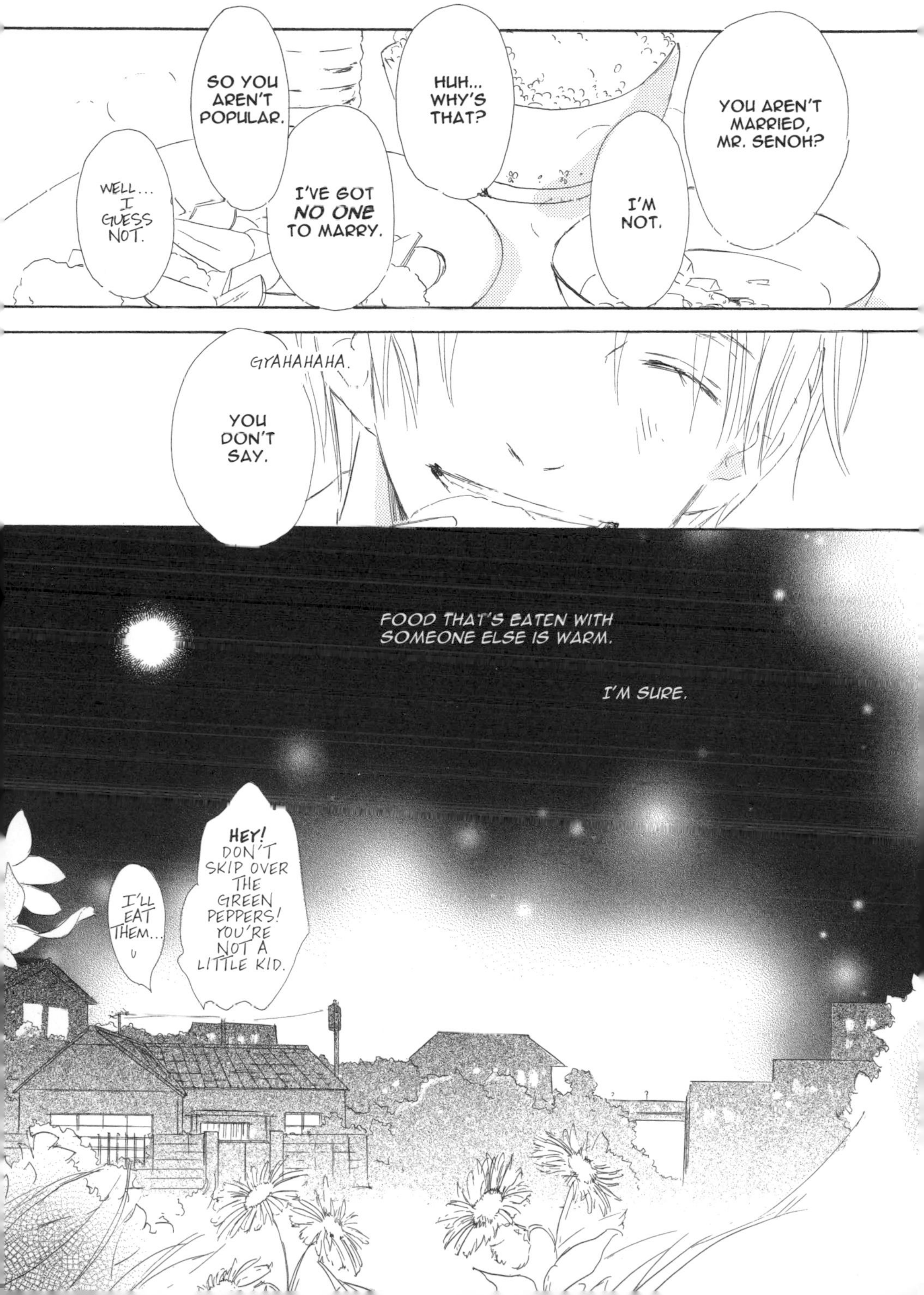
YOU AREN'T MARRIED, MR. SENOH?
I'M NOT.
HUH... WHY'S THAT?
I'VE GOT **NO ONE** TO MARRY.
SO YOU AREN'T POPULAR.
WELL... I GUESS NOT.
GYAHAHAHA.
YOU DON'T SAY.
FOOD THAT'S EATEN WITH SOMEONE ELSE IS WARM.
I'M SURE.
HEY! DON'T SKIP OVER THE GREEN PEPPERS! YOU'RE NOT A LITTLE KID.
I'LL EAT THEM...

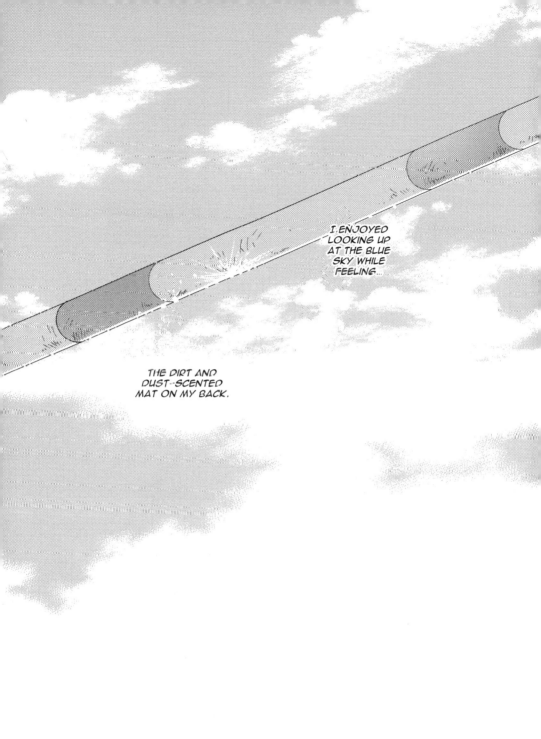

I ENJOYED
LOOKING UP
AT THE BLUE
SKY WHILE
FEELING...

THE DIRT AND
DUST-SCENTED
MAT ON MY BACK.

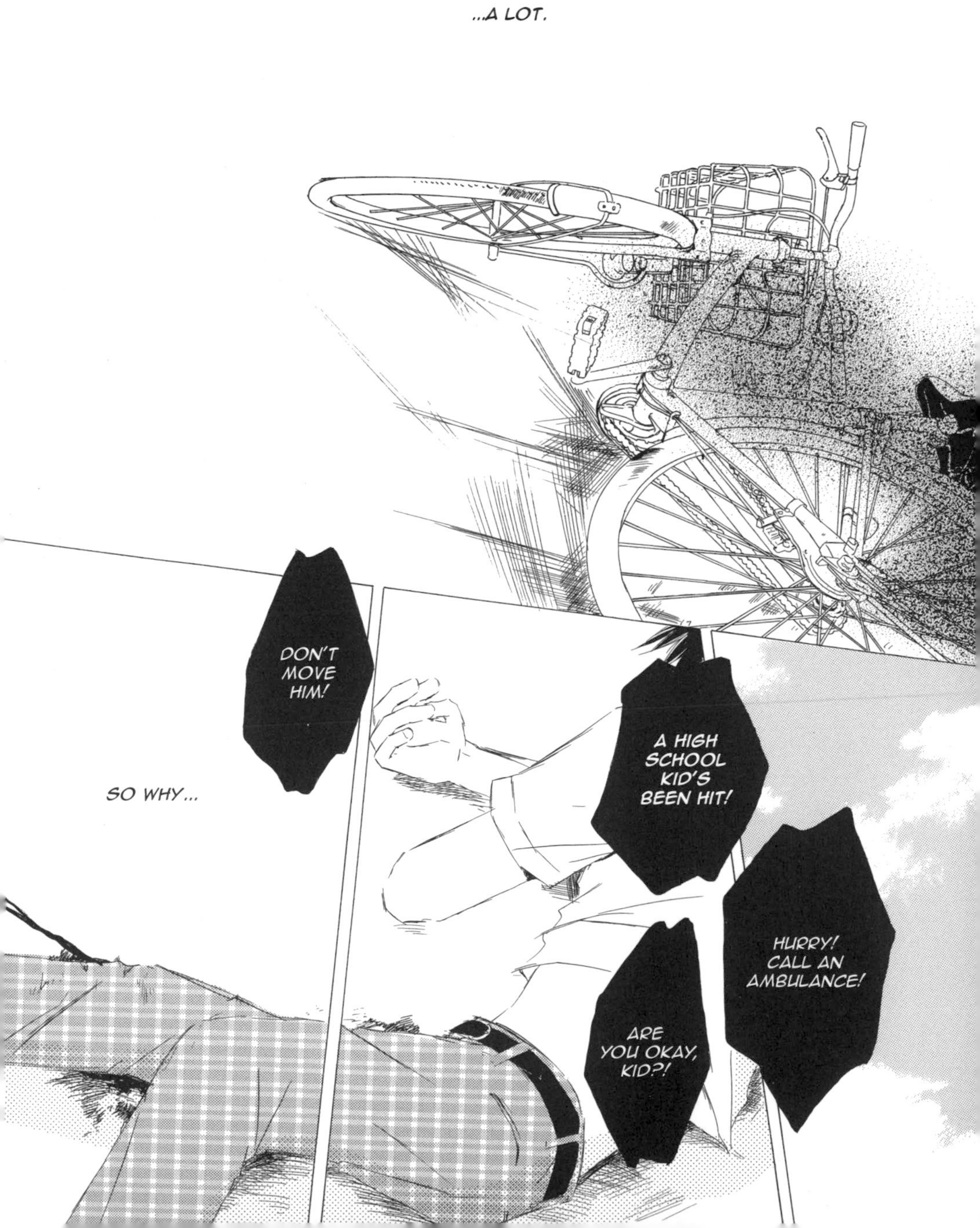
...A LOT.
A HIGH SCHOOL KID'S BEEN HIT!
HURRY! CALL AN AMBULANCE!
ARE YOU OKAY, KID?!
DON'T MOVE HIM!
SO WHY...

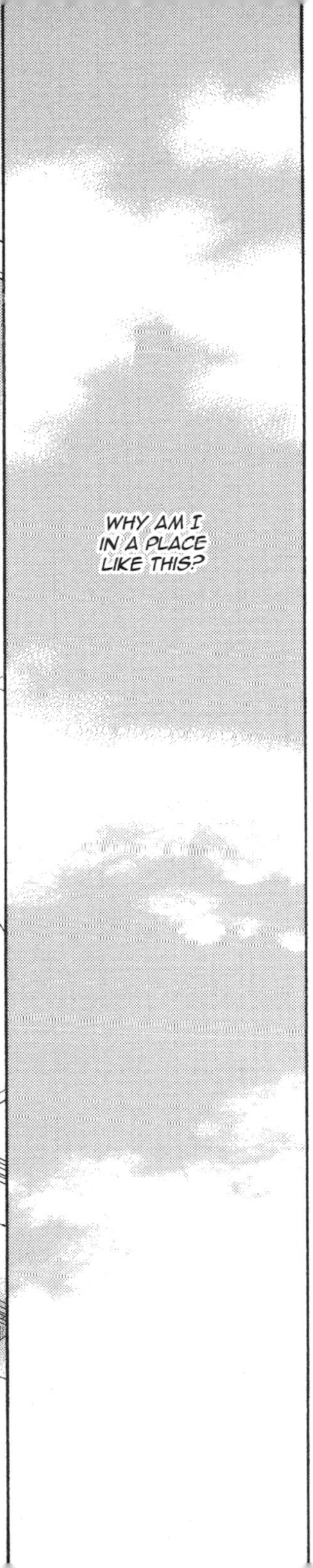
WHY AM I IN A PLACE LIKE THIS?
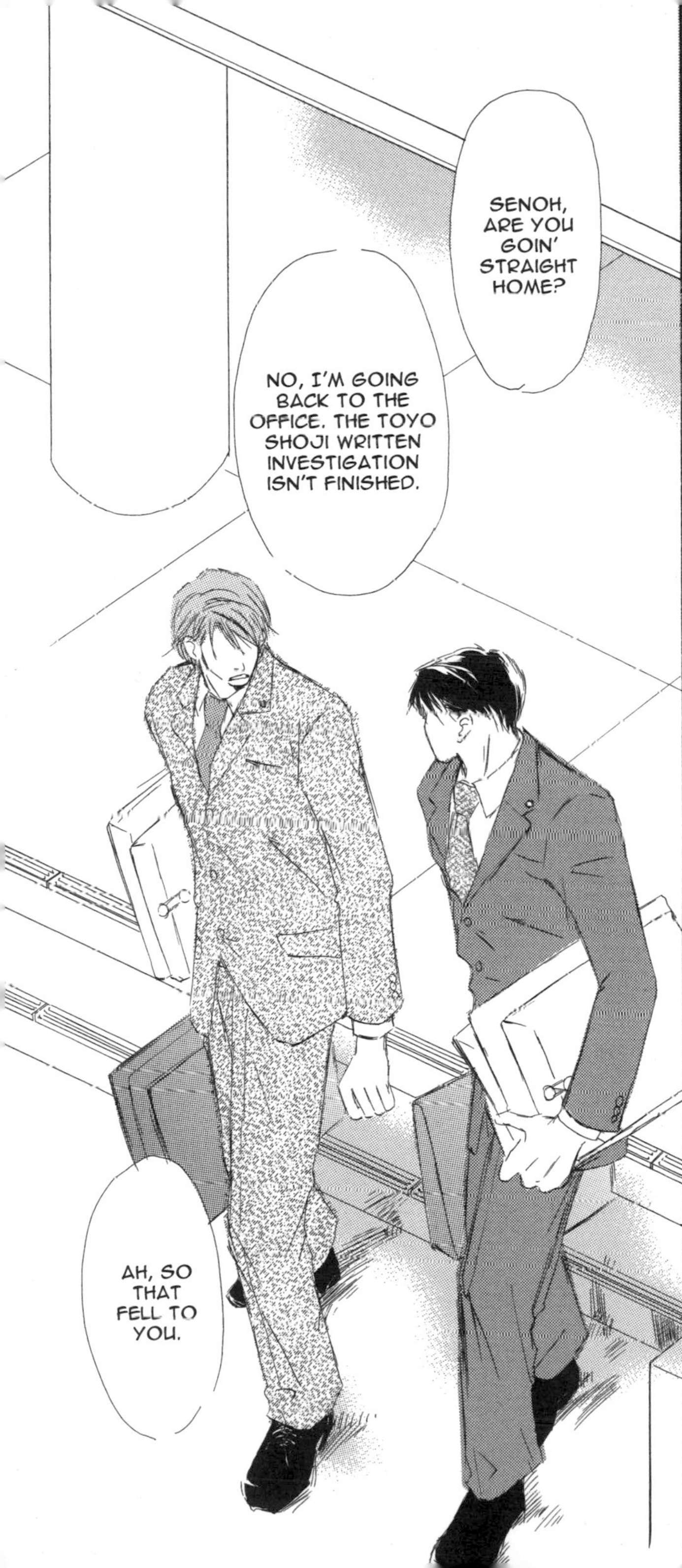
SENOH, ARE YOU GOIN' STRAIGHT HOME?
NO, I'M GOING BACK TO THE OFFICE. THE TOYO SHOJI WRITTEN INVESTIGATION ISN'T FINISHED.
AH, SO THAT FELL TO YOU.

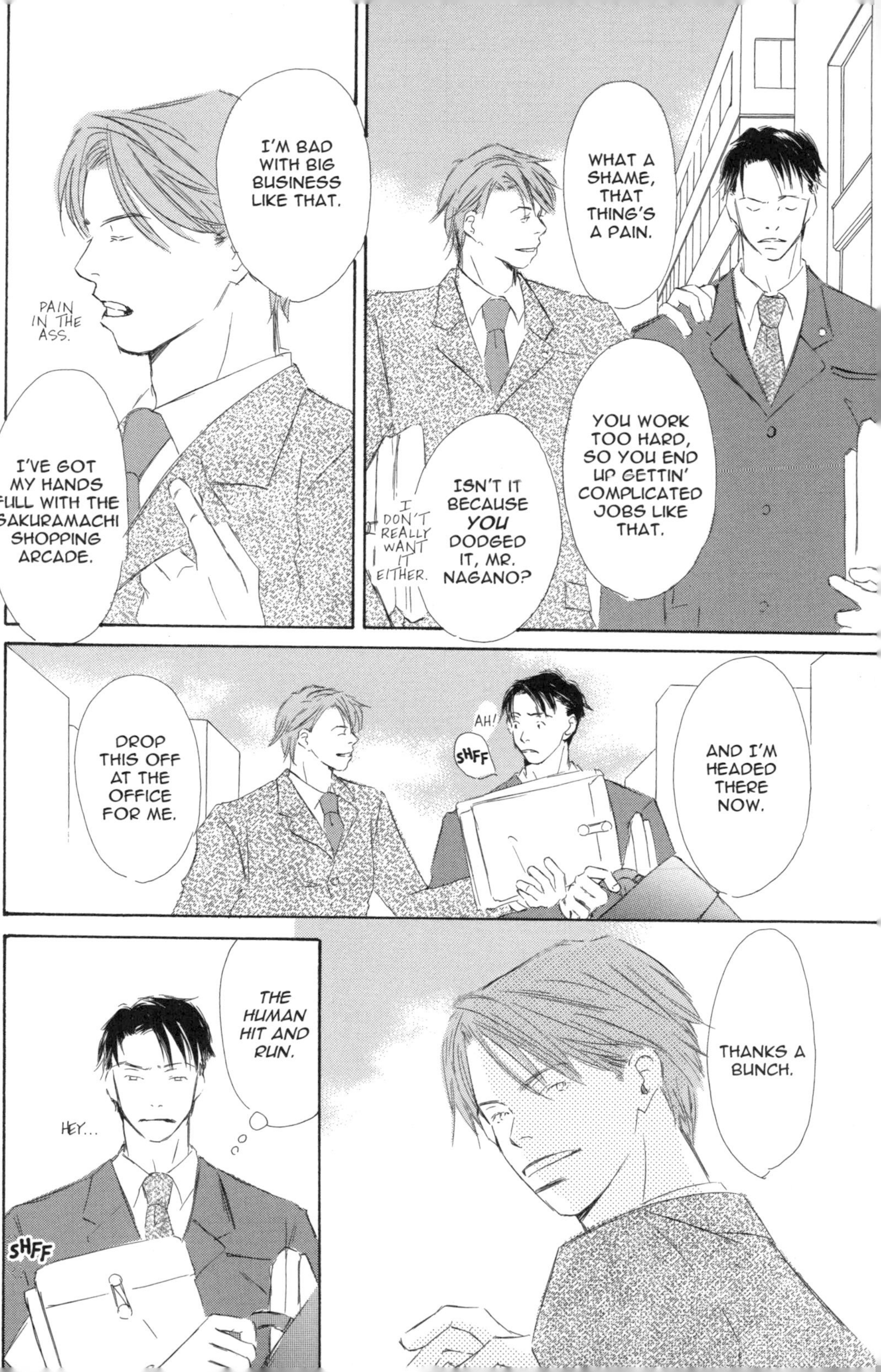
WHAT A SHAME, THAT THING'S A PAIN.
YOU WORK TOO HARD, SO YOU END UP GETTIN' COMPLICATED JOBS LIKE THAT.
ISN'T IT BECAUSE *YOU* DODGED IT, MR. NAGANO?
I DON'T REALLY WANT IT EITHER.
I'M BAD WITH BIG BUSINESS LIKE THAT.
PAIN IN THE ASS.
I'VE GOT MY HANDS FULL WITH THE SAKURAMACHI SHOPPING ARCADE.
AND I'M HEADED THERE NOW.
AH!
SHFF
DROP THIS OFF AT THE OFFICE FOR ME.
THANKS A BUNCH.
THE HUMAN HIT AND RUN.
HEY...
SHFF

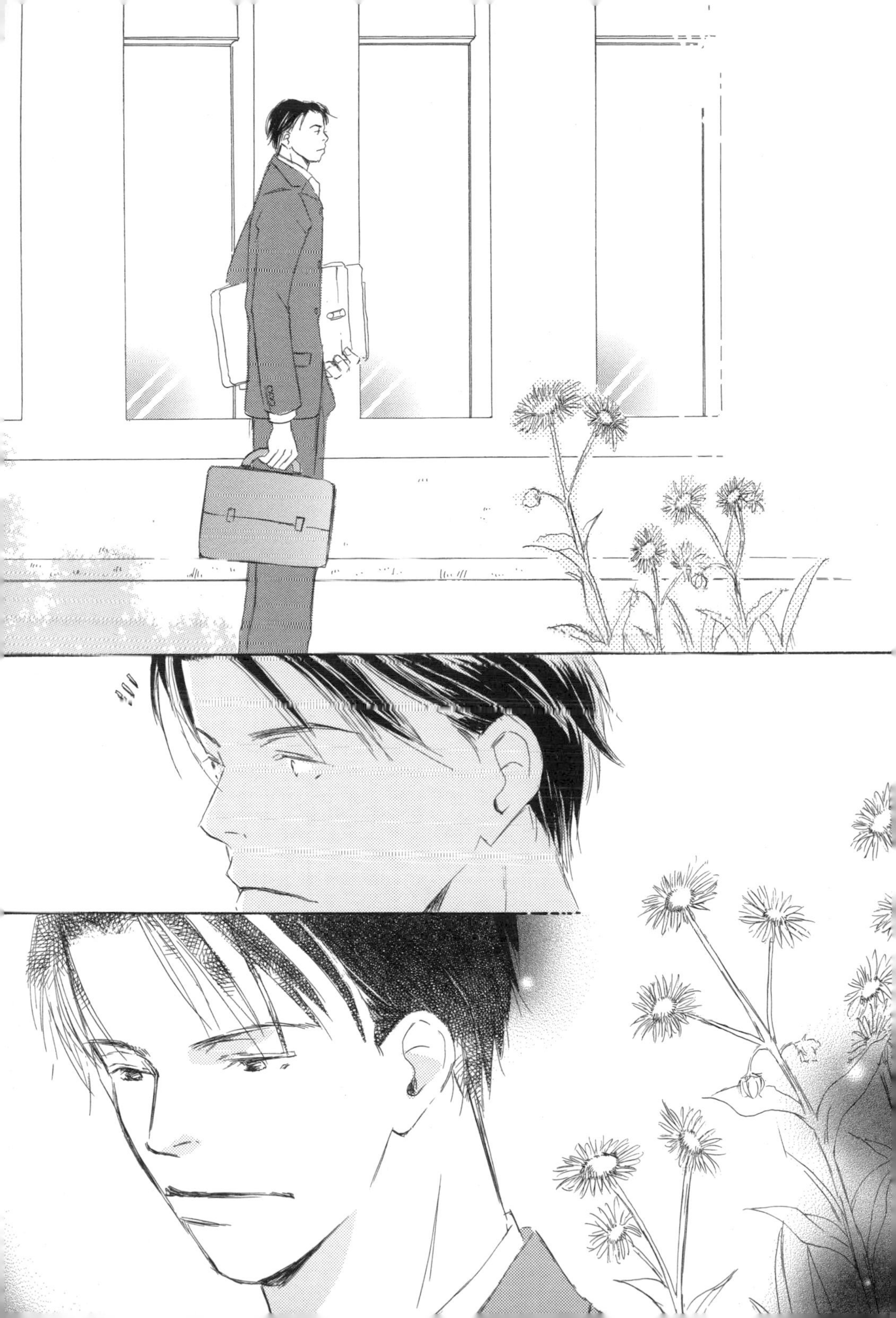

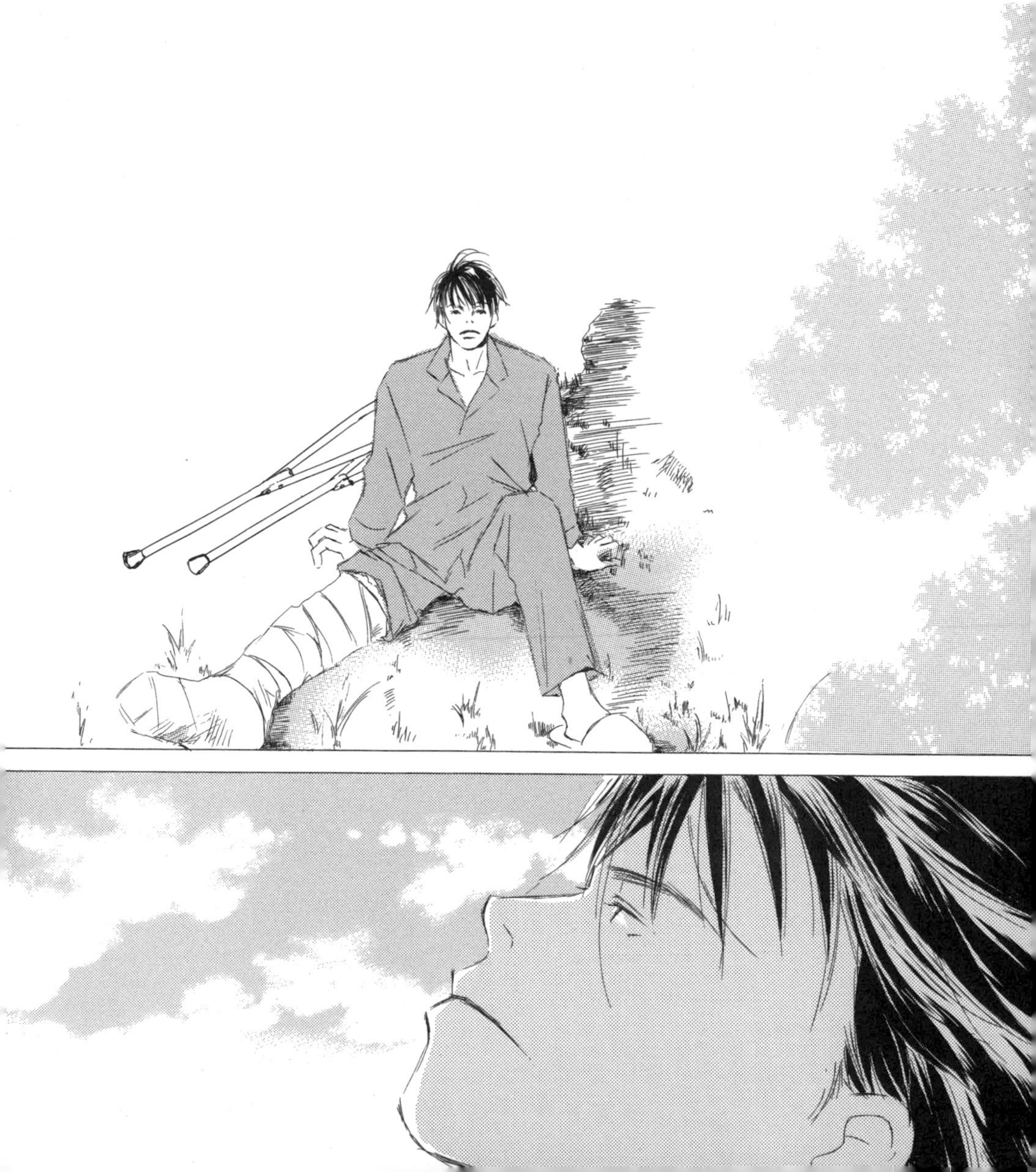

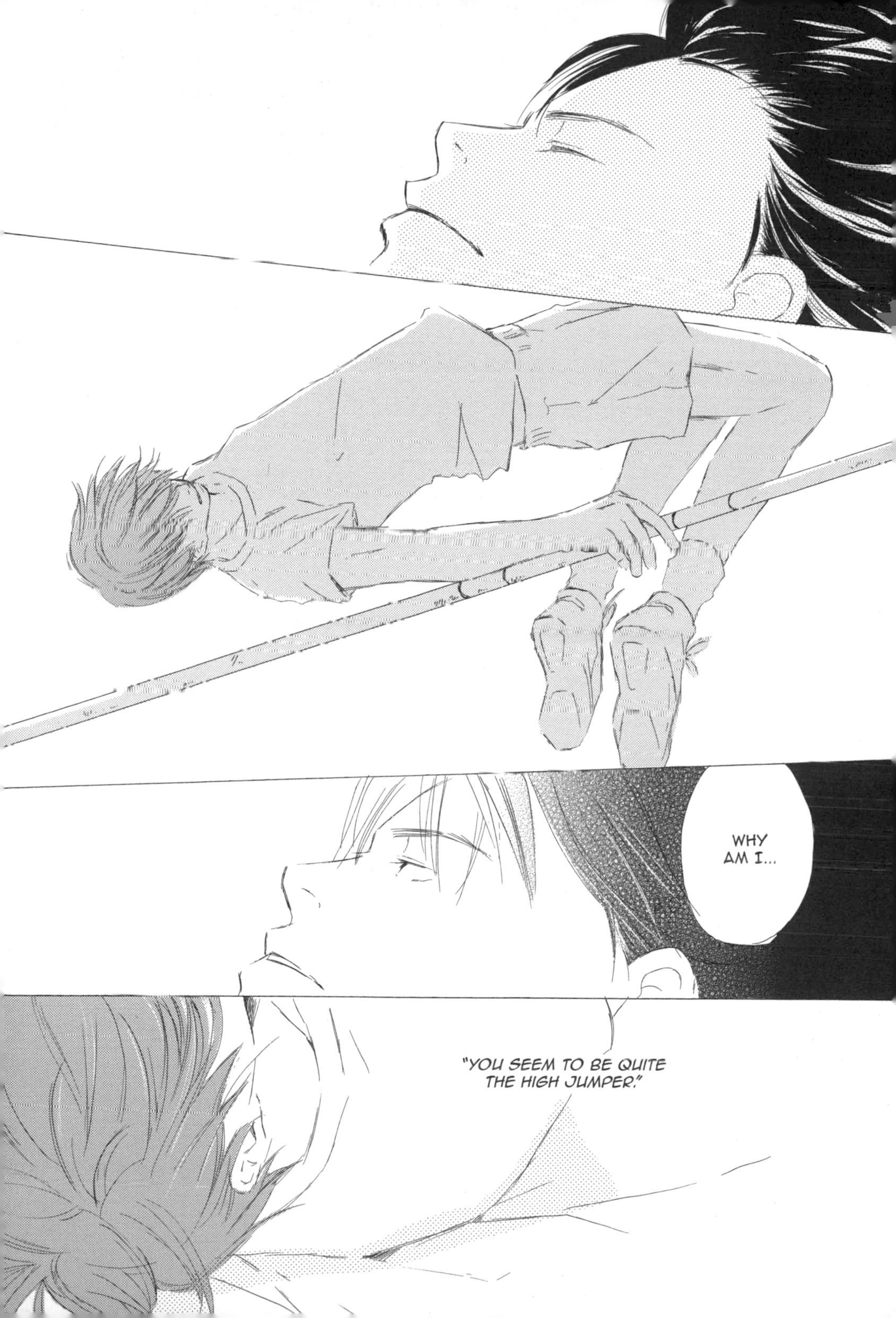
WHY AM I...
"YOU SEEM TO BE QUITE THE HIGH JUMPER."

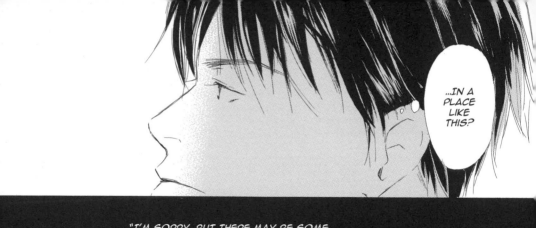

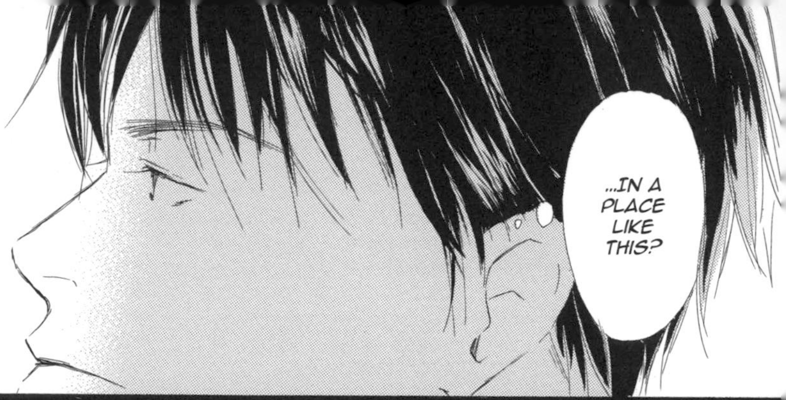
...IN A PLACE LIKE THIS?

"I'M SORRY, BUT THERE MAY BE SOME AFTEREFFECTS IN YOUR RIGHT LEG."

"EVEN AFTER REHABILITATION."

AS FOR JUMPING...

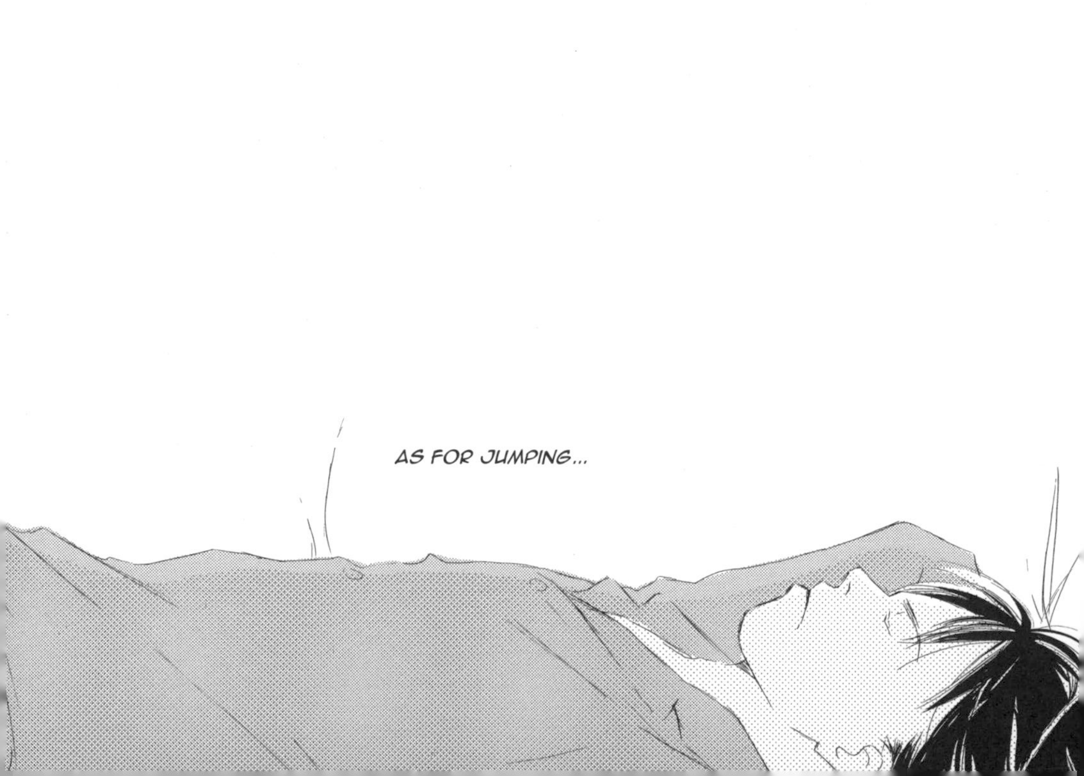

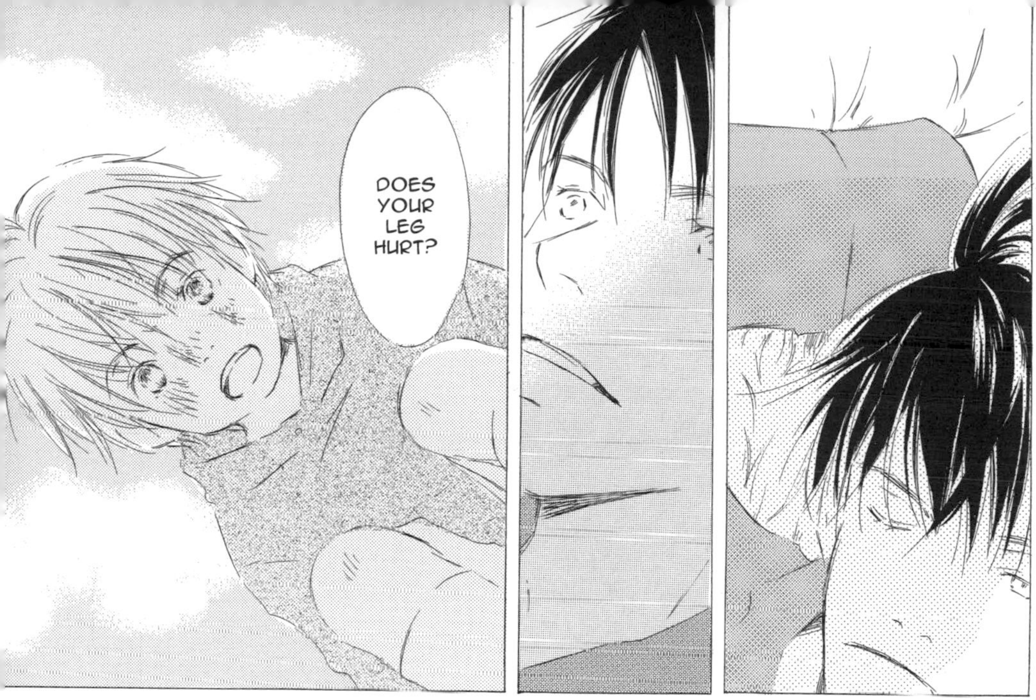
DOES YOUR LEG HURT?

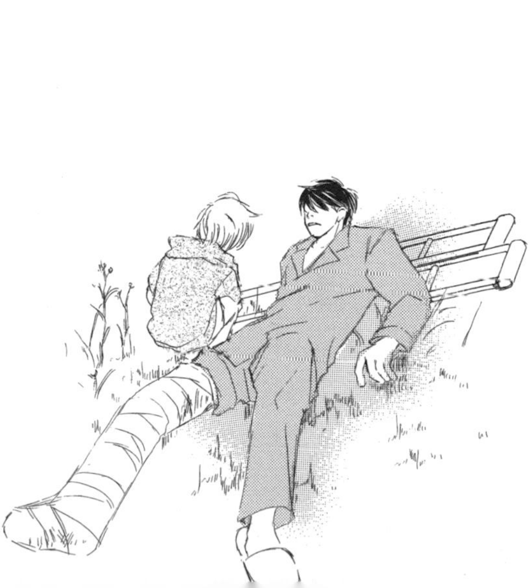

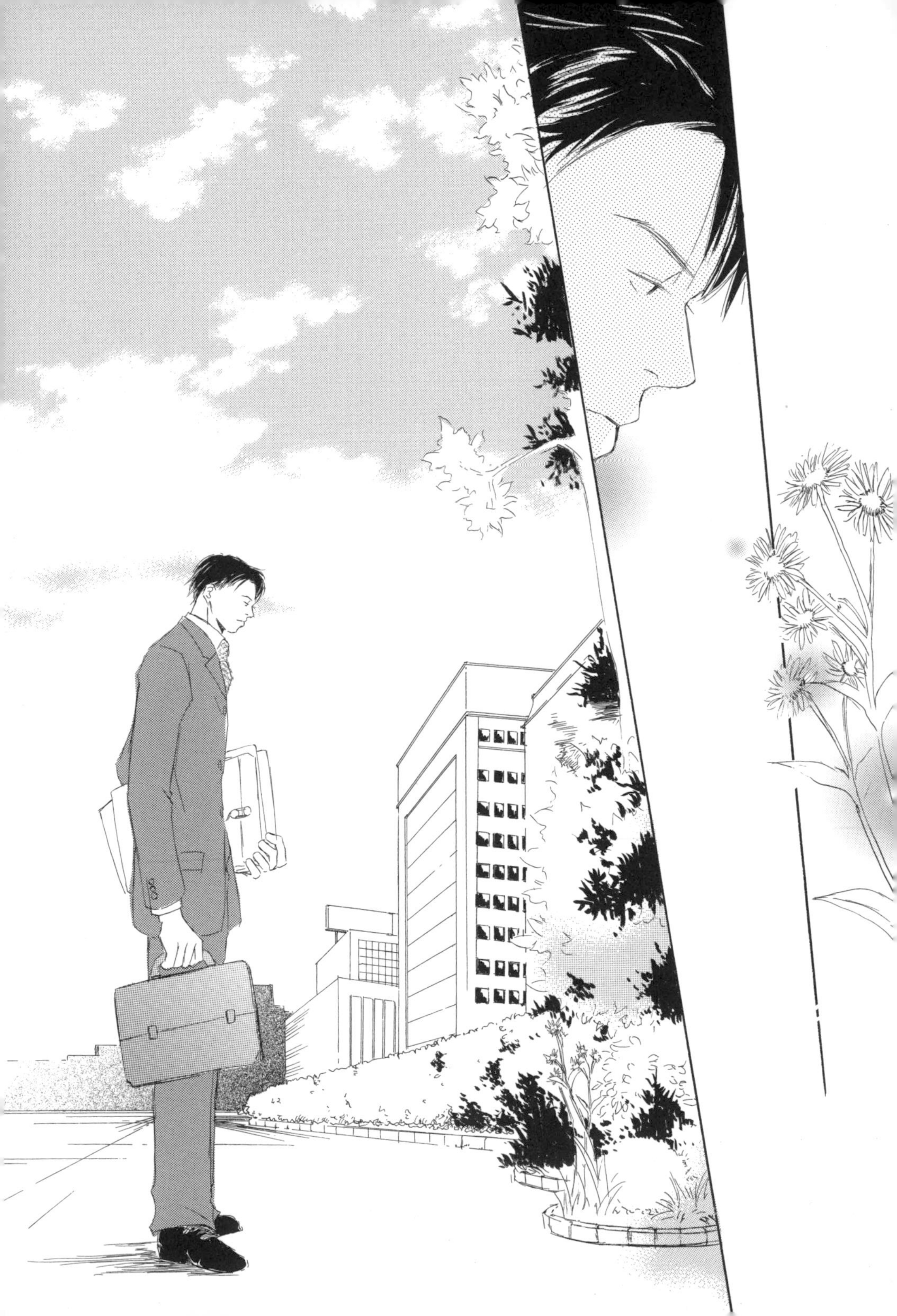

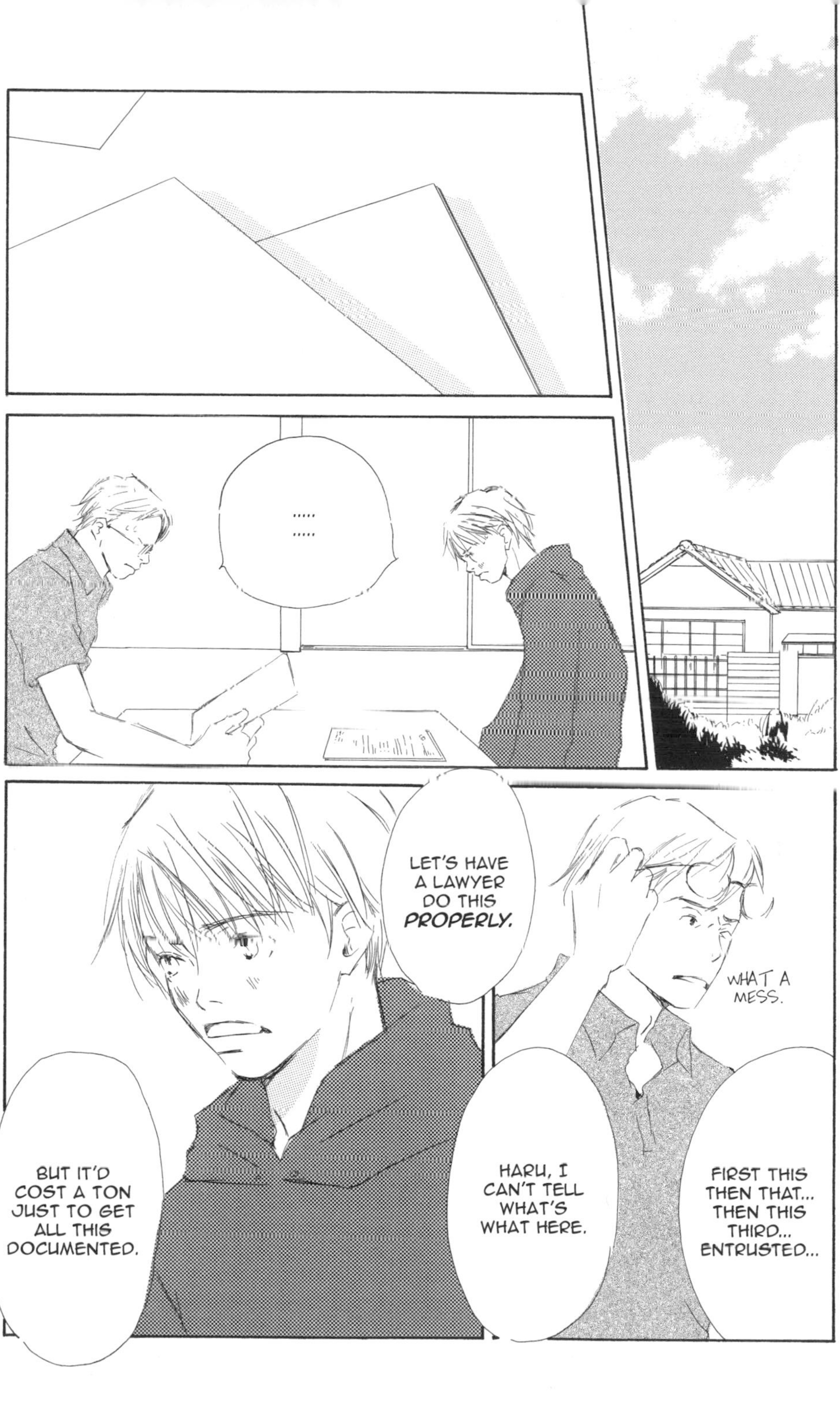
......
......
FIRST THIS THEN THAT... THEN THIS THIRD... ENTRUSTED...
WHAT A MESS.
HARU, I CAN'T TELL WHAT'S WHAT HERE.
LET'S HAVE A LAWYER DO THIS PROPERLY.
BUT IT'D COST A TON JUST TO GET ALL THIS DOCUMENTED.

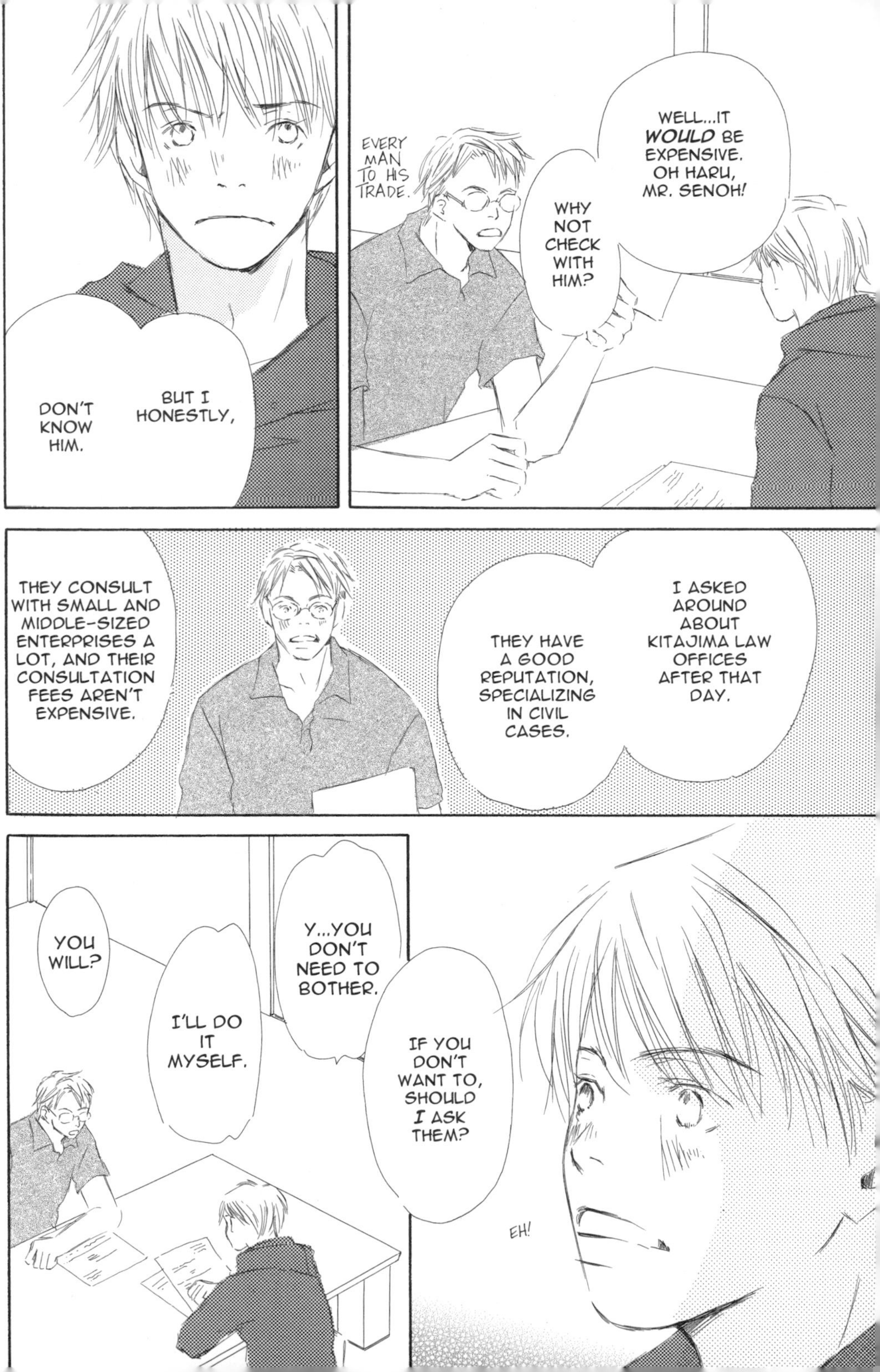
WELL...IT ***WOULD*** BE EXPENSIVE. OH HARU, MR. SENOH!
WHY NOT CHECK WITH HIM?
EVERY MAN TO HIS TRADE.
BUT I HONESTLY,
DON'T KNOW HIM.
I ASKED AROUND ABOUT KITAJIMA LAW OFFICES AFTER THAT DAY.
THEY HAVE A GOOD REPUTATION, SPECIALIZING IN CIVIL CASES.
THEY CONSULT WITH SMALL AND MIDDLE-SIZED ENTERPRISES A LOT, AND THEIR CONSULTATION FEES AREN'T EXPENSIVE.
IF YOU DON'T WANT TO, SHOULD *I* ASK THEM?
EH!
Y...YOU DON'T NEED TO BOTHER.
I'LL DO IT MYSELF.
YOU WILL?

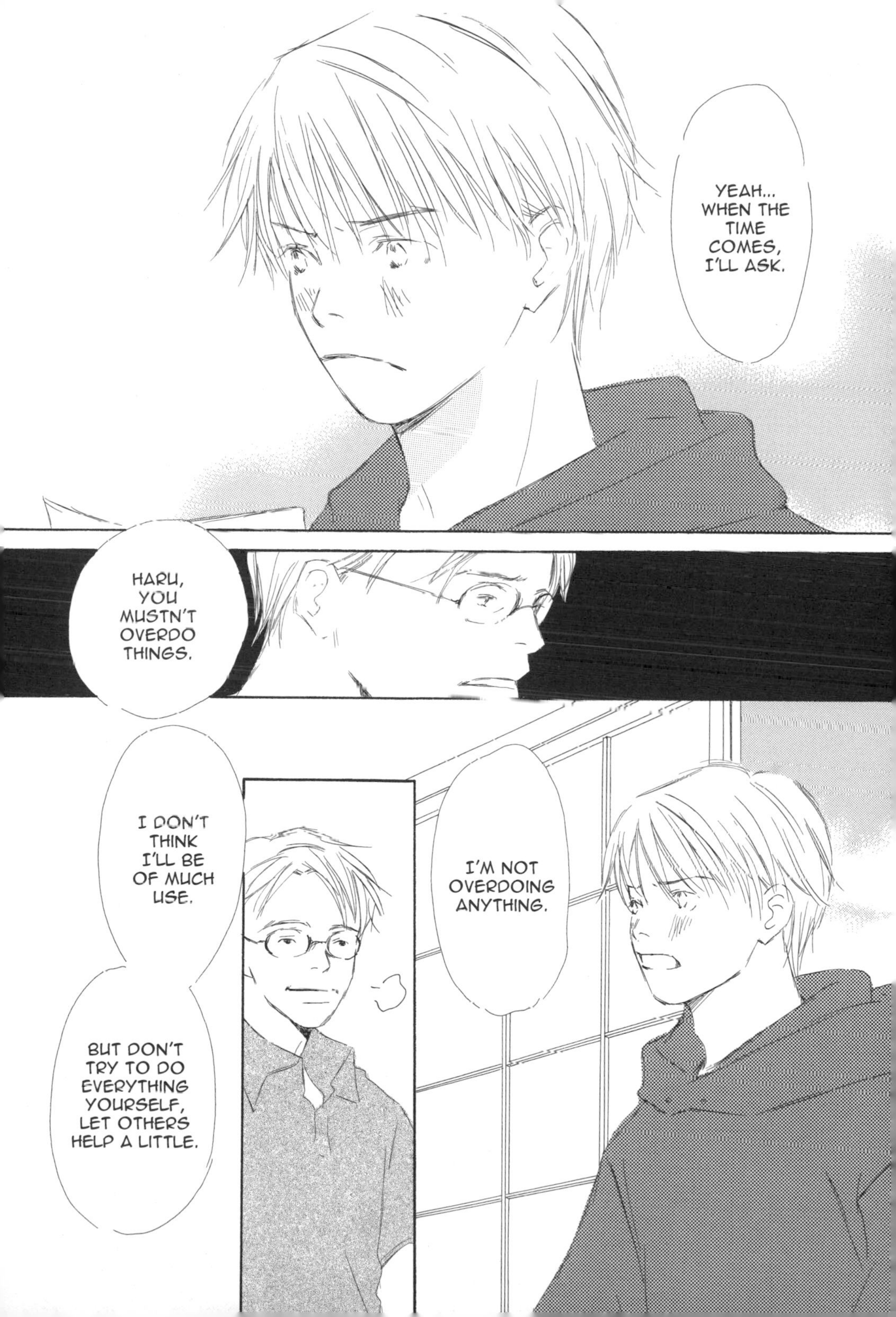
YEAH... WHEN THE TIME COMES, I'LL ASK.
HARU, YOU MUSTN'T OVERDO THINGS.
I'M NOT OVERDOING ANYTHING.
I DON'T THINK I'LL BE OF MUCH USE.
BUT DON'T TRY TO DO EVERYTHING YOURSELF, LET OTHERS HELP A LITTLE.

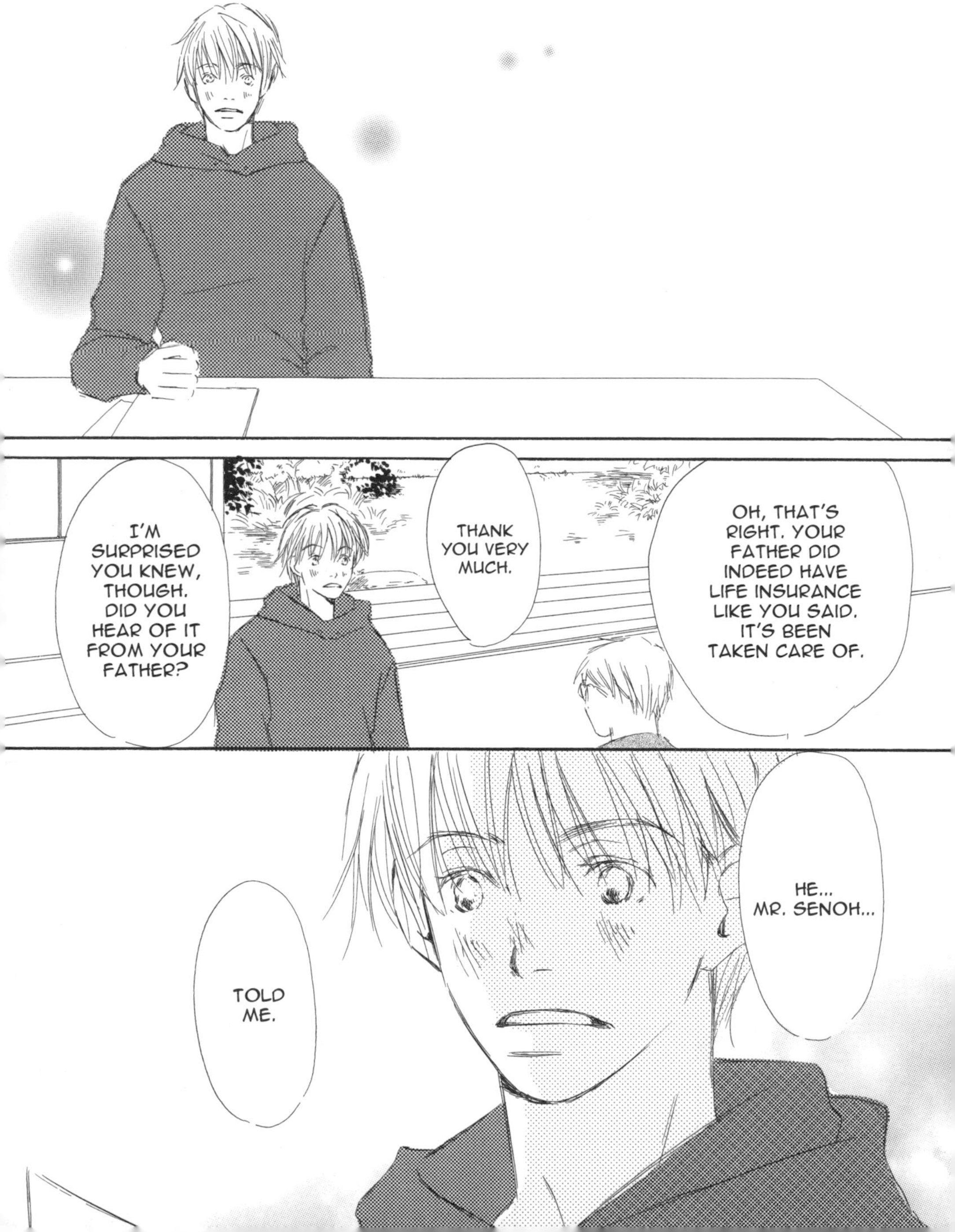
OH, THAT'S RIGHT. YOUR FATHER DID INDEED HAVE LIFE INSURANCE LIKE YOU SAID. IT'S BEEN TAKEN CARE OF.
THANK YOU VERY MUCH.
I'M SURPRISED YOU KNEW, THOUGH. DID YOU HEAR OF IT FROM YOUR FATHER?
HE... MR. SENOH...
TOLD ME.

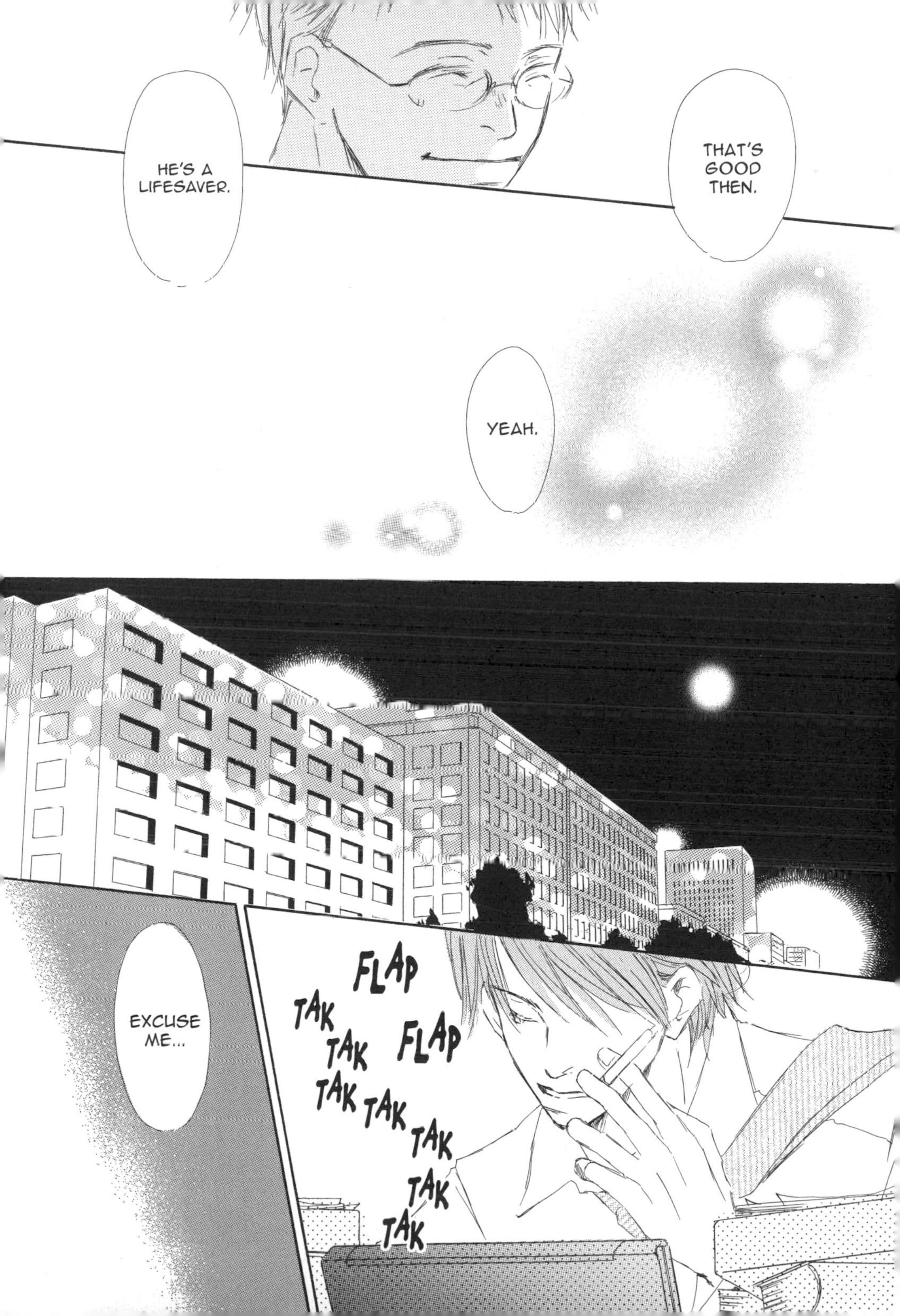
HE'S A LIFESAVER.
THAT'S GOOD THEN.
YEAH.
FLAP
TAK
FLAP
TAK
TAK
TAK
TAK
TAK
TAK
EXCUSE ME...

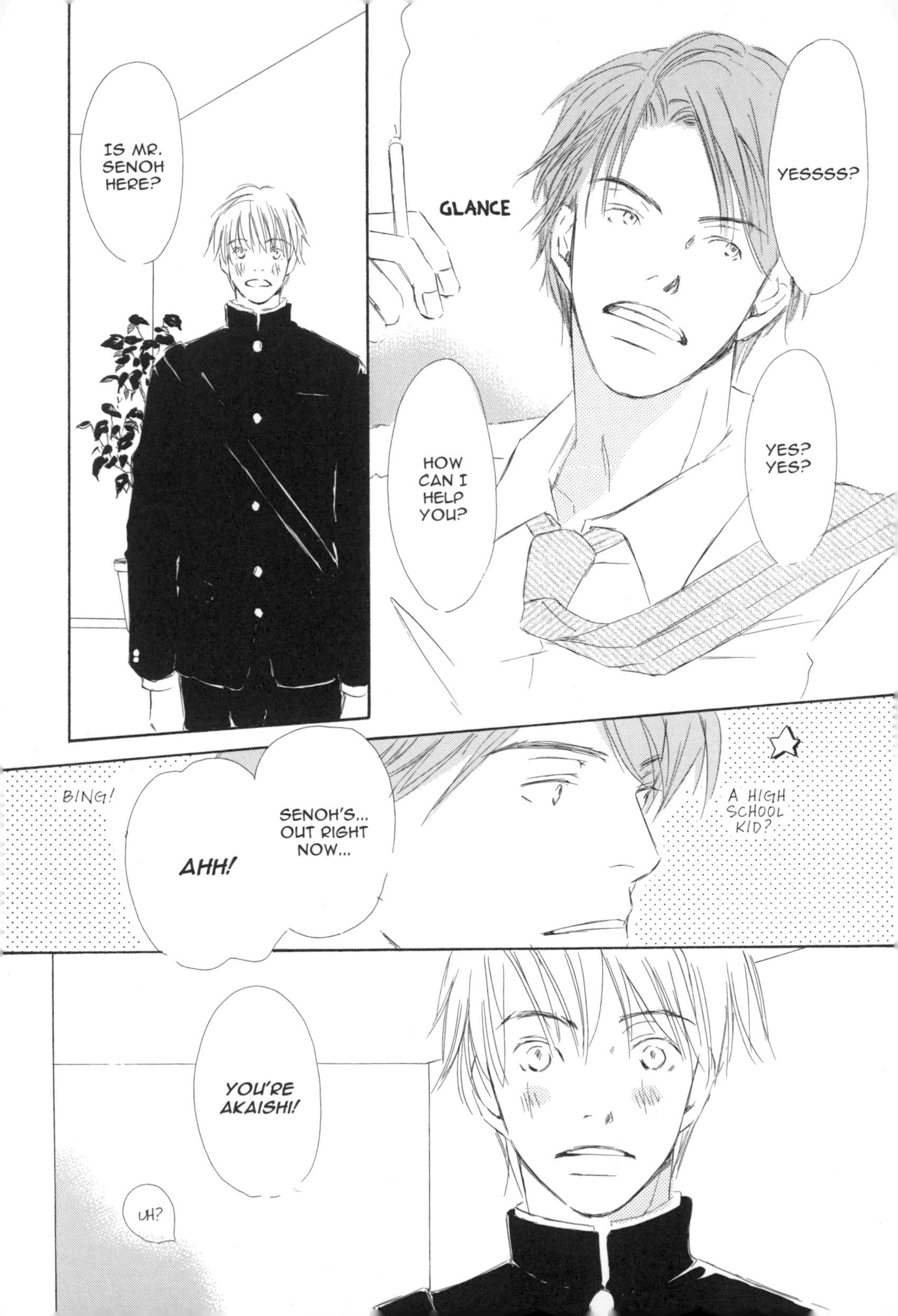
YESSSS?
GLANCE
YES? YES?
HOW CAN I HELP YOU?
IS MR. SENOH HERE?
A HIGH SCHOOL KID?
SENOH'S... OUT RIGHT NOW...
AHH!
BING!
YOU'RE AKAISHI!
UH?

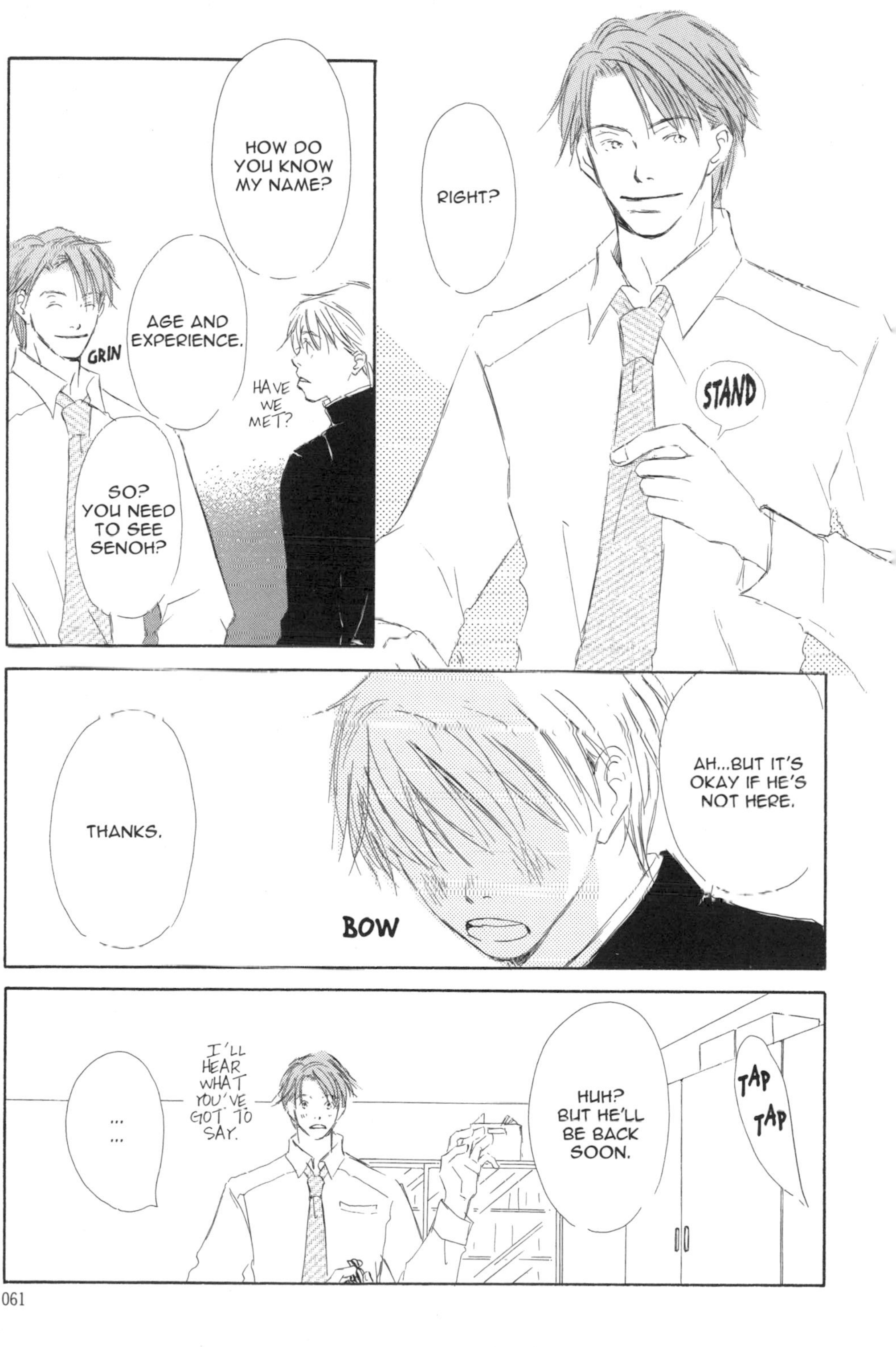
RIGHT?
STAND
HOW DO YOU KNOW MY NAME?
HAVE WE MET?
AGE AND EXPERIENCE.
GRIN
SO? YOU NEED TO SEE SENOH?
AH...BUT IT'S OKAY IF HE'S NOT HERE.
BOW
THANKS.
TAP TAP
HUH? BUT HE'LL BE BACK SOON.
I'LL HEAR WHAT YOU'VE GOT TO SAY.
... ...

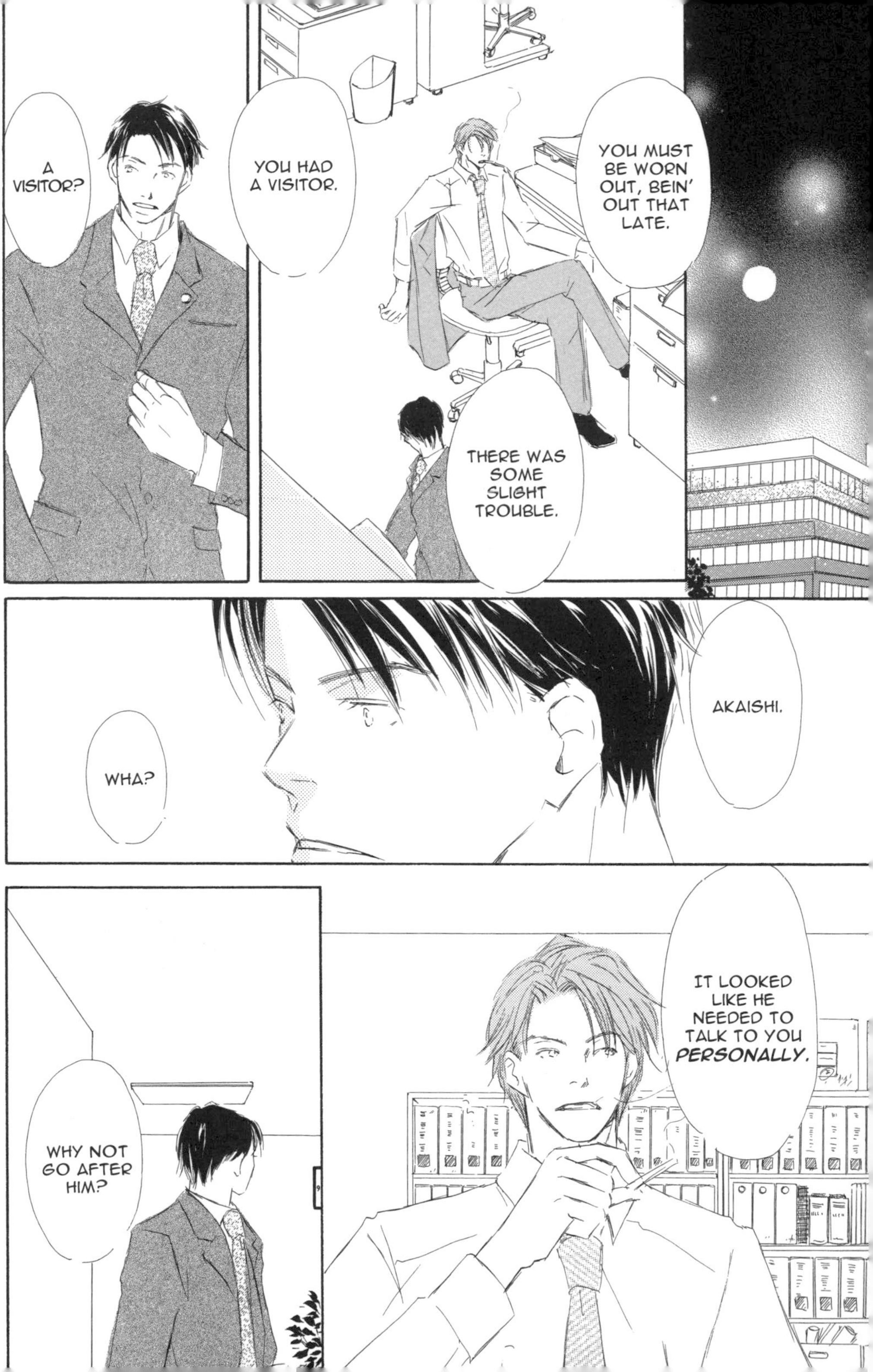
YOU MUST BE WORN OUT, BEIN' OUT THAT LATE.
THERE WAS SOME SLIGHT TROUBLE.
YOU HAD A VISITOR.
A VISITOR?
AKAISHI.
WHA?
IT LOOKED LIKE HE NEEDED TO TALK TO YOU PERSONALLY.
WHY NOT GO AFTER HIM?

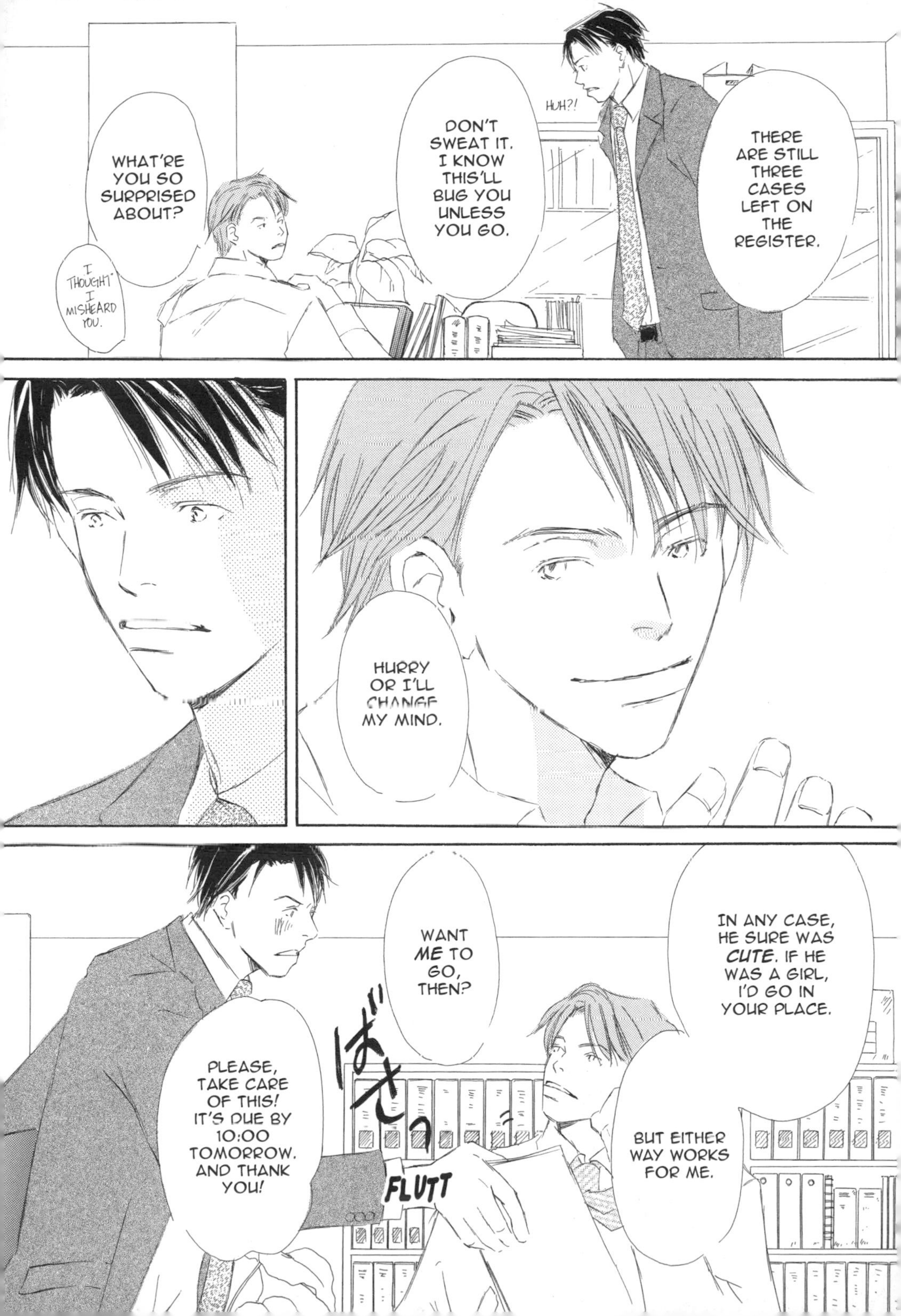
THERE ARE STILL THREE CASES LEFT ON THE REGISTER.
HUH?!
DON'T SWEAT IT. I KNOW THIS'LL BUG YOU UNLESS YOU GO.
WHAT'RE YOU SO SURPRISED ABOUT?
I THOUGHT I MISHEARD YOU.
HURRY OR I'LL CHANGE MY MIND.
WANT ME TO GO, THEN?
IN ANY CASE, HE SURE WAS CUTE. IF HE WAS A GIRL, I'D GO IN YOUR PLACE.
BUT EITHER WAY WORKS FOR ME.
PLEASE, TAKE CARE OF THIS! IT'S DUE BY 10:00 TOMORROW. AND THANK YOU!
ばさっ
FLUTT

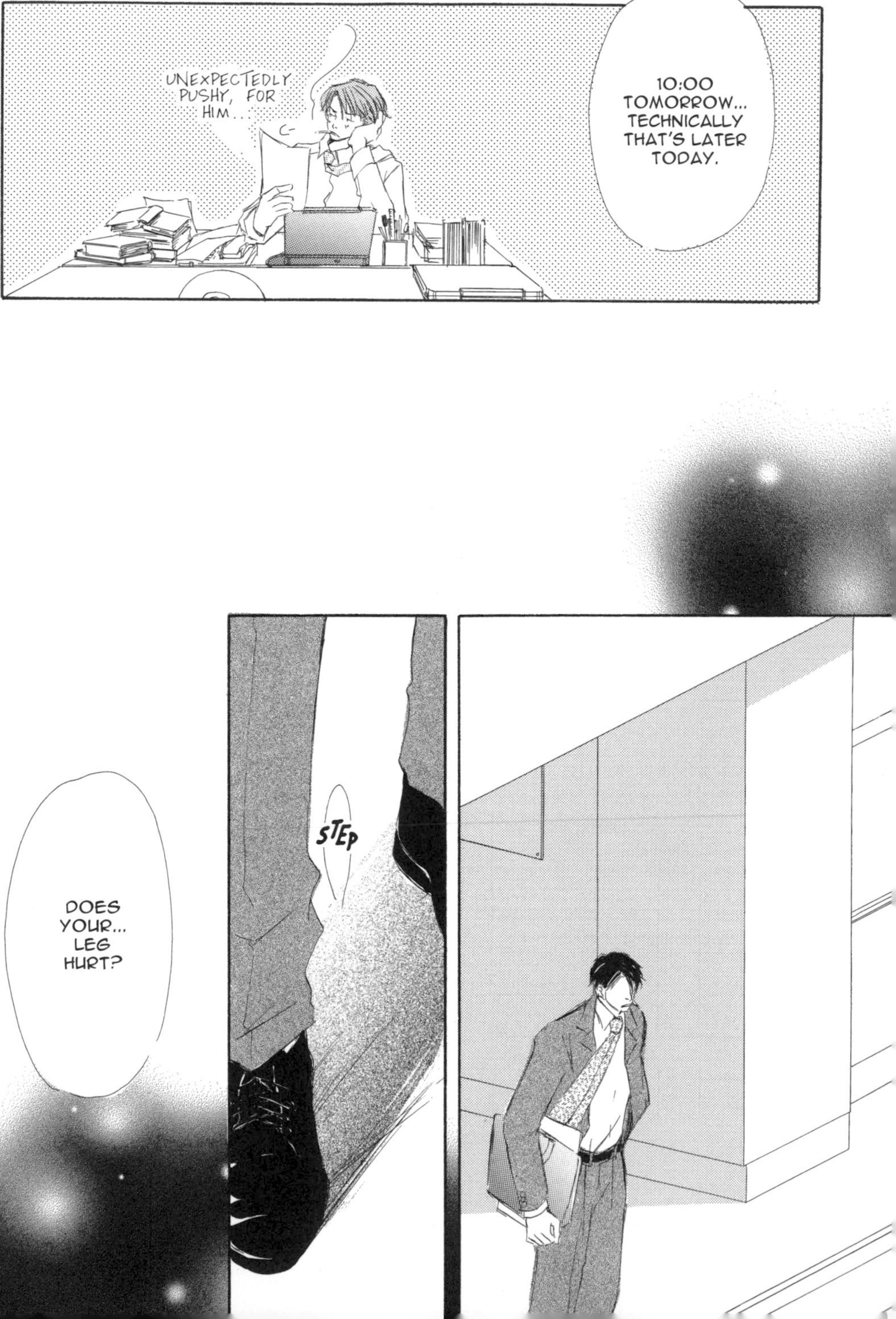
10:00 TOMORROW... TECHNICALLY THAT'S LATER TODAY.
UNEXPECTEDLY PUSHY, FOR HIM...
STEP
DOES YOUR... LEG HURT?

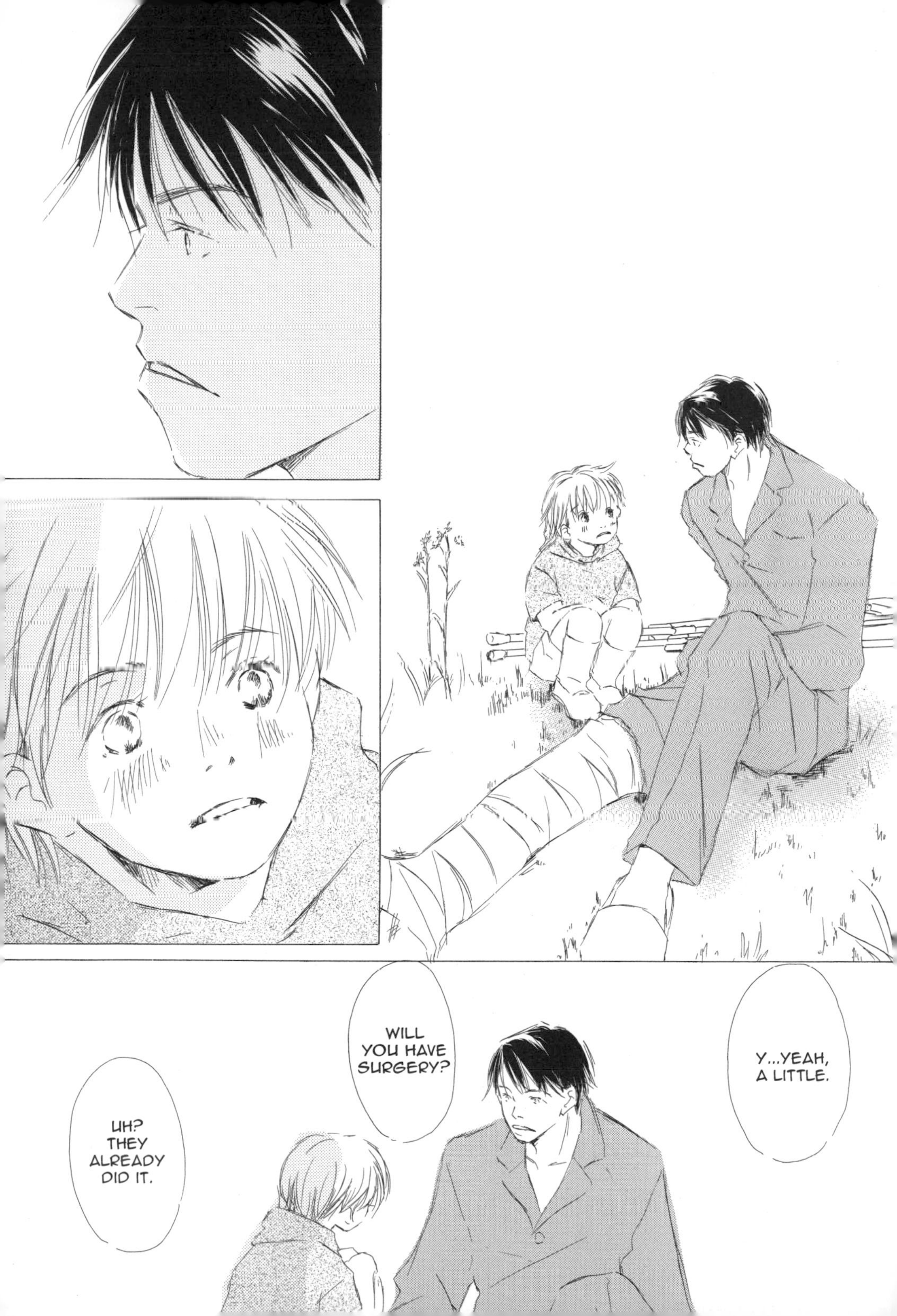
Y...YEAH, A LITTLE.
WILL YOU HAVE SURGERY?
UH? THEY ALREADY DID IT.

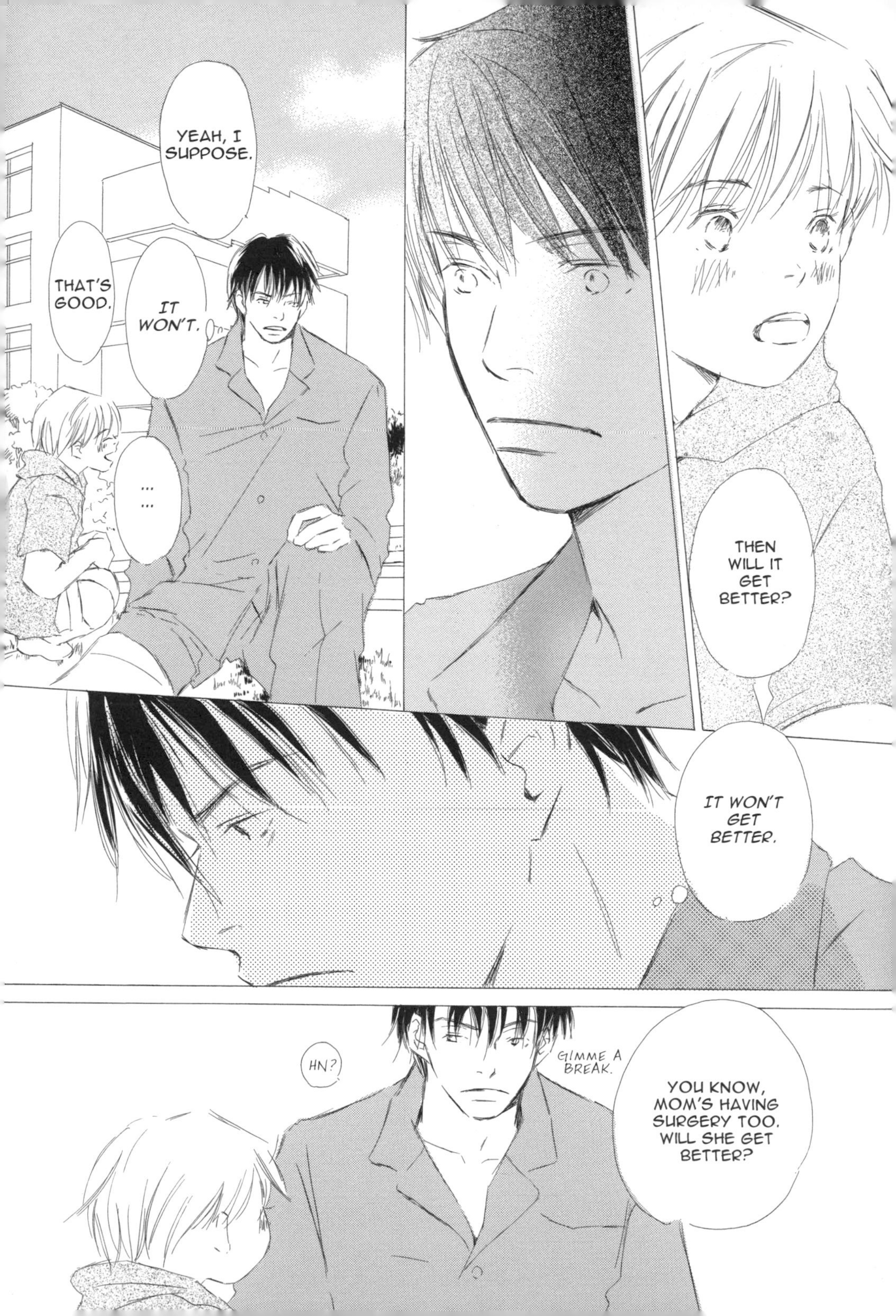
YEAH, I SUPPOSE.
IT WON'T.
THAT'S GOOD.
……
THEN WILL IT GET BETTER?
IT WON'T GET BETTER.
YOU KNOW, MOM'S HAVING SURGERY TOO. WILL SHE GET BETTER?
GIMME A BREAK.
HN?

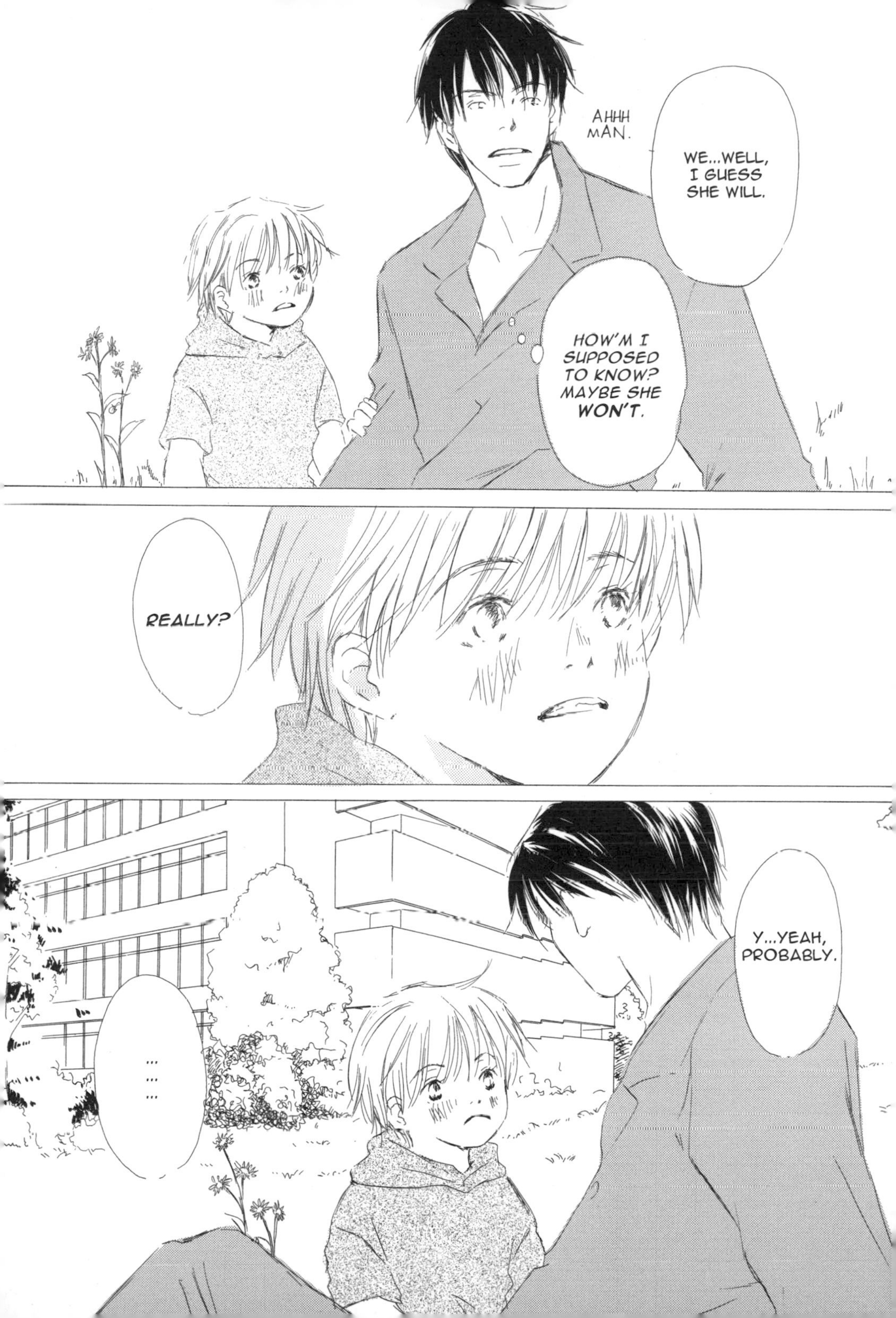
WE...WELL, I GUESS SHE WILL.
AHHH MAN.
HOW'M I SUPPOSED TO KNOW? MAYBE SHE WON'T.
REALLY?
Y...YEAH, PROBABLY.
... ...

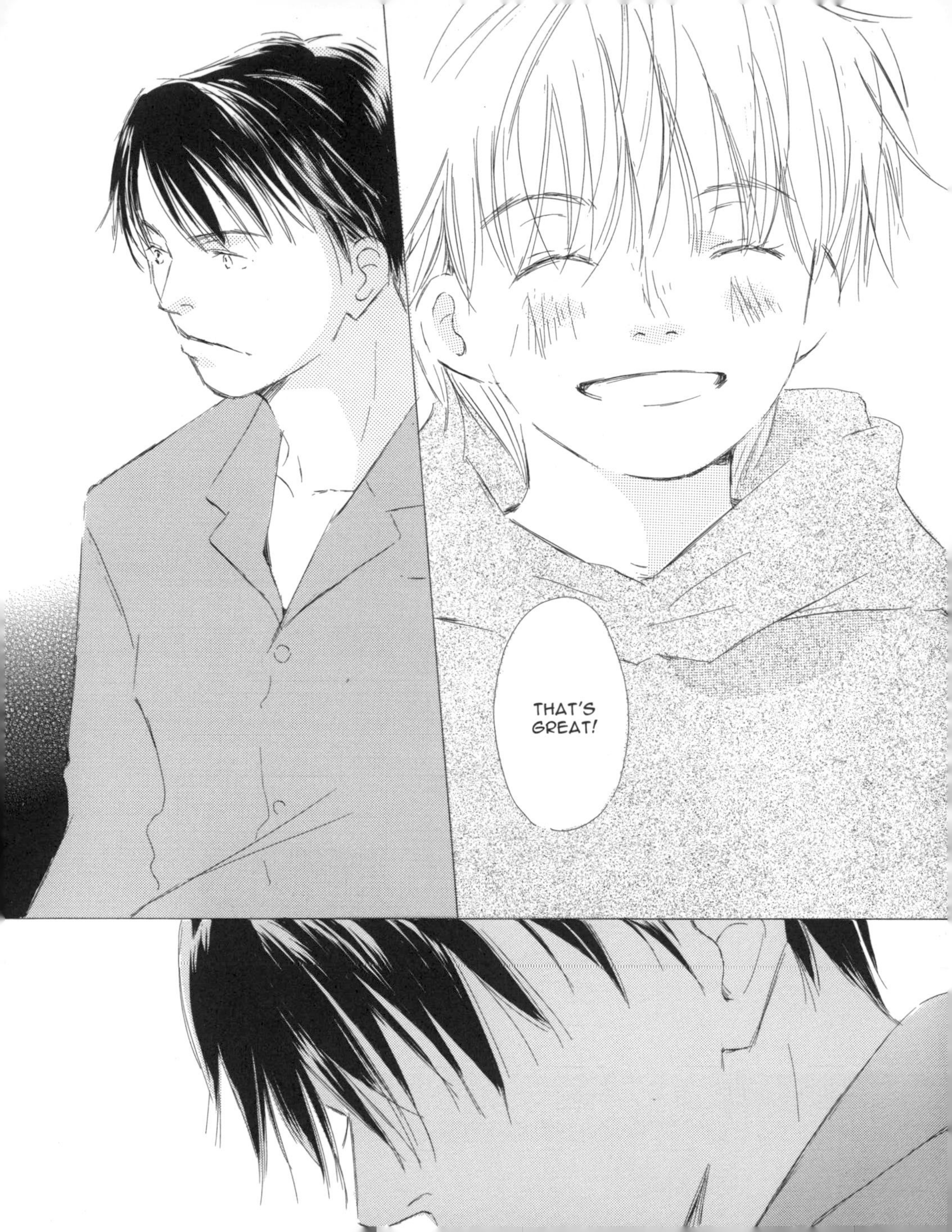
THAT'S GREAT!

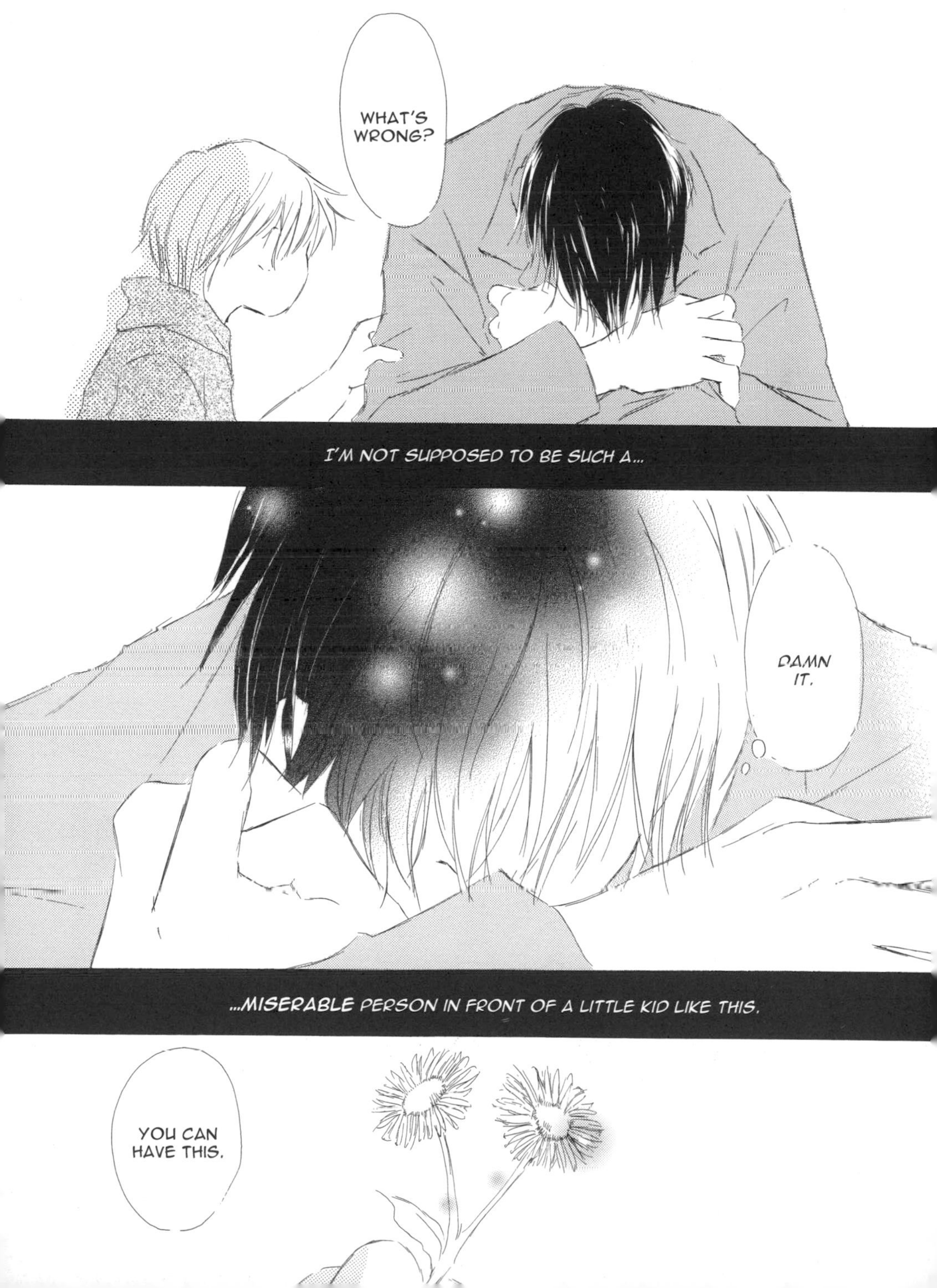
WHAT'S WRONG?
I'M NOT SUPPOSED TO BE SUCH A...
DAMN IT.
...MISERABLE PERSON IN FRONT OF A LITTLE KID LIKE THIS.
YOU CAN HAVE THIS.

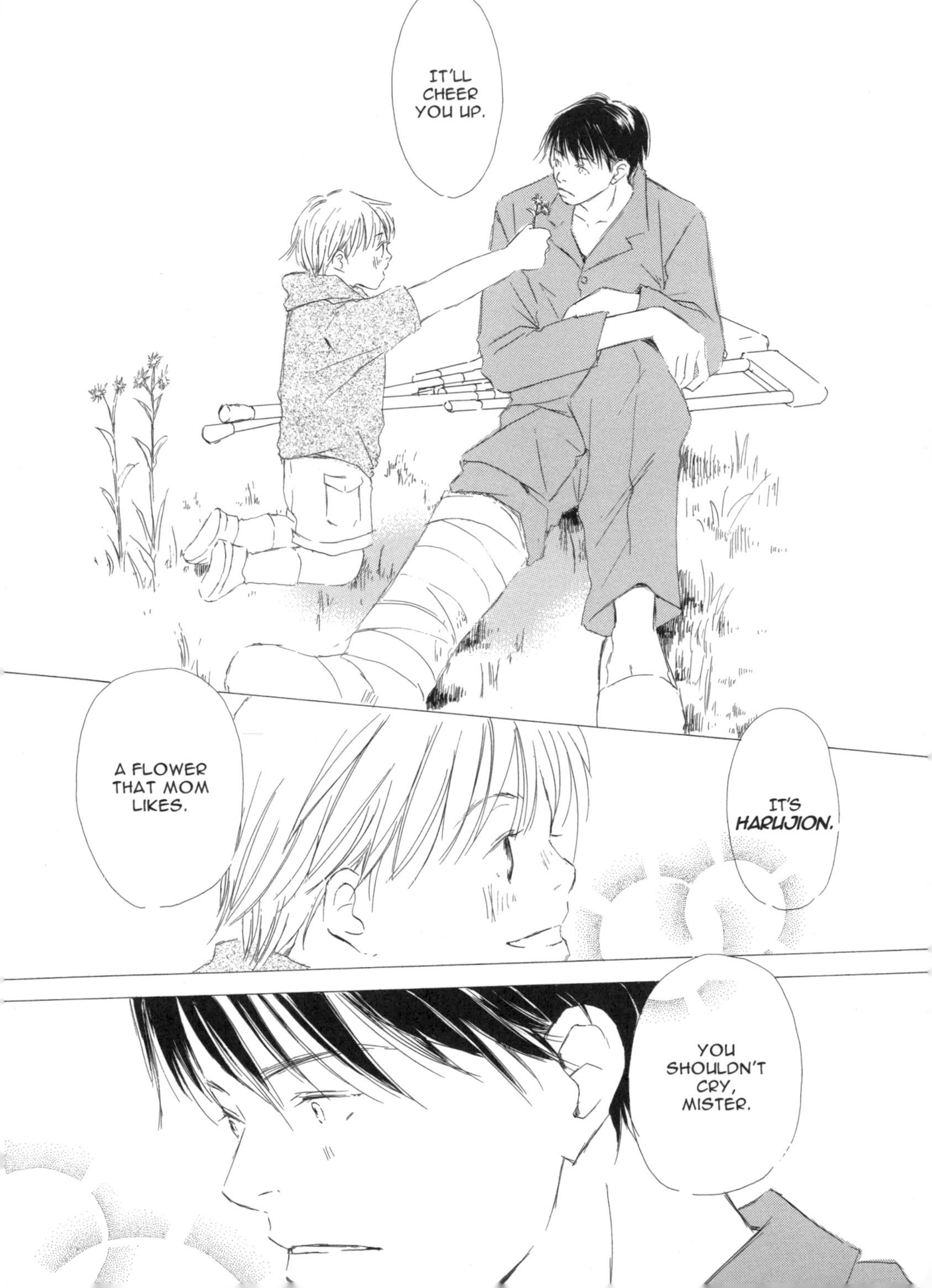
IT'LL CHEER YOU UP.
IT'S *HARUJION.*
A FLOWER THAT MOM LIKES.
YOU SHOULDN'T CRY, MISTER.

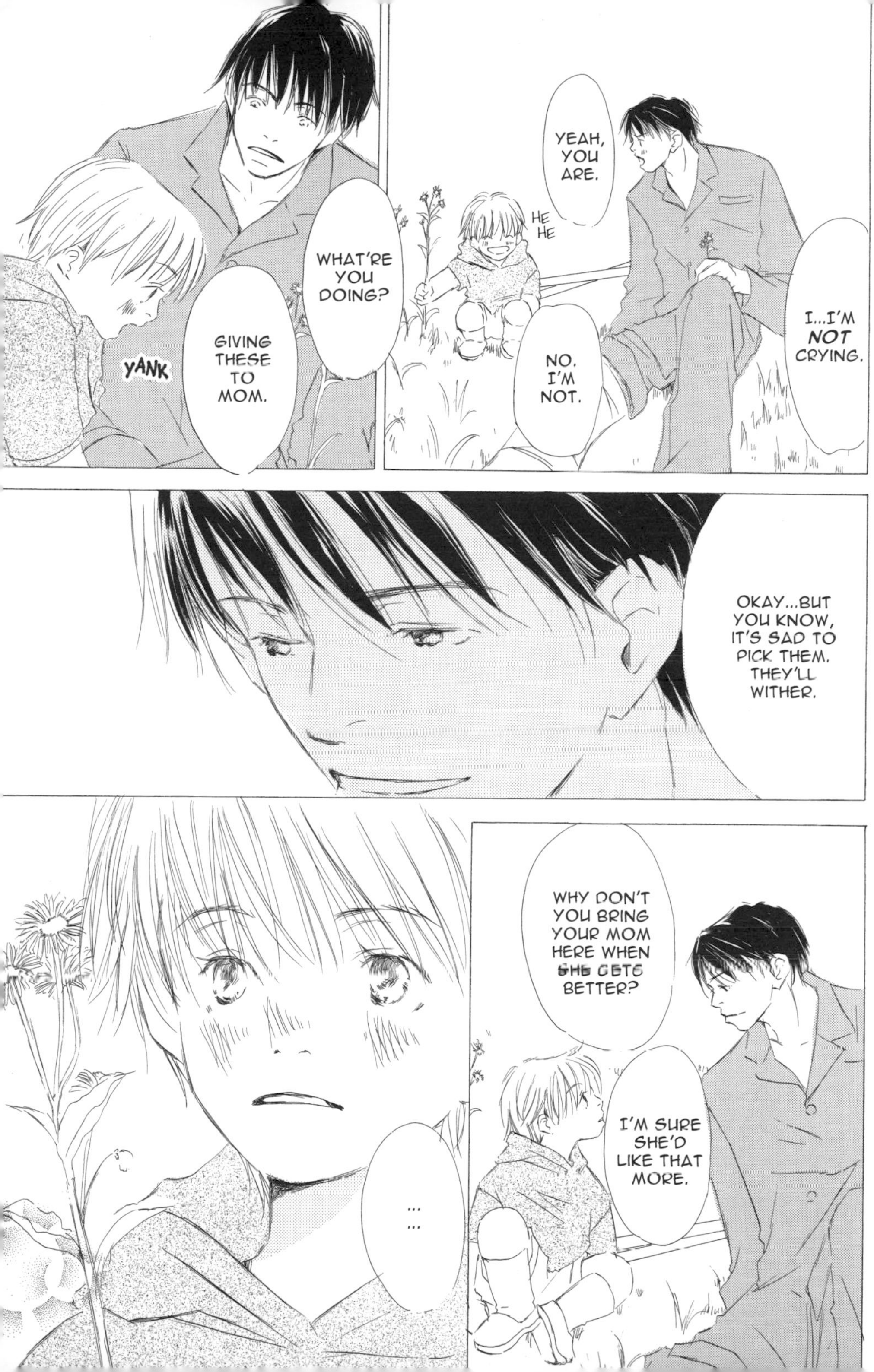
I...I'M NOT CRYING.
YEAH, YOU ARE.
HE HE
NO. I'M NOT.
WHAT'RE YOU DOING?
GIVING THESE TO MOM.
YANK
OKAY...BUT YOU KNOW, IT'S SAD TO PICK THEM. THEY'LL WITHER.
WHY DON'T YOU BRING YOUR MOM HERE WHEN SHE GETS BETTER?
I'M SURE SHE'D LIKE THAT MORE.
... ...

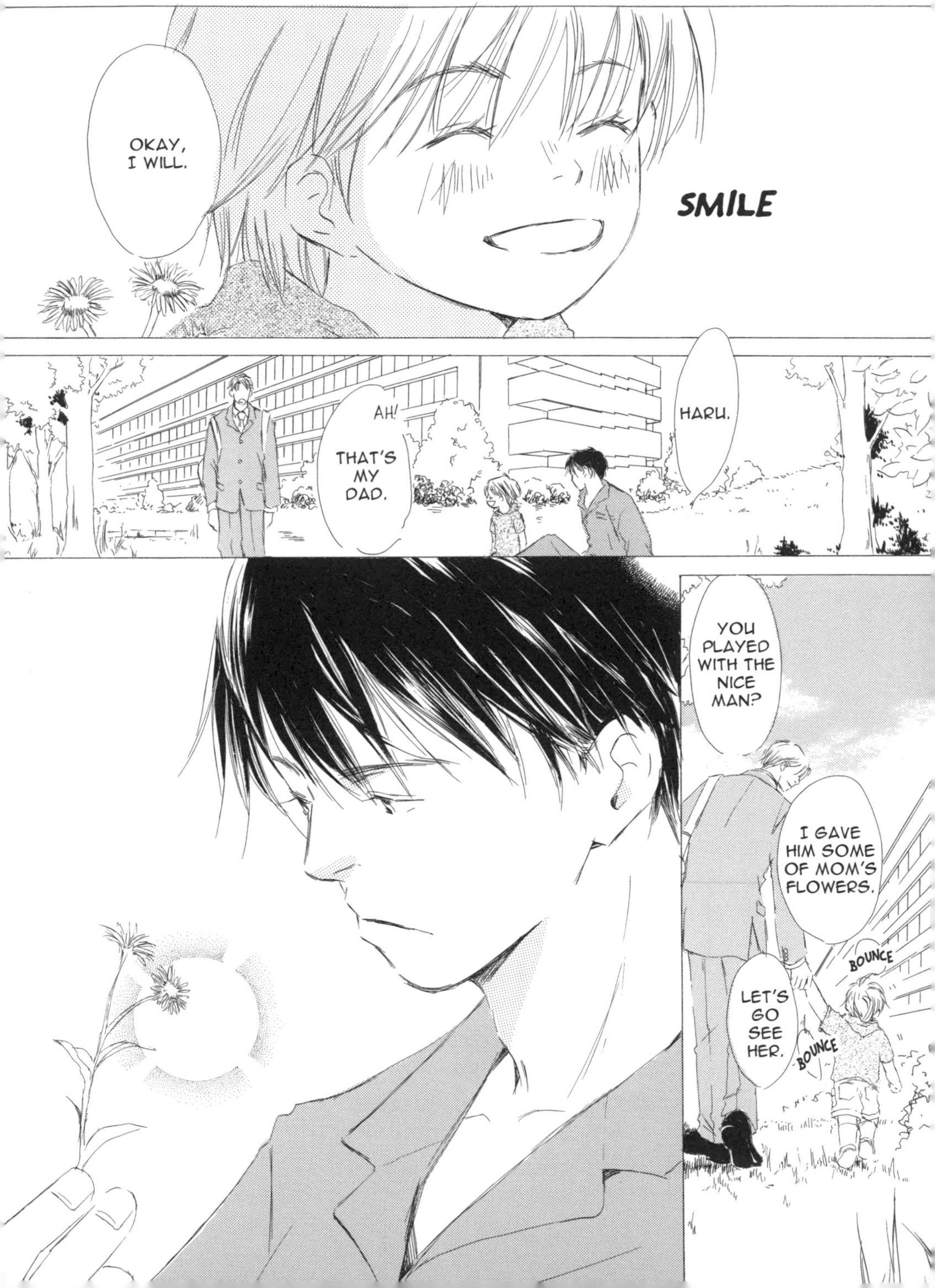
OKAY, I WILL.
SMILE
HARU.
AH!
THAT'S MY DAD.
YOU PLAYED WITH THE NICE MAN?
I GAVE HIM SOME OF MOM'S FLOWERS.
BOUNCE
LET'S GO SEE HER.
BOUNCE

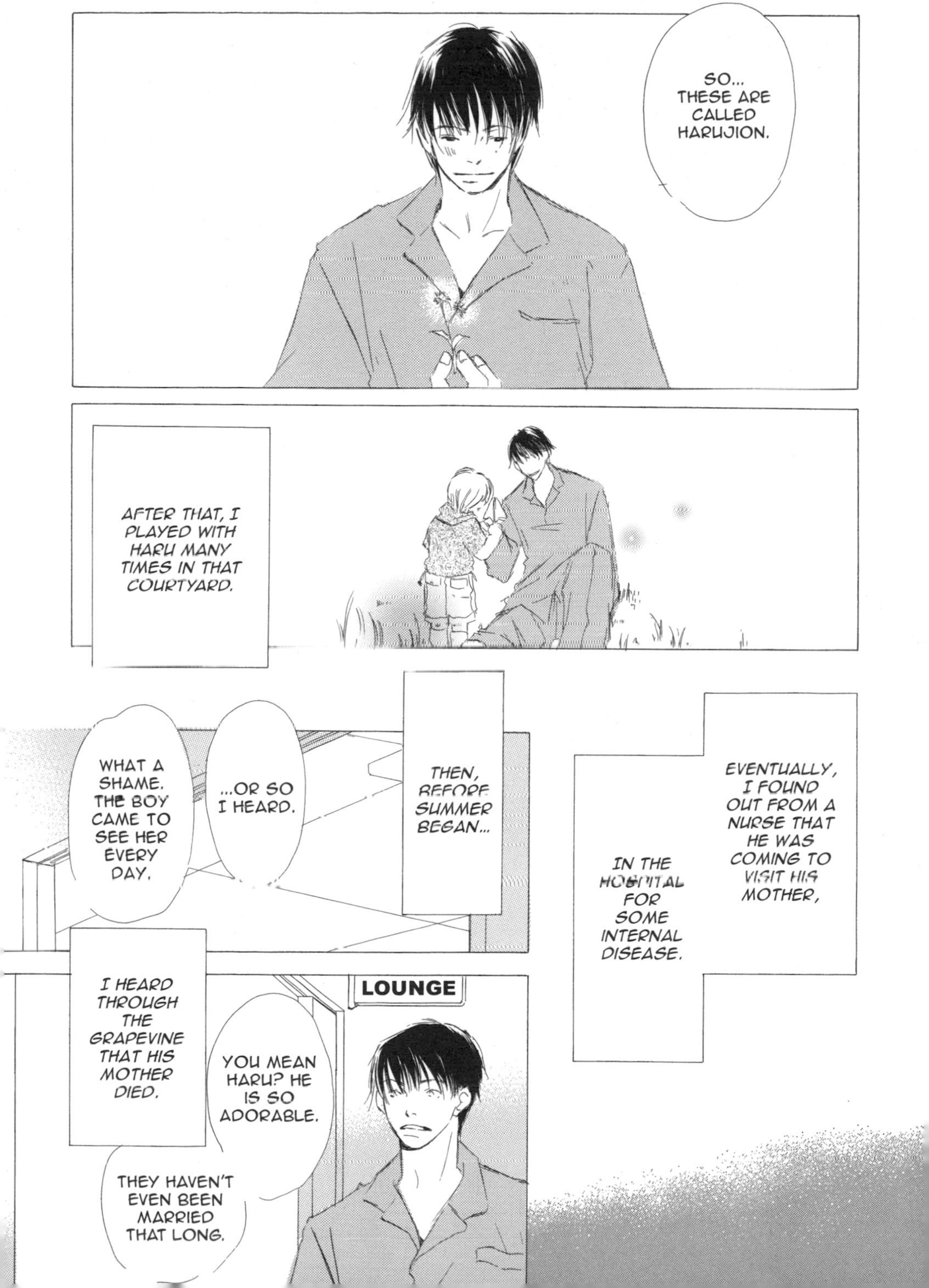
SO... THESE ARE CALLED HARUJION.
AFTER THAT, I PLAYED WITH HARU MANY TIMES IN THAT COURTYARD.
EVENTUALLY, I FOUND OUT FROM A NURSE THAT HE WAS COMING TO VISIT HIS MOTHER,
IN THE HOSPITAL FOR SOME INTERNAL DISEASE.
THEN, BEFORE SUMMER BEGAN...
...OR SO I HEARD.
WHAT A SHAME. THE BOY CAME TO SEE HER EVERY DAY.
LOUNGE
I HEARD THROUGH THE GRAPEVINE THAT HIS MOTHER DIED.
YOU MEAN HARU? HE IS SO ADORABLE.
THEY HAVEN'T EVEN BEEN MARRIED THAT LONG.

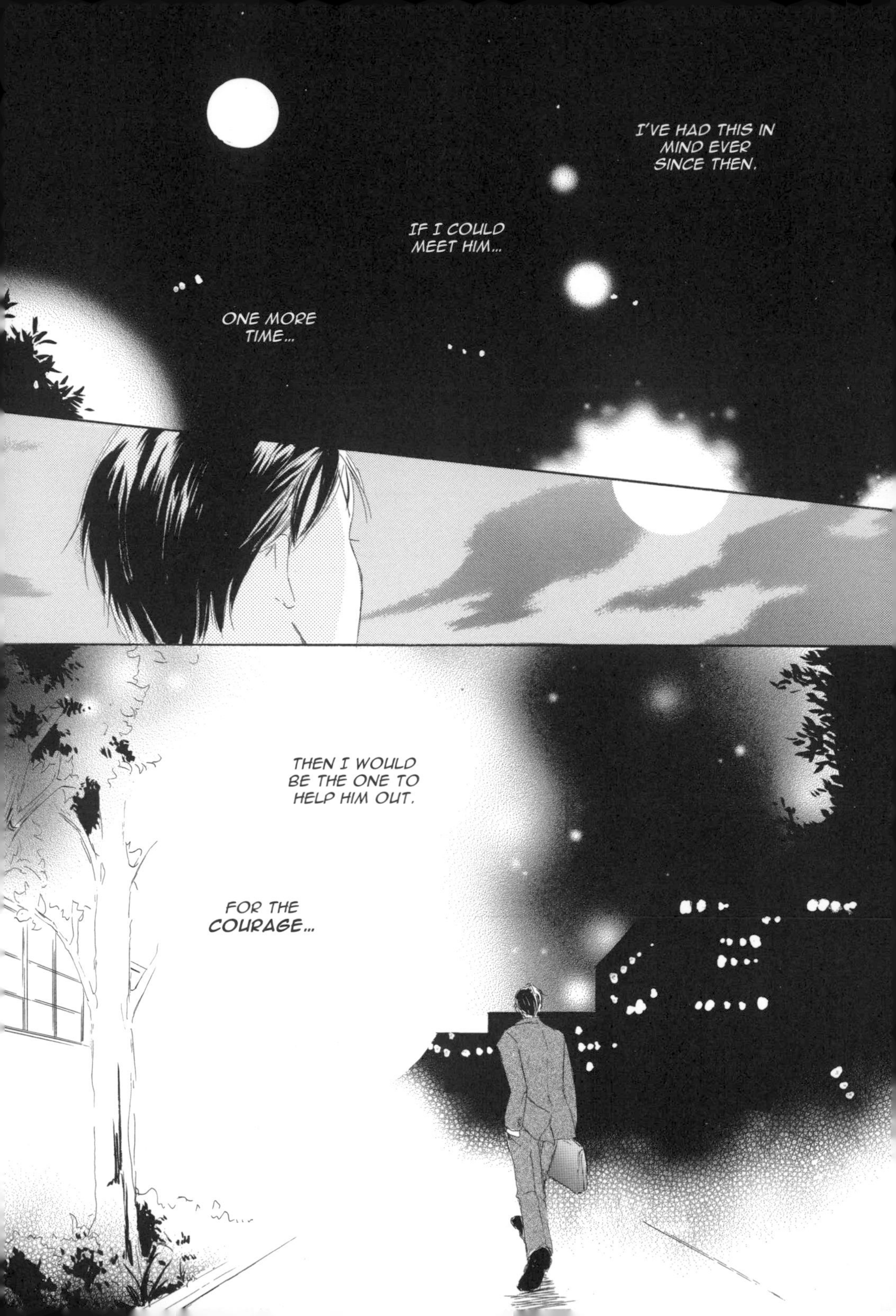
I'VE HAD THIS IN MIND EVER SINCE THEN.
IF I COULD MEET HIM...
ONE MORE TIME...
THEN I WOULD BE THE ONE TO HELP HIM OUT.
FOR THE COURAGE...

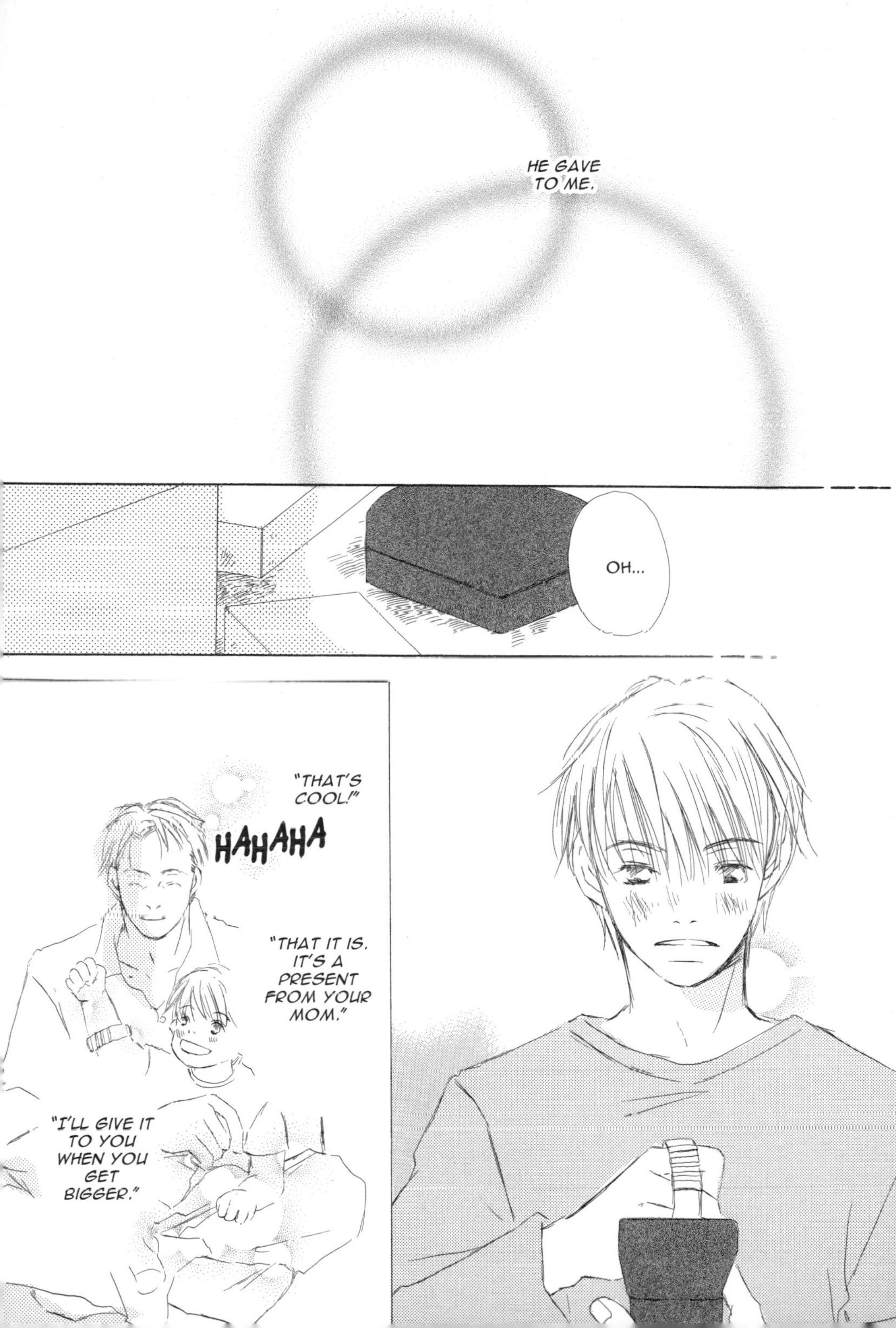
HE GAVE TO ME.
OH...
"THAT'S COOL!"
HAHAHA
"THAT IT IS. IT'S A PRESENT FROM YOUR MOM."
"I'LL GIVE IT TO YOU WHEN YOU GET BIGGER."

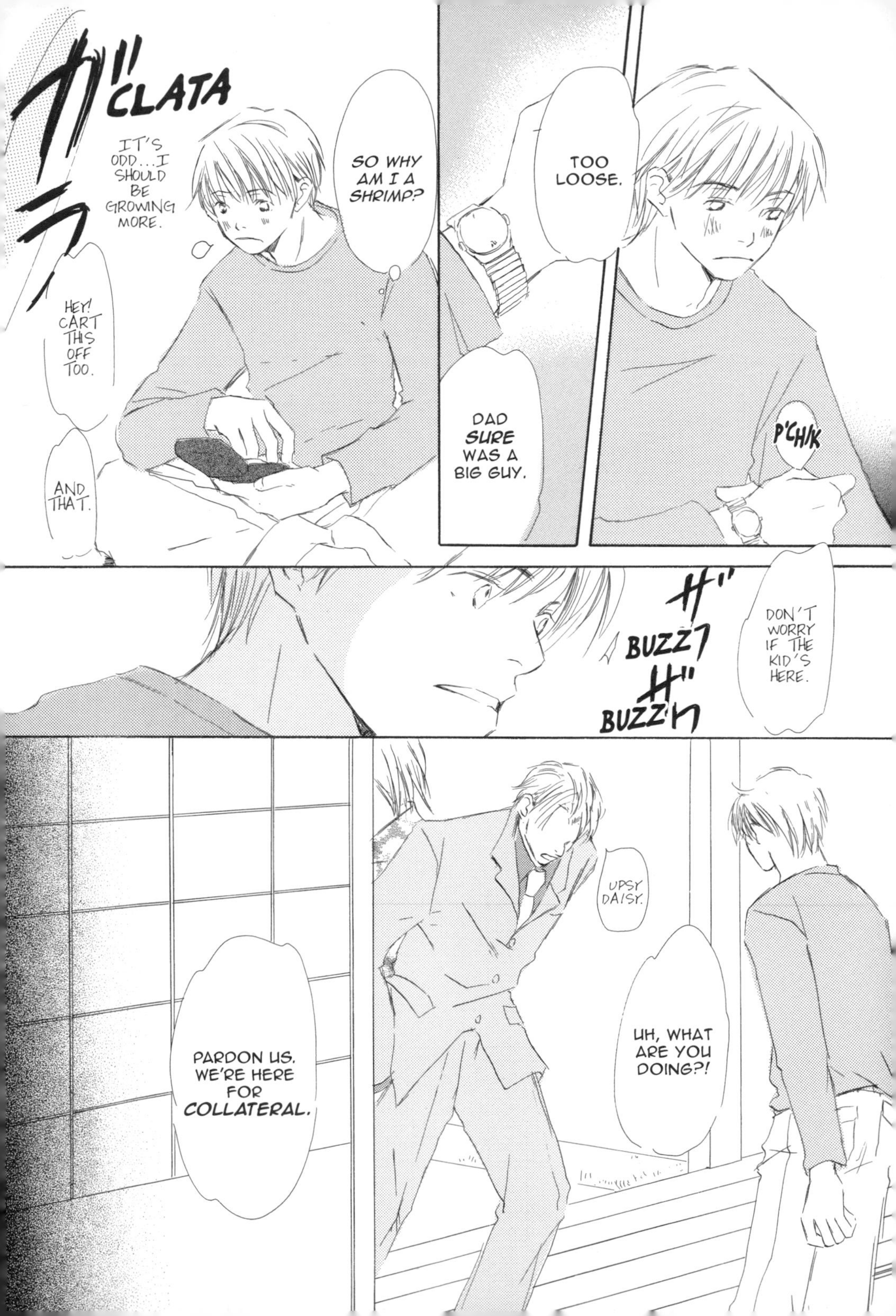
P'CHIK
TOO LOOSE.
DAD SURE WAS A BIG GUY.
SO WHY AM I A SHRIMP?
IT'S ODD... I SHOULD BE GROWING MORE.
CLATA
HEY! CART THIS OFF TOO.
AND THAT.
DON'T WORRY IF THE KID'S HERE.
BUZZ
BUZZ
UH, WHAT ARE YOU DOING?!
UPSY DAISY.
PARDON US. WE'RE HERE FOR COLLATERAL.

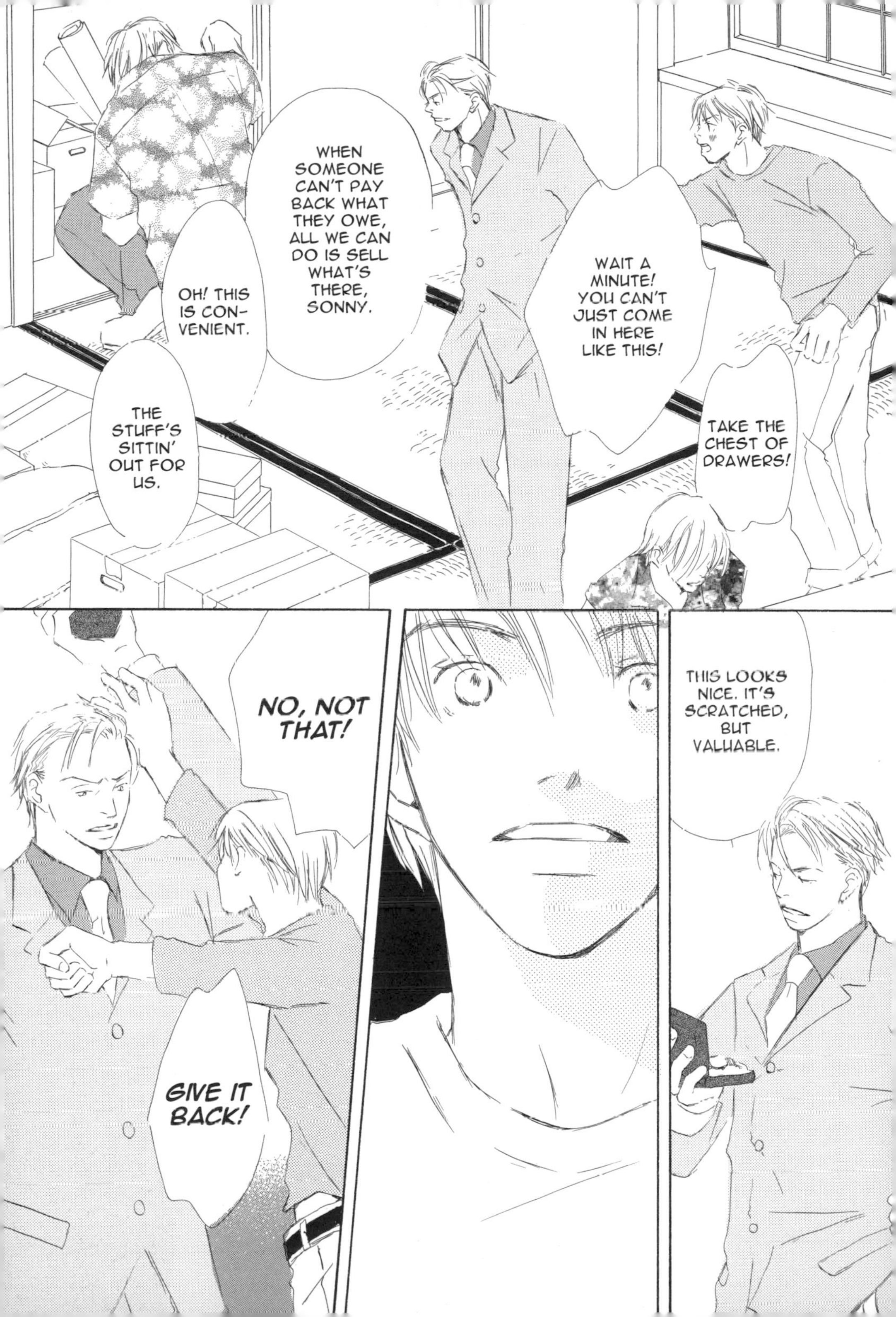
WAIT A MINUTE! YOU CAN'T JUST COME IN HERE LIKE THIS!
WHEN SOMEONE CAN'T PAY BACK WHAT THEY OWE, ALL WE CAN DO IS SELL WHAT'S THERE, SONNY.
TAKE THE CHEST OF DRAWERS!
OH! THIS IS CON-VENIENT.
THE STUFF'S SITTIN' OUT FOR US.
THIS LOOKS NICE. IT'S SCRATCHED, BUT VALUABLE.
NO, NOT THAT!
GIVE IT BACK!

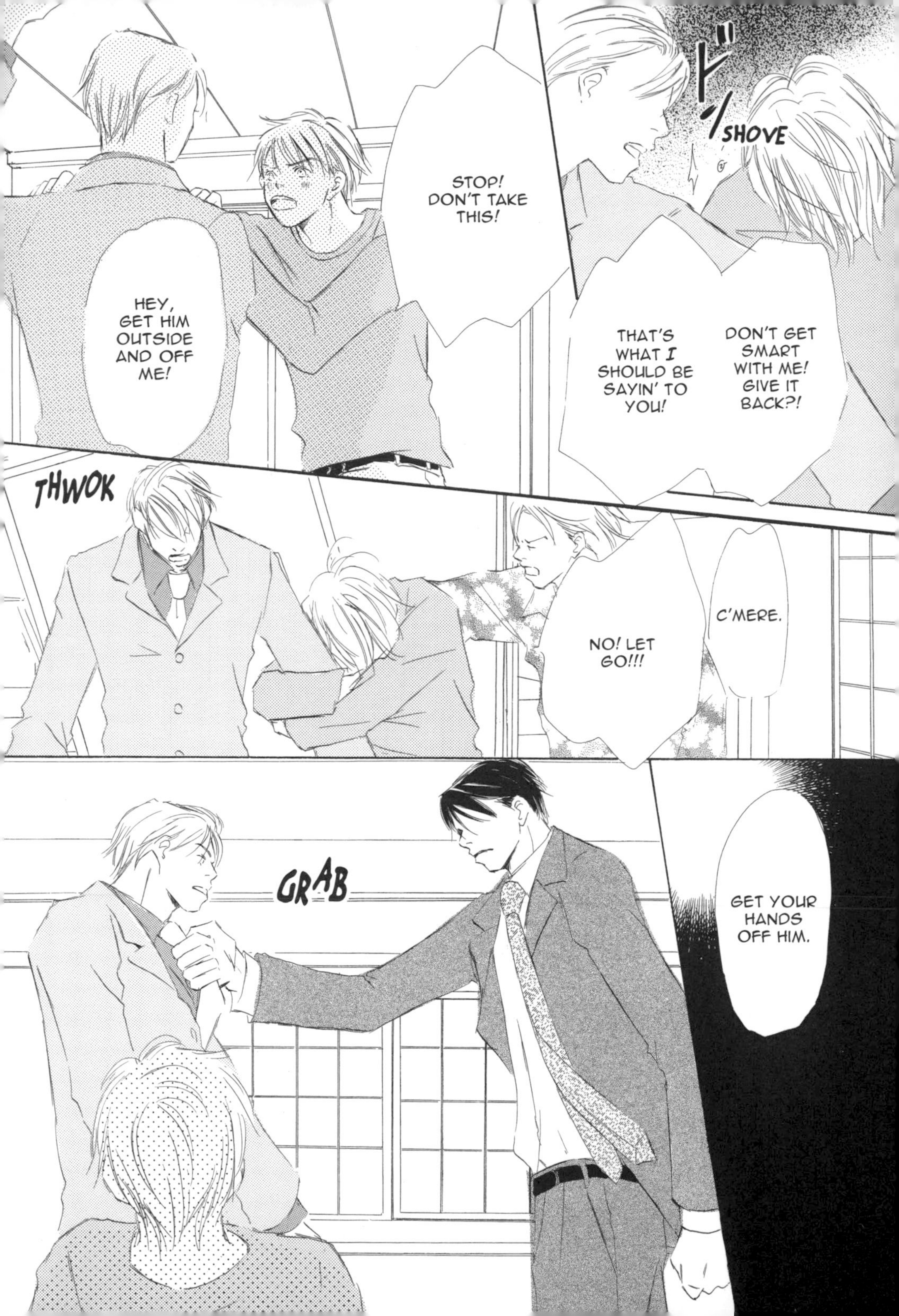
SHOVE
DON'T GET SMART WITH ME! GIVE IT BACK?!
THAT'S WHAT I SHOULD BE SAYIN' TO YOU!
STOP! DON'T TAKE THIS!
HEY, GET HIM OUTSIDE AND OFF ME!
C'MERE.
NO! LET GO!!!
THWOK
GET YOUR HANDS OFF HIM.
GRAB

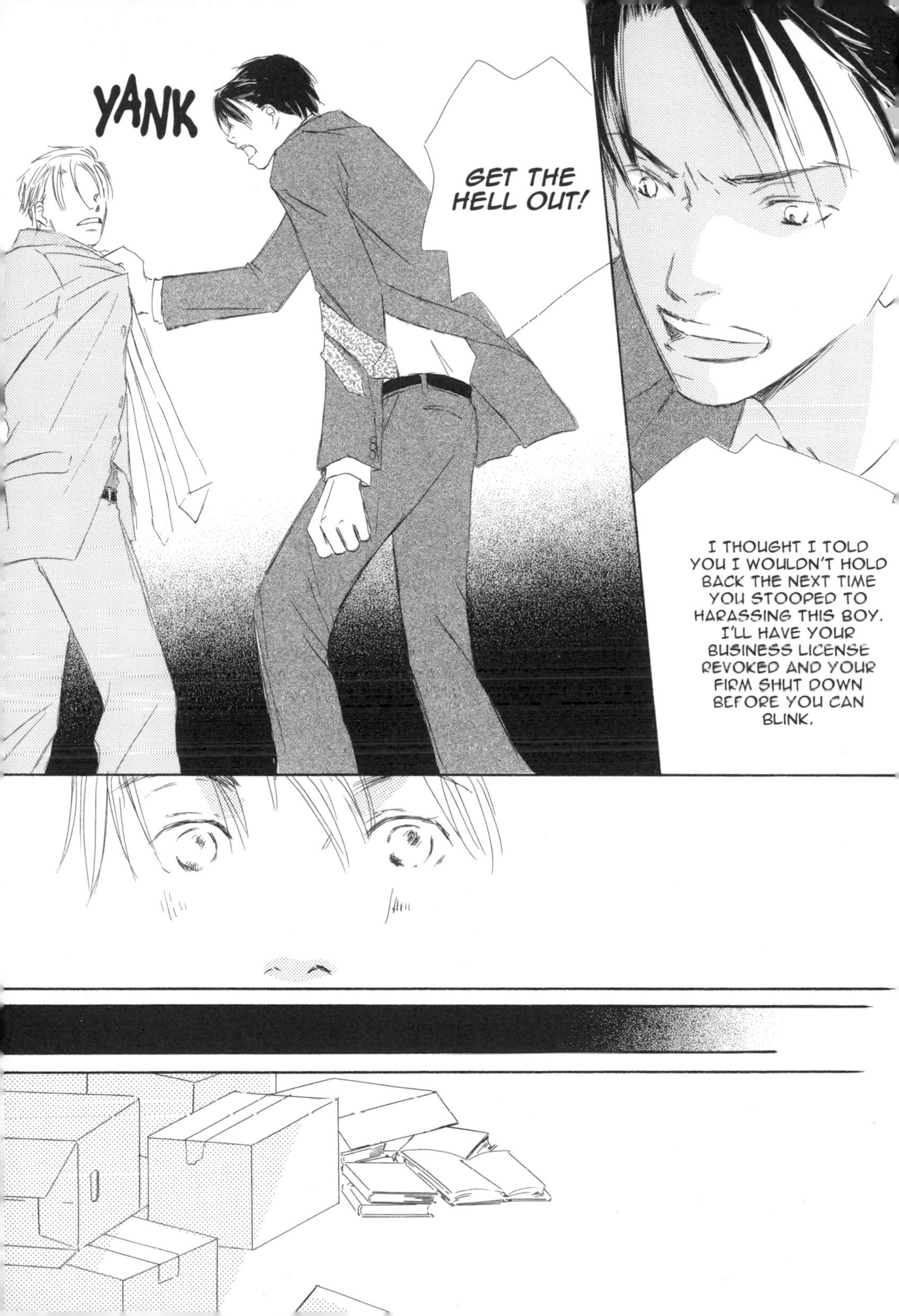
I THOUGHT I TOLD YOU I WOULDN'T HOLD BACK THE NEXT TIME YOU STOOPED TO HARASSING THIS BOY. I'LL HAVE YOUR BUSINESS LICENSE REVOKED AND YOUR FIRM SHUT DOWN BEFORE YOU CAN BLINK.
YANK
GET THE HELL OUT!

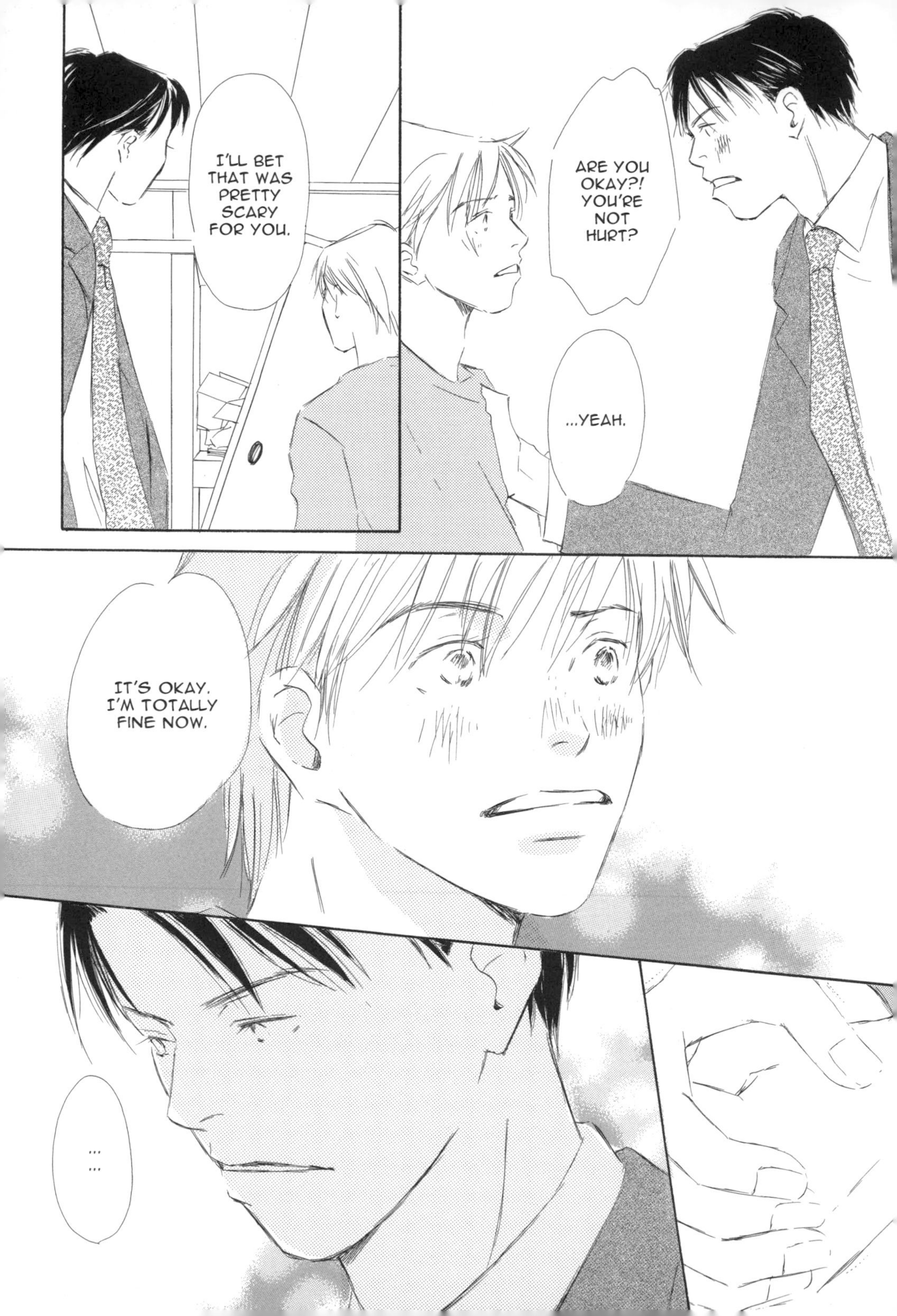
ARE YOU OKAY?! YOU'RE NOT HURT?
...YEAH.
I'LL BET THAT WAS PRETTY SCARY FOR YOU.
IT'S OKAY. I'M TOTALLY FINE NOW.
... ...

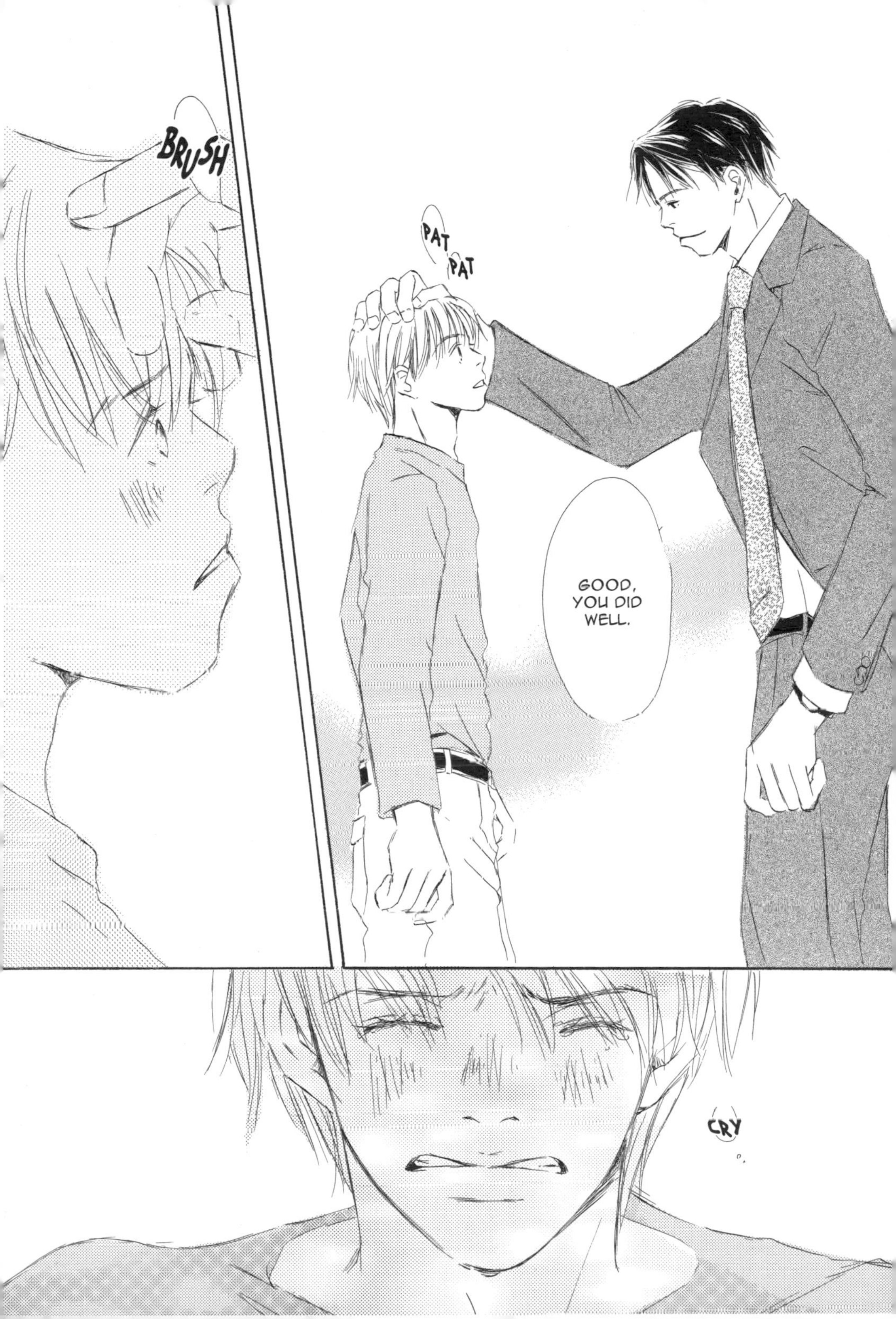
PAT PAT
GOOD, YOU DID WELL.
BRUSH
CRY

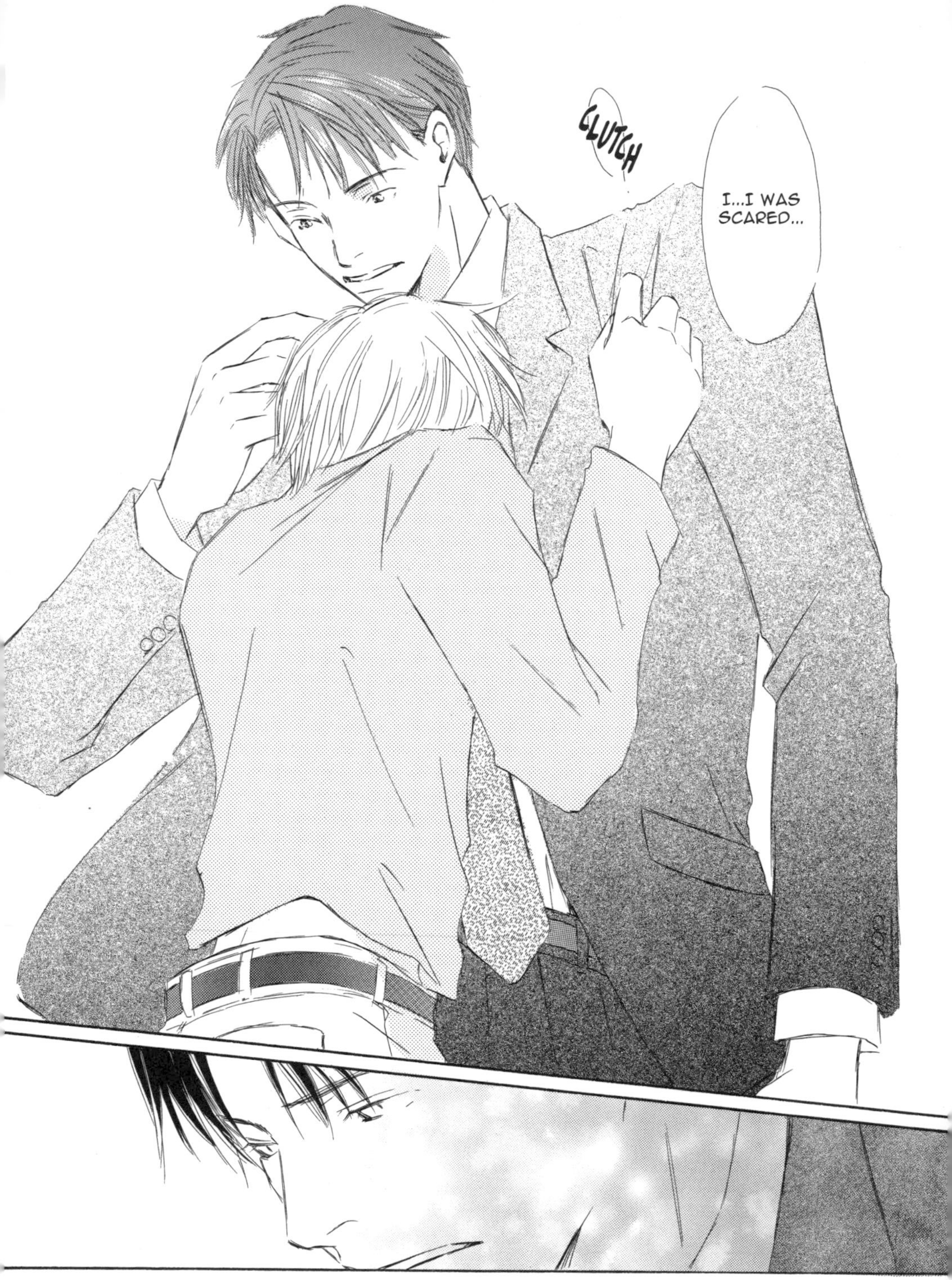
CLUTCH
I...I WAS SCARED...

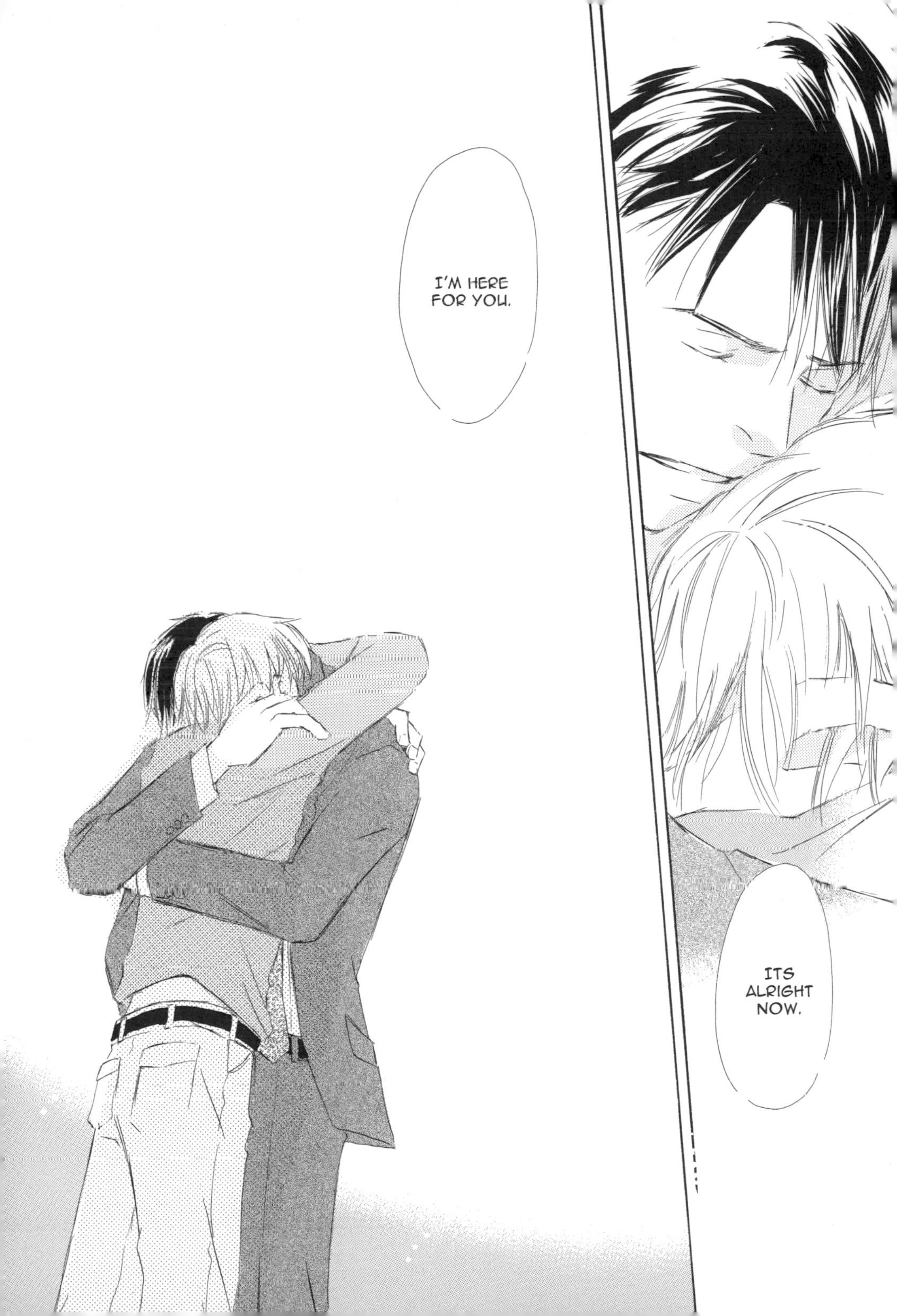
ITS ALRIGHT NOW.
I'M HERE FOR YOU.

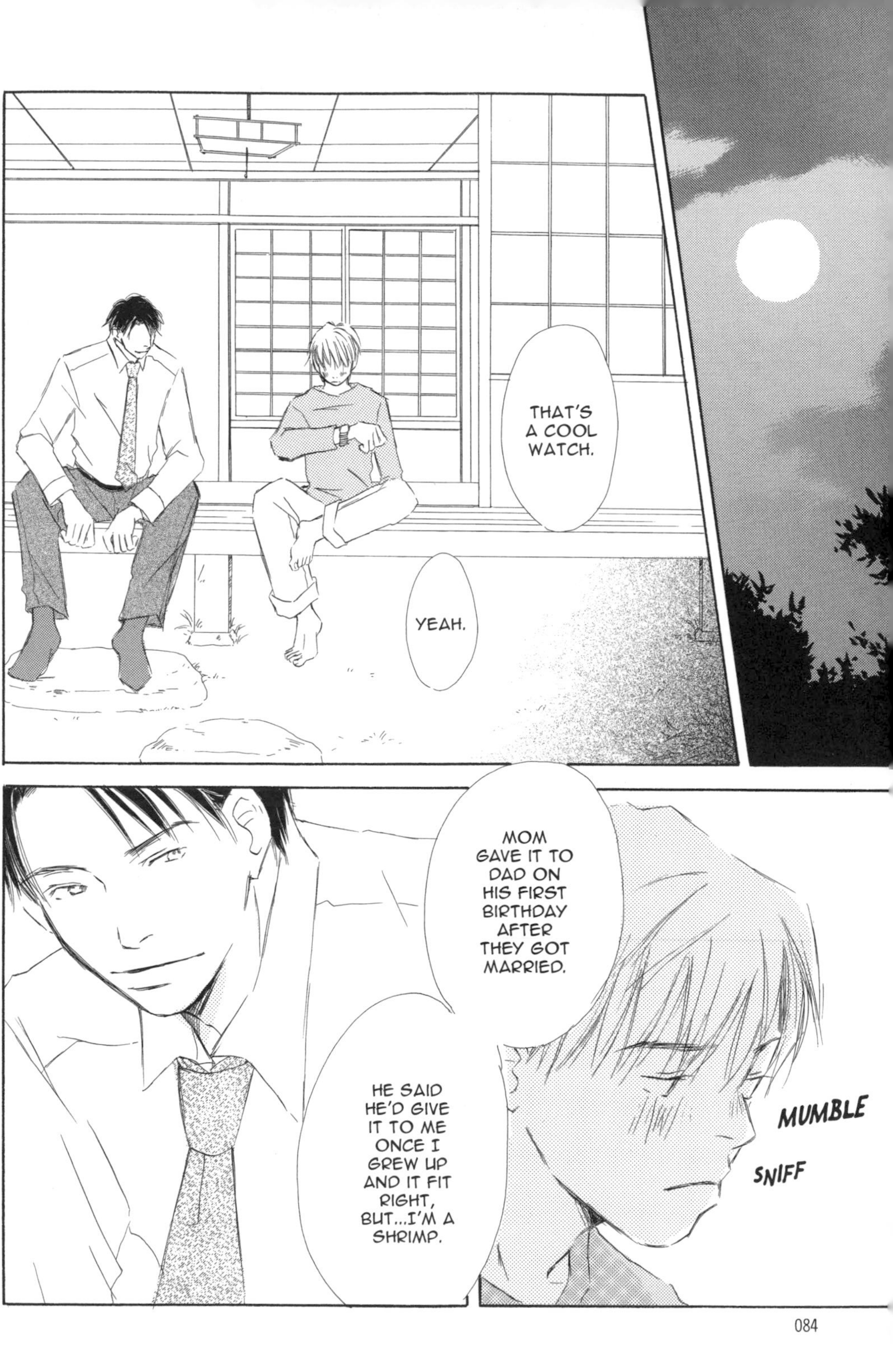
THAT'S A COOL WATCH.
YEAH.
MOM GAVE IT TO DAD ON HIS FIRST BIRTHDAY AFTER THEY GOT MARRIED.
HE SAID HE'D GIVE IT TO ME ONCE I GREW UP AND IT FIT RIGHT, BUT...I'M A SHRIMP.
MUMBLE
SNIFF

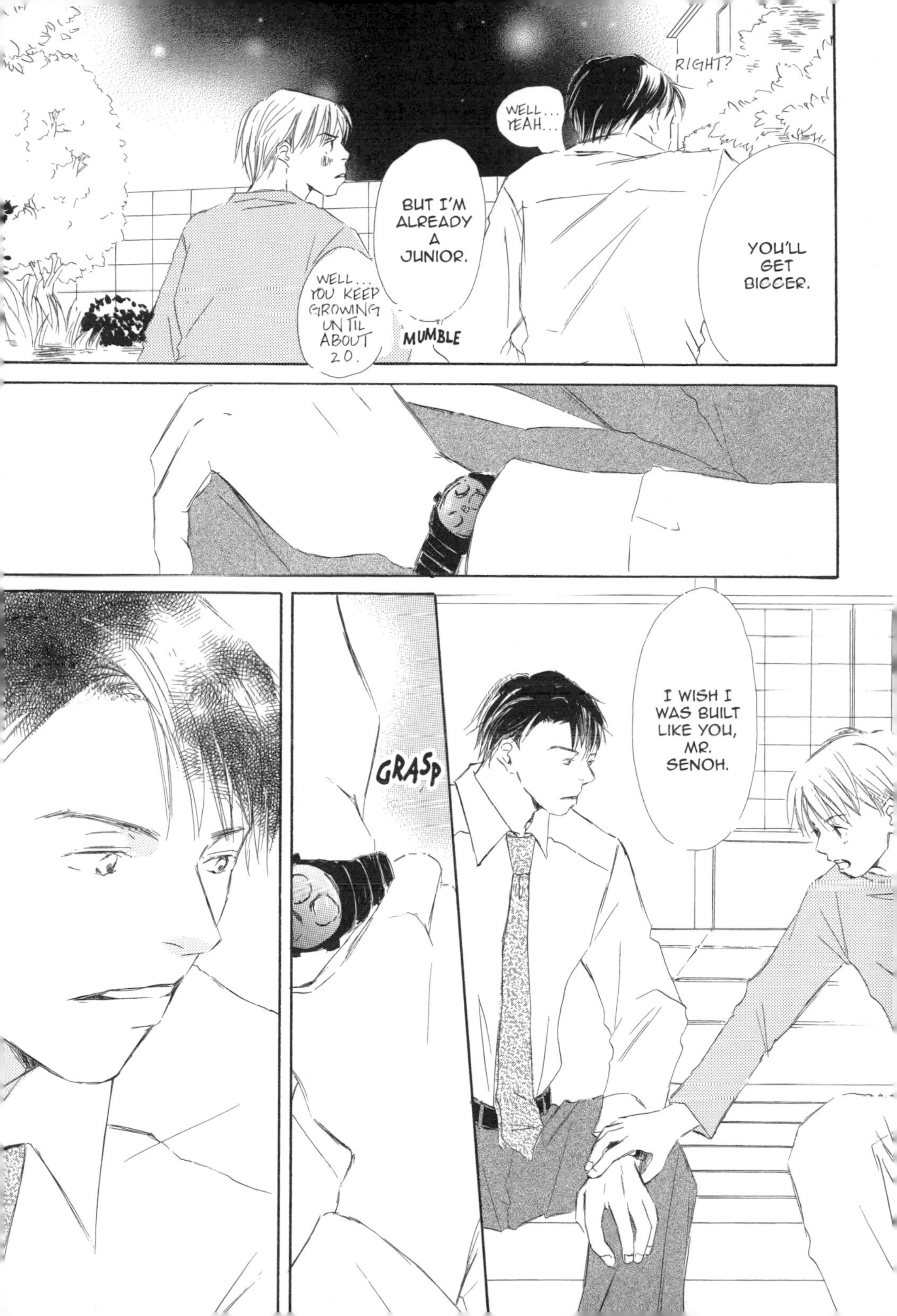
YOU'LL GET BIGGER.
RIGHT?
WELL... YEAH...
BUT I'M ALREADY A JUNIOR.
WELL... YOU KEEP GROWING UNTIL ABOUT 20.
MUMBLE
I WISH I WAS BUILT LIKE YOU, MR. SENOH.
GRASP

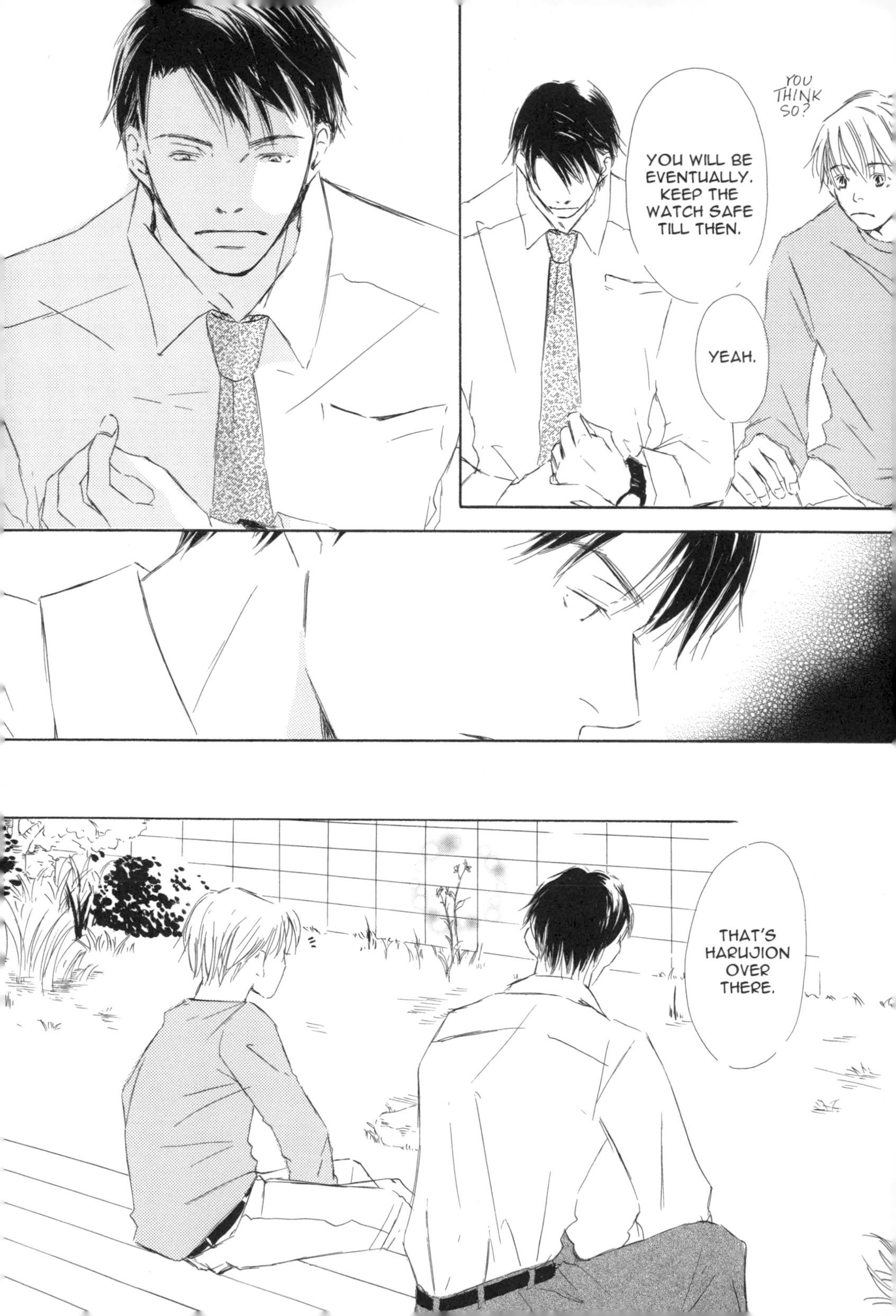
YOU THINK SO?
YOU WILL BE EVENTUALLY. KEEP THE WATCH SAFE TILL THEN.
YEAH.
THAT'S HARUJION OVER THERE.

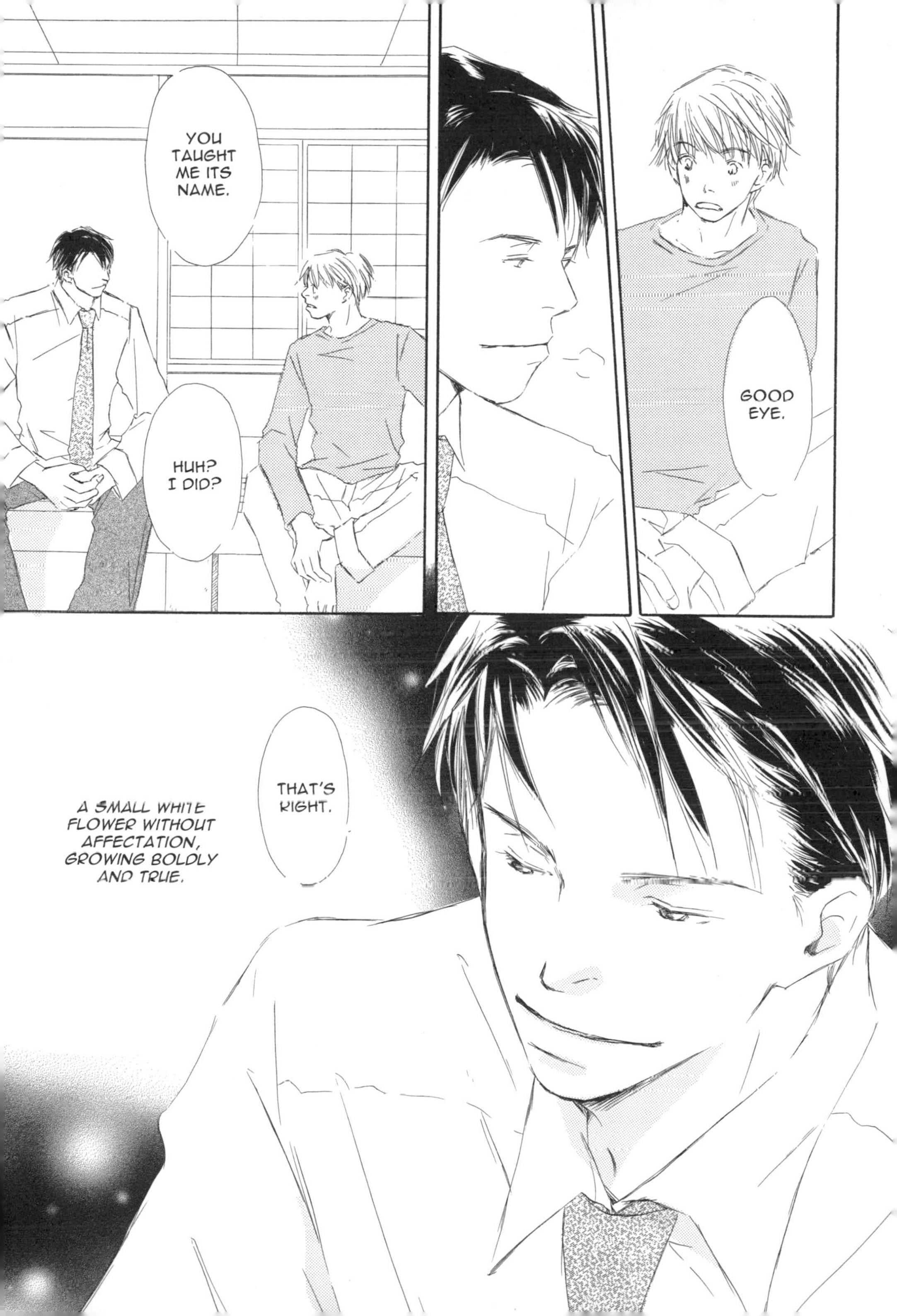
GOOD EYE.
YOU TAUGHT ME ITS NAME.
HUH? I DID?
THAT'S RIGHT.
A SMALL WHITE FLOWER WITHOUT AFFECTATION, GROWING BOLDLY AND TRUE.

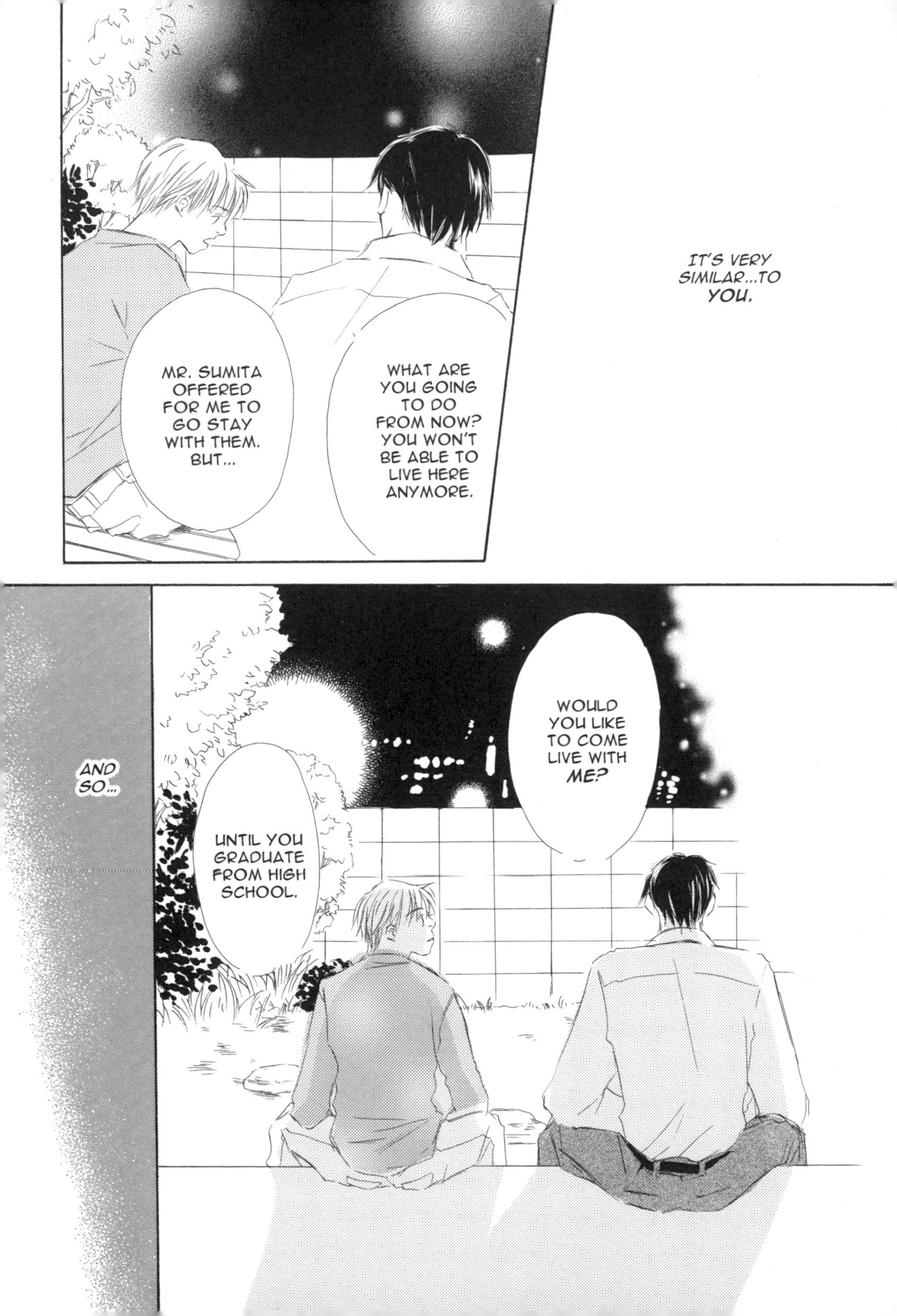
IT'S VERY SIMILAR...TO YOU.
WHAT ARE YOU GOING TO DO FROM NOW? YOU WON'T BE ABLE TO LIVE HERE ANYMORE.
MR. SUMITA OFFERED FOR ME TO GO STAY WITH THEM. BUT...
WOULD YOU LIKE TO COME LIVE WITH ME?
UNTIL YOU GRADUATE FROM HIGH SCHOOL.
AND SO...

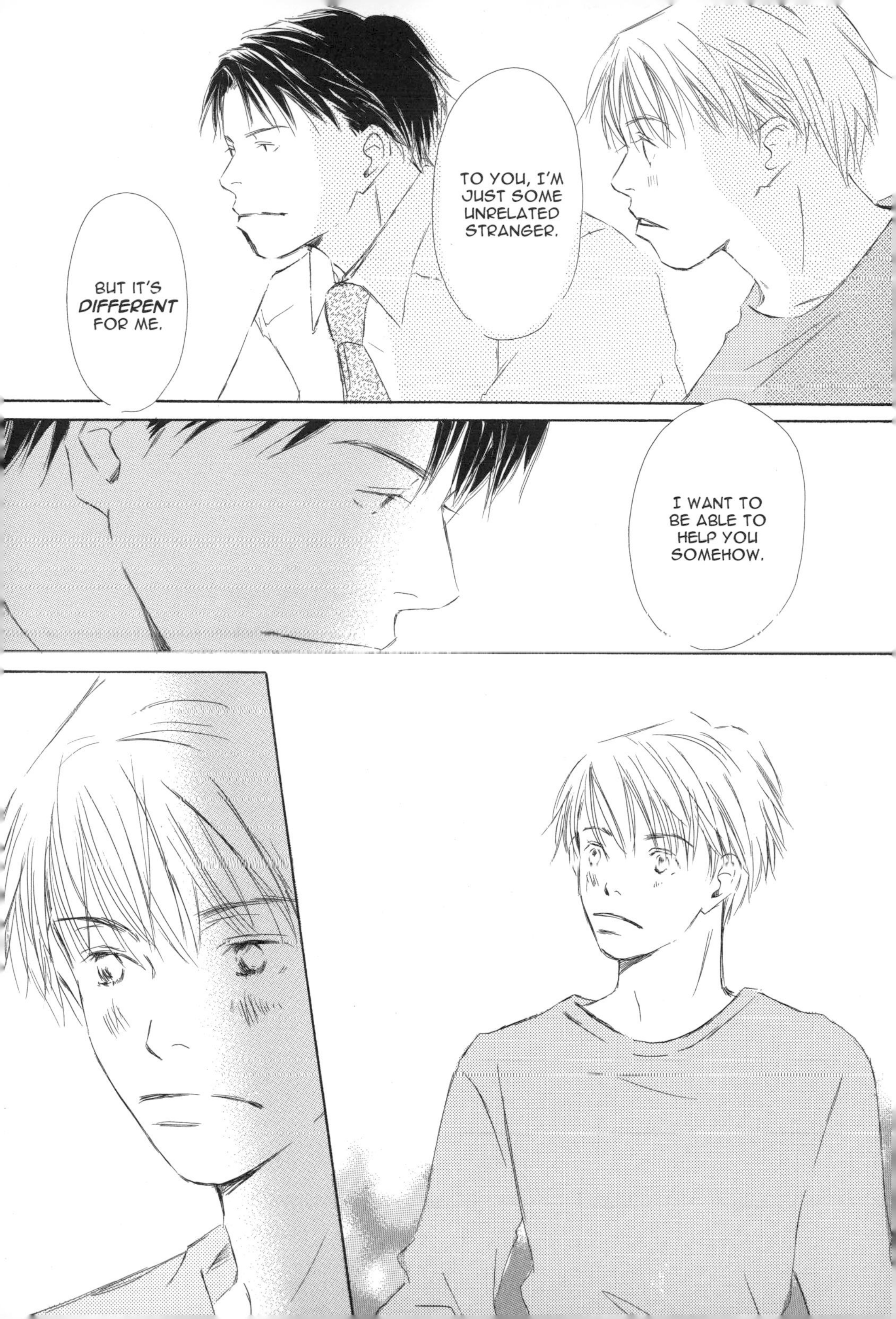
TO YOU, I'M JUST SOME UNRELATED STRANGER.
BUT IT'S DIFFERENT FOR ME.
I WANT TO BE ABLE TO HELP YOU SOMEHOW.

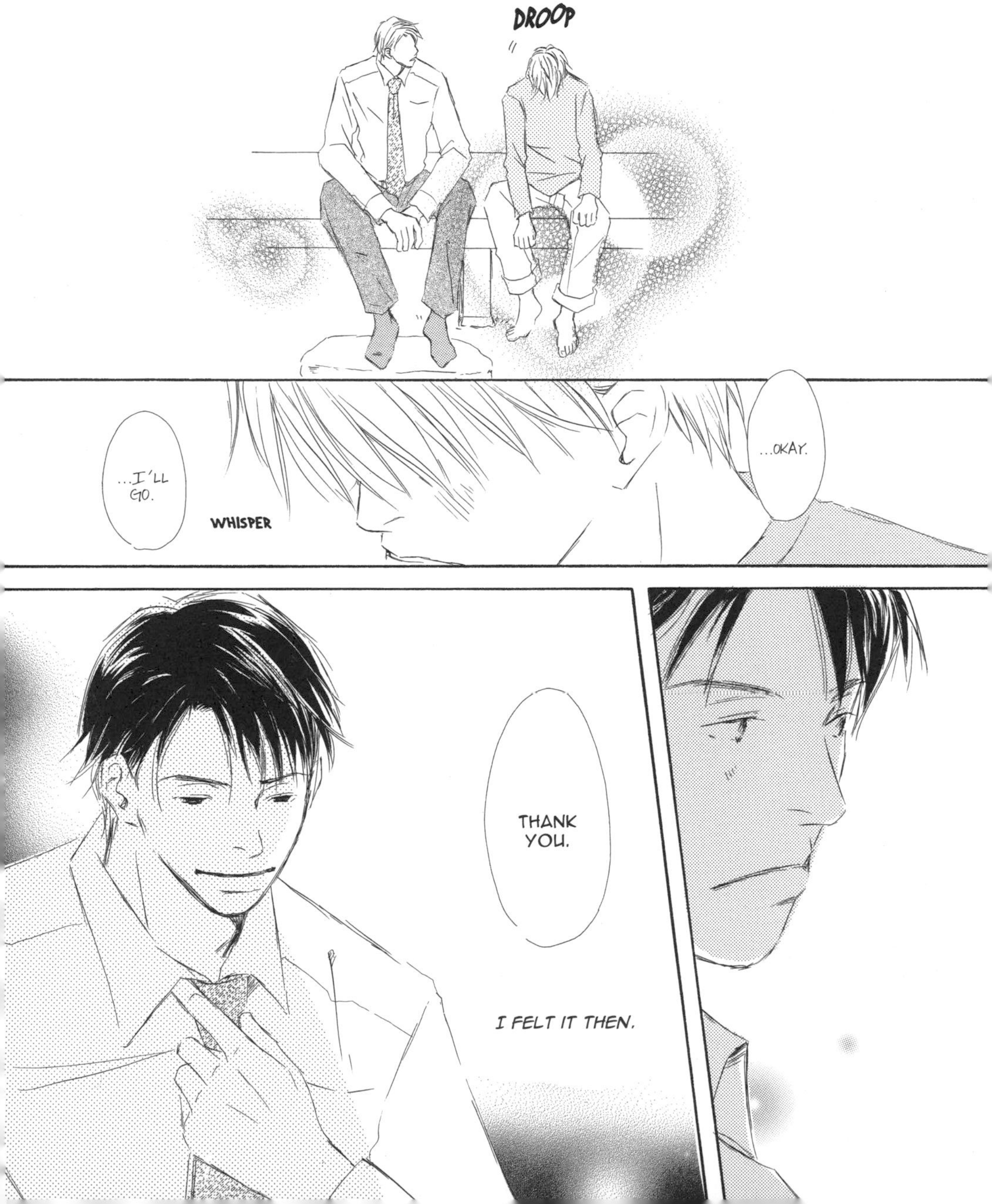
DROOP
...OKAY.
...I'LL GO.
WHISPER
THANK YOU.
I FELT IT THEN.

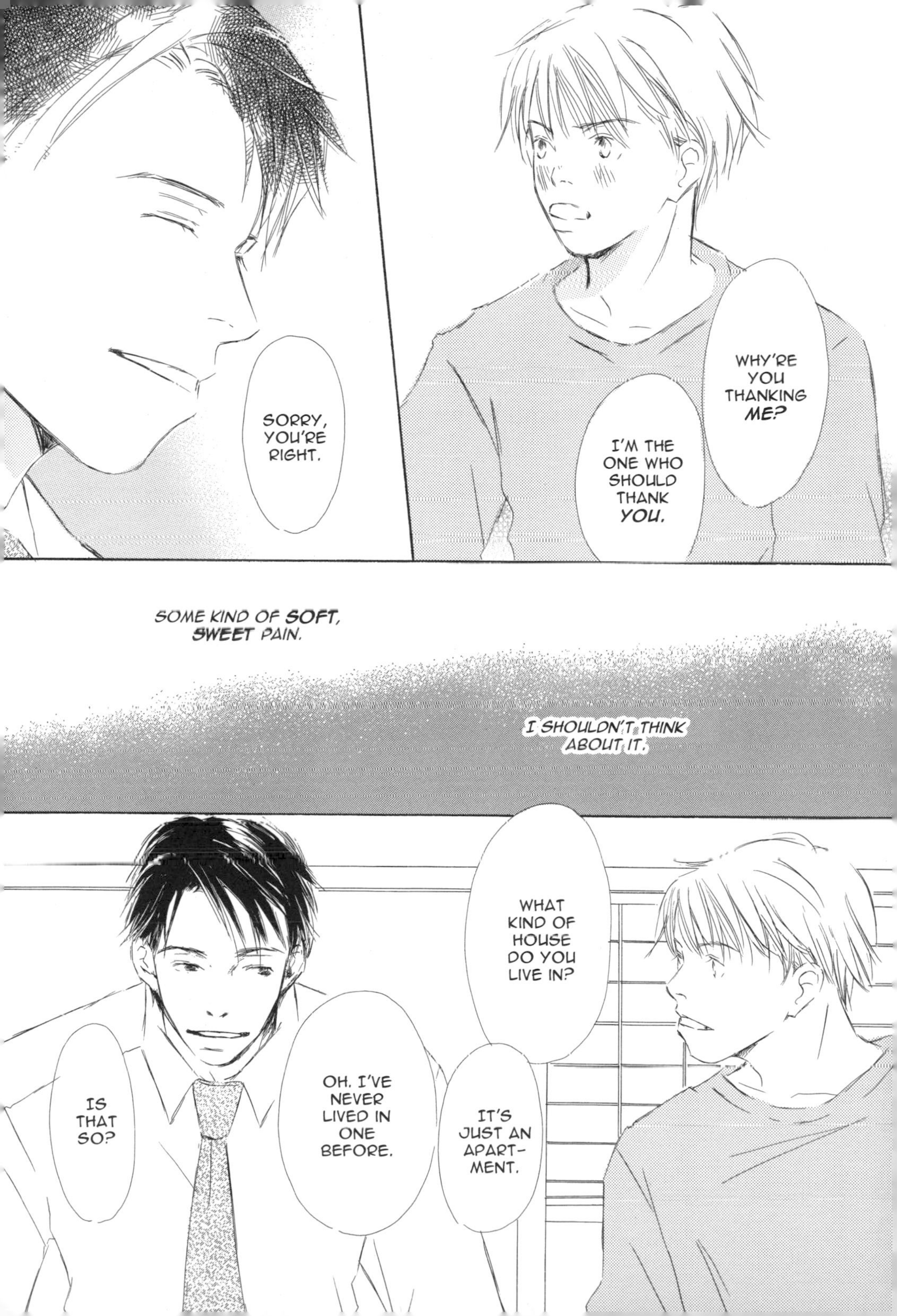
WHY'RE YOU THANKING ***ME?***
I'M THE ONE WHO SHOULD THANK ***YOU.***
SORRY, YOU'RE RIGHT.
*SOME KIND OF **SOFT, SWEET** PAIN.*
I SHOULDN'T THINK ABOUT IT.
WHAT KIND OF HOUSE DO YOU LIVE IN?
IT'S JUST AN APART-MENT.
OH. I'VE NEVER LIVED IN ONE BEFORE.
IS THAT SO?

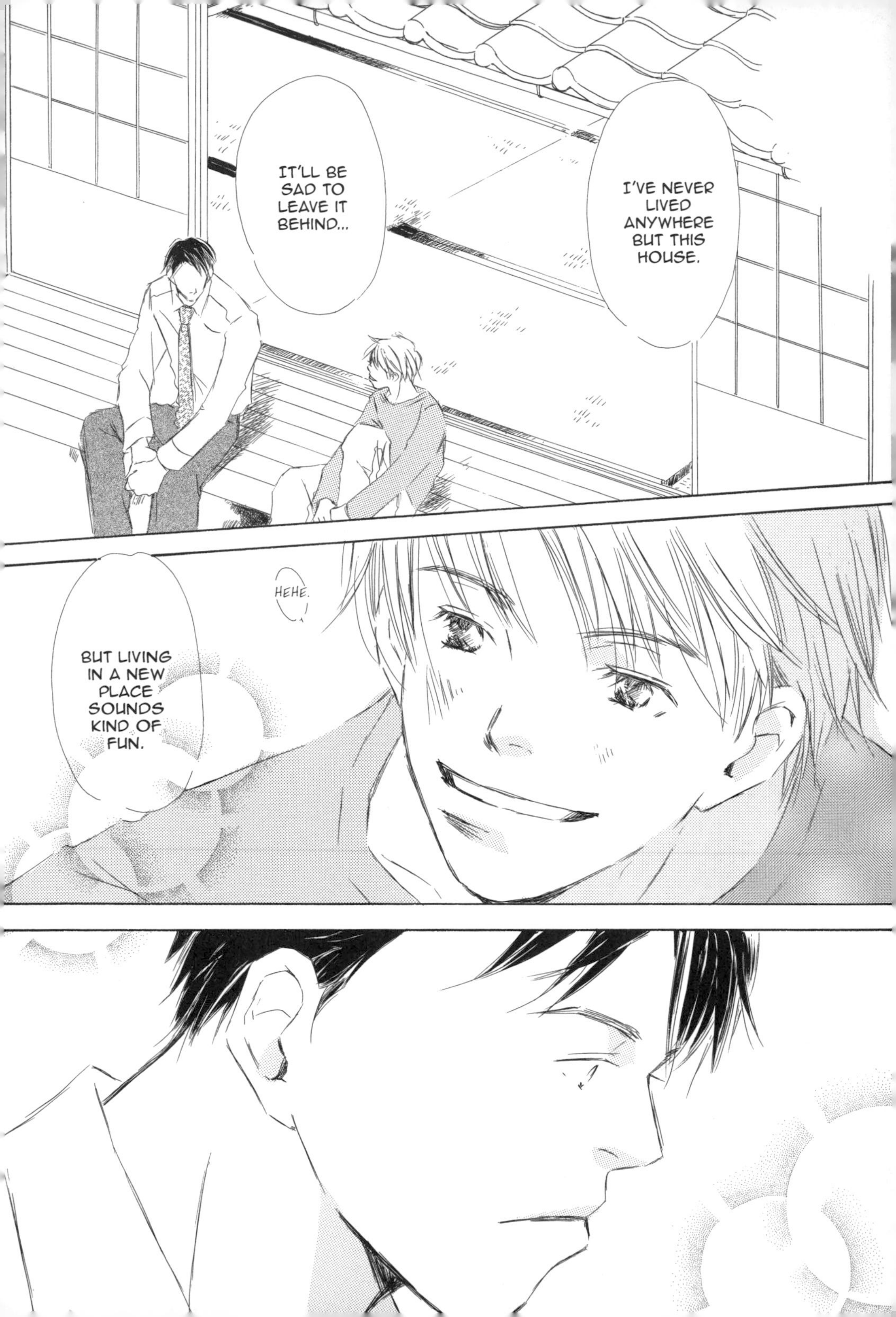
I'VE NEVER LIVED ANYWHERE BUT THIS HOUSE.
IT'LL BE SAD TO LEAVE IT BEHIND...
HEHE.
BUT LIVING IN A NEW PLACE SOUNDS KIND OF FUN.

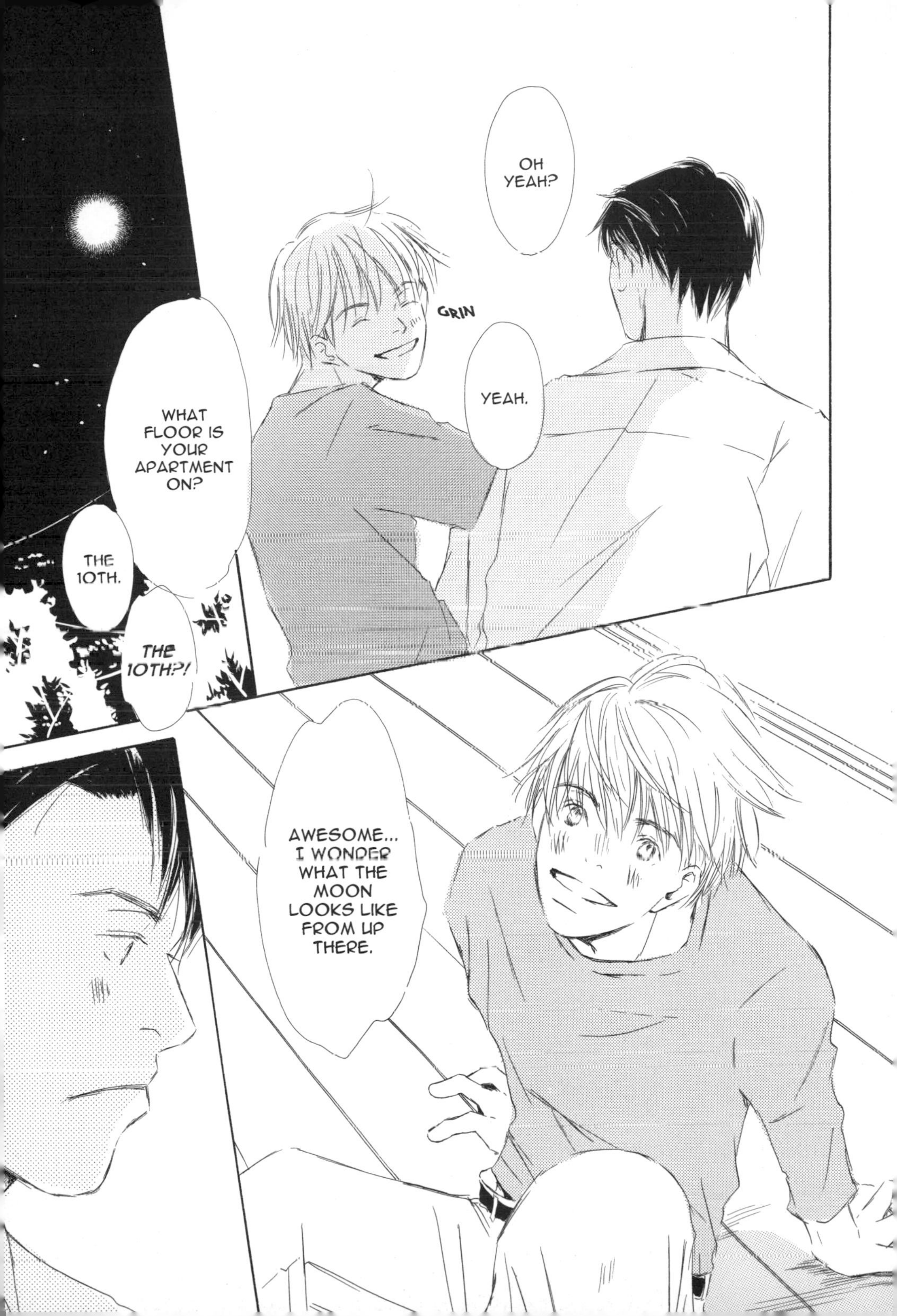
OH YEAH?
GRIN
YEAH.
WHAT FLOOR IS YOUR APARTMENT ON?
THE 10TH.
THE 10TH?!
AWESOME... I WONDER WHAT THE MOON LOOKS LIKE FROM UP THERE.

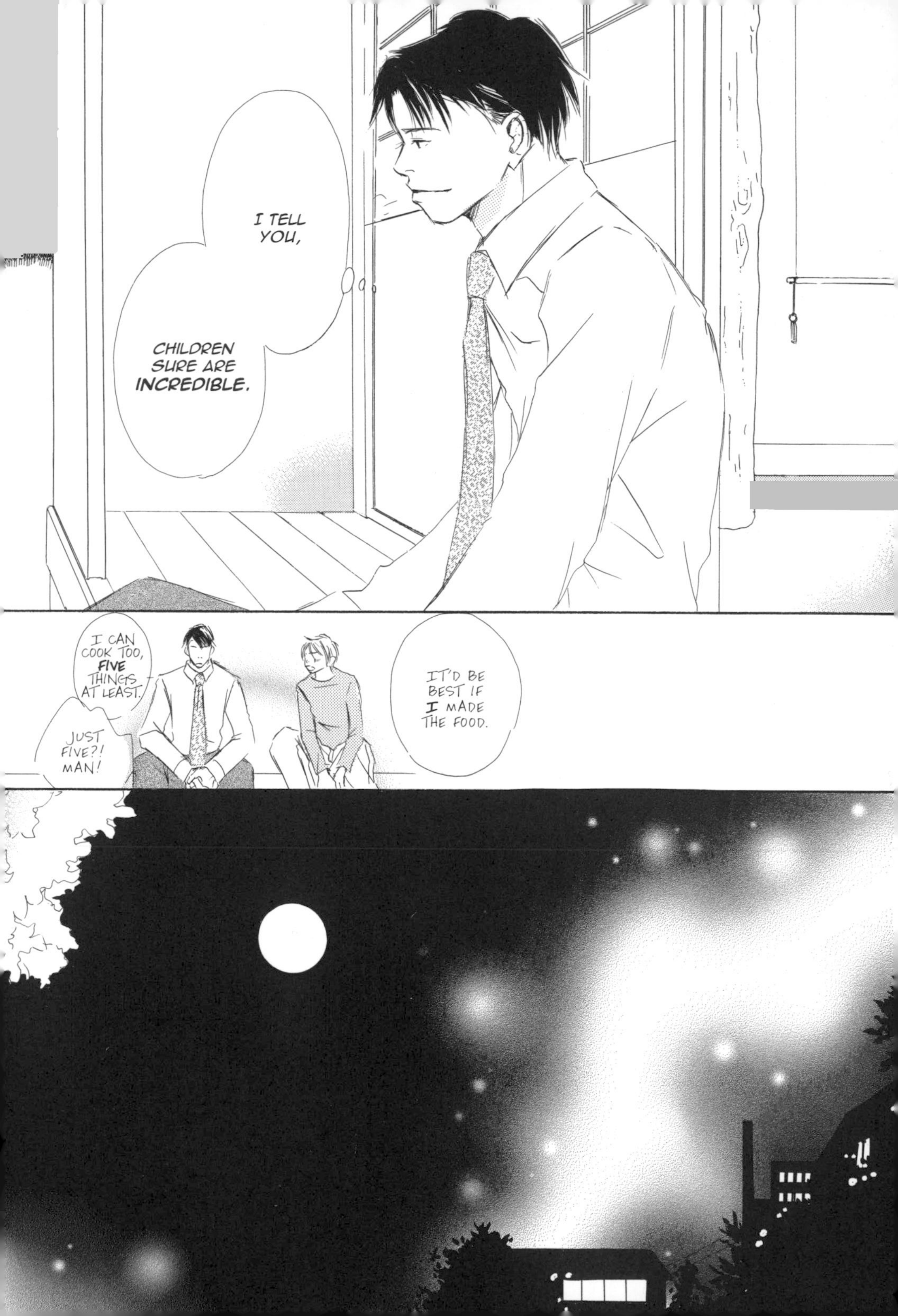
I TELL YOU,
CHILDREN SURE ARE INCREDIBLE.
IT'D BE BEST IF I MADE THE FOOD.
I CAN COOK TOO, FIVE THINGS AT LEAST.
JUST FIVE?! MAN!

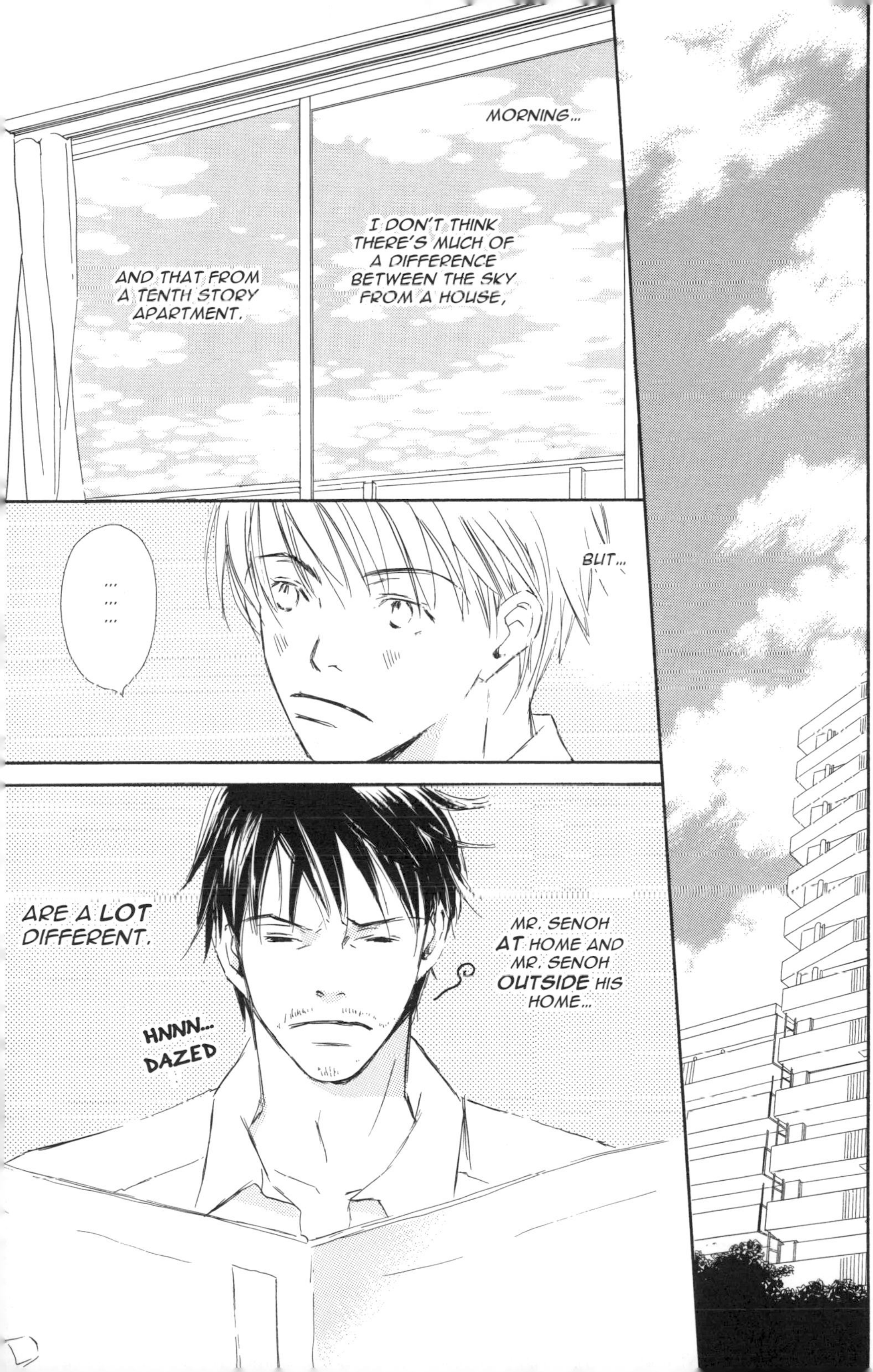
MORNING...
I DON'T THINK THERE'S MUCH OF A DIFFERENCE BETWEEN THE SKY FROM A HOUSE,
AND THAT FROM A TENTH STORY APARTMENT.
BUT...
... ...
MR. SENOH AT HOME AND MR. SENOH OUTSIDE HIS HOME...
ARE A LOT DIFFERENT.
HNNN... DAZED

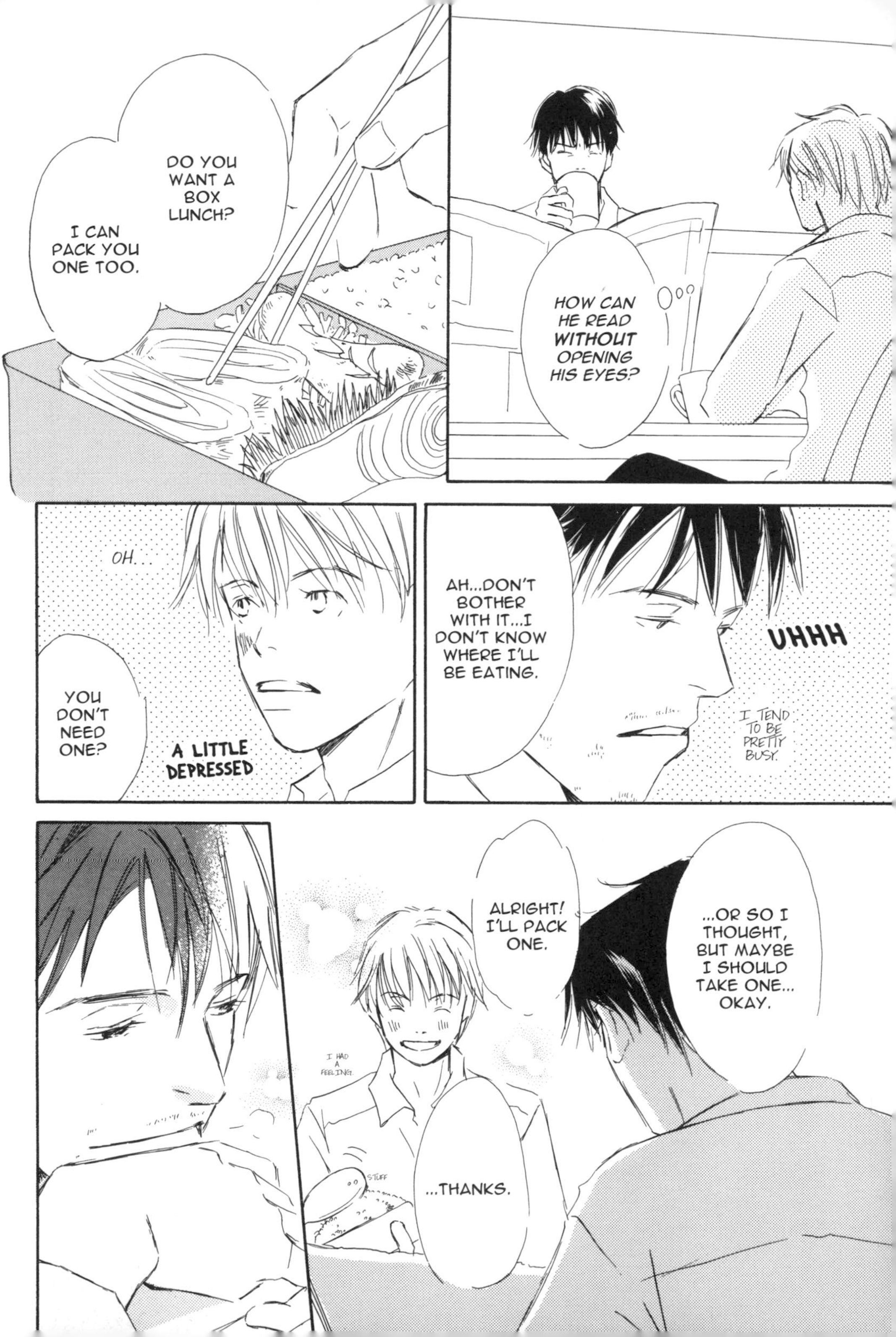
HOW CAN HE READ WITHOUT OPENING HIS EYES?
DO YOU WANT A BOX LUNCH?
I CAN PACK YOU ONE TOO.
UHHH
AH...DON'T BOTHER WITH IT...I DON'T KNOW WHERE I'LL BE EATING.
I TEND TO BE PRETTY BUSY.
OH...
YOU DON'T NEED ONE?
A LITTLE DEPRESSED
...OR SO I THOUGHT, BUT MAYBE I SHOULD TAKE ONE... OKAY.
ALRIGHT! I'LL PACK ONE.
I HAD A FEELING.
STUFF
...THANKS.

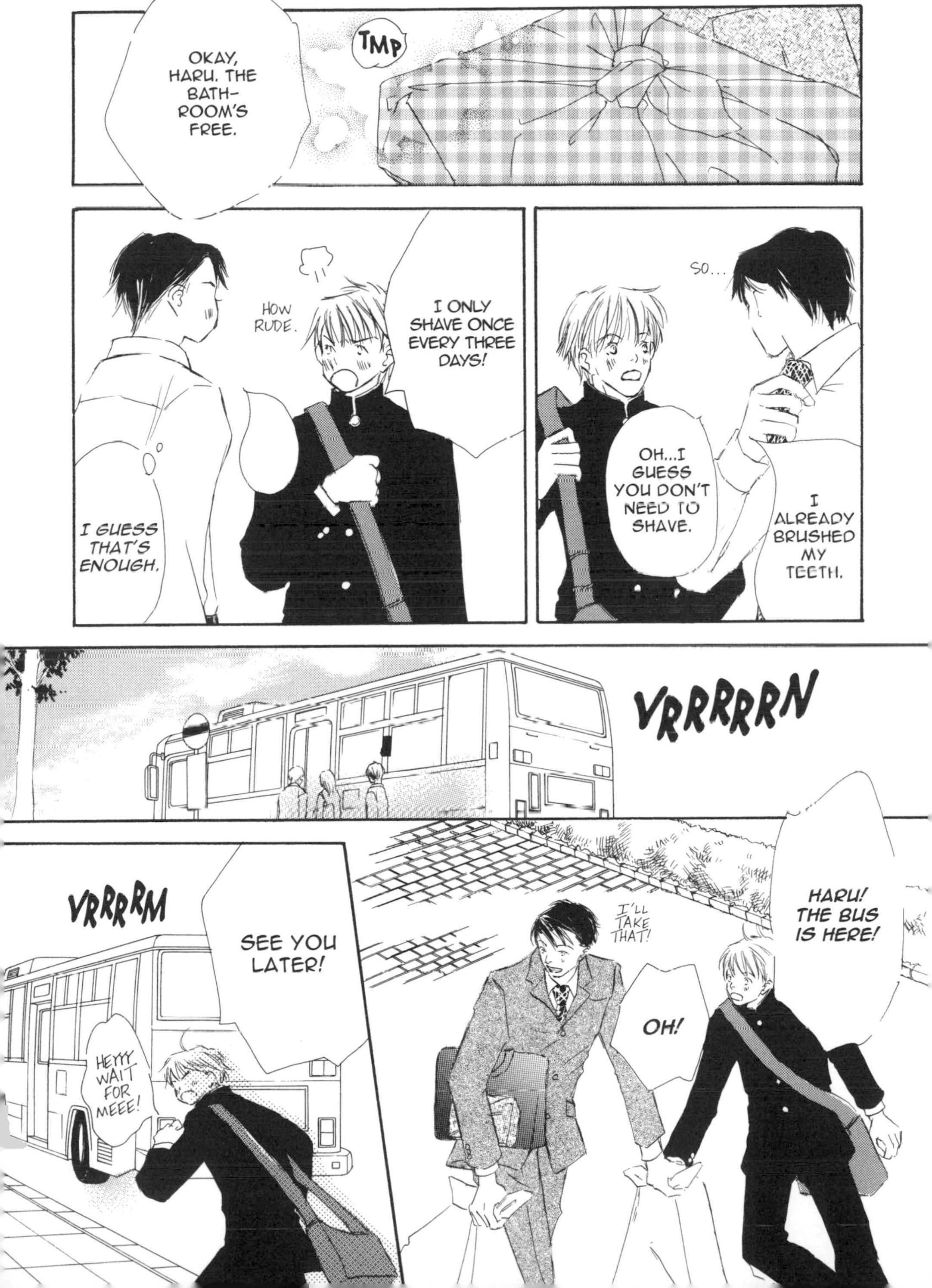
TMP
OKAY, HARU. THE BATH-ROOM'S FREE.
SO...
I ALREADY BRUSHED MY TEETH.
OH...I GUESS YOU DON'T NEED TO SHAVE.
I ONLY SHAVE ONCE EVERY THREE DAYS!
HOW RUDE.
I GUESS THAT'S ENOUGH.
VRRRRRN
HARU! THE BUS IS HERE!
OH!
I'LL TAKE THAT!
SEE YOU LATER!
VRRRRM
HEYYY WAIT FOR MEEE!

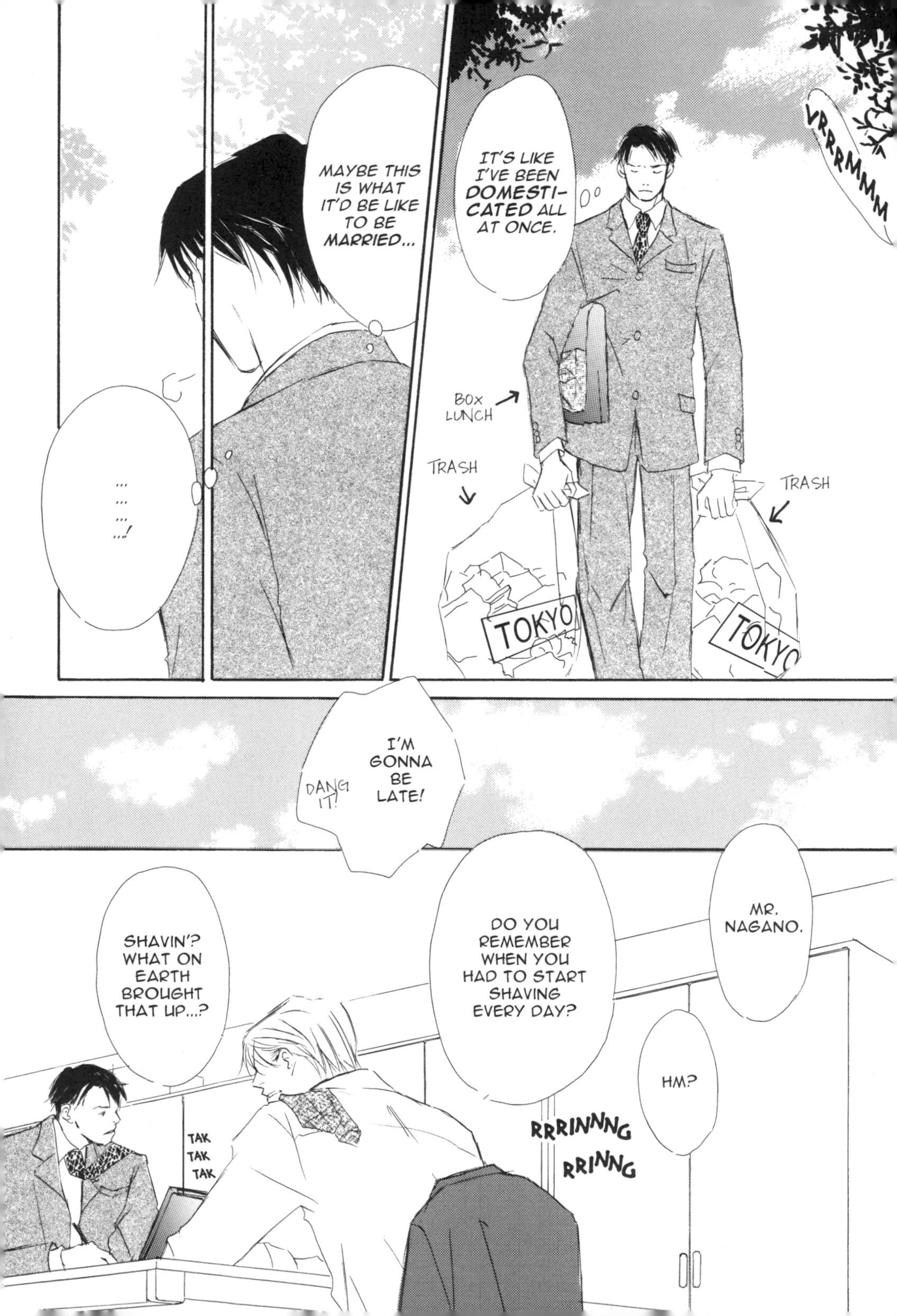
VRRRRMMMM
IT'S LIKE I'VE BEEN DOMESTI-CATED ALL AT ONCE.
BOX LUNCH
TRASH
TRASH
MAYBE THIS IS WHAT IT'D BE LIKE TO BE MARRIED...
... ...!
I'M GONNA BE LATE!
DANG IT!
MR. NAGANO.
DO YOU REMEMBER WHEN YOU HAD TO START SHAVING EVERY DAY?
HM?
RRRINNNG
RRINNG
SHAVIN'? WHAT ON EARTH BROUGHT THAT UP...?
TAK TAK TAK

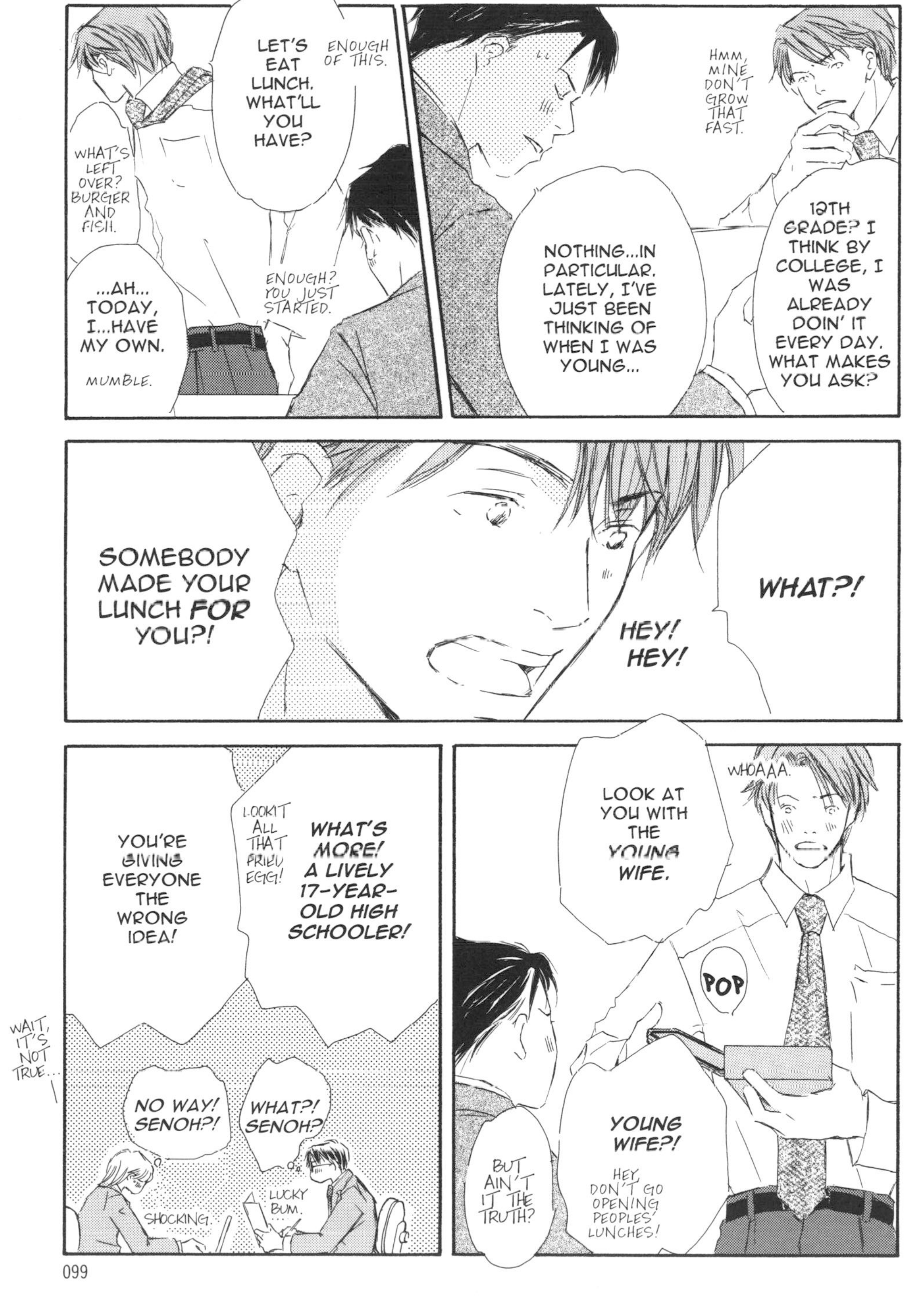
HMM, MINE DON'T GROW THAT FAST.
12TH GRADE? I THINK BY COLLEGE, I WAS ALREADY DOIN' IT EVERY DAY. WHAT MAKES YOU ASK?
NOTHING...IN PARTICULAR. LATELY, I'VE JUST BEEN THINKING OF WHEN I WAS YOUNG...
ENOUGH OF THIS.
LET'S EAT LUNCH. WHAT'LL YOU HAVE?
WHAT'S LEFT OVER? BURGER AND FISH.
ENOUGH? YOU JUST STARTED.
...AH... TODAY, I...HAVE MY OWN.
MUMBLE.
WHAT?!
HEY! HEY!
SOMEBODY MADE YOUR LUNCH FOR YOU?!
WHOAAA.
LOOK AT YOU WITH THE YOUNG WIFE.
POP
YOUNG WIFE?!
HEY, DON'T GO OPENING PEOPLES' LUNCHES!
BUT AIN'T IT THE TRUTH?
WHAT'S MORE! A LIVELY 17-YEAR-OLD HIGH SCHOOLER!
LOOKIT ALL THAT FRIED EGG!
YOU'RE GIVING EVERYONE THE WRONG IDEA!
WHAT?! SENOH?!
NO WAY! SENOH?!
LUCKY BUM.
SHOCKING.
WAIT, IT'S NOT TRUE...

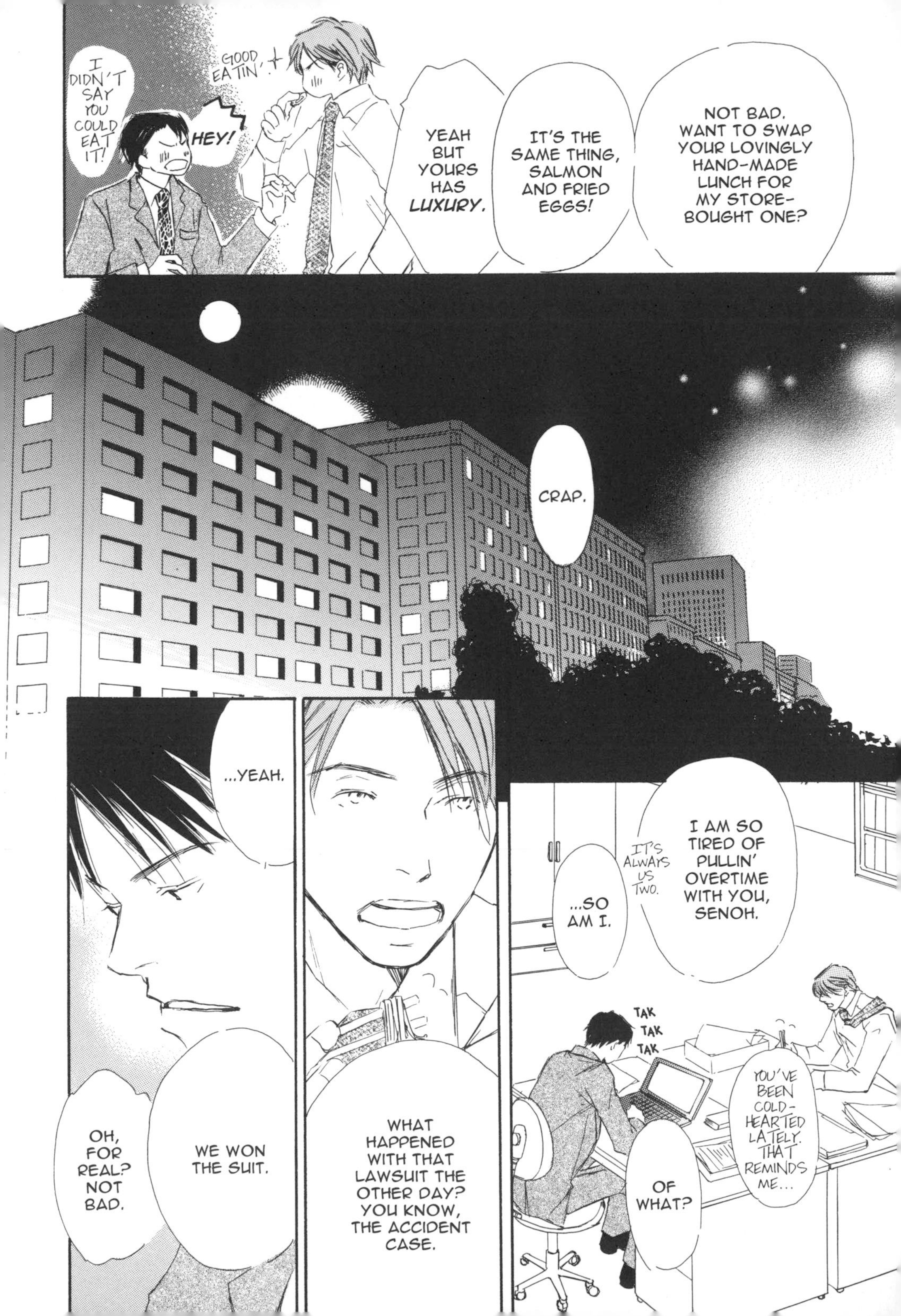
NOT BAD. WANT TO SWAP YOUR LOVINGLY HAND-MADE LUNCH FOR MY STORE-BOUGHT ONE?
IT'S THE SAME THING, SALMON AND FRIED EGGS!
YEAH BUT YOURS HAS LUXURY.
GOOD EATIN'.
HEY!
I DIDN'T SAY YOU COULD EAT IT!
CRAP.
I AM SO TIRED OF PULLIN' OVERTIME WITH YOU, SENOH.
IT'S ALWAYS US TWO.
...SO AM I.
TAK TAK TAK
YOU'VE BEEN COLD-HEARTED LATELY. THAT REMINDS ME...
OF WHAT?
WHAT HAPPENED WITH THAT LAWSUIT THE OTHER DAY? YOU KNOW, THE ACCIDENT CASE.
...YEAH.
WE WON THE SUIT.
OH, FOR REAL? NOT BAD.

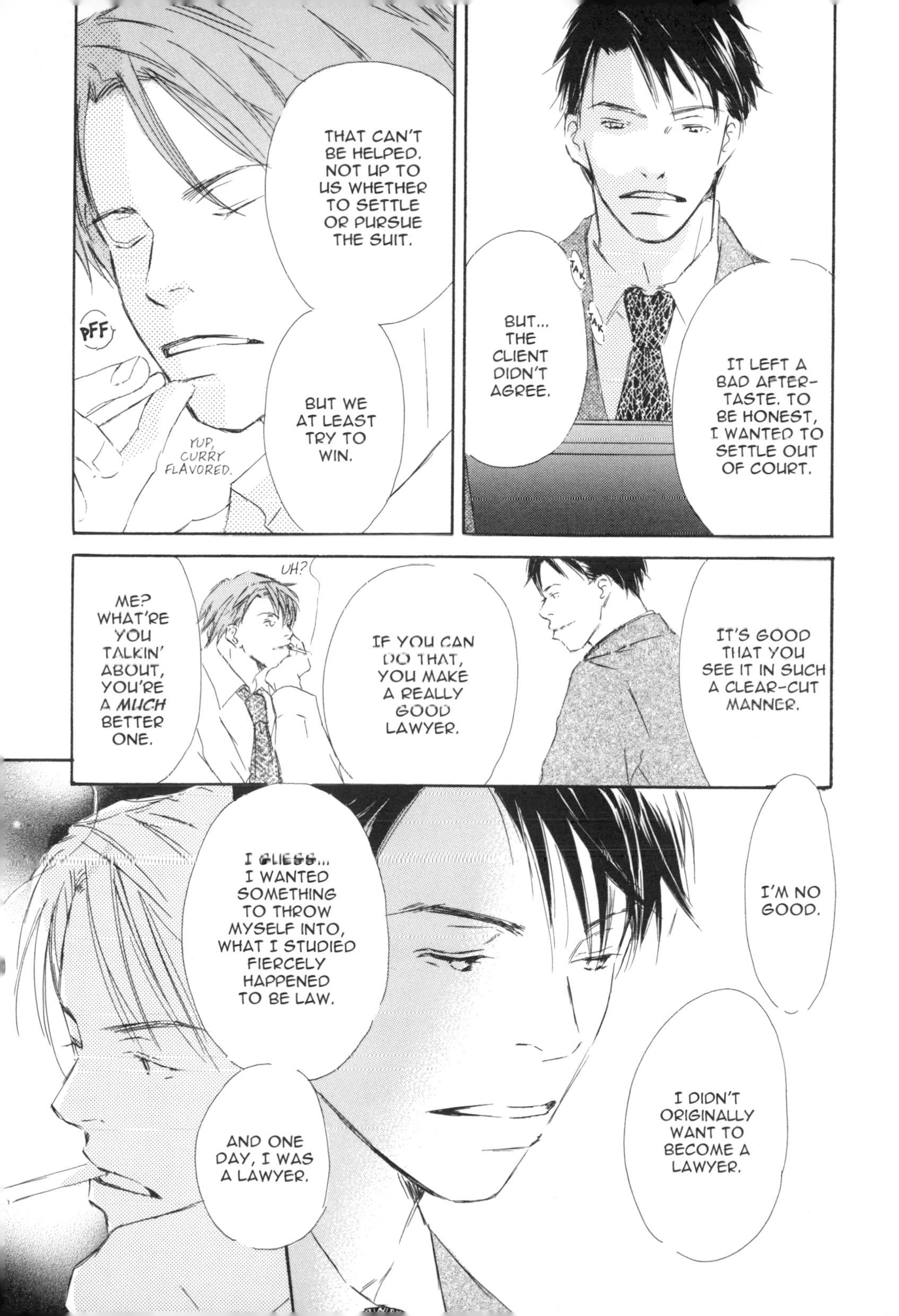
IT LEFT A BAD AFTER-TASTE. TO BE HONEST, I WANTED TO SETTLE OUT OF COURT.
TAK
TAK
BUT... THE CLIENT DIDN'T AGREE.
THAT CAN'T BE HELPED. NOT UP TO US WHETHER TO SETTLE OR PURSUE THE SUIT.
BUT WE AT LEAST TRY TO WIN.
PFF
YUP, CURRY FLAVORED.
IT'S GOOD THAT YOU SEE IT IN SUCH A CLEAR-CUT MANNER.
IF YOU CAN DO THAT, YOU MAKE A REALLY GOOD LAWYER.
UH?
ME? WHAT'RE YOU TALKIN' ABOUT, YOU'RE A *MUCH* BETTER ONE.
I'M NO GOOD.
I DIDN'T ORIGINALLY WANT TO BECOME A LAWYER.
I GUESS... I WANTED SOMETHING TO THROW MYSELF INTO, WHAT I STUDIED FIERCELY HAPPENED TO BE LAW.
AND ONE DAY, I WAS A LAWYER.

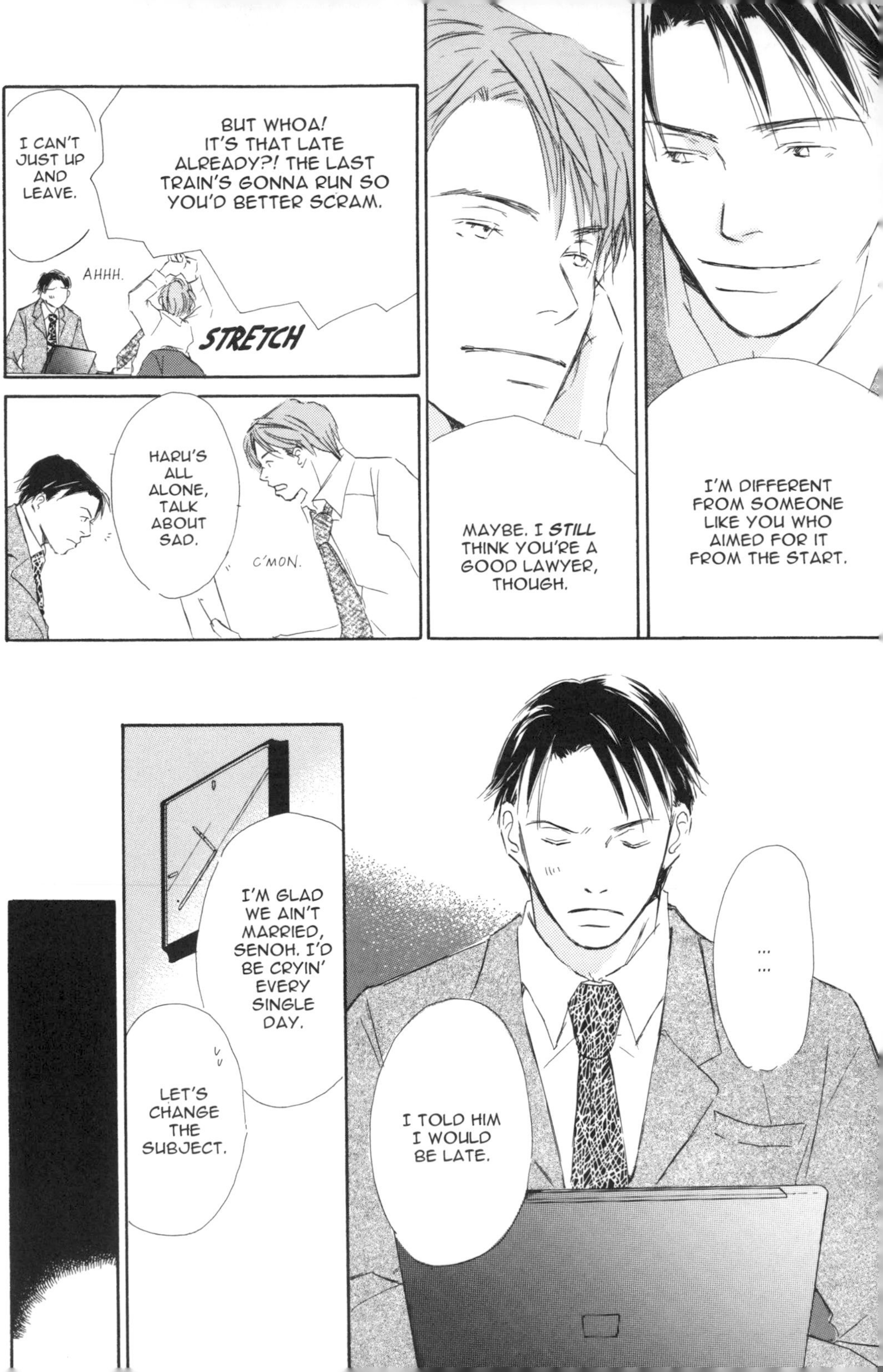
I'M DIFFERENT FROM SOMEONE LIKE YOU WHO AIMED FOR IT FROM THE START.
MAYBE. I STILL THINK YOU'RE A GOOD LAWYER, THOUGH.
BUT WHOA! IT'S THAT LATE ALREADY?! THE LAST TRAIN'S GONNA RUN SO YOU'D BETTER SCRAM.
AHHH.
STRETCH
I CAN'T JUST UP AND LEAVE.
HARU'S ALL ALONE, TALK ABOUT SAD.
C'MON.
... ...
I TOLD HIM I WOULD BE LATE.
I'M GLAD WE AIN'T MARRIED, SENOH. I'D BE CRYIN' EVERY SINGLE DAY.
LET'S CHANGE THE SUBJECT.

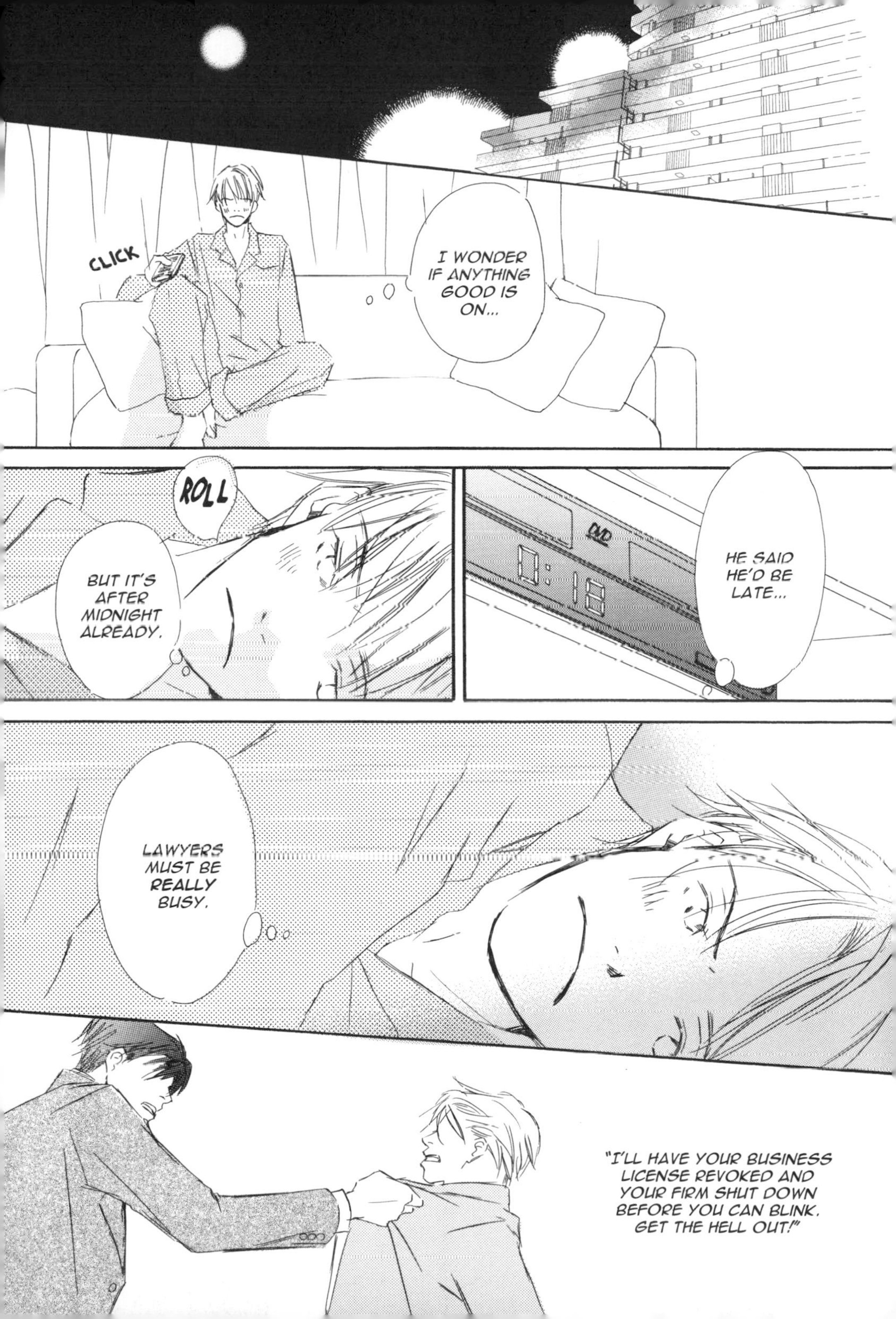
CLICK
I WONDER IF ANYTHING GOOD IS ON...
HE SAID HE'D BE LATE...
DVD
0:18
ROLL
BUT IT'S AFTER MIDNIGHT ALREADY.
LAWYERS MUST BE REALLY BUSY.
"I'LL HAVE YOUR BUSINESS LICENSE REVOKED AND YOUR FIRM SHUT DOWN BEFORE YOU CAN BLINK. GET THE HELL OUT!"

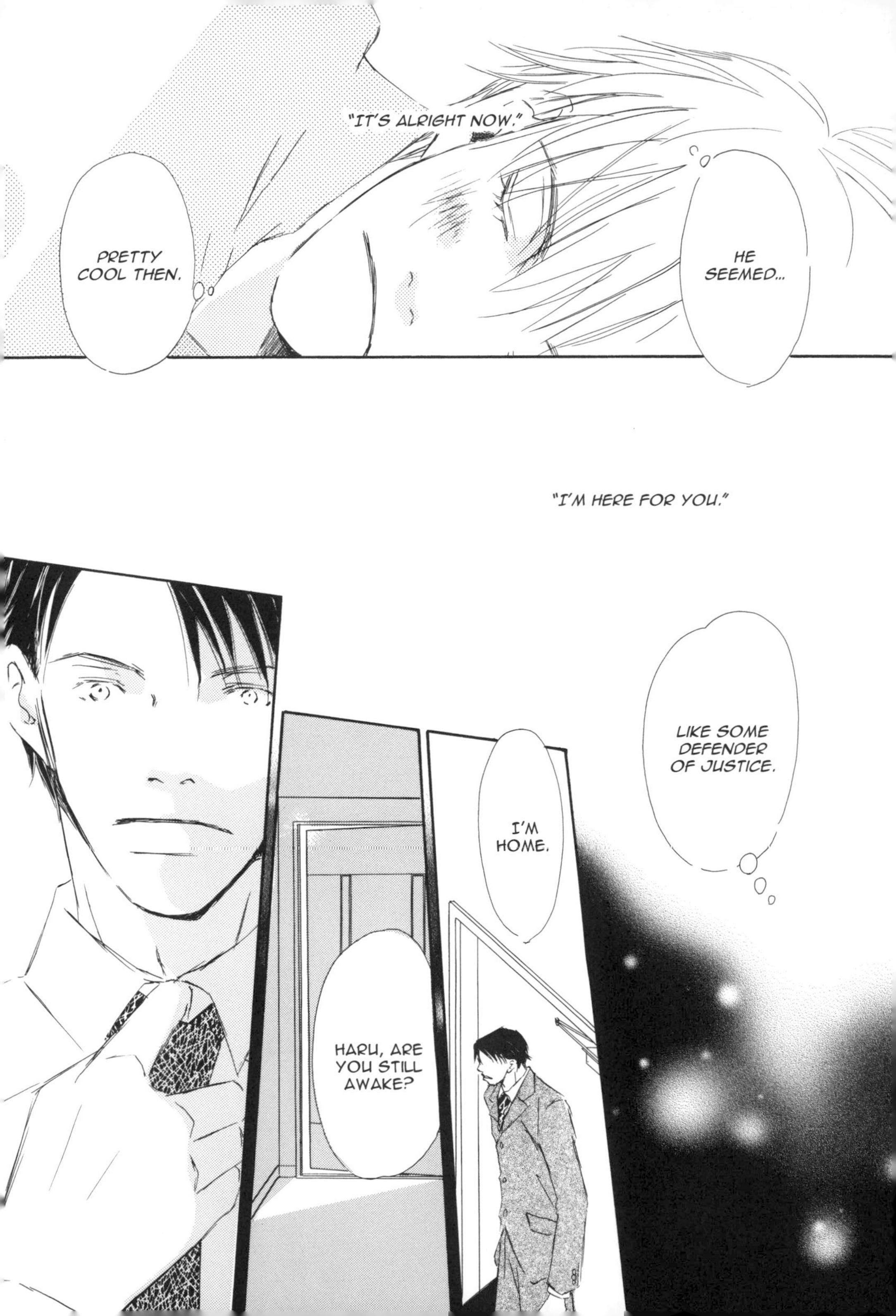
"IT'S ALRIGHT NOW."
HE SEEMED...
PRETTY COOL THEN.
"I'M HERE FOR YOU."
LIKE SOME DEFENDER OF JUSTICE.
I'M HOME.
HARU, ARE YOU STILL AWAKE?

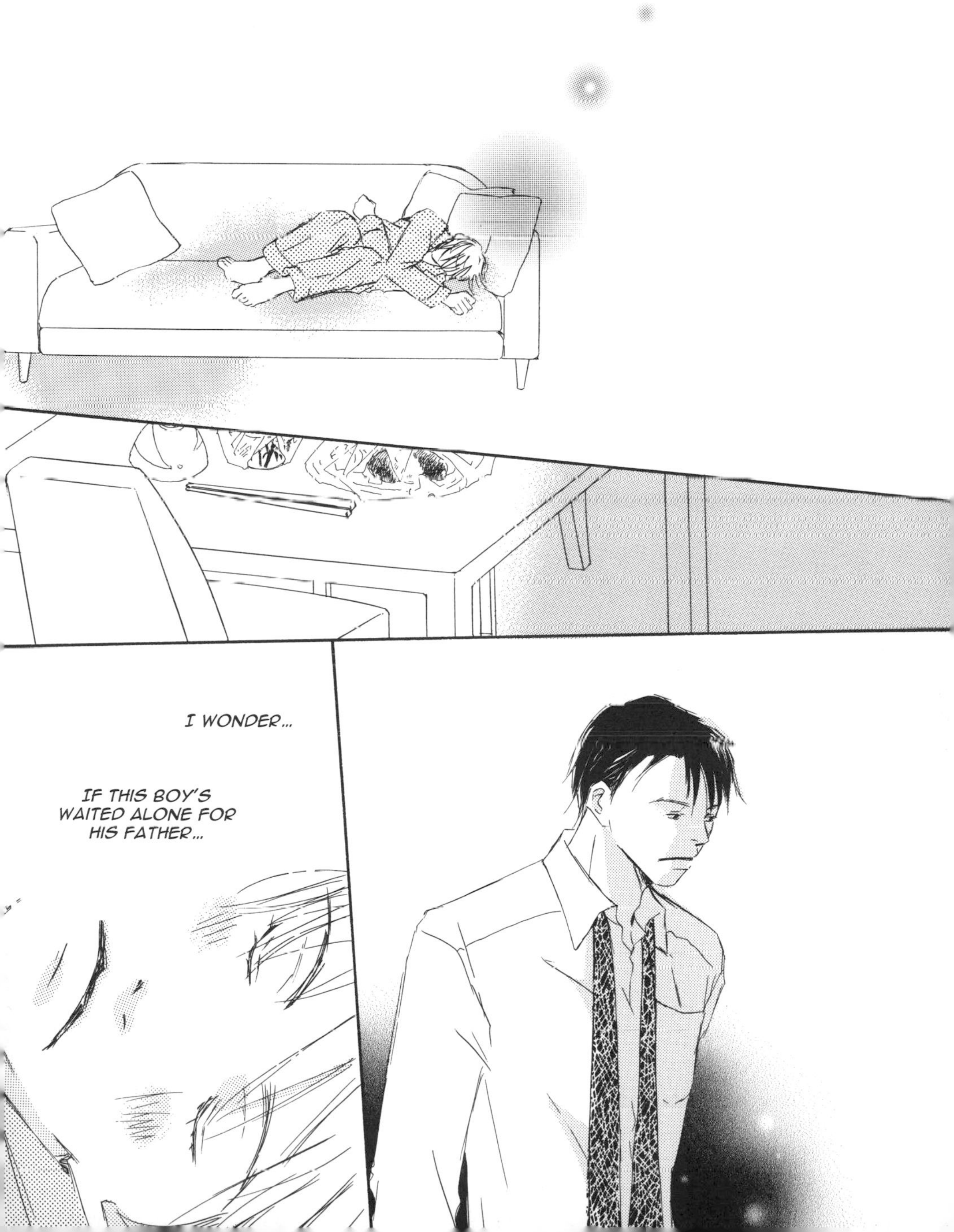
I WONDER...
IF THIS BOY'S WAITED ALONE FOR HIS FATHER...

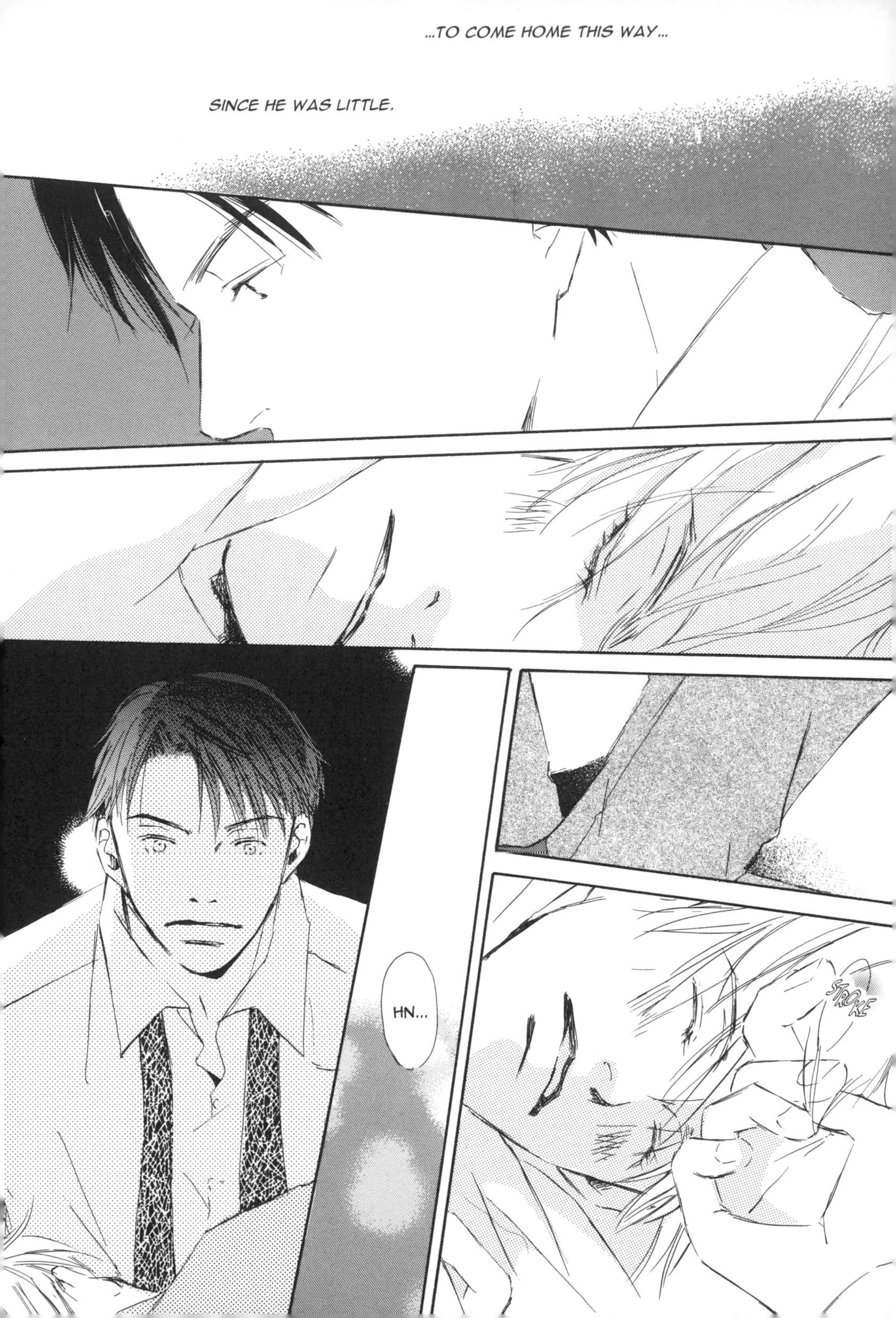

...TO COME HOME THIS WAY...
SINCE HE WAS LITTLE.
HN...
STROKE

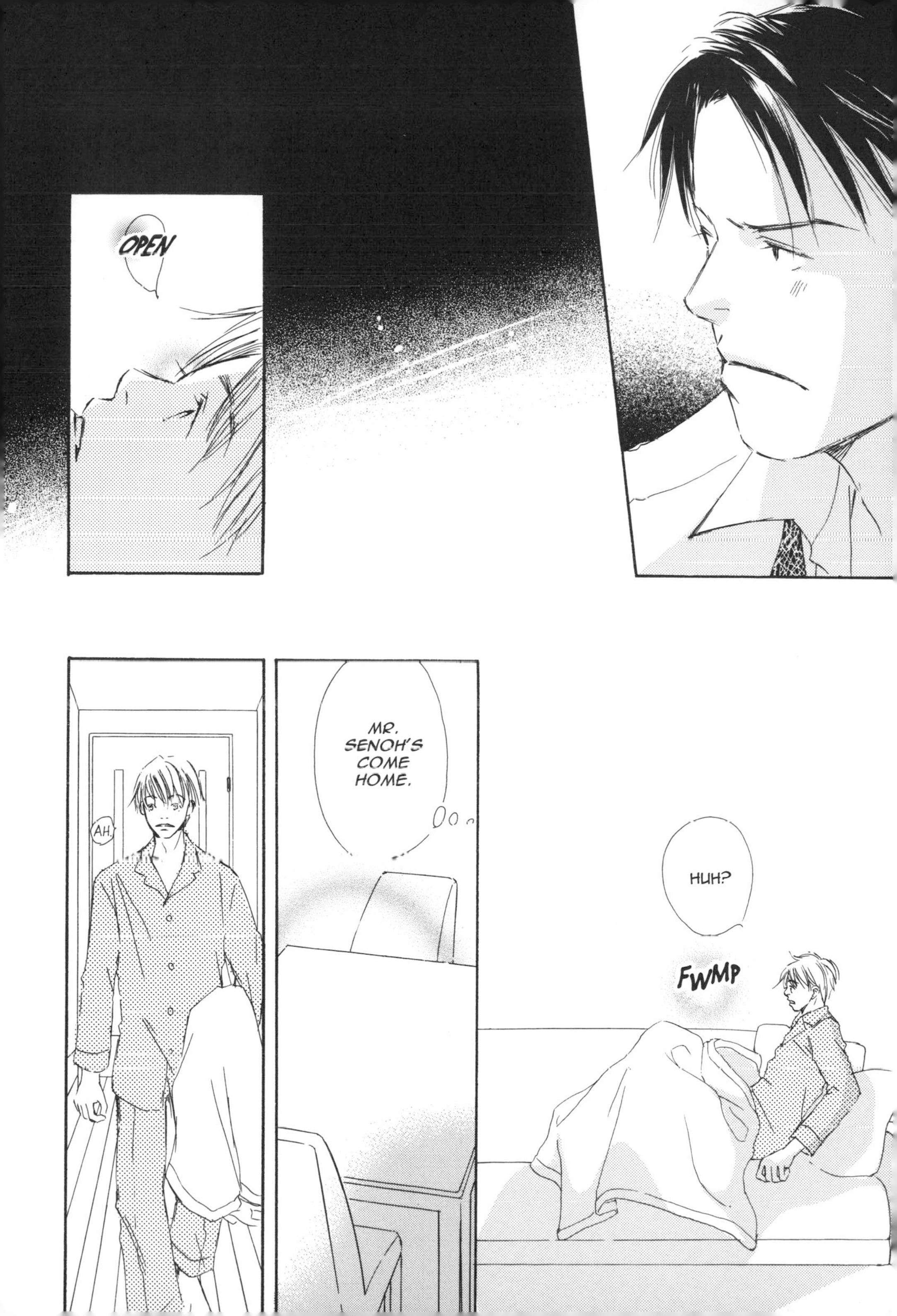
OPEN
HUH?
FWMP
MR. SENOH'S COME HOME.
AH.

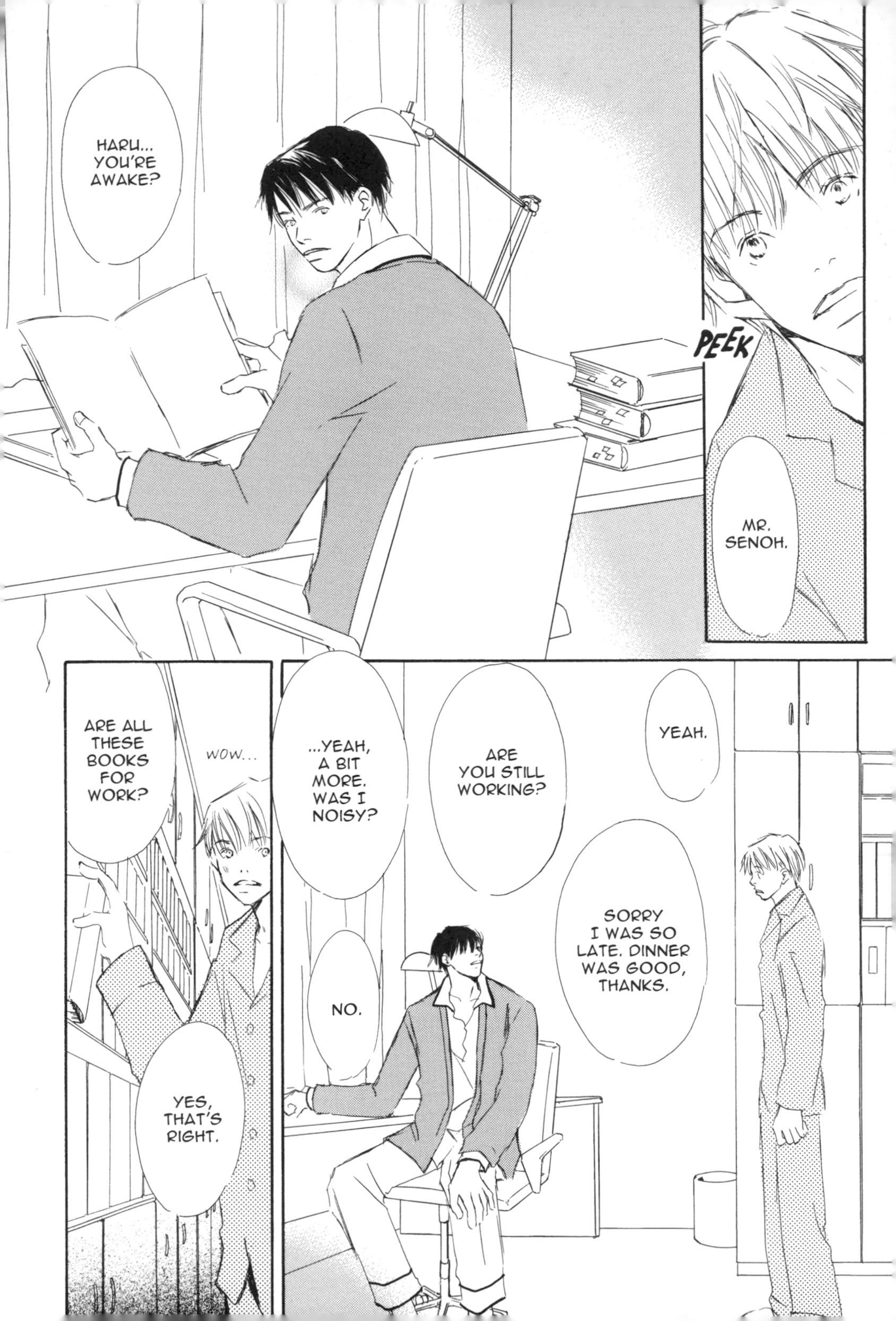
PEEK
MR. SENOH.
HARU... YOU'RE AWAKE?
YEAH.
ARE YOU STILL WORKING?
SORRY I WAS SO LATE. DINNER WAS GOOD, THANKS.
...YEAH, A BIT MORE. WAS I NOISY?
NO.
WOW...
ARE ALL THESE BOOKS FOR WORK?
YES, THAT'S RIGHT.

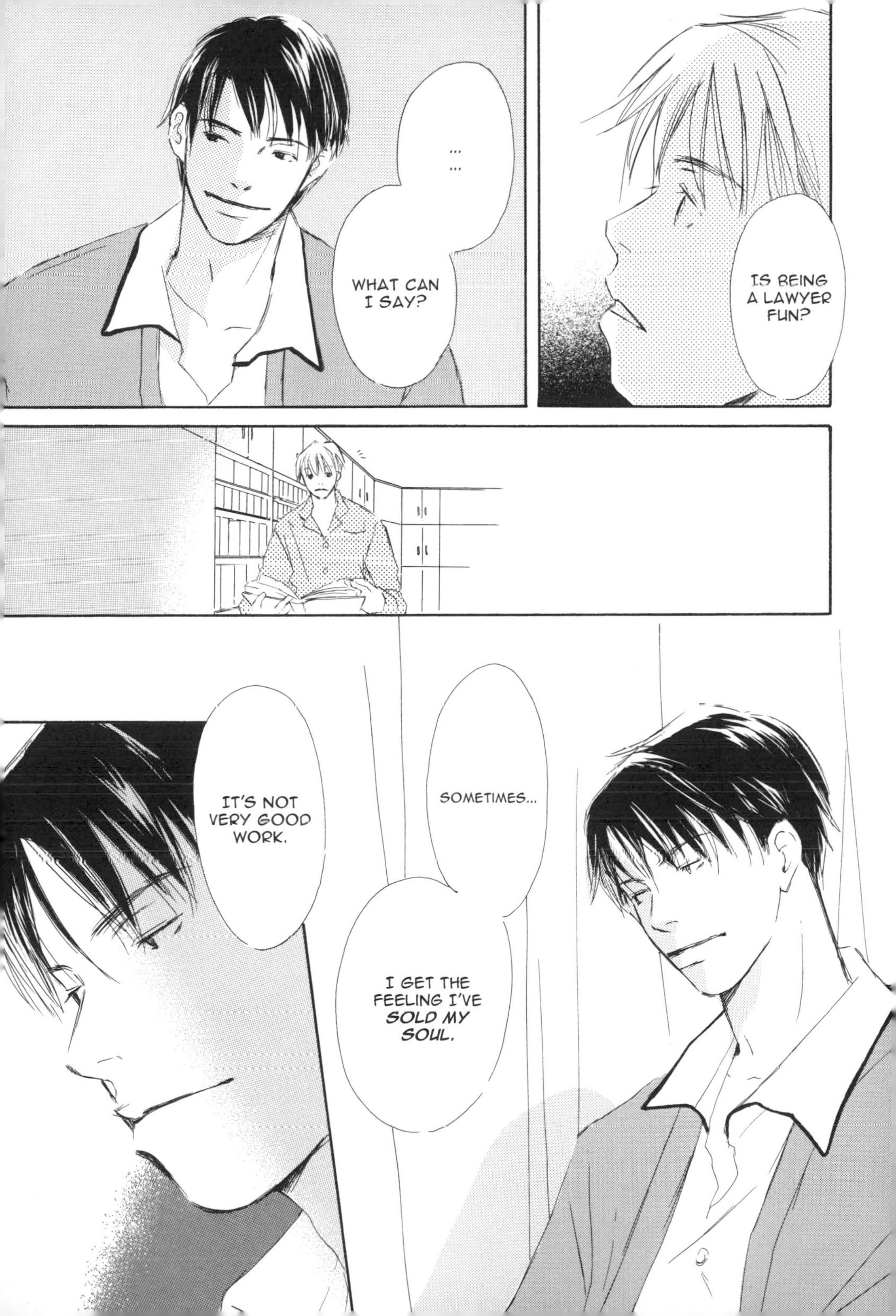
IS BEING A LAWYER FUN?
... ...
WHAT CAN I SAY?
SOMETIMES...
I GET THE FEELING I'VE SOLD MY SOUL.
IT'S NOT VERY GOOD WORK.

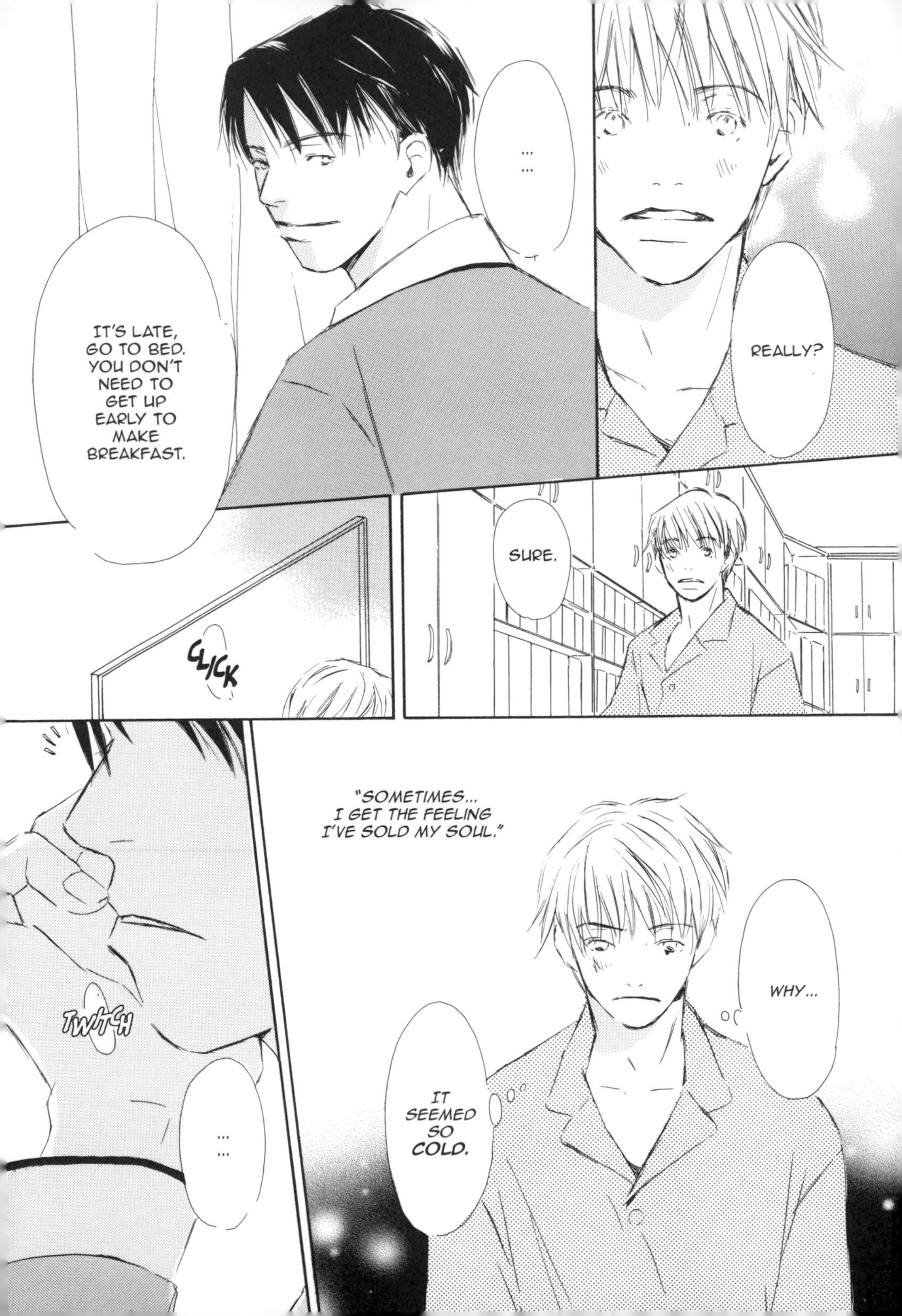
REALLY?
...
...
IT'S LATE, GO TO BED. YOU DON'T NEED TO GET UP EARLY TO MAKE BREAKFAST.
SURE.
CLICK
"SOMETIMES... I GET THE FEELING I'VE SOLD MY SOUL."
WHY...
IT SEEMED SO COLD.
TWITCH
...
...

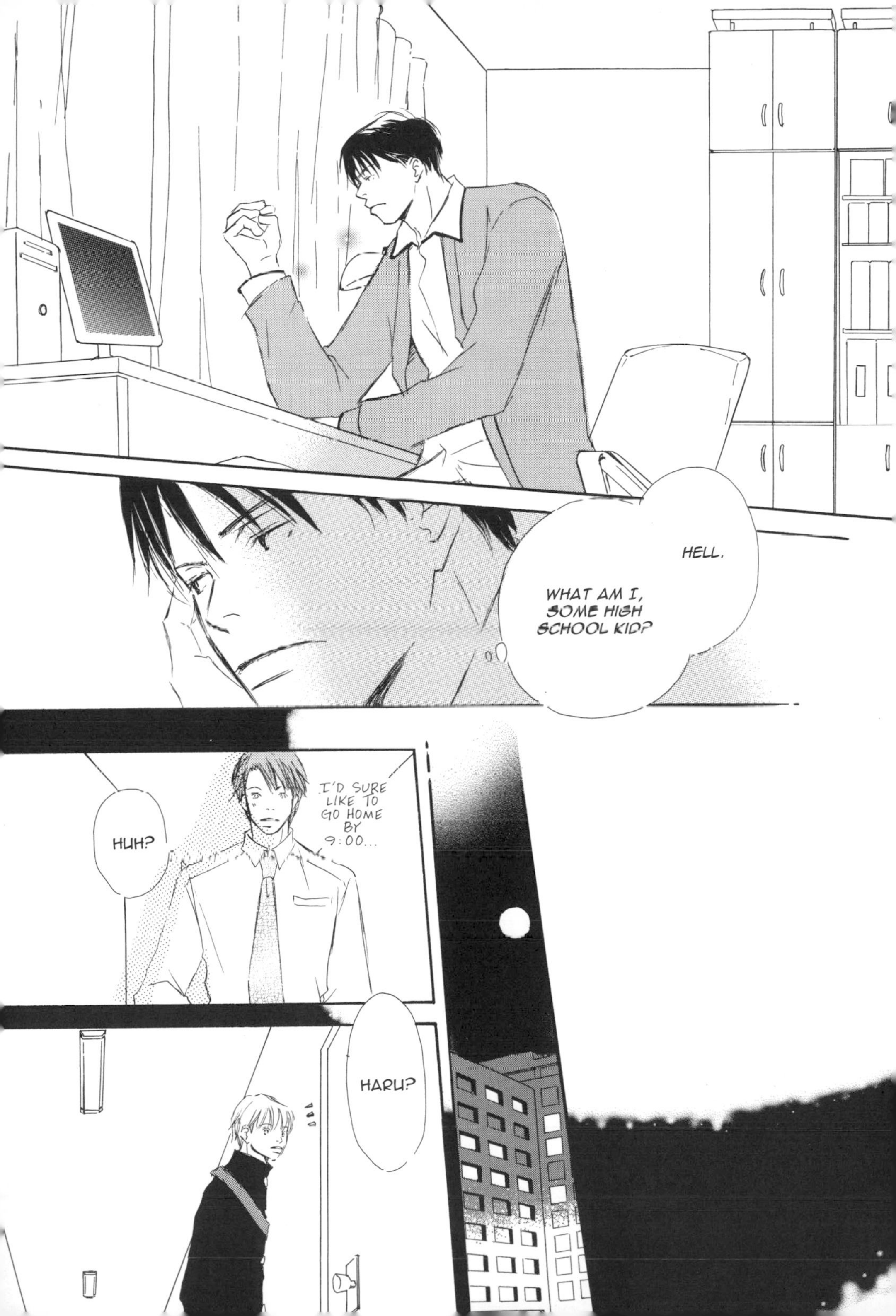
HELL.
WHAT AM I, SOME HIGH SCHOOL KID?
I'D SURE LIKE TO GO HOME BY 9:00...
HUH?
HARU?

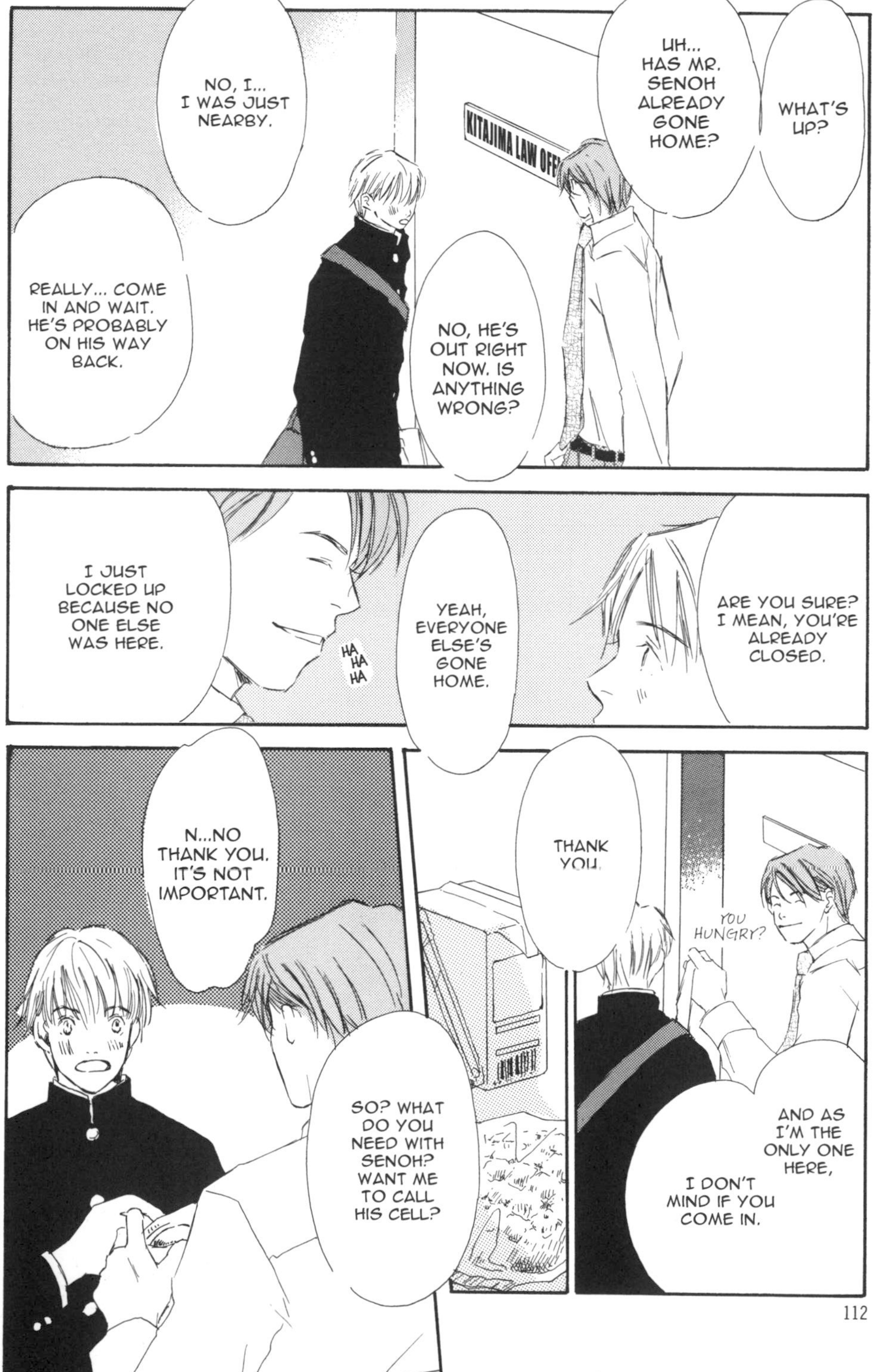
WHAT'S UP?
UH... HAS MR. SENOH ALREADY GONE HOME?
KITAJIMA LAW OFF
NO, HE'S OUT RIGHT NOW. IS ANYTHING WRONG?
NO, I... I WAS JUST NEARBY.
REALLY... COME IN AND WAIT. HE'S PROBABLY ON HIS WAY BACK.
ARE YOU SURE? I MEAN, YOU'RE ALREADY CLOSED.
YEAH, EVERYONE ELSE'S GONE HOME.
HA HA HA
I JUST LOCKED UP BECAUSE NO ONE ELSE WAS HERE.
AND AS I'M THE ONLY ONE HERE,
I DON'T MIND IF YOU COME IN.
THANK YOU.
YOU HUNGRY?
SO? WHAT DO YOU NEED WITH SENOH? WANT ME TO CALL HIS CELL?
N...NO THANK YOU. IT'S NOT IMPORTANT.

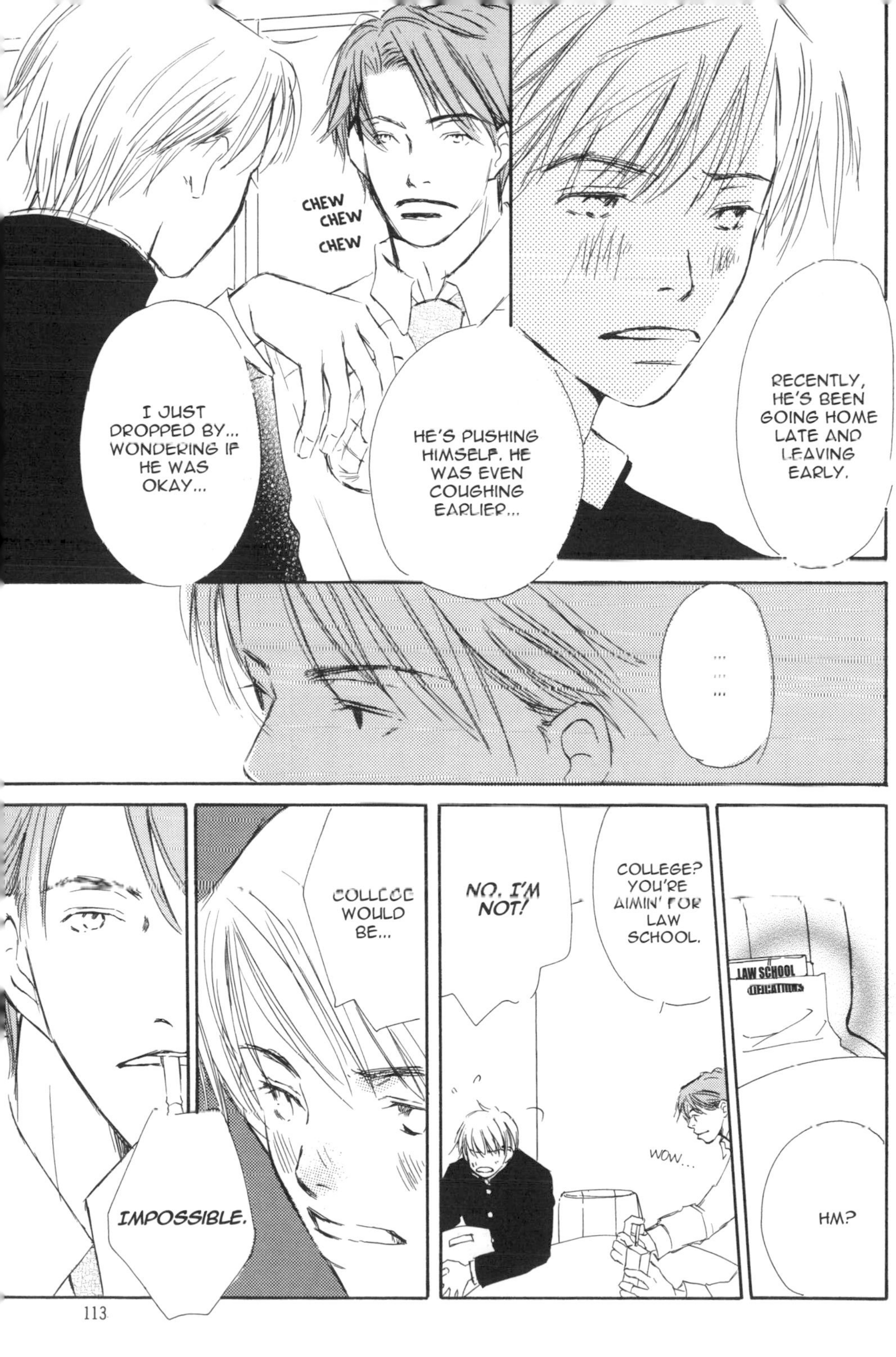
RECENTLY, HE'S BEEN GOING HOME LATE AND LEAVING EARLY.
CHEW CHEW CHEW
HE'S PUSHING HIMSELF. HE WAS EVEN COUGHING EARLIER...
I JUST DROPPED BY... WONDERING IF HE WAS OKAY...
... ...
HM?
LAW SCHOOL
COLLEGE? YOU'RE AIMIN' FOR LAW SCHOOL.
WOW...
NO. I'M NOT!
COLLEGE WOULD BE...
IMPOSSIBLE.

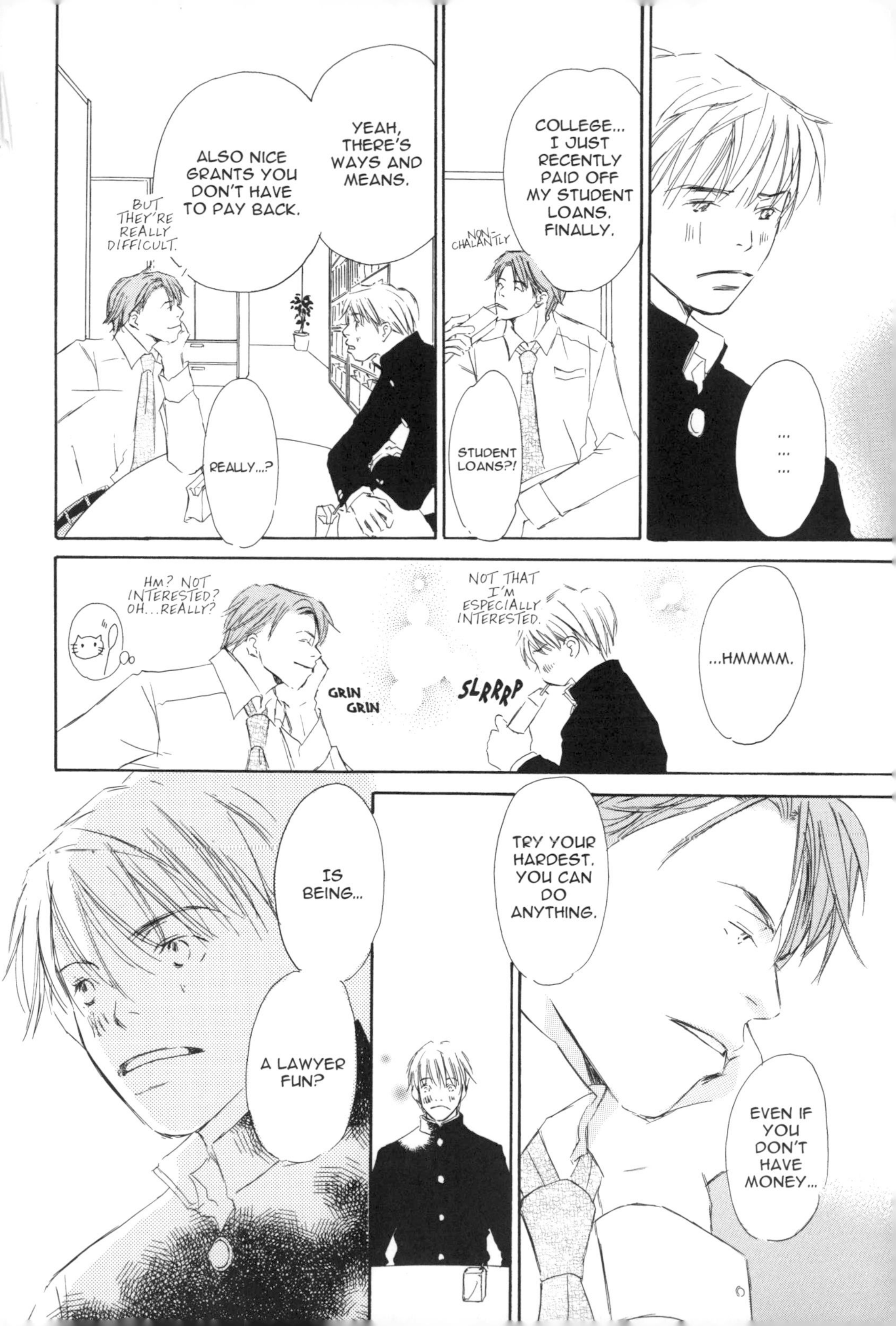
......
COLLEGE... I JUST RECENTLY PAID OFF MY STUDENT LOANS. FINALLY.
NON-CHALANTLY
STUDENT LOANS?!
YEAH, THERE'S WAYS AND MEANS.
ALSO NICE GRANTS YOU DON'T HAVE TO PAY BACK.
BUT THEY'RE REALLY DIFFICULT.
REALLY...?
...HMMMM.
NOT THAT I'M ESPECIALLY INTERESTED.
SLRRRP
GRIN GRIN
HM? NOT INTERESTED? OH...REALLY?
TRY YOUR HARDEST. YOU CAN DO ANYTHING.
EVEN IF YOU DON'T HAVE MONEY...
IS BEING...
A LAWYER FUN?

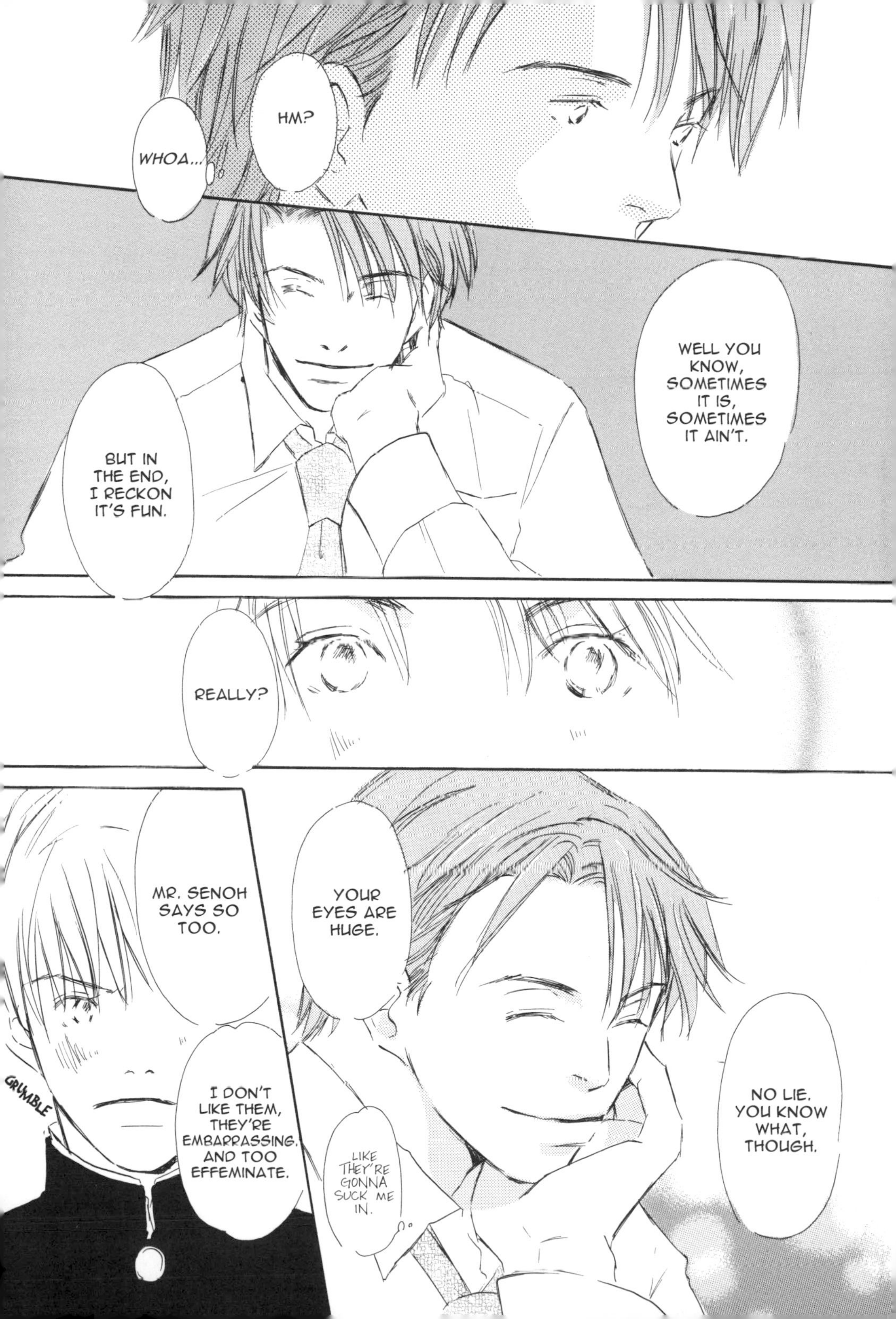
HM?
WHOA...
WELL YOU KNOW, SOMETIMES IT IS, SOMETIMES IT AIN'T.
BUT IN THE END, I RECKON IT'S FUN.
REALLY?
NO LIE. YOU KNOW WHAT, THOUGH.
YOUR EYES ARE HUGE.
LIKE THEY'RE GONNA SUCK ME IN.
MR. SENOH SAYS SO TOO.
I DON'T LIKE THEM, THEY'RE EMBARRASSING. AND TOO EFFEMINATE.
GRUMBLE

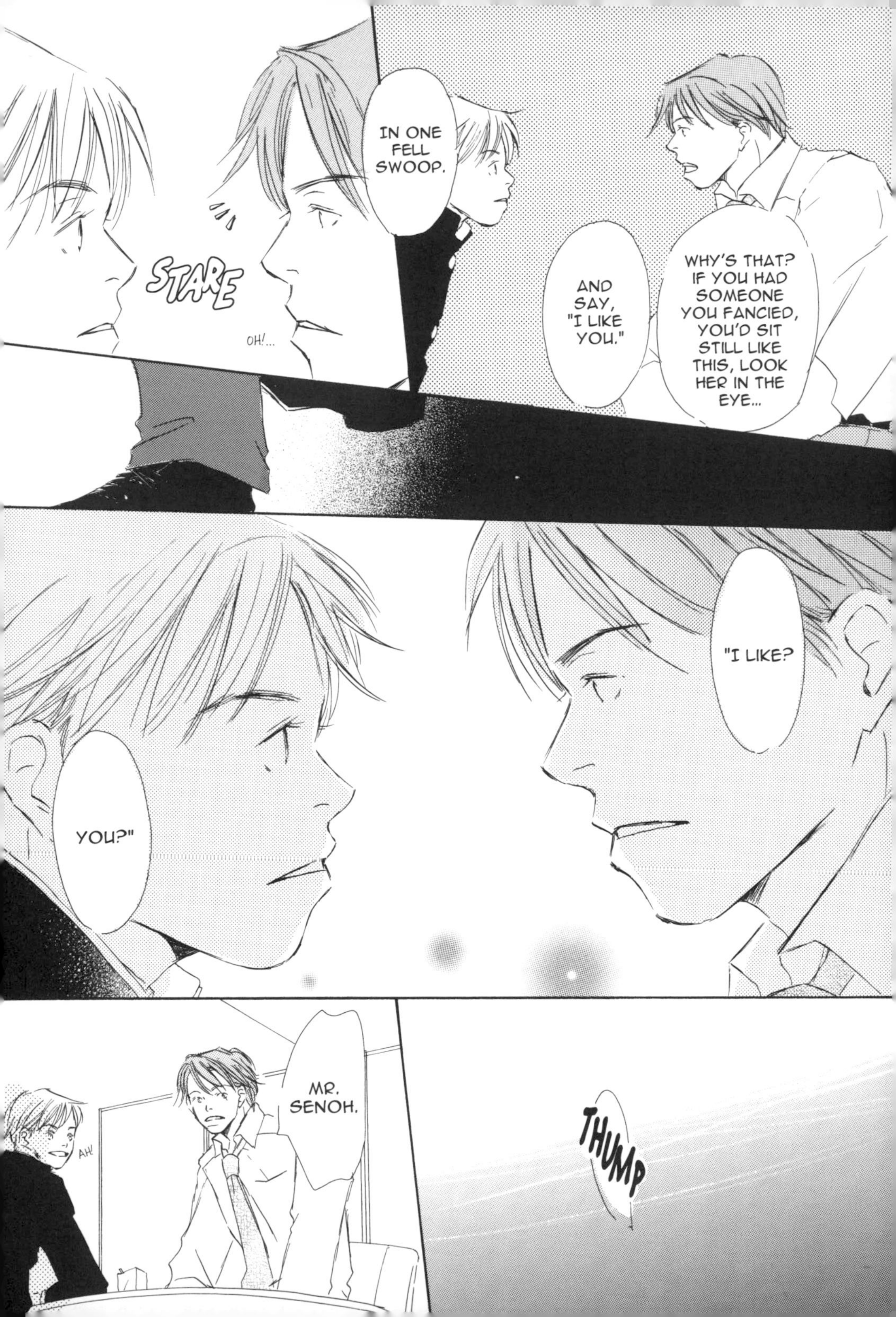
WHY'S THAT? IF YOU HAD SOMEONE YOU FANCIED, YOU'D SIT STILL LIKE THIS, LOOK HER IN THE EYE...
AND SAY, "I LIKE YOU."
IN ONE FELL SWOOP.
STARE
OH!...
"I LIKE?
YOU?"
THUMP
MR. SENOH.
AH!

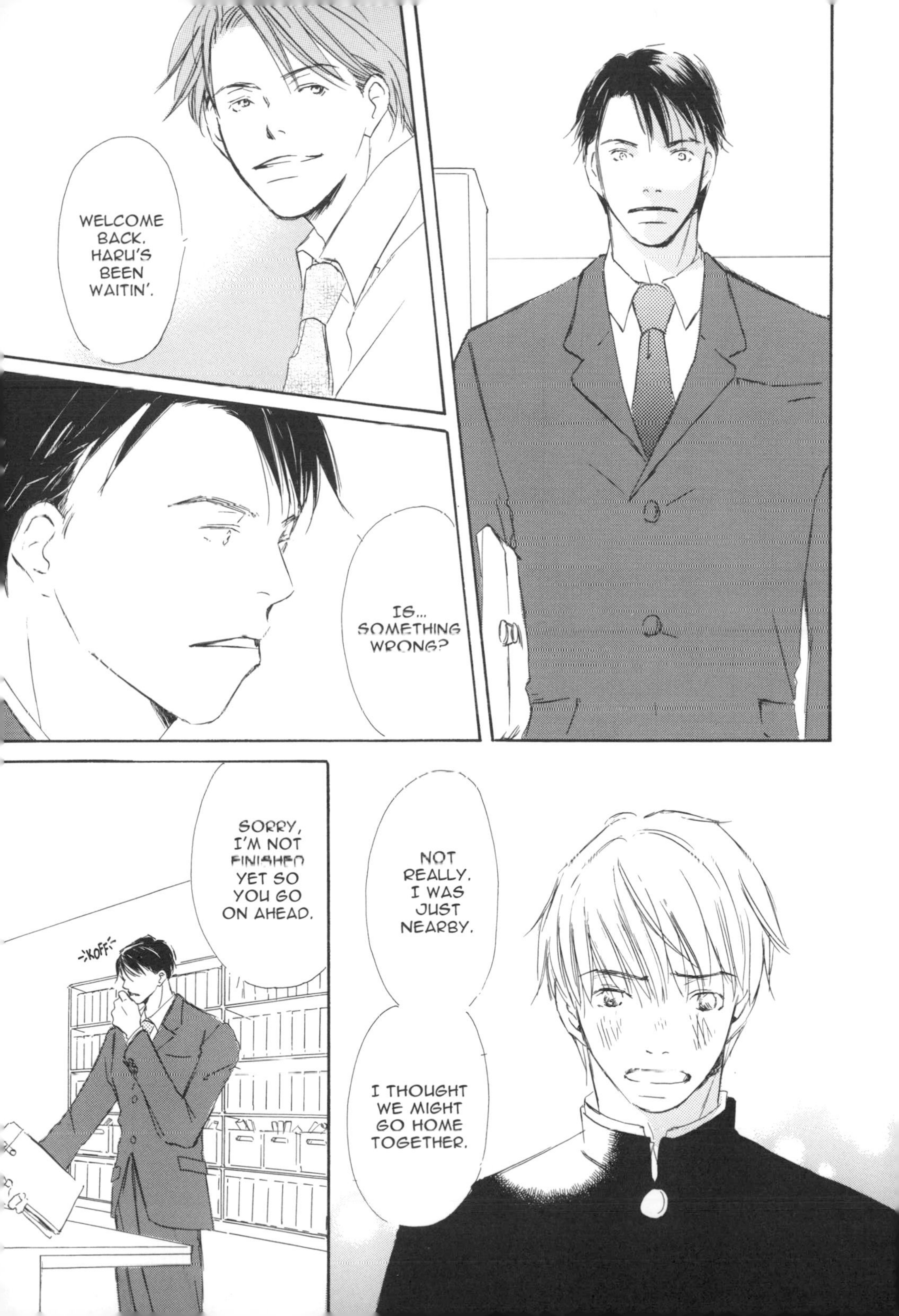
WELCOME BACK. HARU'S BEEN WAITIN'.
IS... SOMETHING WRONG?
NOT REALLY. I WAS JUST NEARBY.
I THOUGHT WE MIGHT GO HOME TOGETHER.
SORRY, I'M NOT FINISHED YET SO YOU GO ON AHEAD.
KOFF

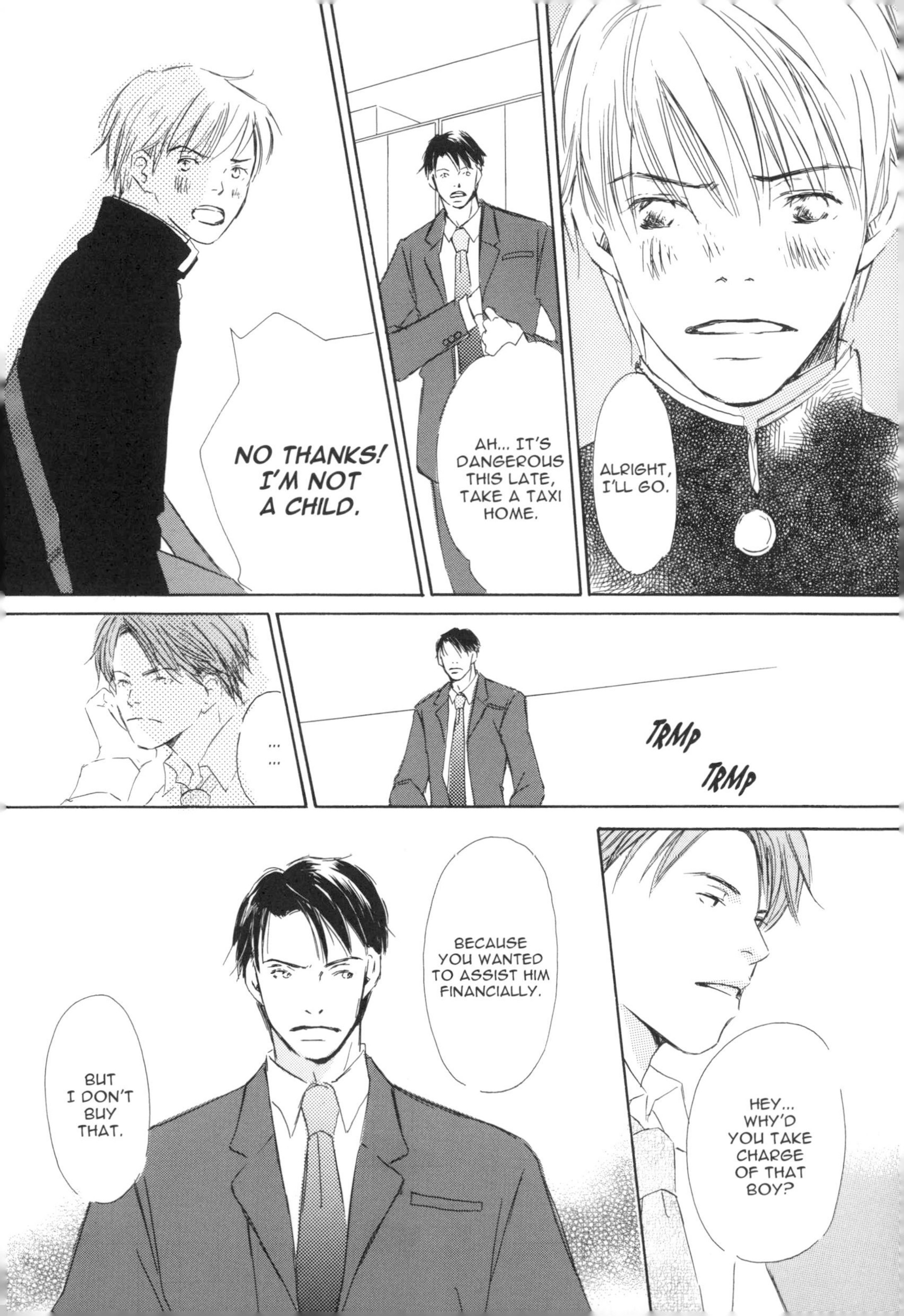
ALRIGHT, I'LL GO.
AH... IT'S DANGEROUS THIS LATE, TAKE A TAXI HOME.
NO THANKS! I'M NOT A CHILD.
TRMP
TRMP
... ...
HEY... WHY'D YOU TAKE CHARGE OF THAT BOY?
BECAUSE YOU WANTED TO ASSIST HIM FINANCIALLY.
BUT I DON'T BUY THAT.

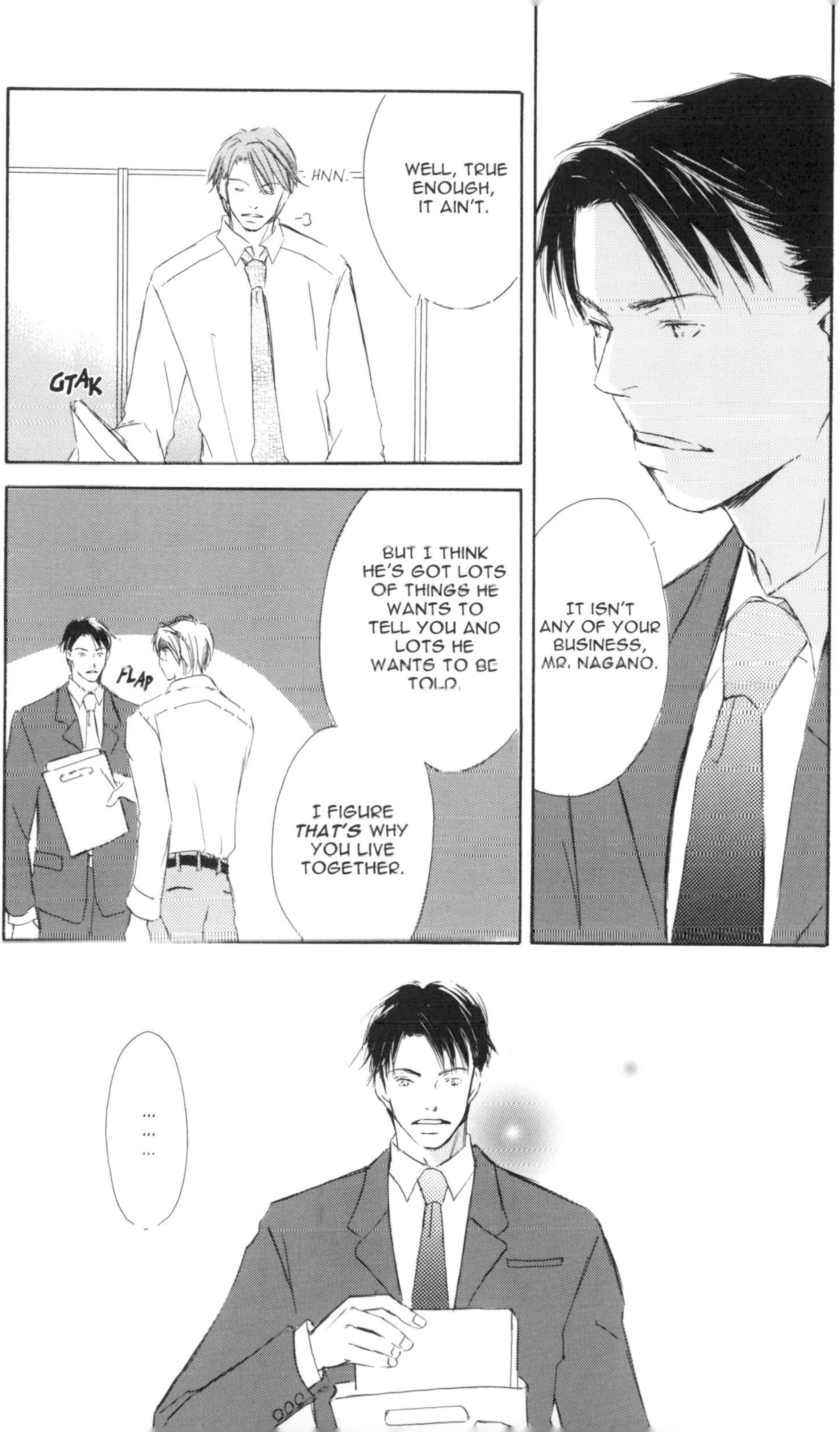
IT ISN'T ANY OF YOUR BUSINESS, MR. NAGANO.
HNN.
WELL, TRUE ENOUGH, IT AIN'T.
GTAK
BUT I THINK HE'S GOT LOTS OF THINGS HE WANTS TO TELL YOU AND LOTS HE WANTS TO BE TOLD.
FLAP
I FIGURE THAT'S WHY YOU LIVE TOGETHER.
... ...

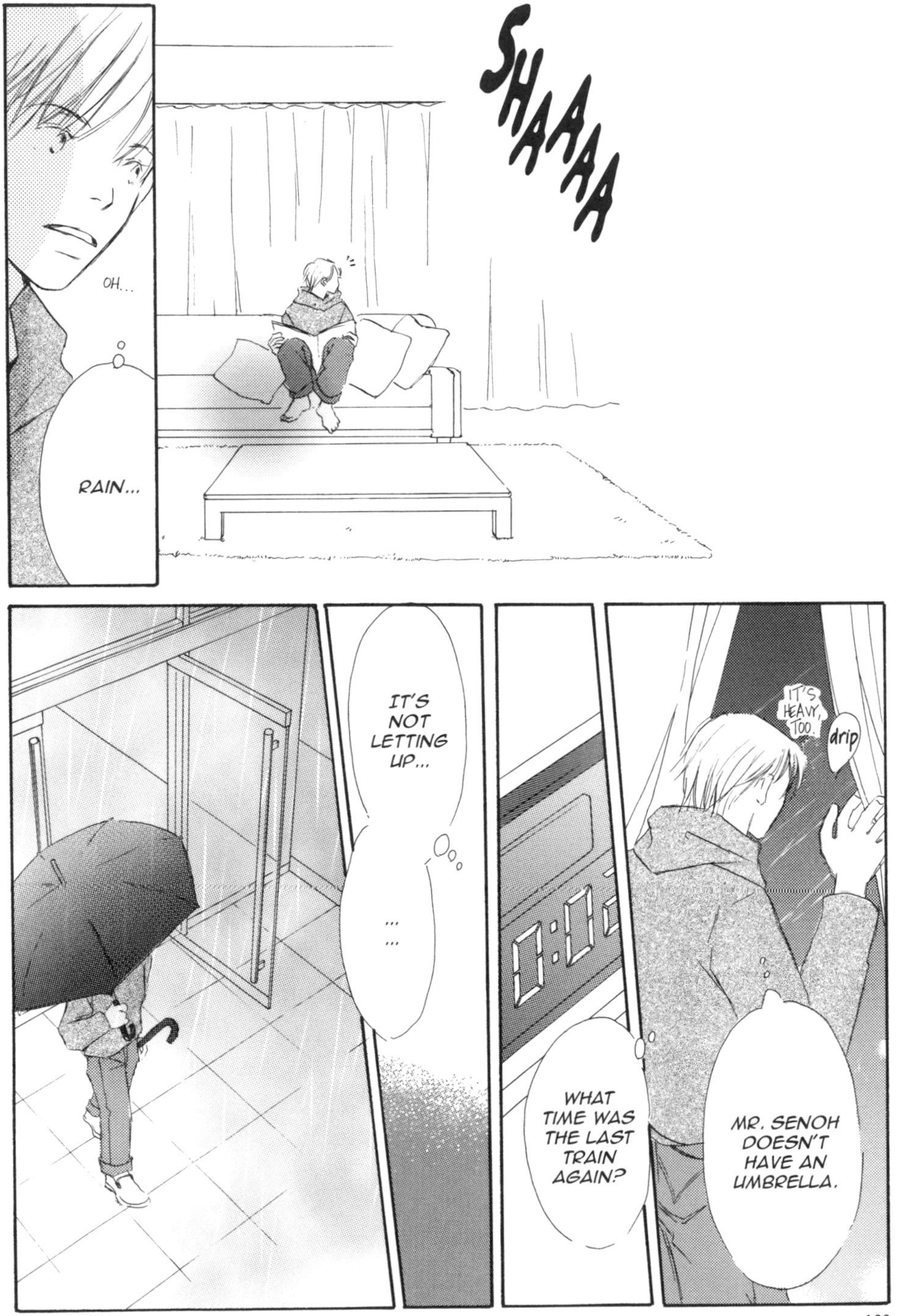
SHAAAA
OH...
RAIN...
drip
IT'S HEAVY, TOO.
MR. SENOH DOESN'T HAVE AN UMBRELLA.
WHAT TIME WAS THE LAST TRAIN AGAIN?
IT'S NOT LETTING UP...
... ...

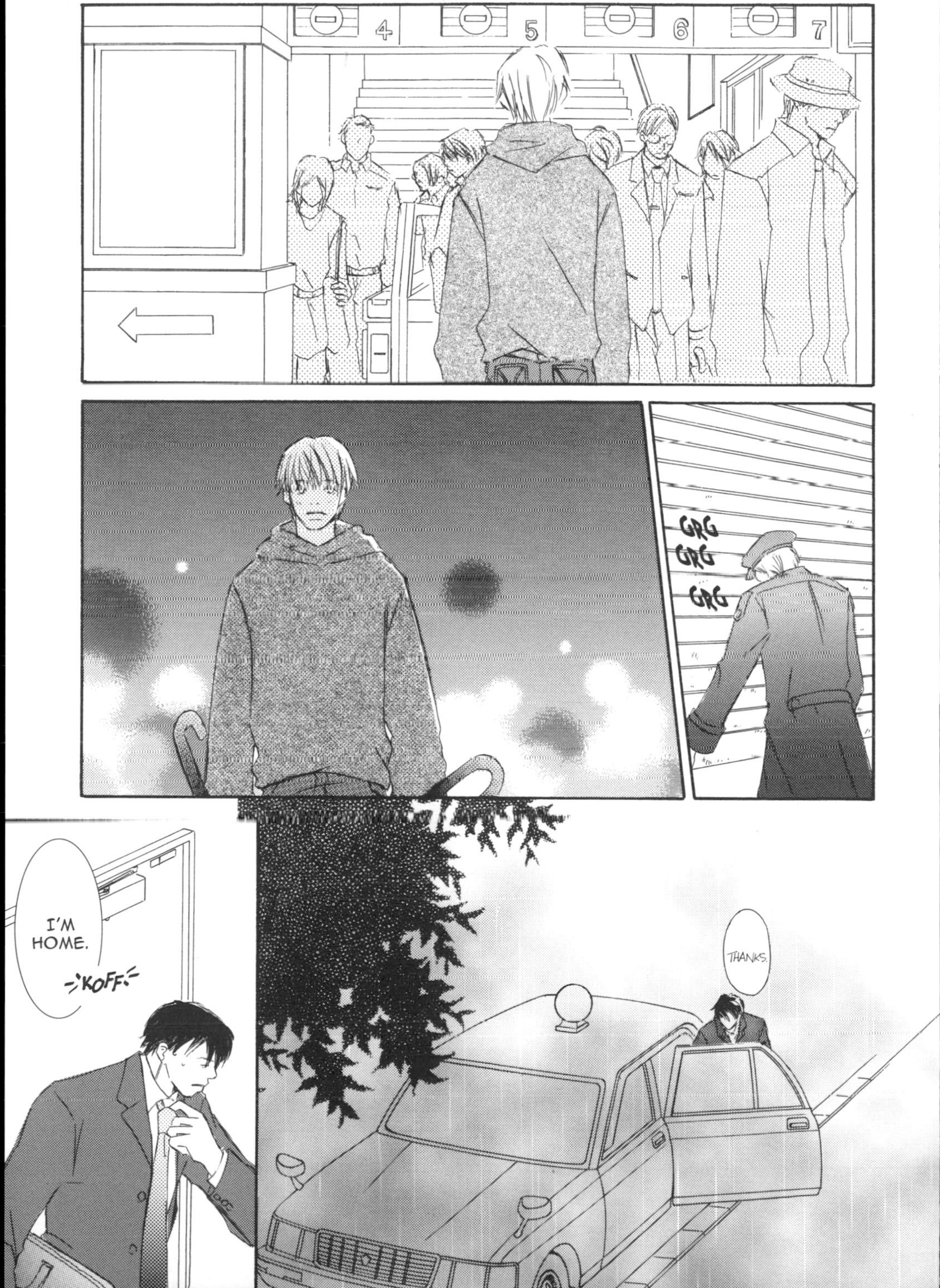
GRG
GRG
GRG
THANKS.
I'M HOME.
-KOFF-

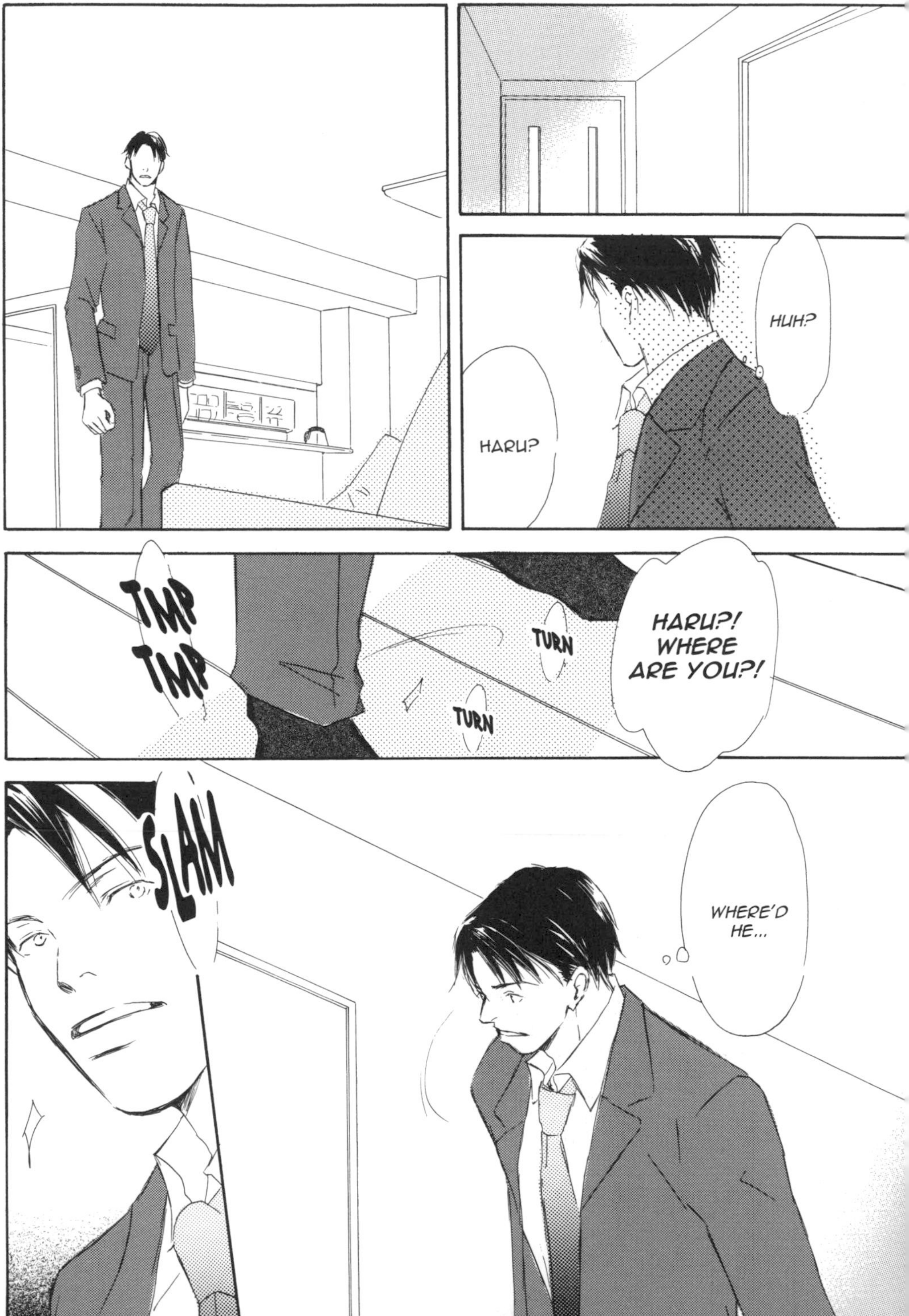
HUH?
HARU?
HARU?! WHERE ARE YOU?!
TURN
TURN
TMP TMP
WHERE'D HE...
SLAM

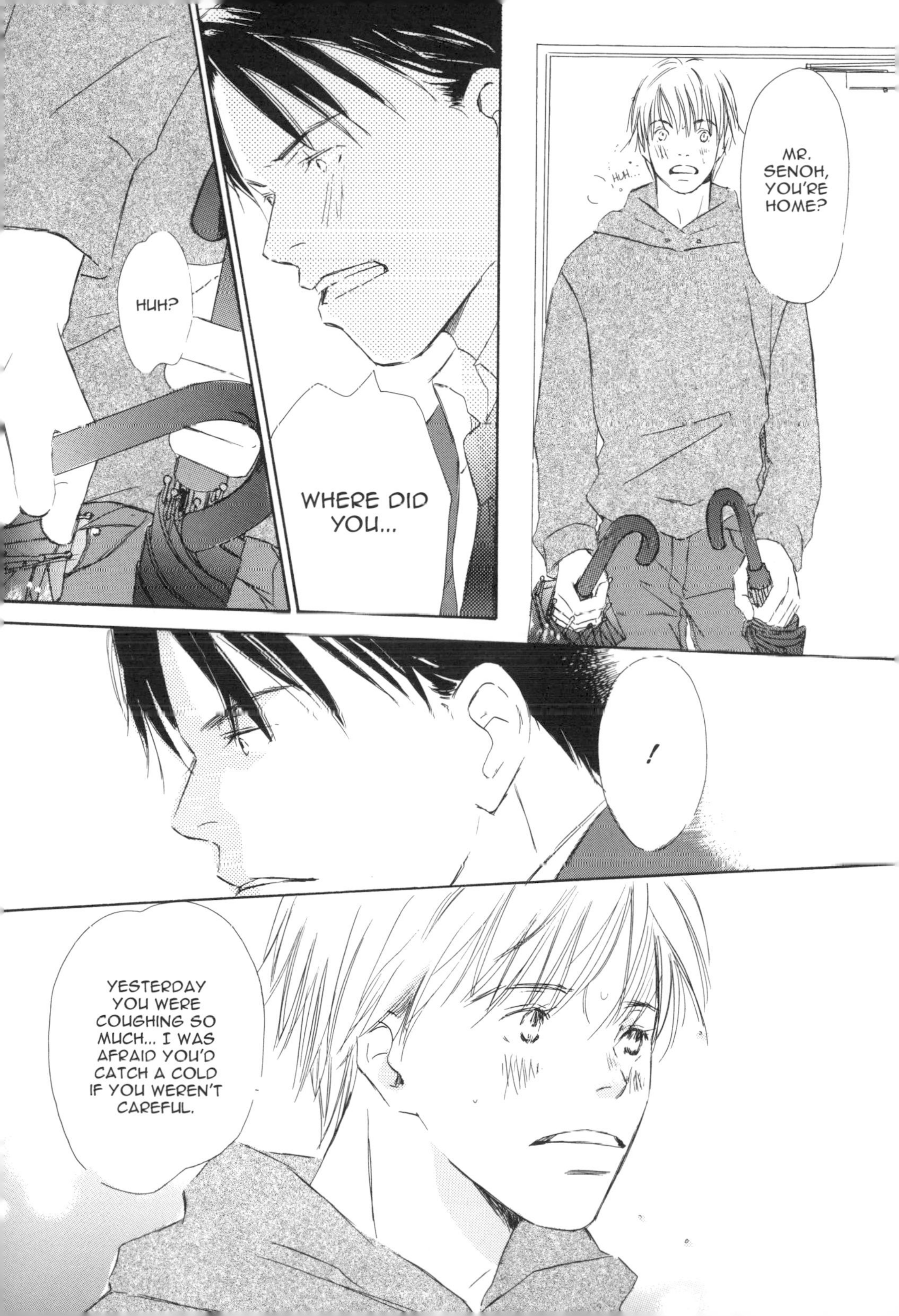
MR. SENOH, YOU'RE HOME?
HUH...
WHERE DID YOU...
HUH?
!
YESTERDAY YOU WERE COUGHING SO MUCH... I WAS AFRAID YOU'D CATCH A COLD IF YOU WEREN'T CAREFUL.

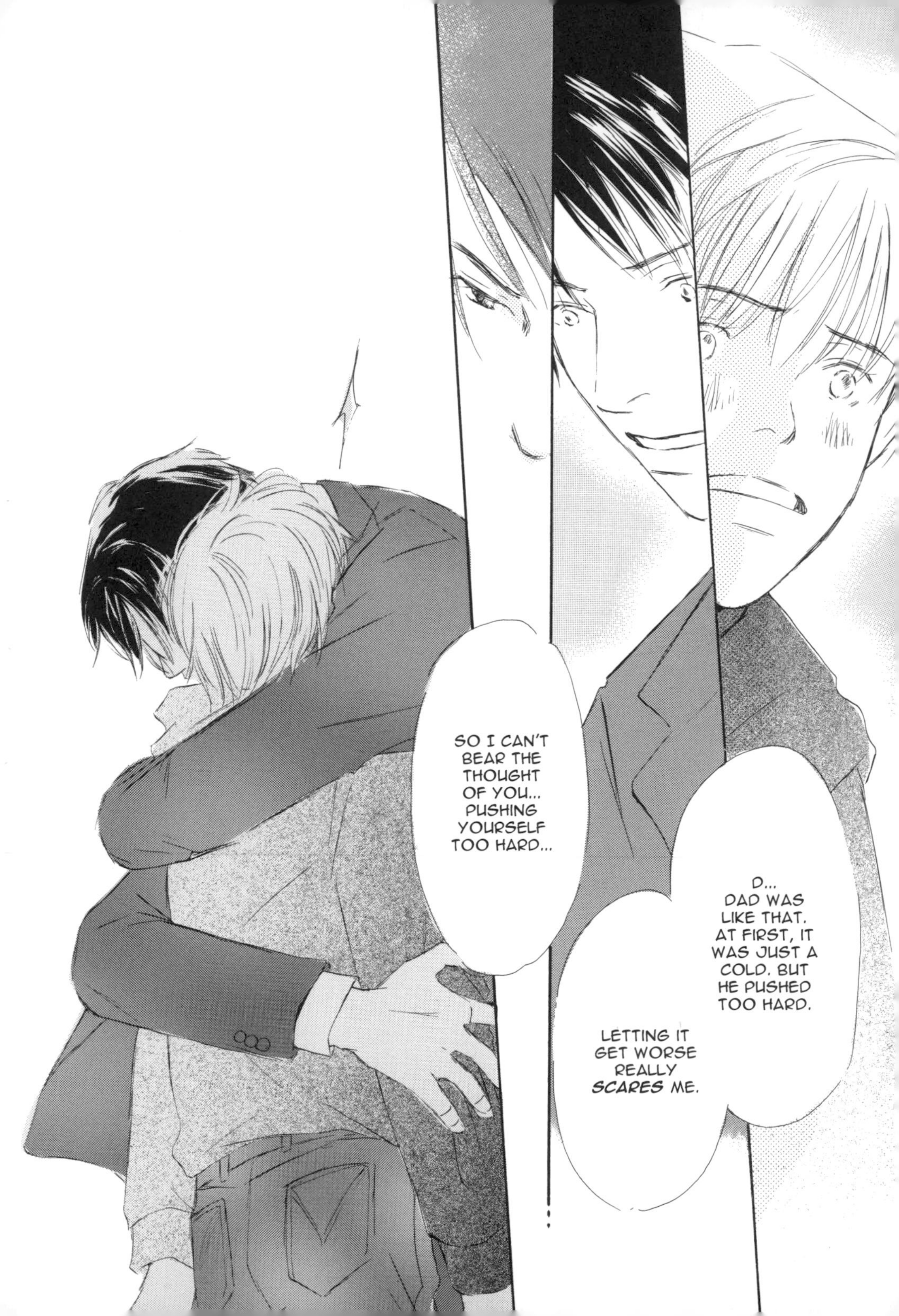

SO I CAN'T BEAR THE THOUGHT OF YOU... PUSHING YOURSELF TOO HARD...
D... DAD WAS LIKE THAT. AT FIRST, IT WAS JUST A COLD. BUT HE PUSHED TOO HARD.
LETTING IT GET WORSE REALLY SCARES ME.

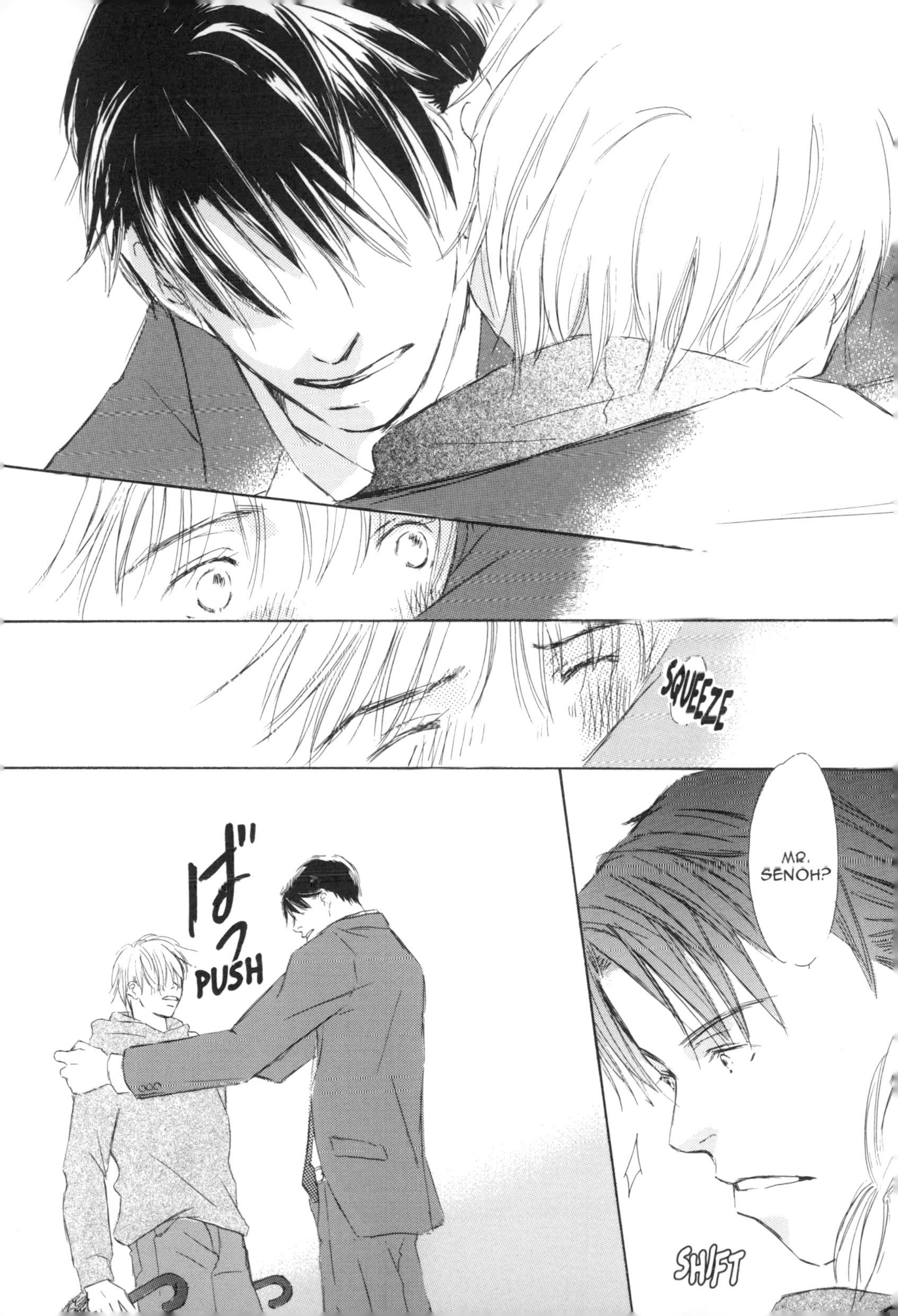
SQUEEZE
MR. SENOH?
SHIFT
ばっ
PUSH

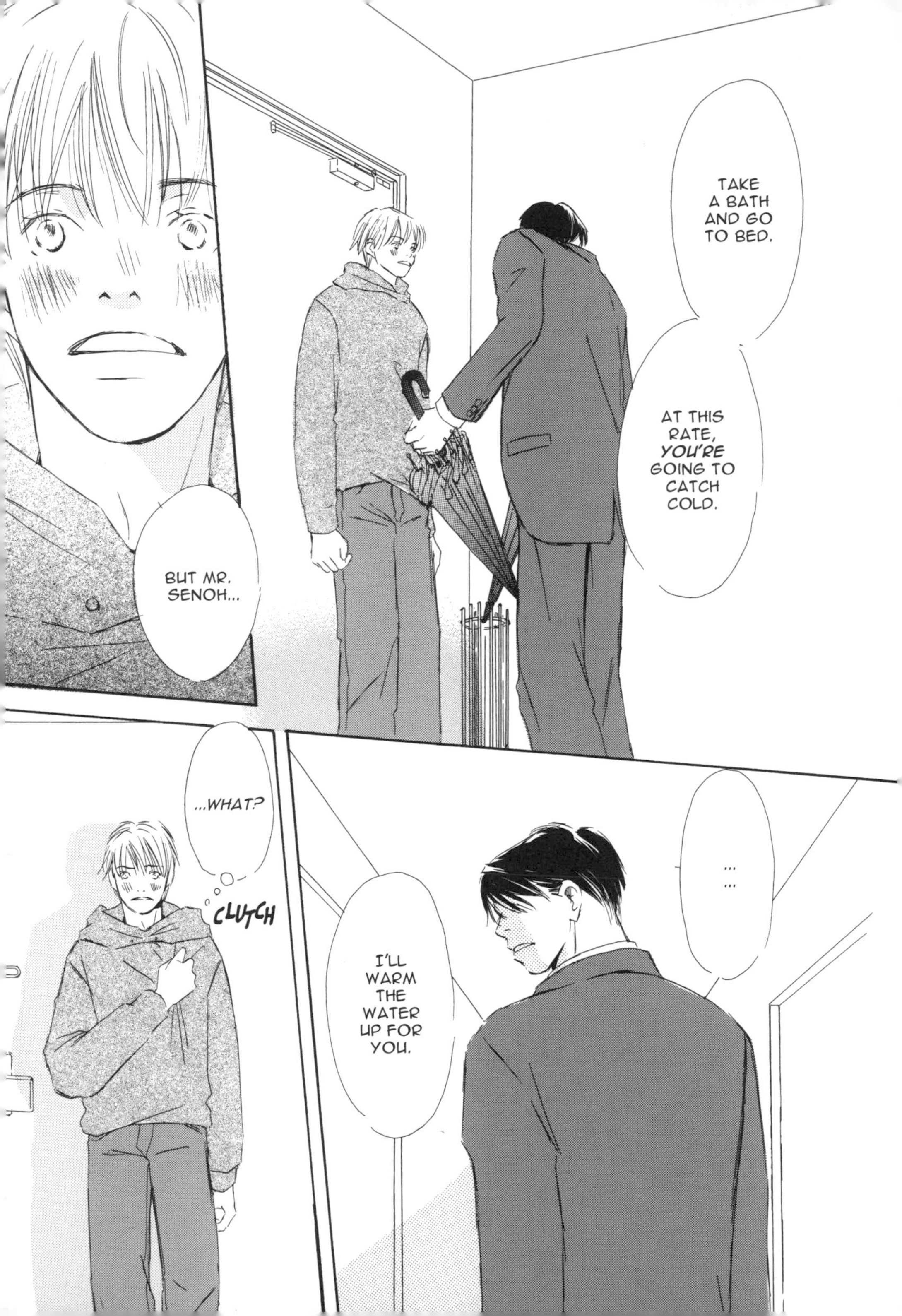
TAKE A BATH AND GO TO BED.
AT THIS RATE, *YOU'RE* GOING TO CATCH COLD.
BUT MR. SENOH...
... ...
I'LL WARM THE WATER UP FOR YOU.
...WHAT?
CLUTCH

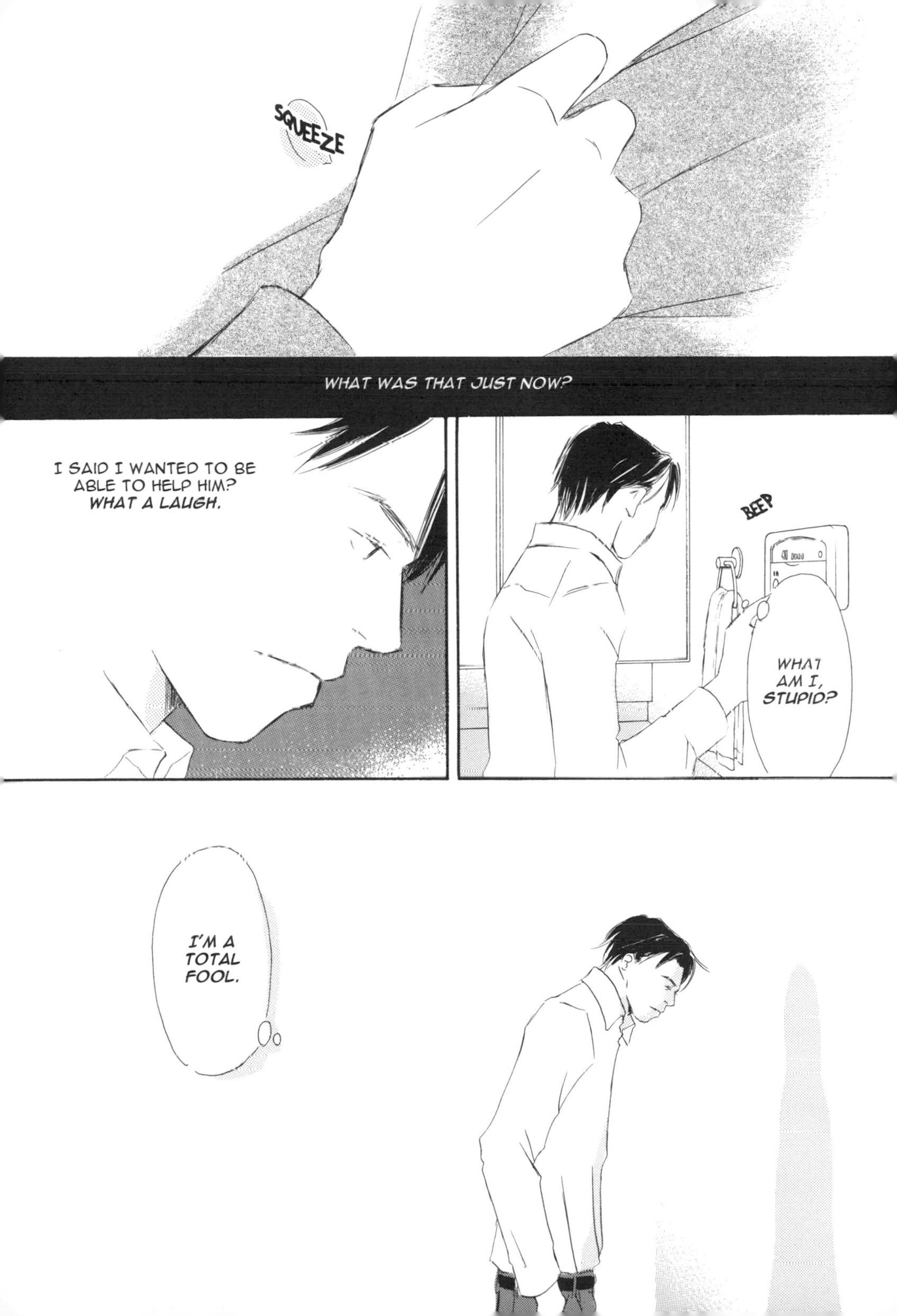
SQUEEZE
WHAT WAS THAT JUST NOW?
BEEP
WHAT AM I, STUPID?
I SAID I WANTED TO BE ABLE TO HELP HIM? WHAT A LAUGH.
I'M A TOTAL FOOL.

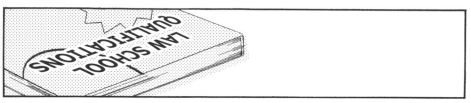

LAW SCHOOL
QUALIFICATIONS
1

I'LL LEAVE...

THE WATER WARMED UP.

YEAH... THANKS.

...

...

YOU LEFT IT AT THE OFFICE.

YOU WANT... TO GO TO COLLEGE?

OH! THAT'S...

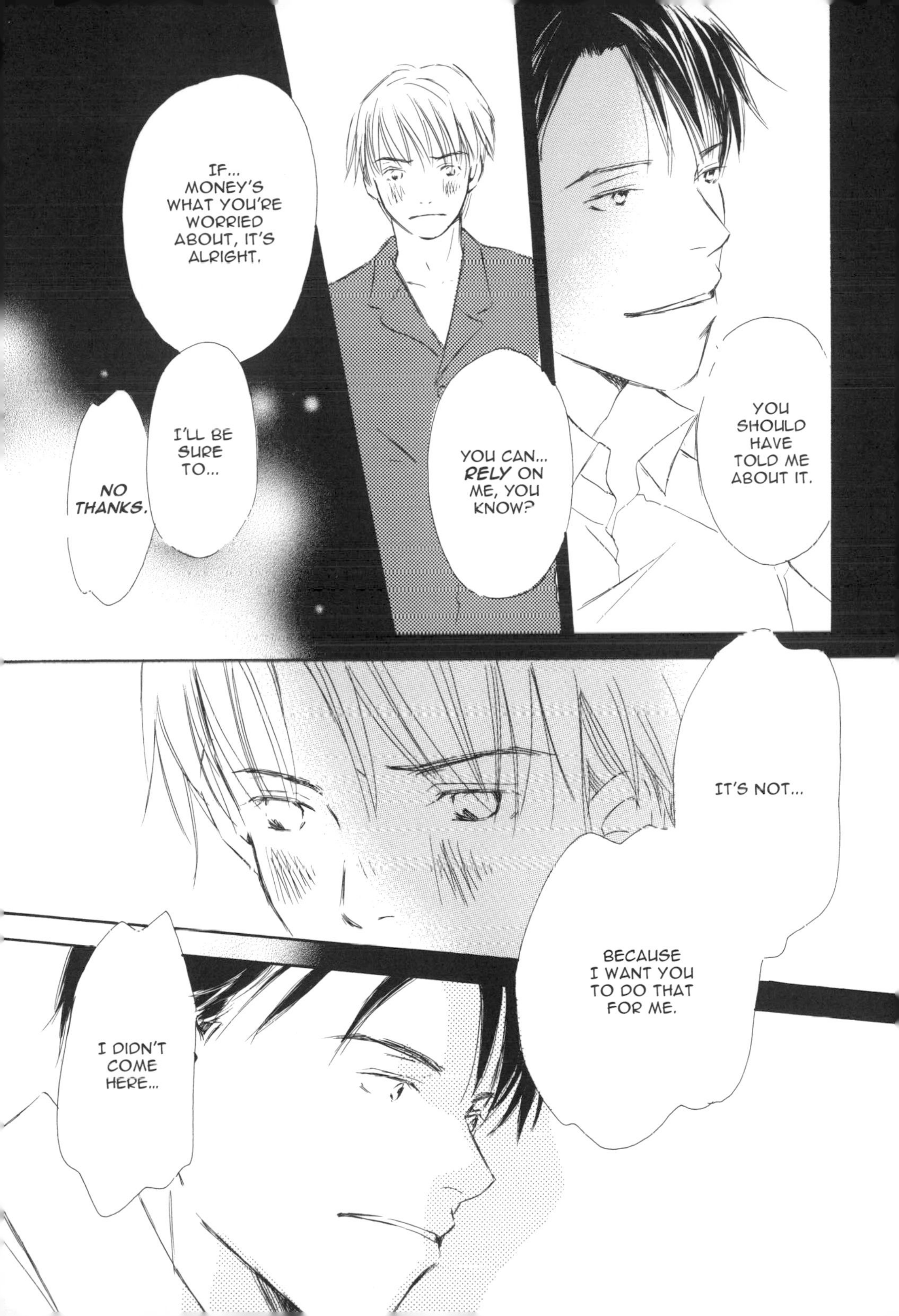
YOU SHOULD HAVE TOLD ME ABOUT IT.
IF... MONEY'S WHAT YOU'RE WORRIED ABOUT, IT'S ALRIGHT.
YOU CAN... **RELY** ON ME, YOU KNOW?
I'LL BE SURE TO...
NO THANKS.
IT'S NOT...
BECAUSE I WANT YOU TO DO THAT FOR ME.
I DIDN'T COME HERE...

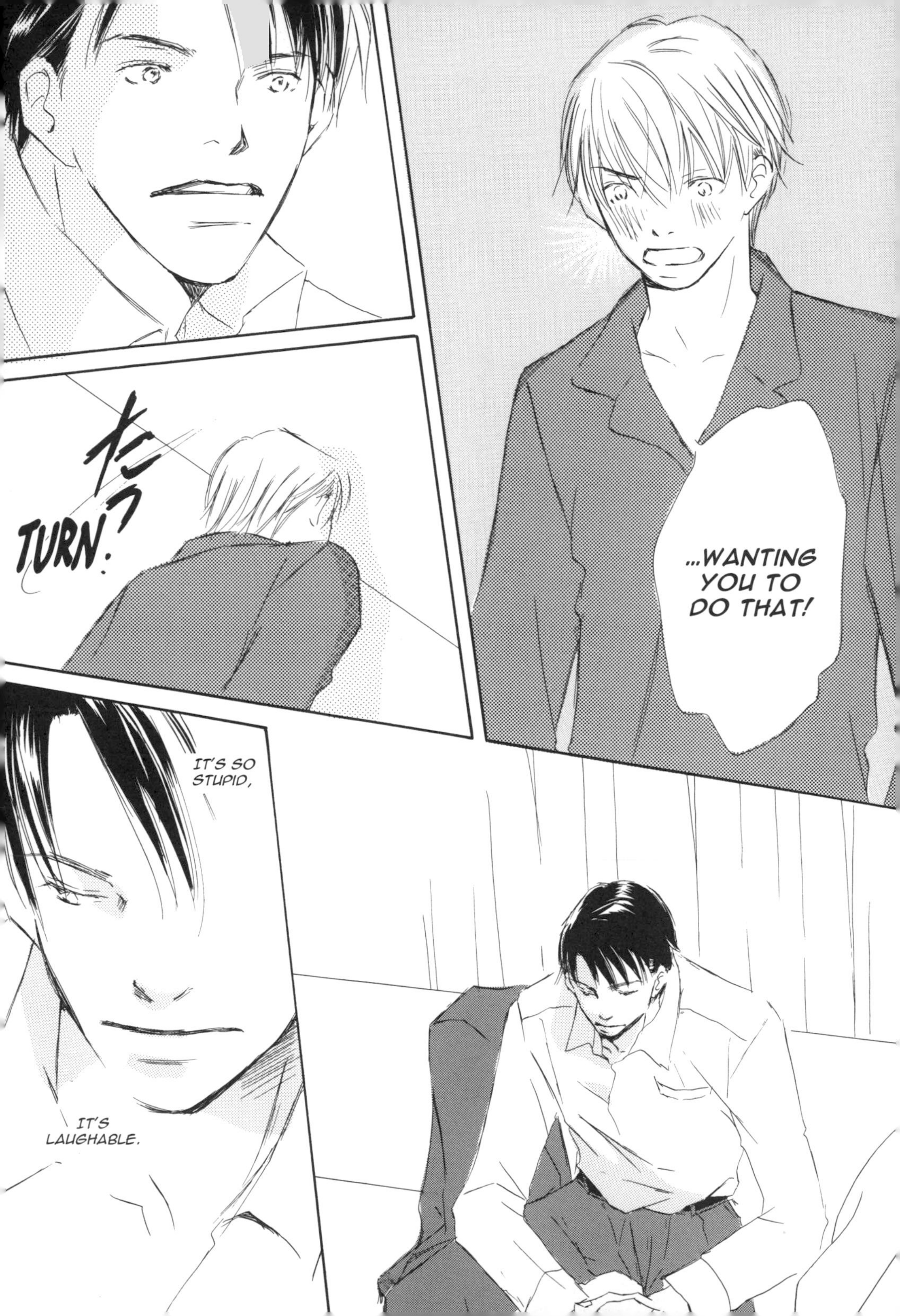
...WANTING YOU TO DO THAT!
たっ
TURN
IT'S SO STUPID,
IT'S LAUGHABLE.

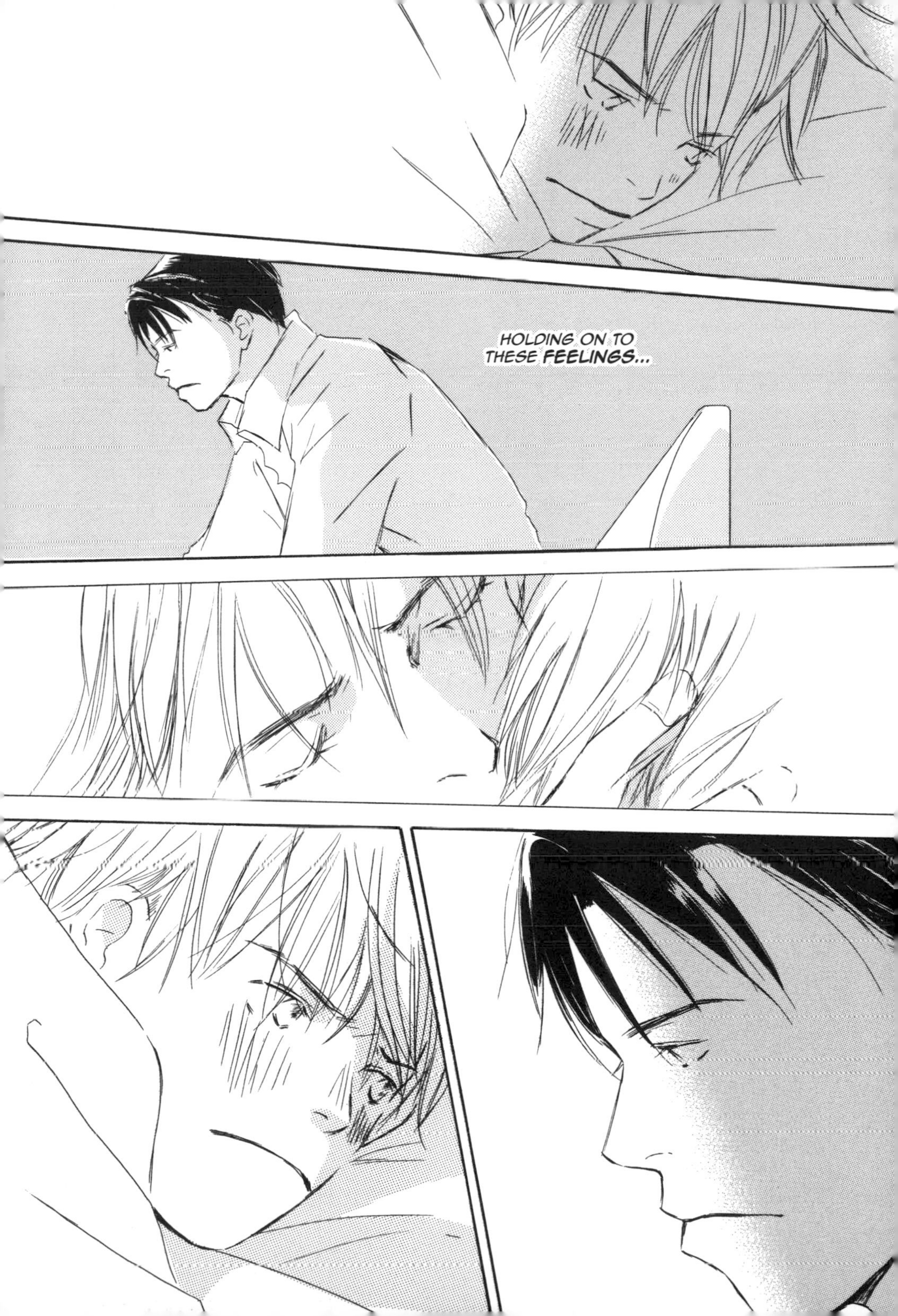
HOLDING ON TO THESE FEELINGS...

WAS I TRYING BE...

SOME SURROGATE FATHER?

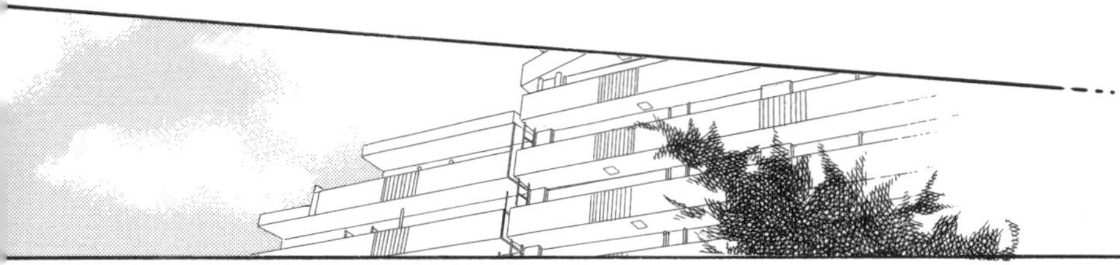

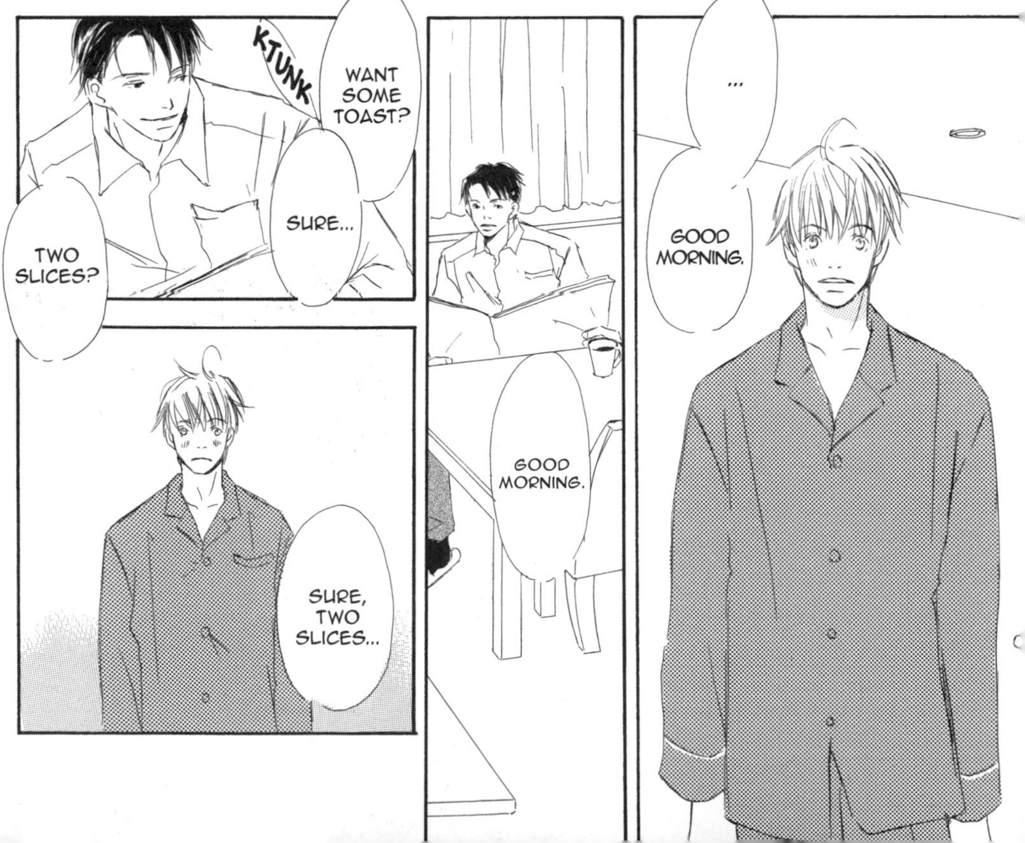
...
GOOD MORNING.
GOOD MORNING.
KTUNK
WANT SOME TOAST?
SURE...
TWO SLICES?
SURE, TWO SLICES...

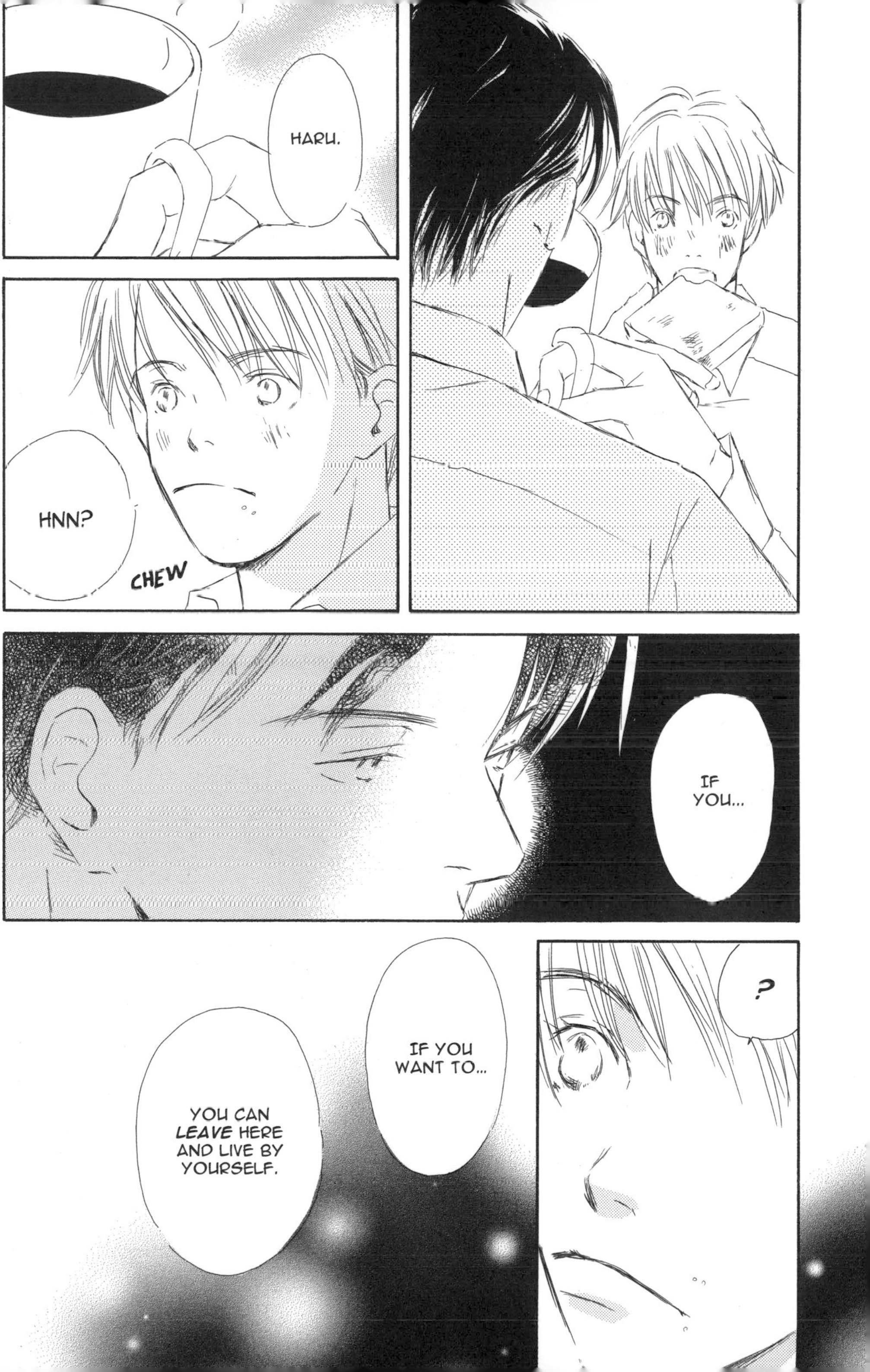
HARU.
HNN?
CHEW
IF YOU...
?
IF YOU WANT TO...
YOU CAN LEAVE HERE AND LIVE BY YOURSELF.

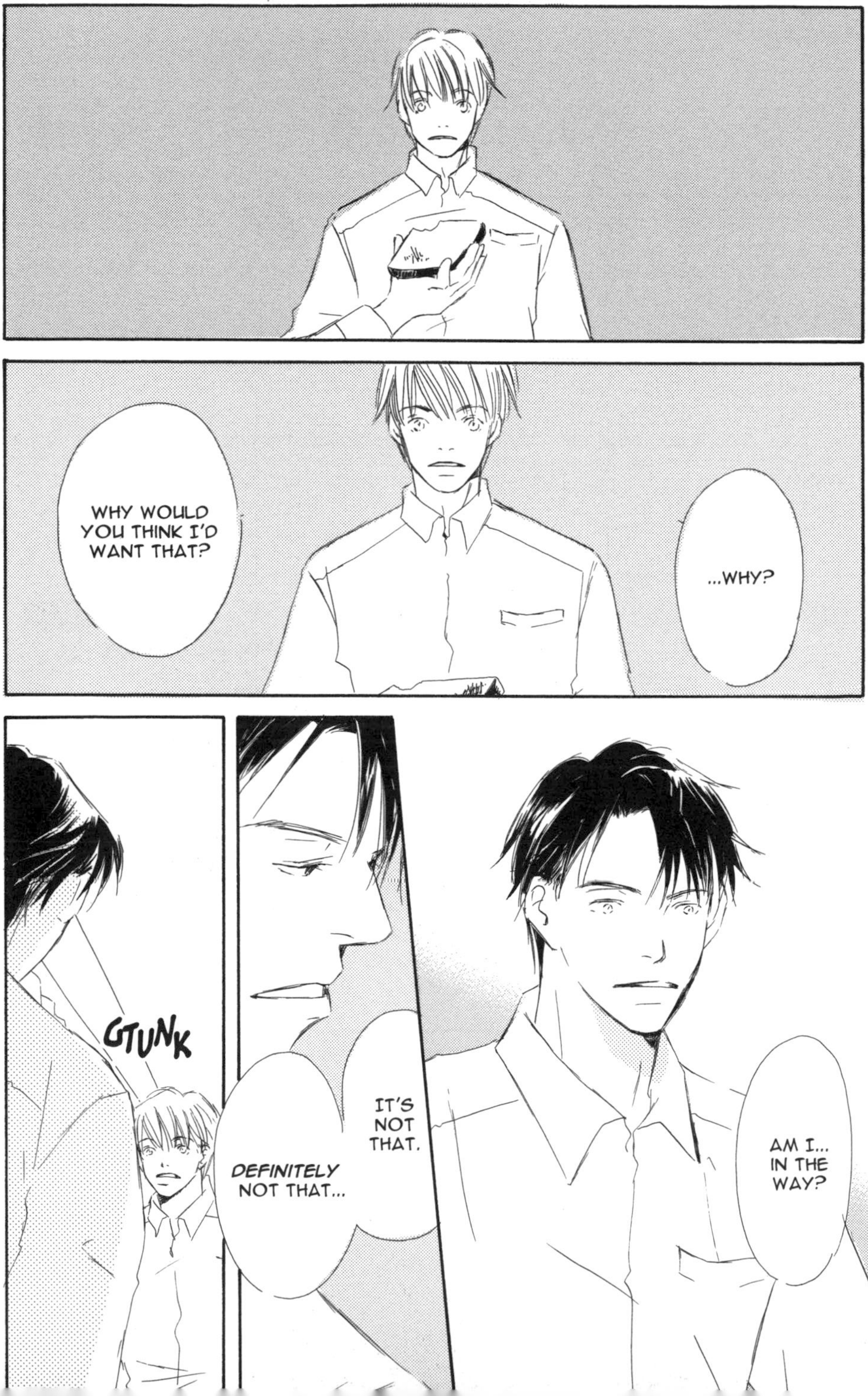
...WHY?
WHY WOULD YOU THINK I'D WANT THAT?
AM I... IN THE WAY?
IT'S NOT THAT.
DEFINITELY NOT THAT...
GTUNK

I'M HEADING OUT.

"MY NAME IS SENOH.
I'M A FRIEND OF HARU'S THERE."

"IT'S ALRIGHT NOW."

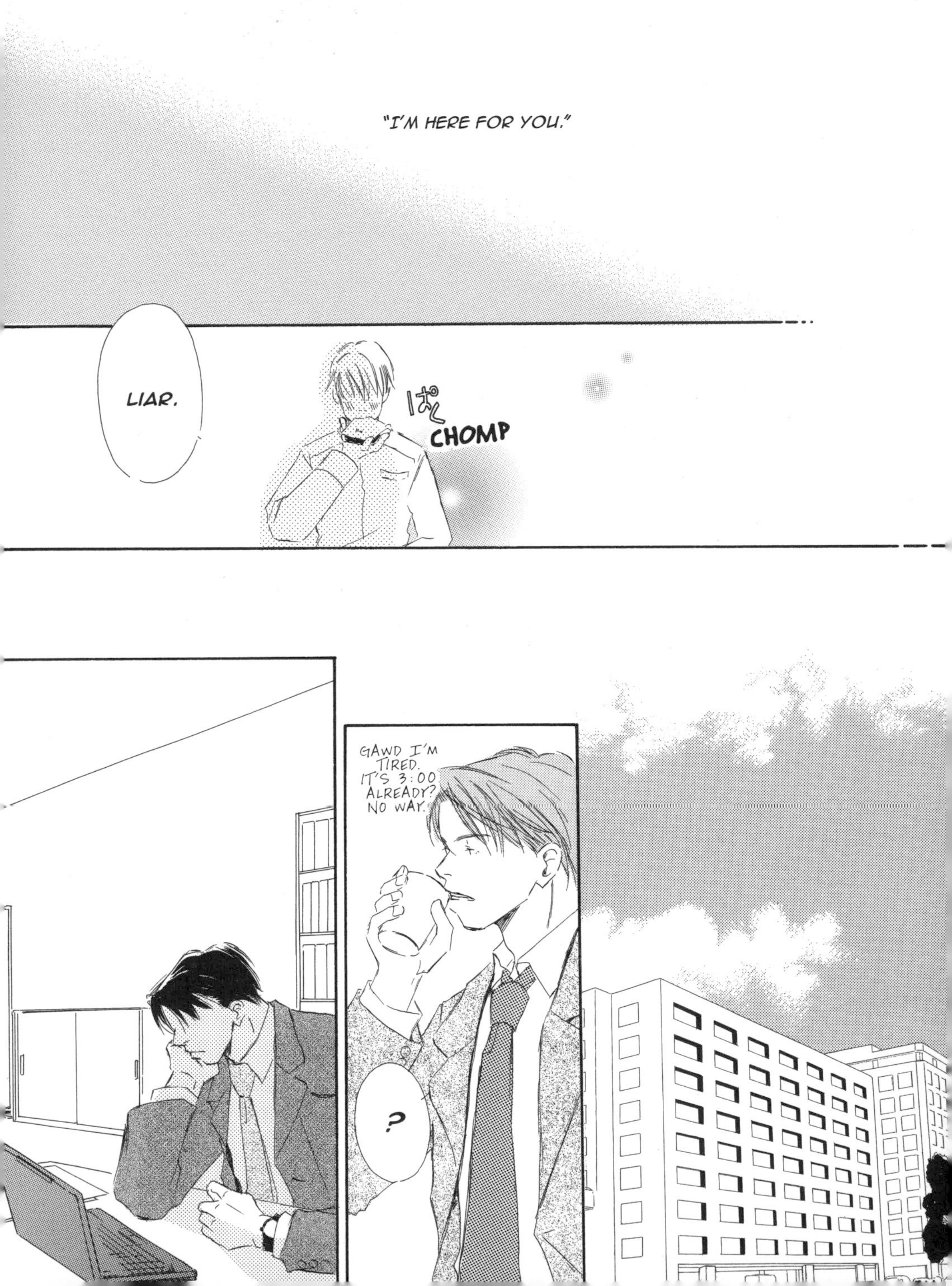
"I'M HERE FOR YOU."
ぱく
CHOMP
LIAR.
GAWD I'M TIRED. IT'S 3:00 ALREADY? NO WAY.
?

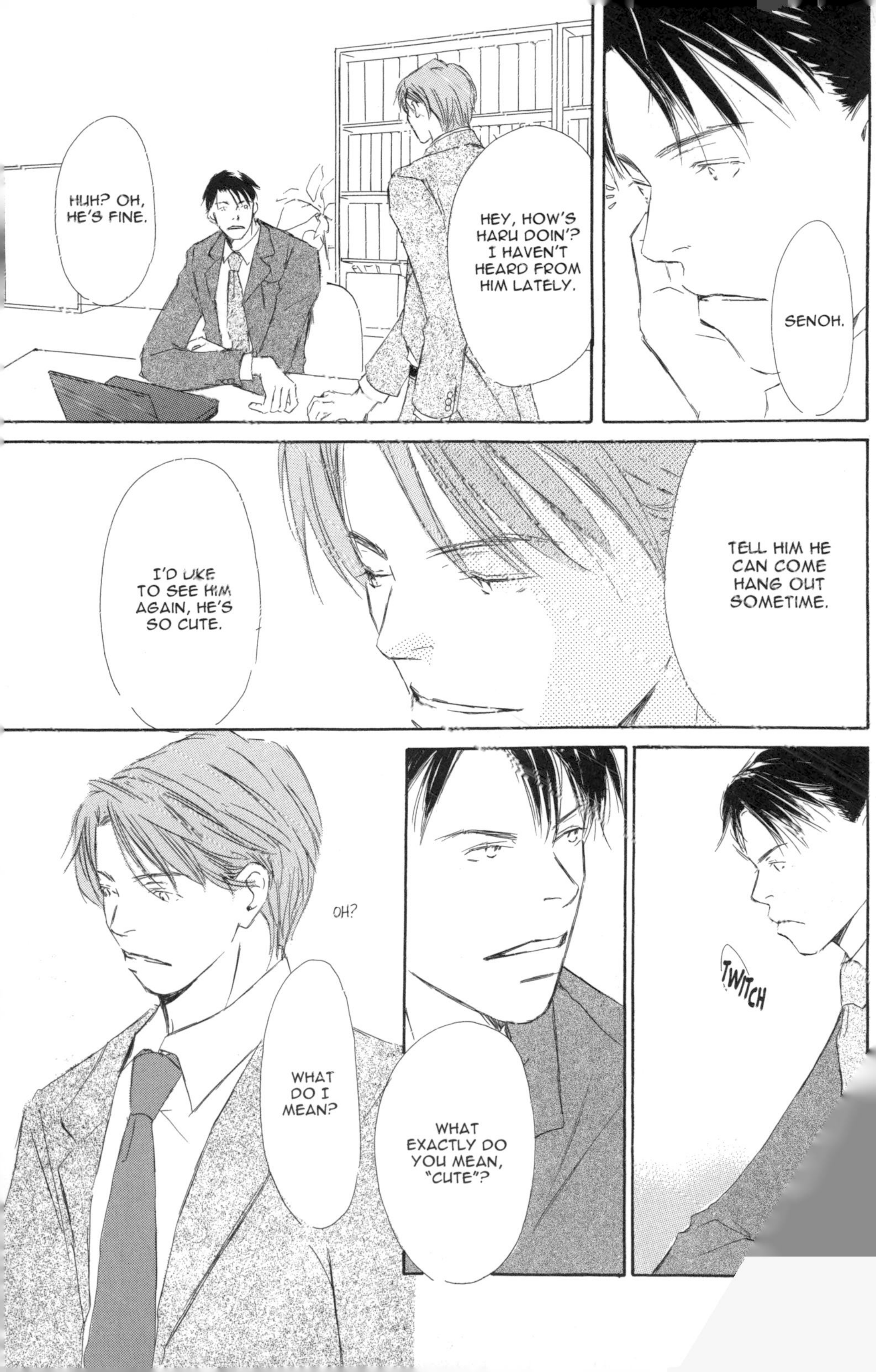
SENOH.
HEY, HOW'S HARU DOIN'? I HAVEN'T HEARD FROM HIM LATELY.
HUH? OH, HE'S FINE.
TELL HIM HE CAN COME HANG OUT SOMETIME.
I'D LIKE TO SEE HIM AGAIN, HE'S SO CUTE.
TWITCH
WHAT EXACTLY DO YOU MEAN, "CUTE"?
OH?
WHAT DO I MEAN?

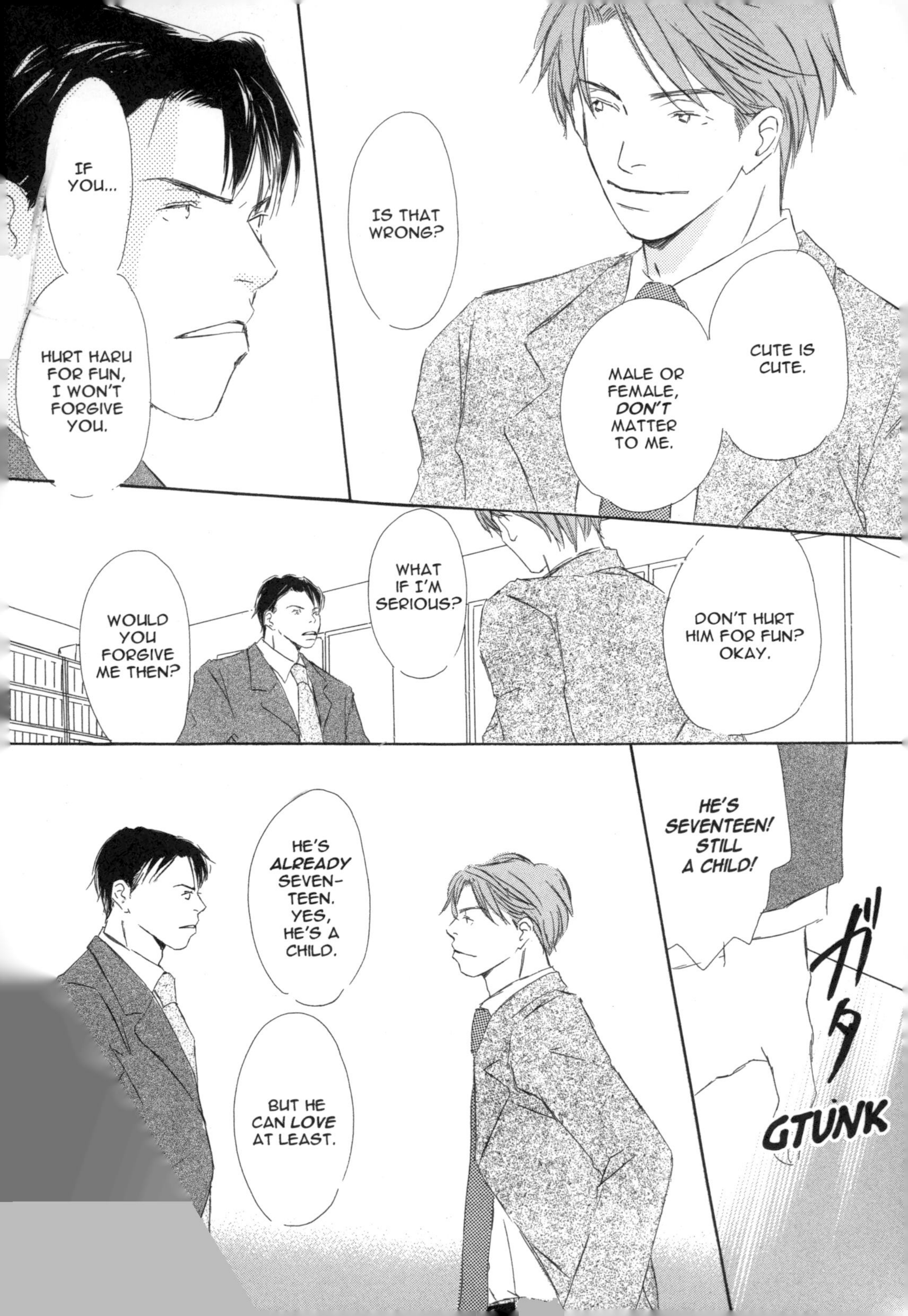
CUTE IS CUTE.
MALE OR FEMALE, *DON'T* MATTER TO ME.
IS THAT WRONG?
IF YOU...
HURT HARU FOR FUN, I WON'T FORGIVE YOU.
DON'T HURT HIM FOR FUN? OKAY.
WHAT IF I'M SERIOUS?
WOULD YOU FORGIVE ME THEN?
HE'S SEVENTEEN! STILL A CHILD!
ガタ
GTUNK
HE'S *ALREADY* SEVENTEEN. YES, HE'S A CHILD.
BUT HE CAN *LOVE* AT LEAST.

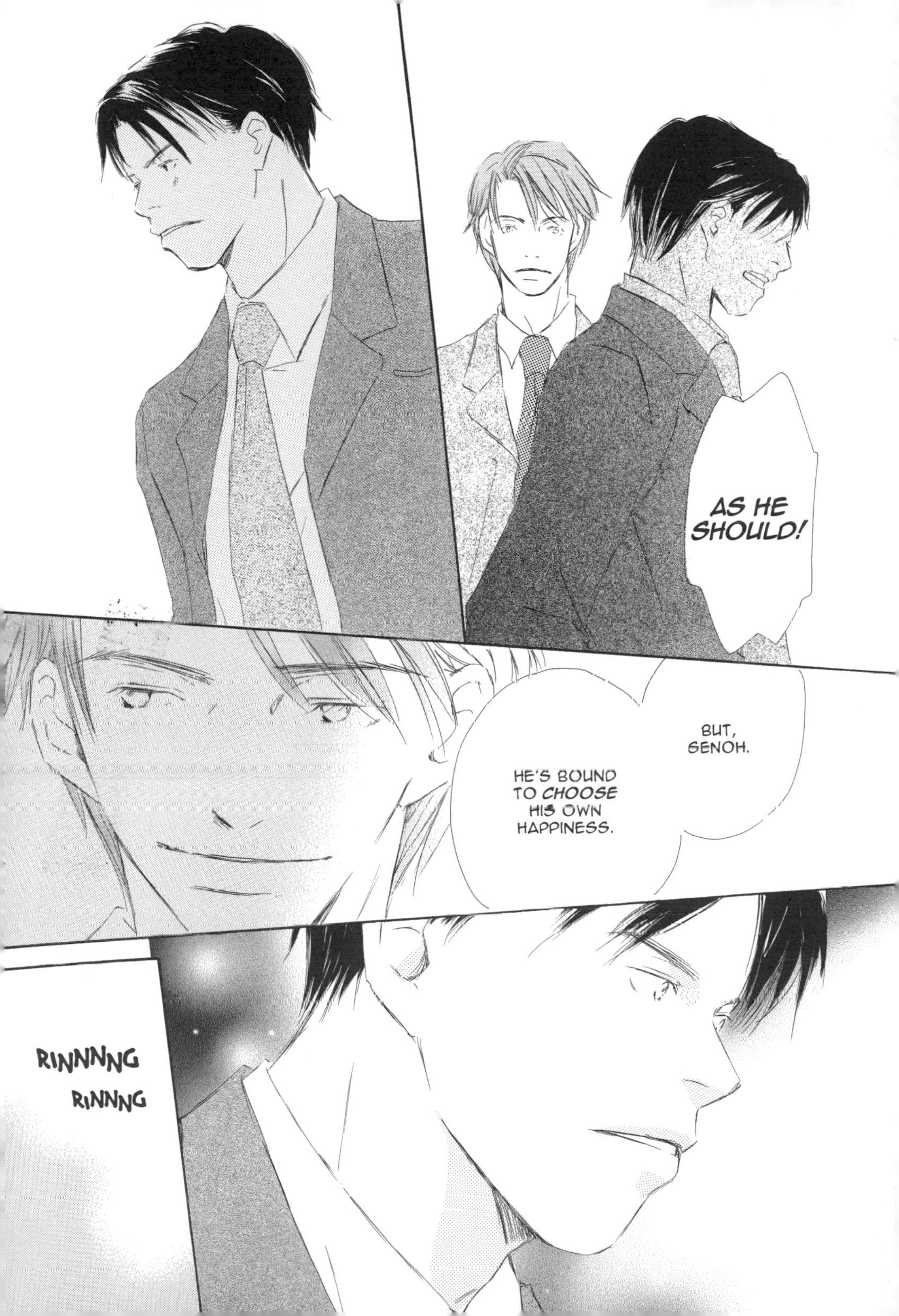
AS HE SHOULD!
BUT, SENOH.
HE'S BOUND TO *CHOOSE* HIS OWN HAPPINESS.
RINNNNG
RINNNG

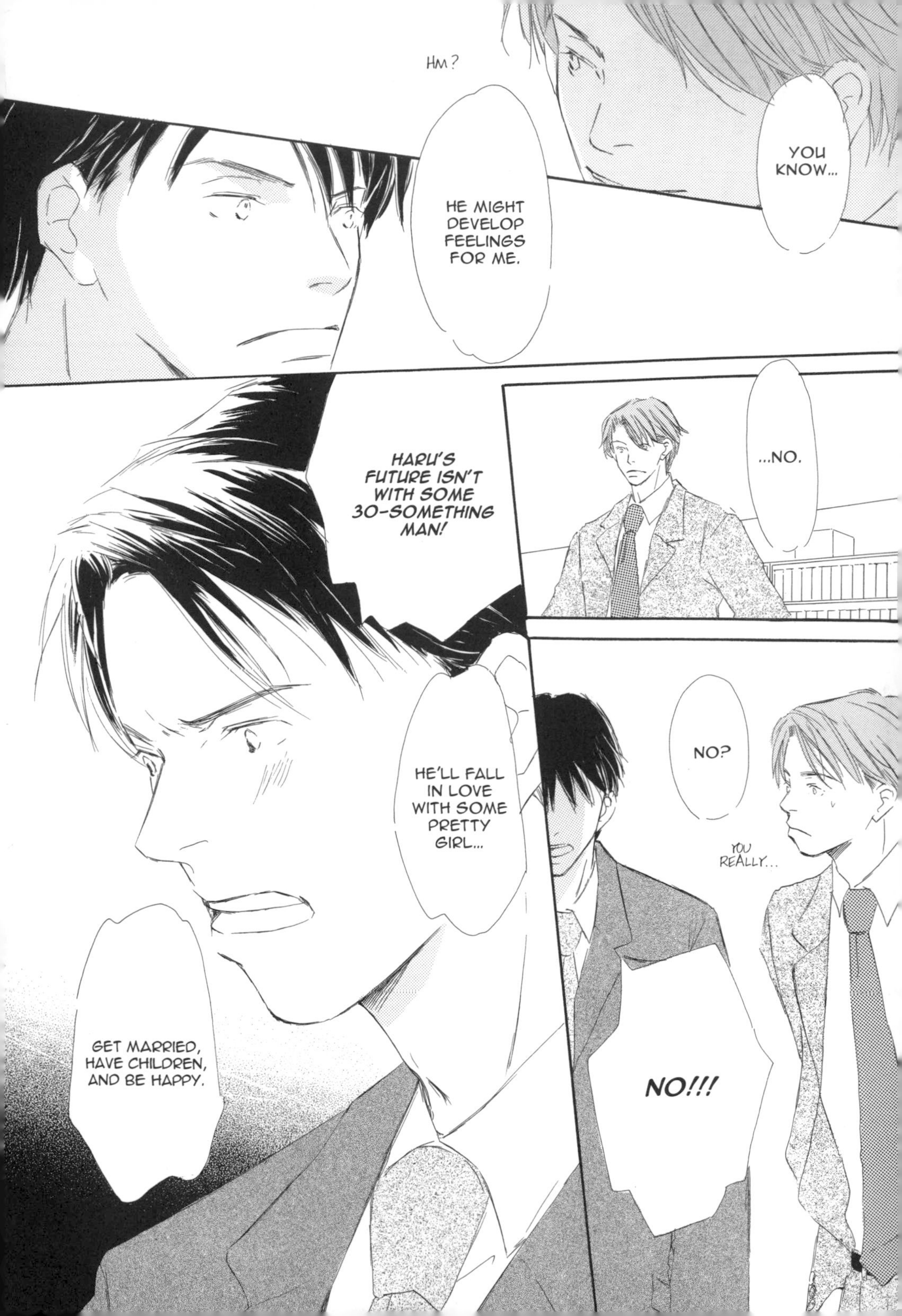
YOU KNOW...
HM?
HE MIGHT DEVELOP FEELINGS FOR ME.
...NO.
NO?
YOU REALLY...
NO!!!
HARU'S FUTURE ISN'T WITH SOME 30-SOMETHING MAN!
HE'LL FALL IN LOVE WITH SOME PRETTY GIRL...
GET MARRIED, HAVE CHILDREN, AND BE HAPPY.

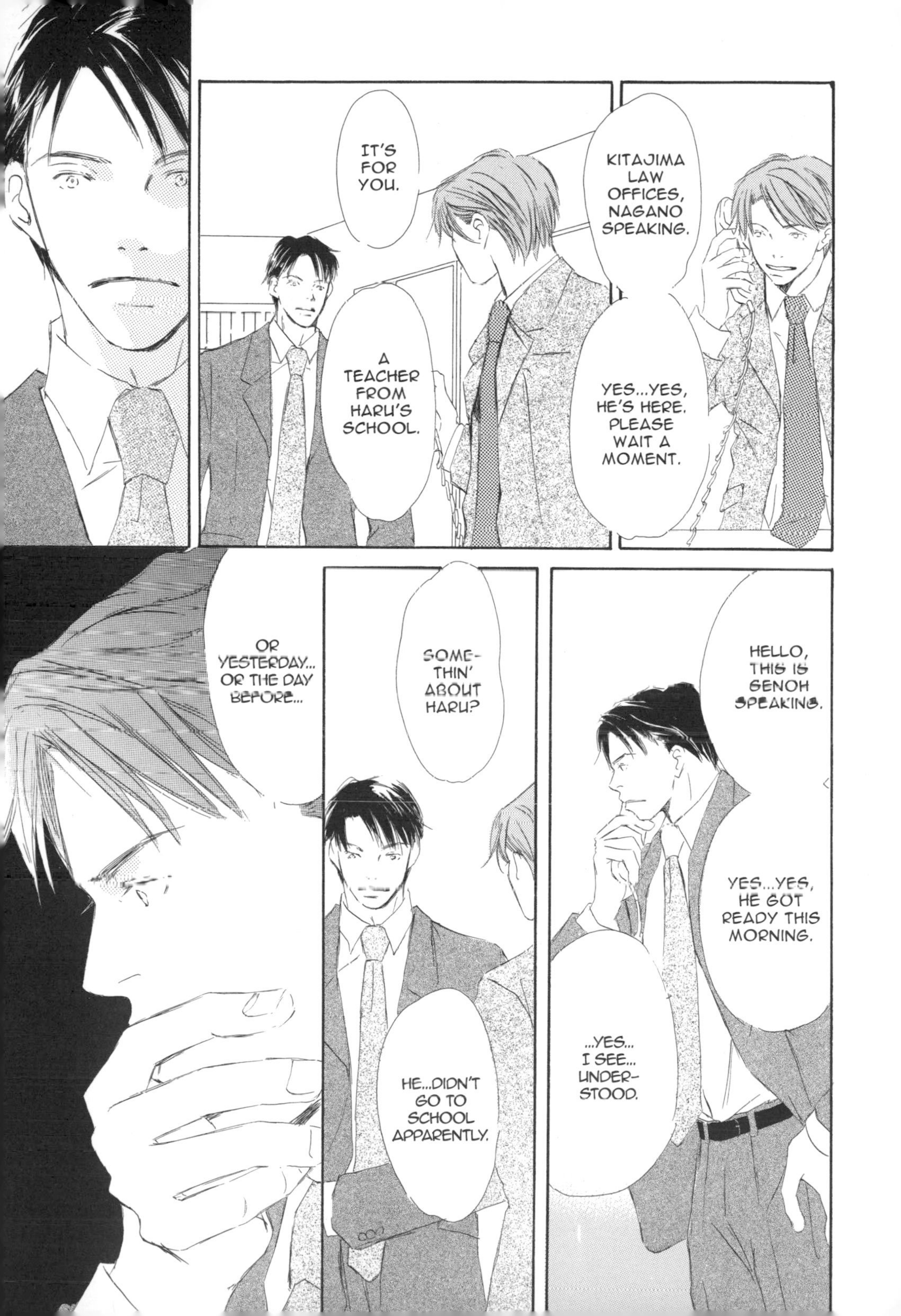
KITAJIMA LAW OFFICES, NAGANO SPEAKING.
YES...YES, HE'S HERE. PLEASE WAIT A MOMENT.
IT'S FOR YOU.
A TEACHER FROM HARU'S SCHOOL.
HELLO, THIS IS GENOH SPEAKING.
YES...YES, HE GOT READY THIS MORNING.
...YES... I SEE... UNDER-STOOD.
SOME-THIN' ABOUT HARU?
HE...DIDN'T GO TO SCHOOL APPARENTLY.
OR YESTERDAY... OR THE DAY BEFORE...

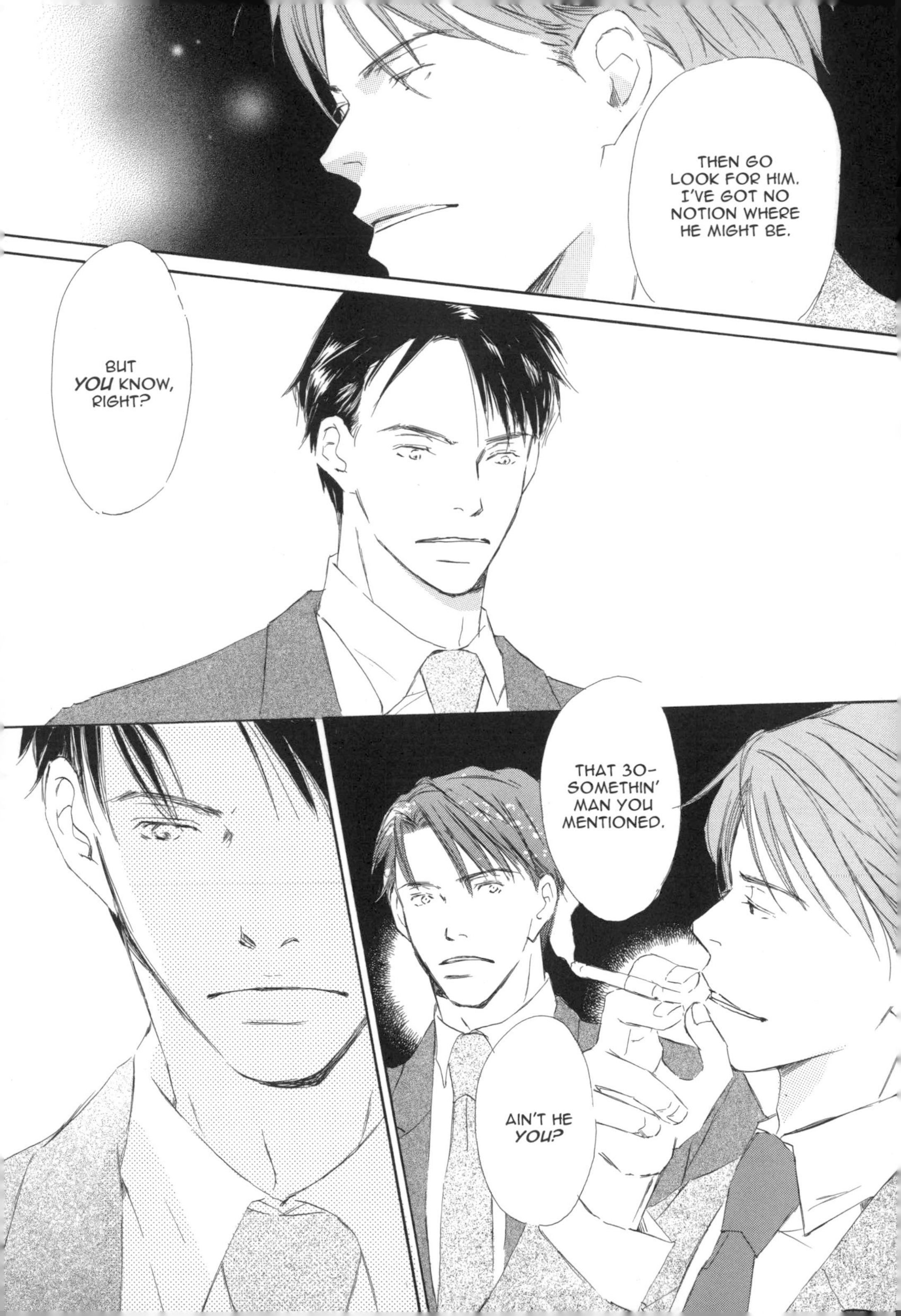
THEN GO LOOK FOR HIM. I'VE GOT NO NOTION WHERE HE MIGHT BE.
BUT *YOU* KNOW, RIGHT?
THAT 30-SOMETHIN' MAN YOU MENTIONED.
AIN'T HE *YOU?*

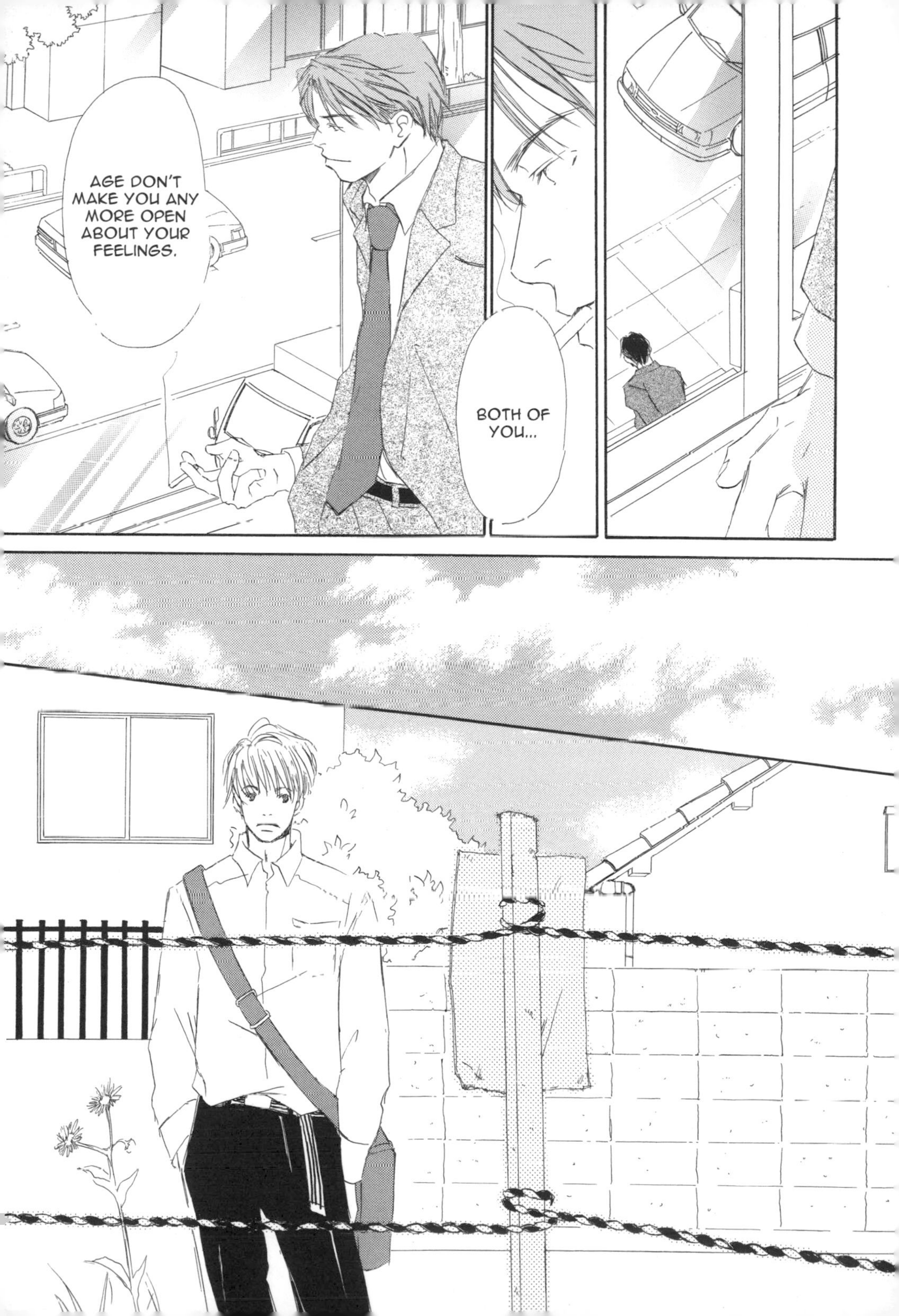
AGE DON'T MAKE YOU ANY MORE OPEN ABOUT YOUR FEELINGS.
BOTH OF YOU...

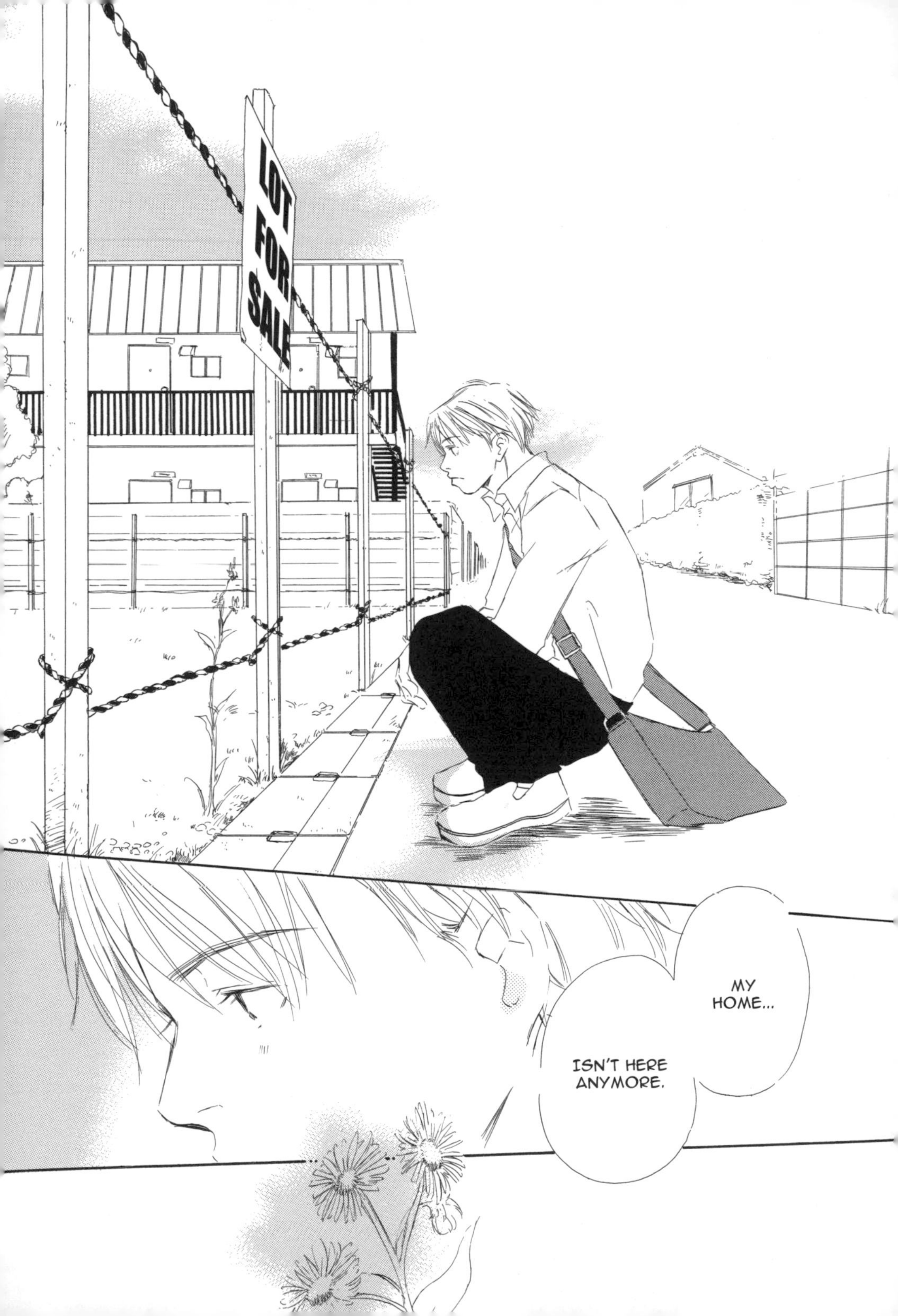
LOT FOR SALE
MY HOME...
ISN'T HERE ANYMORE.

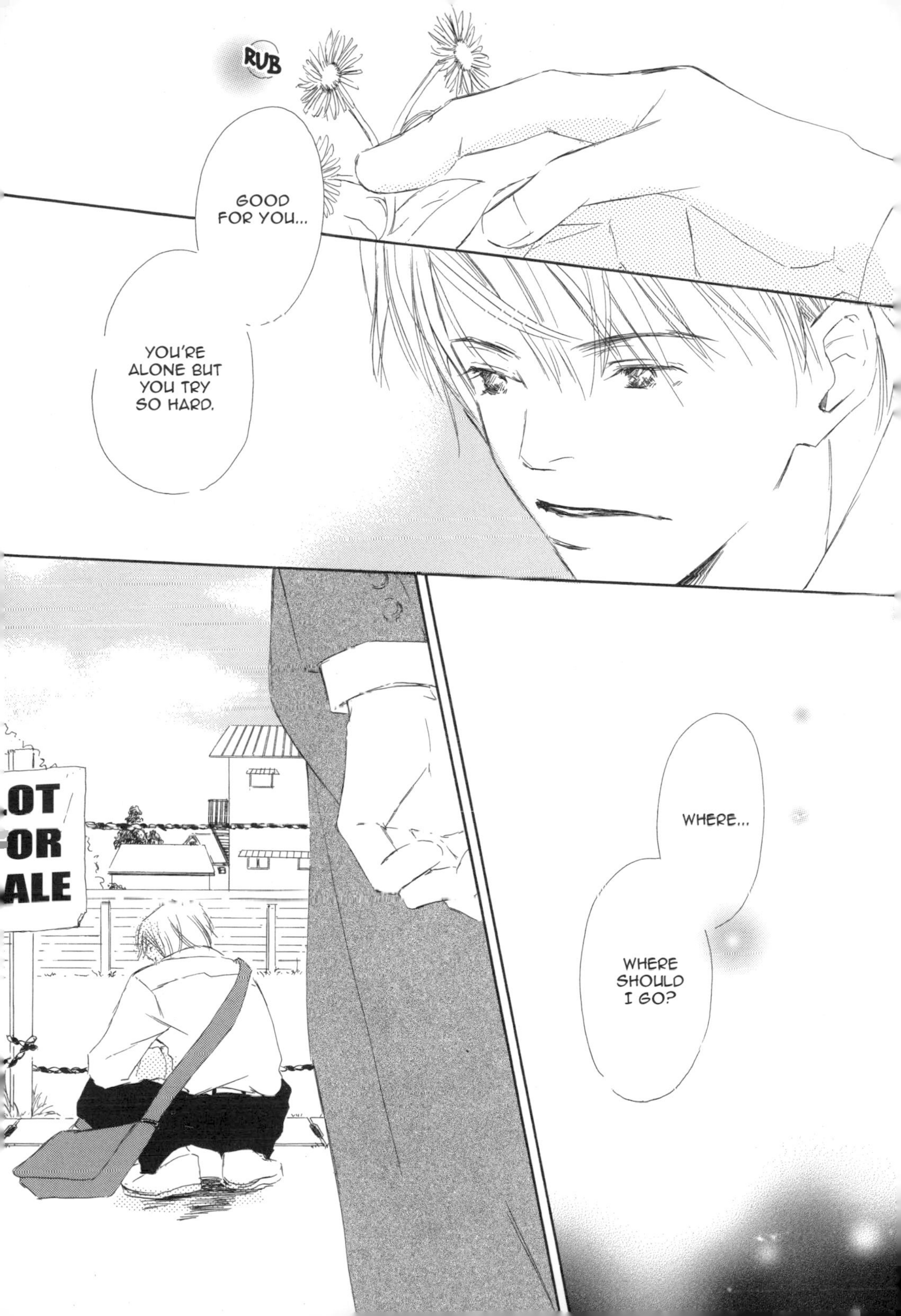
RUB
GOOD FOR YOU...
YOU'RE ALONE BUT YOU TRY SO HARD.
WHERE...
WHERE SHOULD I GO?
OT
OR
ALE

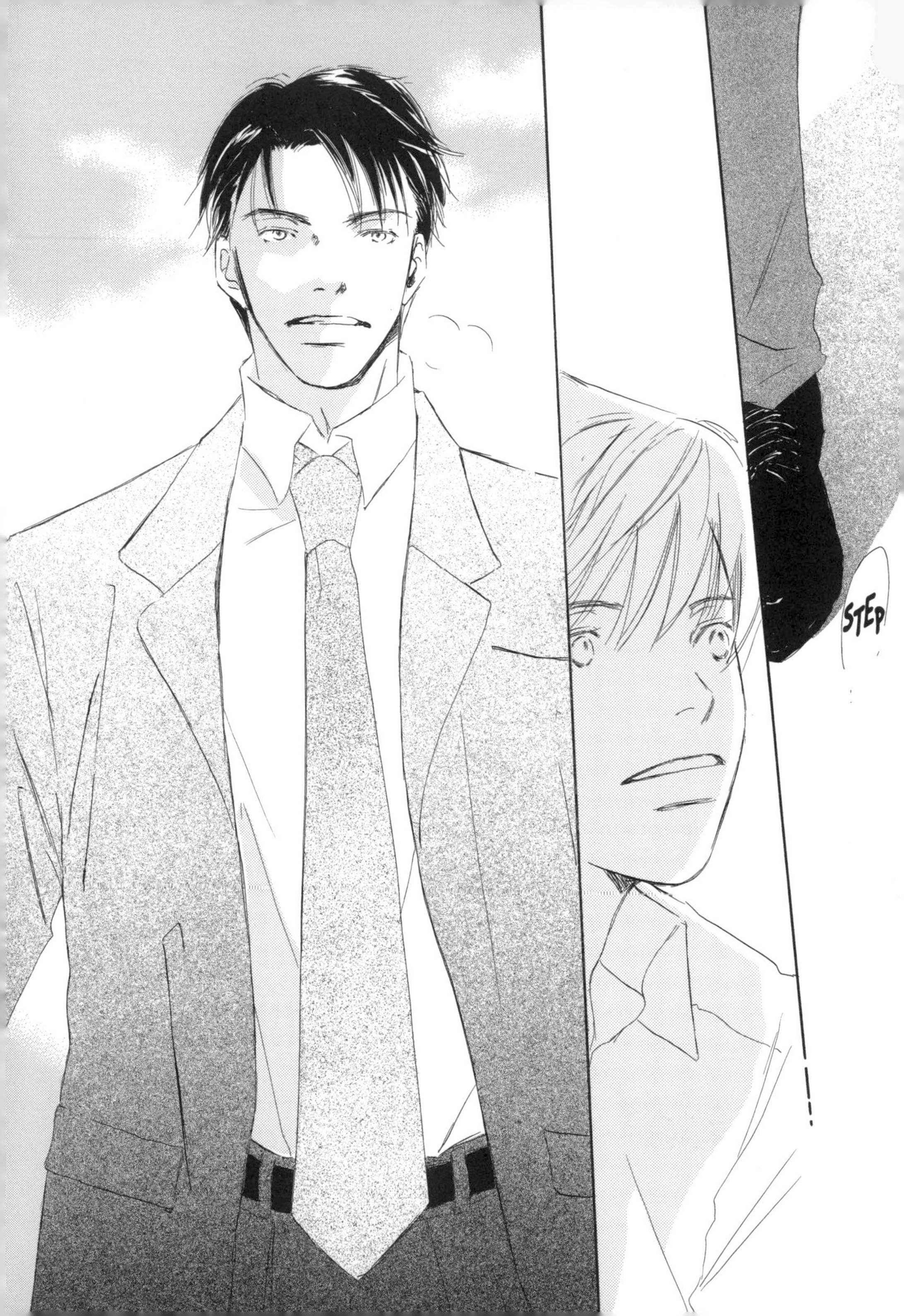
STEP

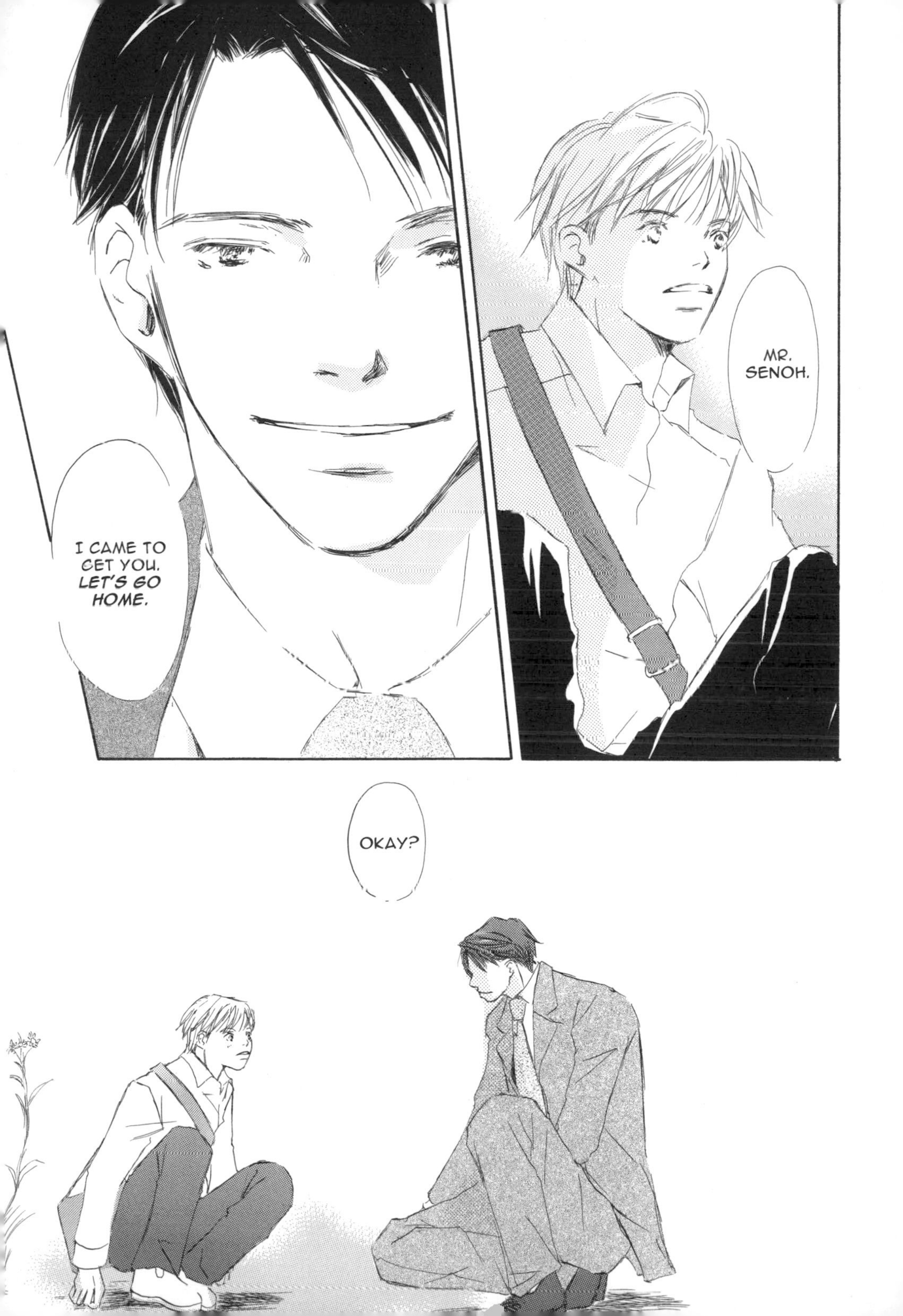
MR. SENOH.
I CAME TO GET YOU. LET'S GO HOME.
OKAY?

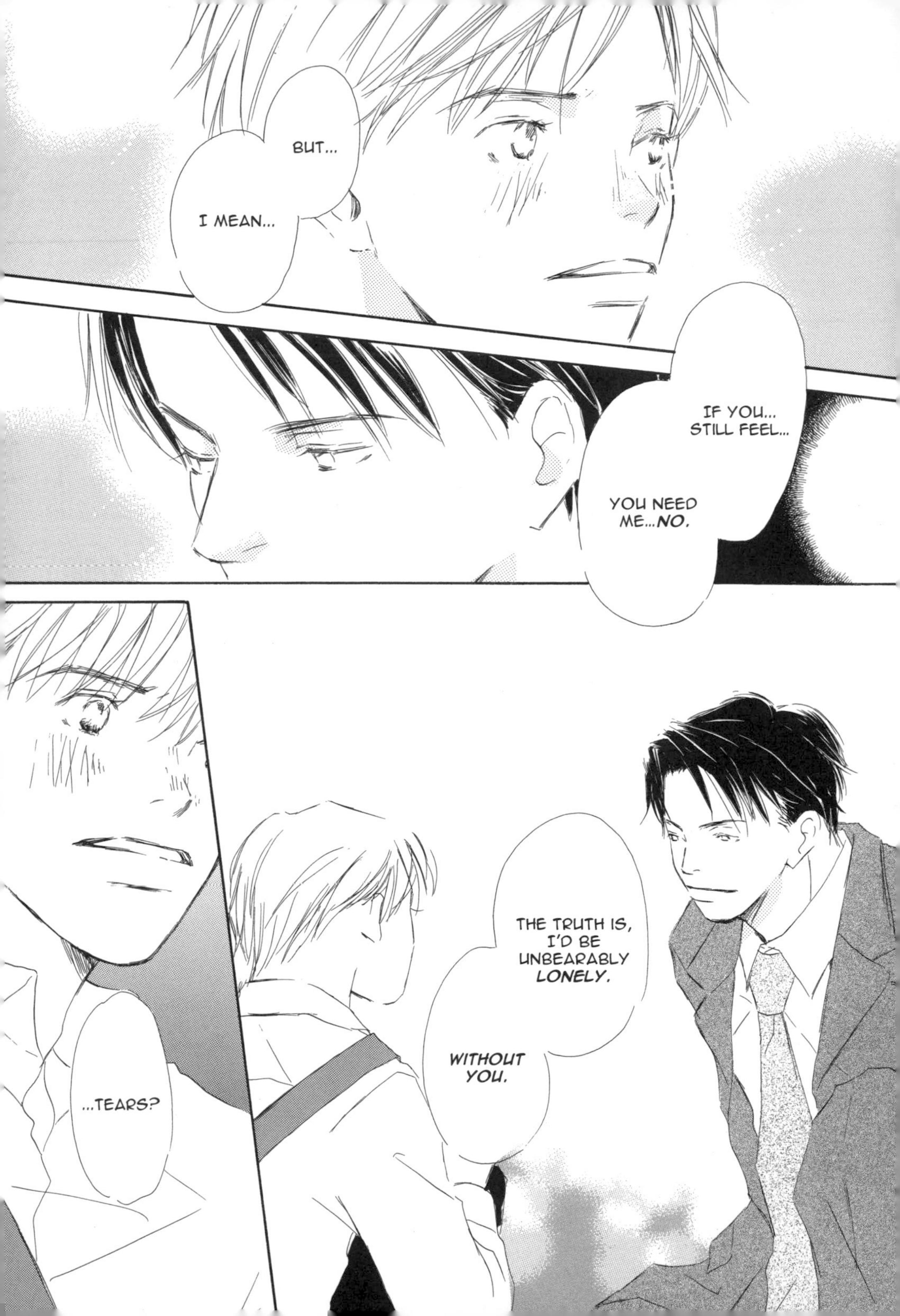
BUT...
I MEAN...
IF YOU... STILL FEEL...
YOU NEED ME...NO.
THE TRUTH IS, I'D BE UNBEARABLY LONELY.
WITHOUT YOU.
...TEARS?

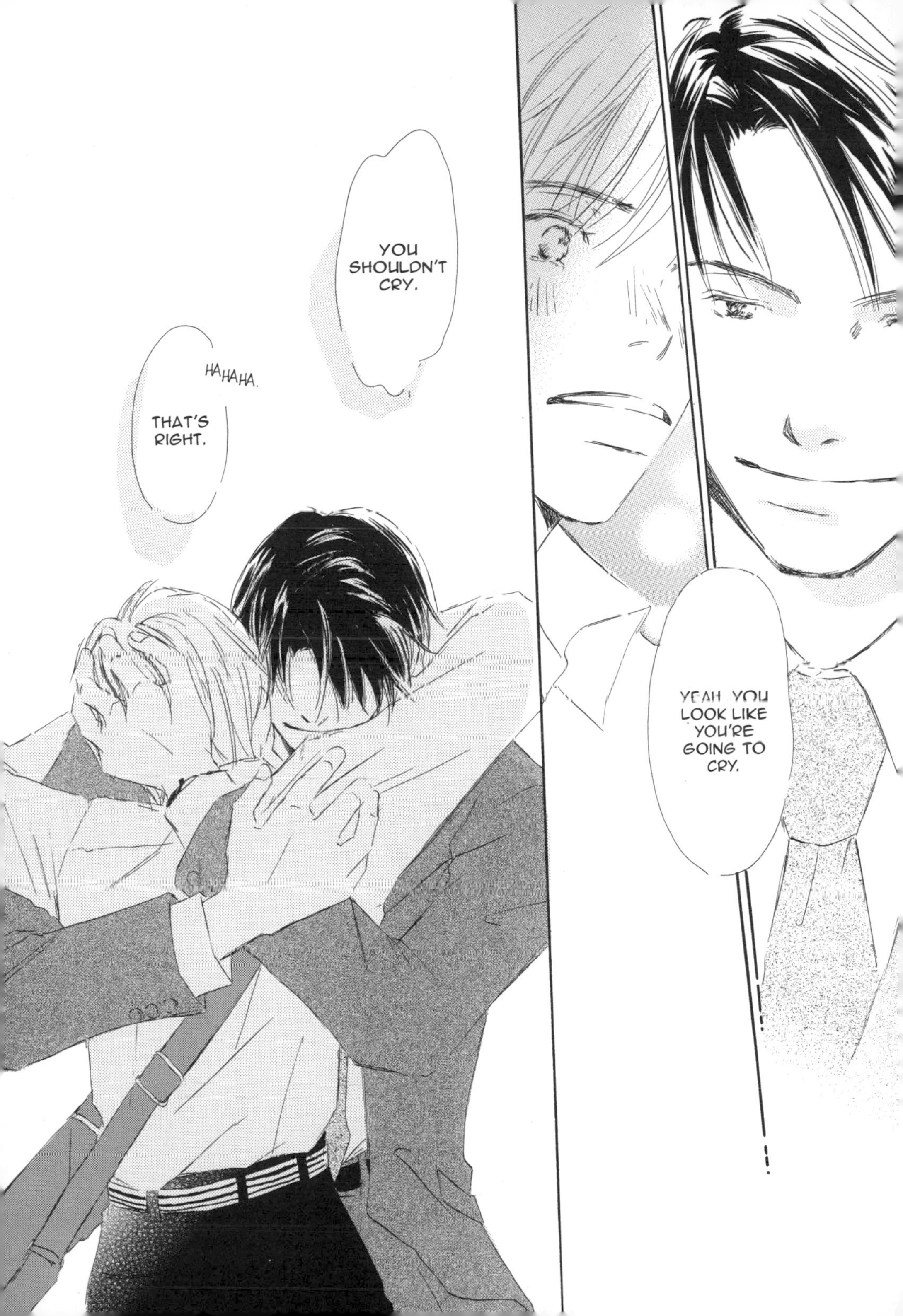
YEAH, YOU LOOK LIKE YOU'RE GOING TO CRY.
YOU SHOULDN'T CRY.
HAHAHA.
THAT'S RIGHT.

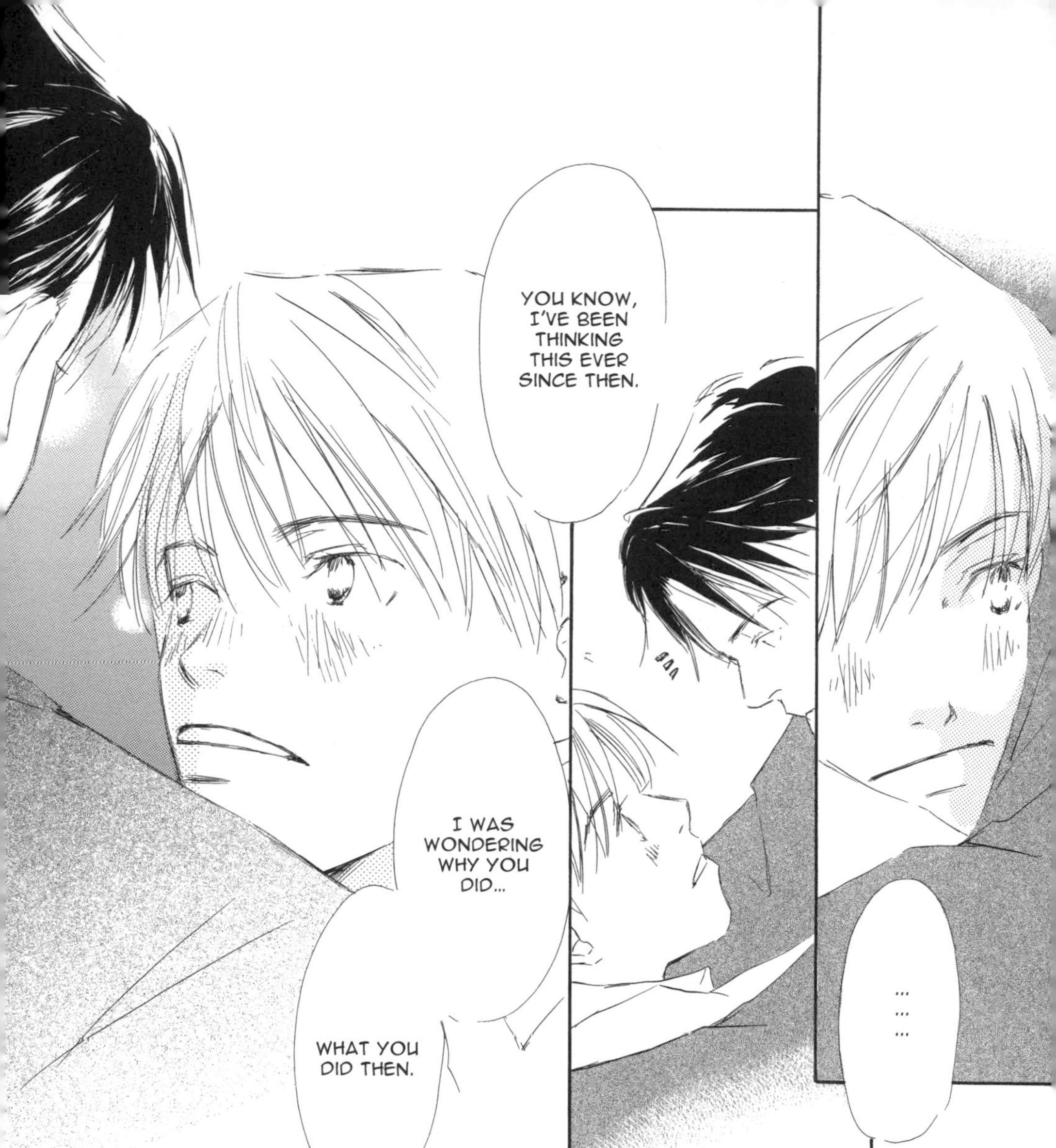
YOU KNOW, I'VE BEEN THINKING THIS EVER SINCE THEN.
I WAS WONDERING WHY YOU DID...
WHAT YOU DID THEN.
... ...

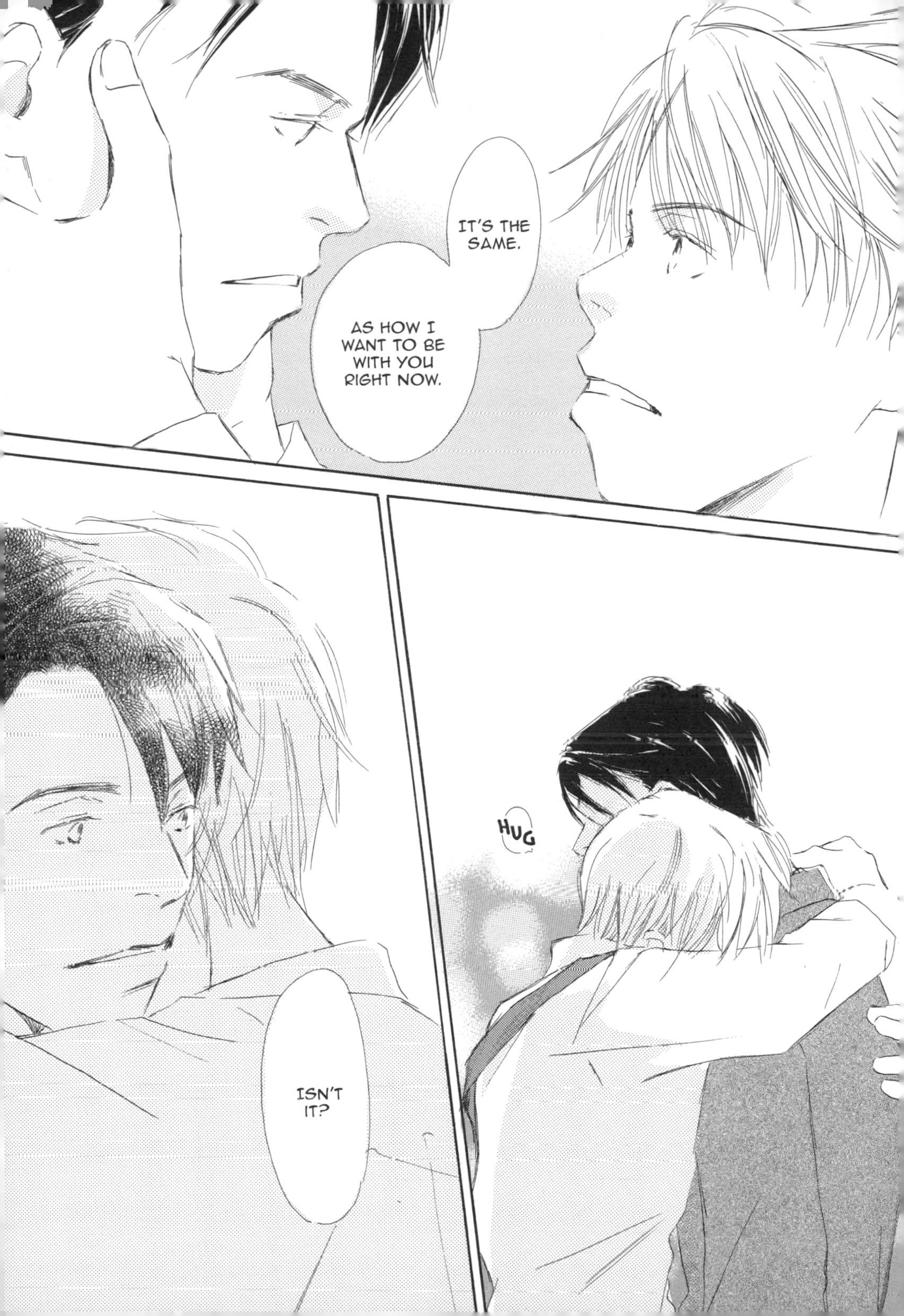
IT'S THE SAME.
AS HOW I WANT TO BE WITH YOU RIGHT NOW.
HUG
ISN'T IT?

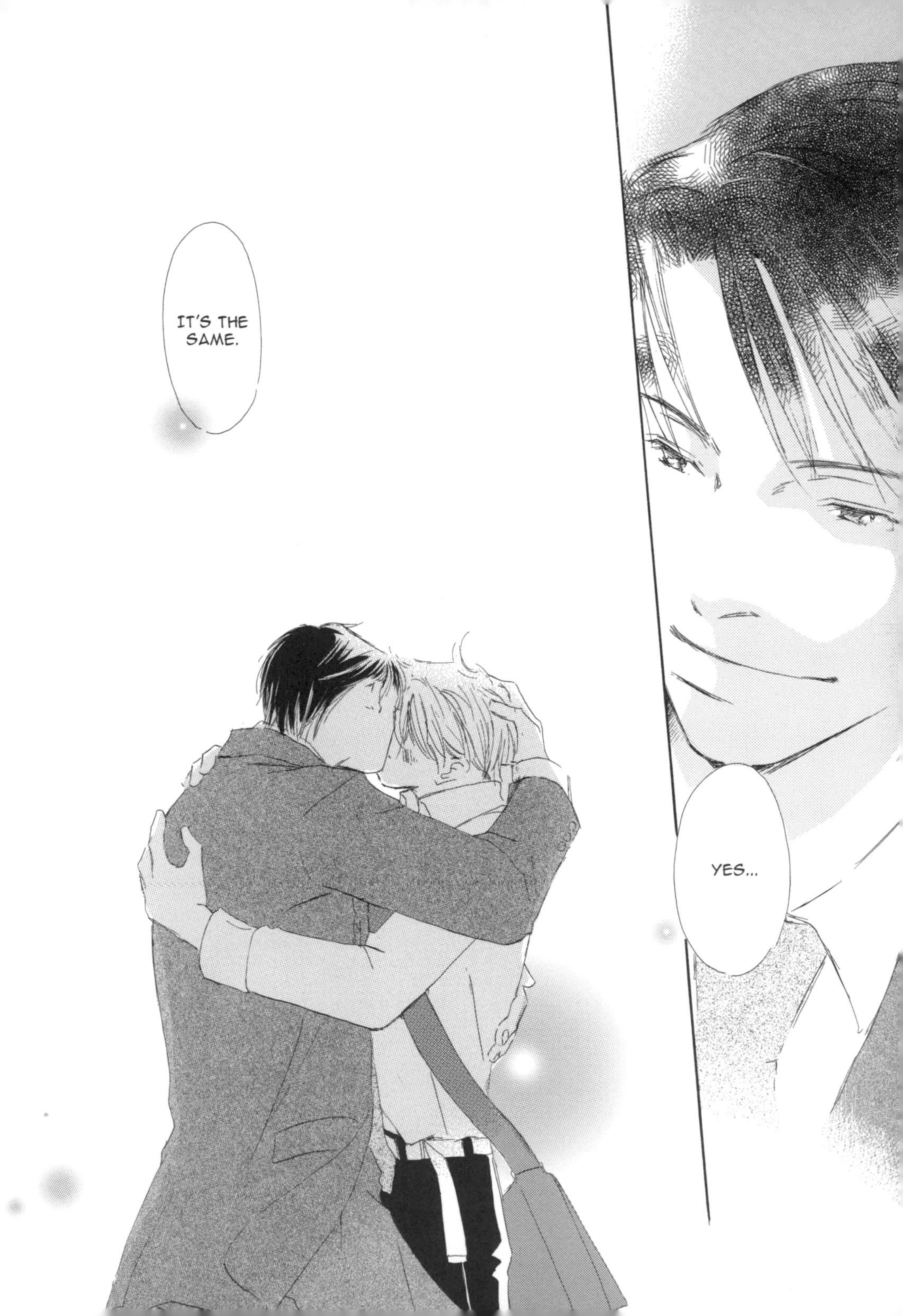
YES...
IT'S THE SAME.

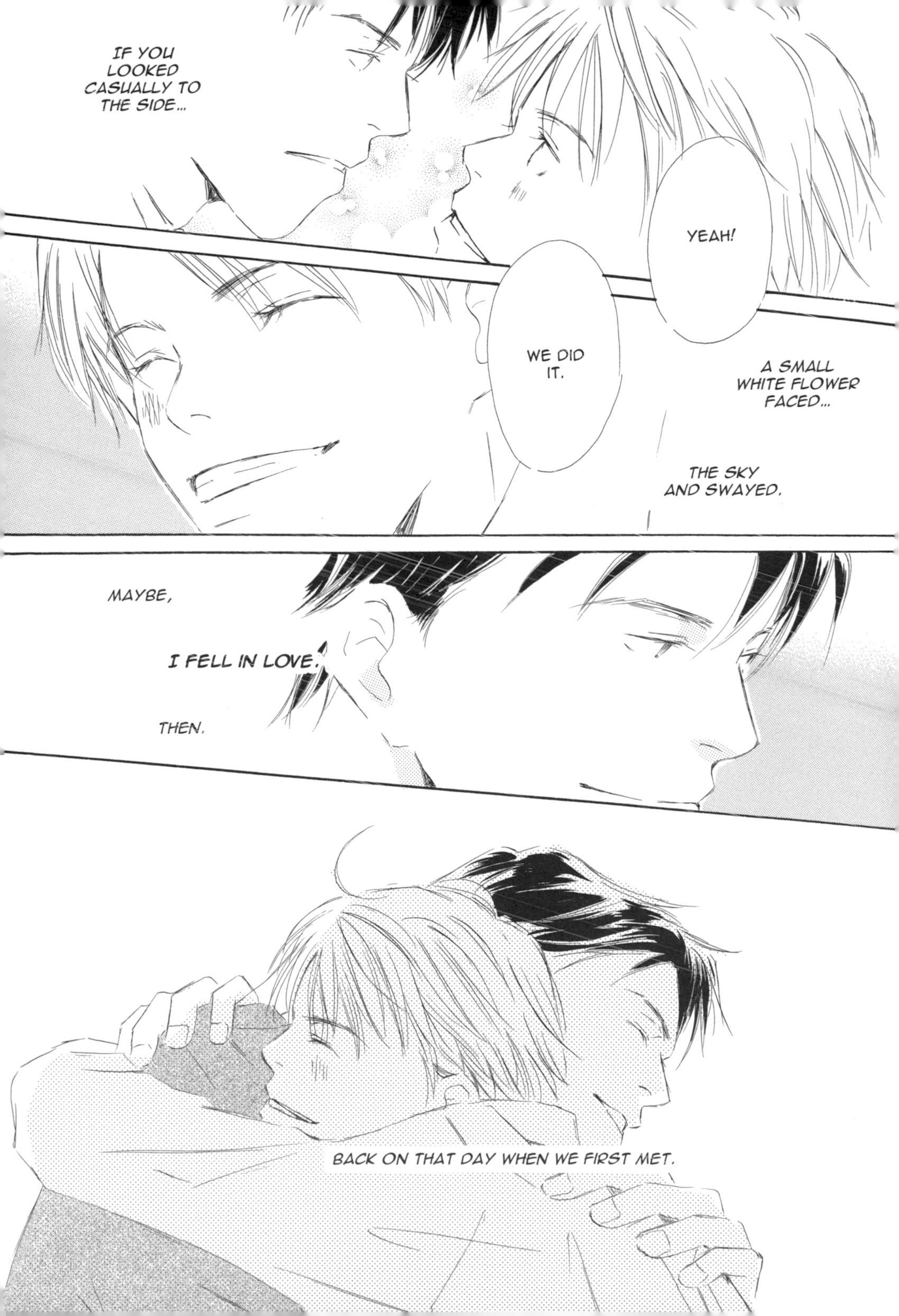
IF YOU LOOKED CASUALLY TO THE SIDE...
WE DID IT.
YEAH!
A SMALL WHITE FLOWER FACED...
THE SKY AND SWAYED.
MAYBE,
I FELL IN LOVE.
THEN.
BACK ON THAT DAY WHEN WE FIRST MET.

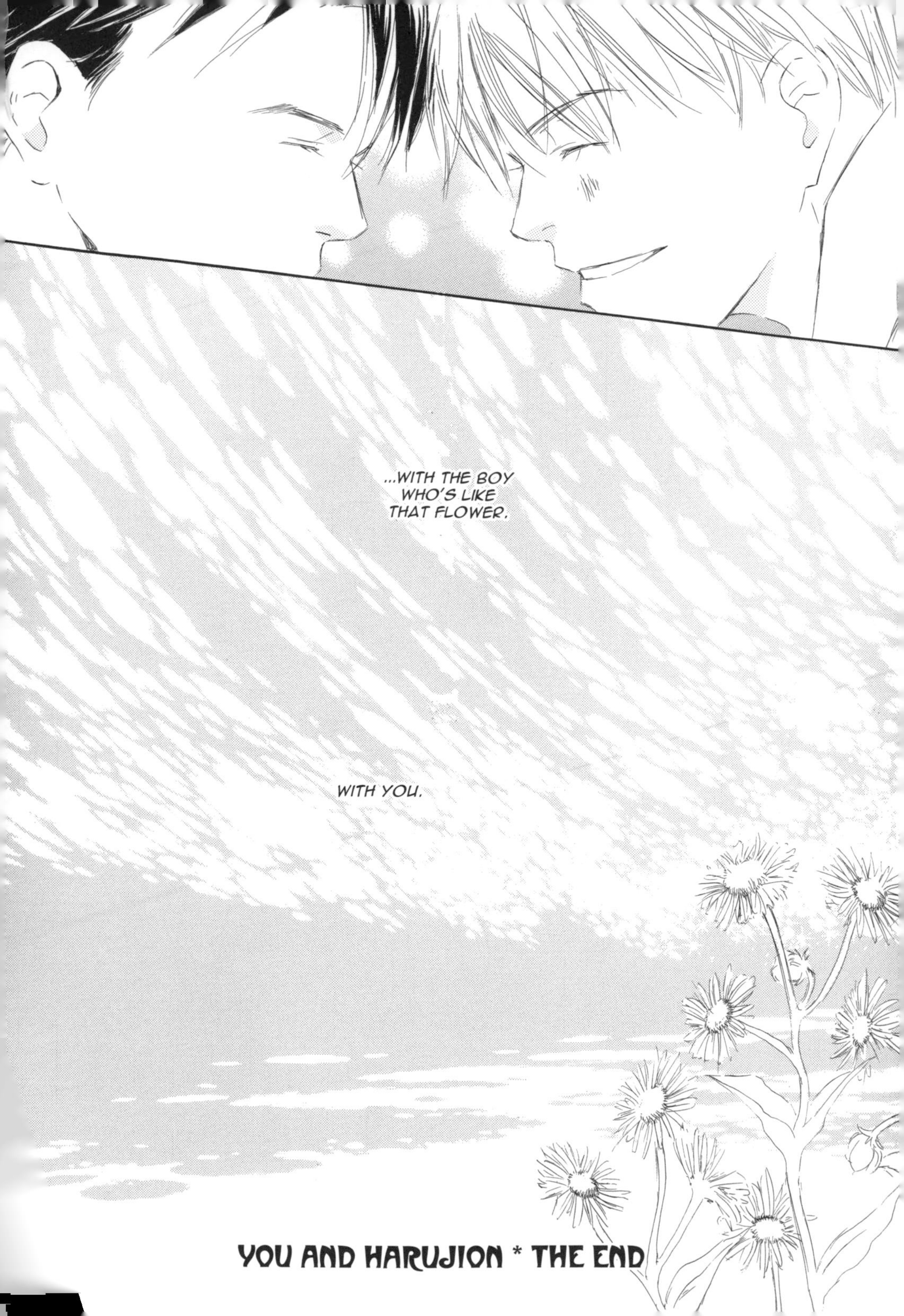
...WITH THE BOY
WHO'S LIKE
THAT FLOWER.
WITH YOU.
YOU AND HARUJION * THE END

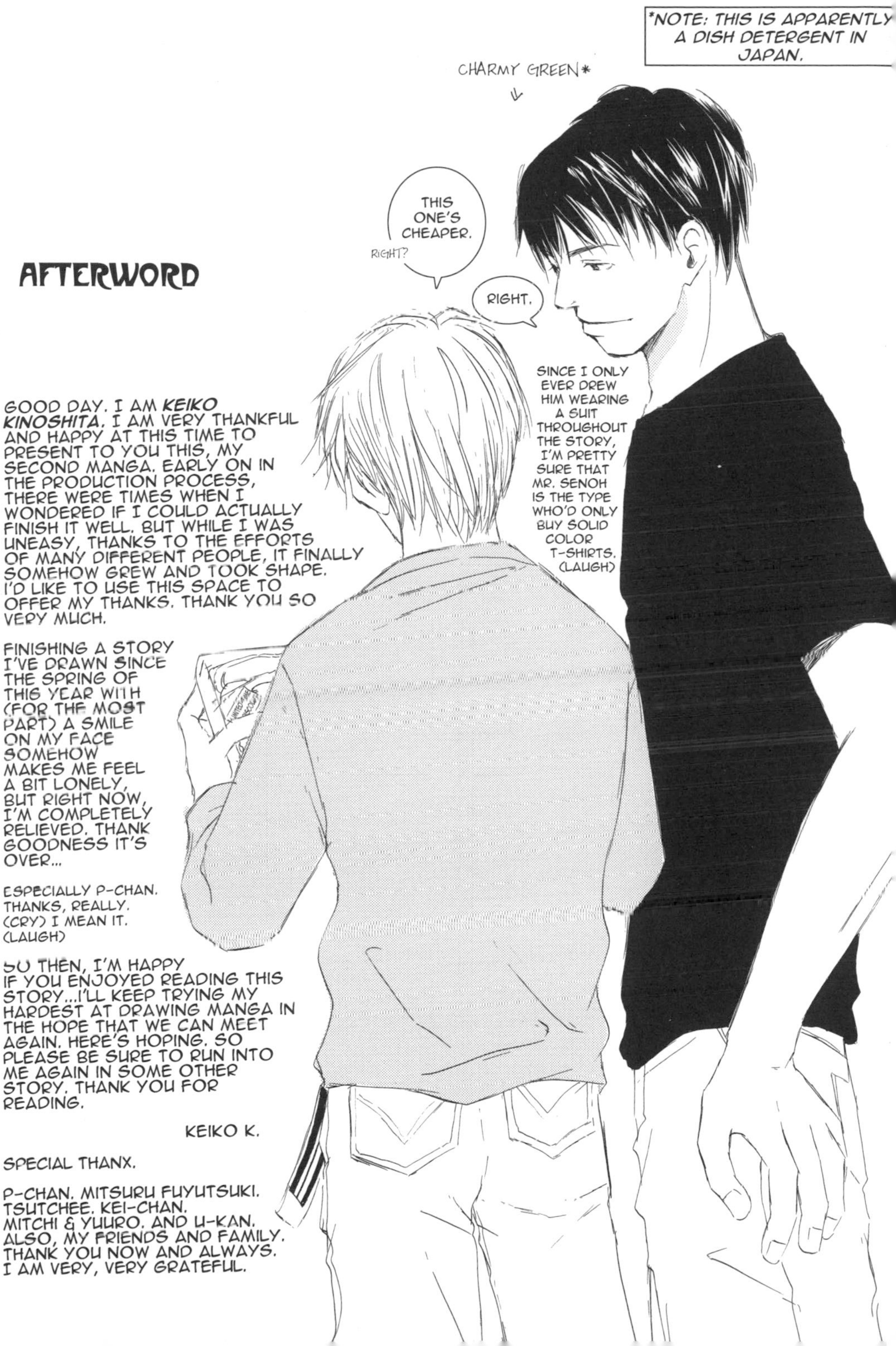
*NOTE: THIS IS APPARENTLY A DISH DETERGENT IN JAPAN.
CHARMY GREEN*
THIS ONE'S CHEAPER.
RIGHT?
RIGHT.
SINCE I ONLY EVER DREW HIM WEARING A SUIT THROUGHOUT THE STORY, I'M PRETTY SURE THAT MR. SENOH IS THE TYPE WHO'D ONLY BUY SOLID COLOR T-SHIRTS. (LAUGH)

AFTERWORD

GOOD DAY. I AM *KEIKO KINOSHITA*. I AM VERY THANKFUL AND HAPPY AT THIS TIME TO PRESENT TO YOU THIS, MY SECOND MANGA. EARLY ON IN THE PRODUCTION PROCESS, THERE WERE TIMES WHEN I WONDERED IF I COULD ACTUALLY FINISH IT WELL. BUT WHILE I WAS UNEASY, THANKS TO THE EFFORTS OF MANY DIFFERENT PEOPLE, IT FINALLY SOMEHOW GREW AND TOOK SHAPE. I'D LIKE TO USE THIS SPACE TO OFFER MY THANKS. THANK YOU SO VERY MUCH.

FINISHING A STORY I'VE DRAWN SINCE THE SPRING OF THIS YEAR WITH (FOR THE MOST PART) A SMILE ON MY FACE SOMEHOW MAKES ME FEEL A BIT LONELY, BUT RIGHT NOW, I'M COMPLETELY RELIEVED. THANK GOODNESS IT'S OVER...

ESPECIALLY P-CHAN. THANKS, REALLY. (CRY) I MEAN IT. (LAUGH)

SO THEN, I'M HAPPY IF YOU ENJOYED READING THIS STORY...I'LL KEEP TRYING MY HARDEST AT DRAWING MANGA IN THE HOPE THAT WE CAN MEET AGAIN. HERE'S HOPING. SO PLEASE BE SURE TO RUN INTO ME AGAIN IN SOME OTHER STORY. THANK YOU FOR READING.

KEIKO K.

SPECIAL THANX.

P-CHAN. MITSURU FUYUTSUKI. TSUTCHEE. KEI-CHAN. MITCHI & YUURO. AND U-KAN. ALSO, MY FRIENDS AND FAMILY. THANK YOU NOW AND ALWAYS. I AM VERY, VERY GRATEFUL.

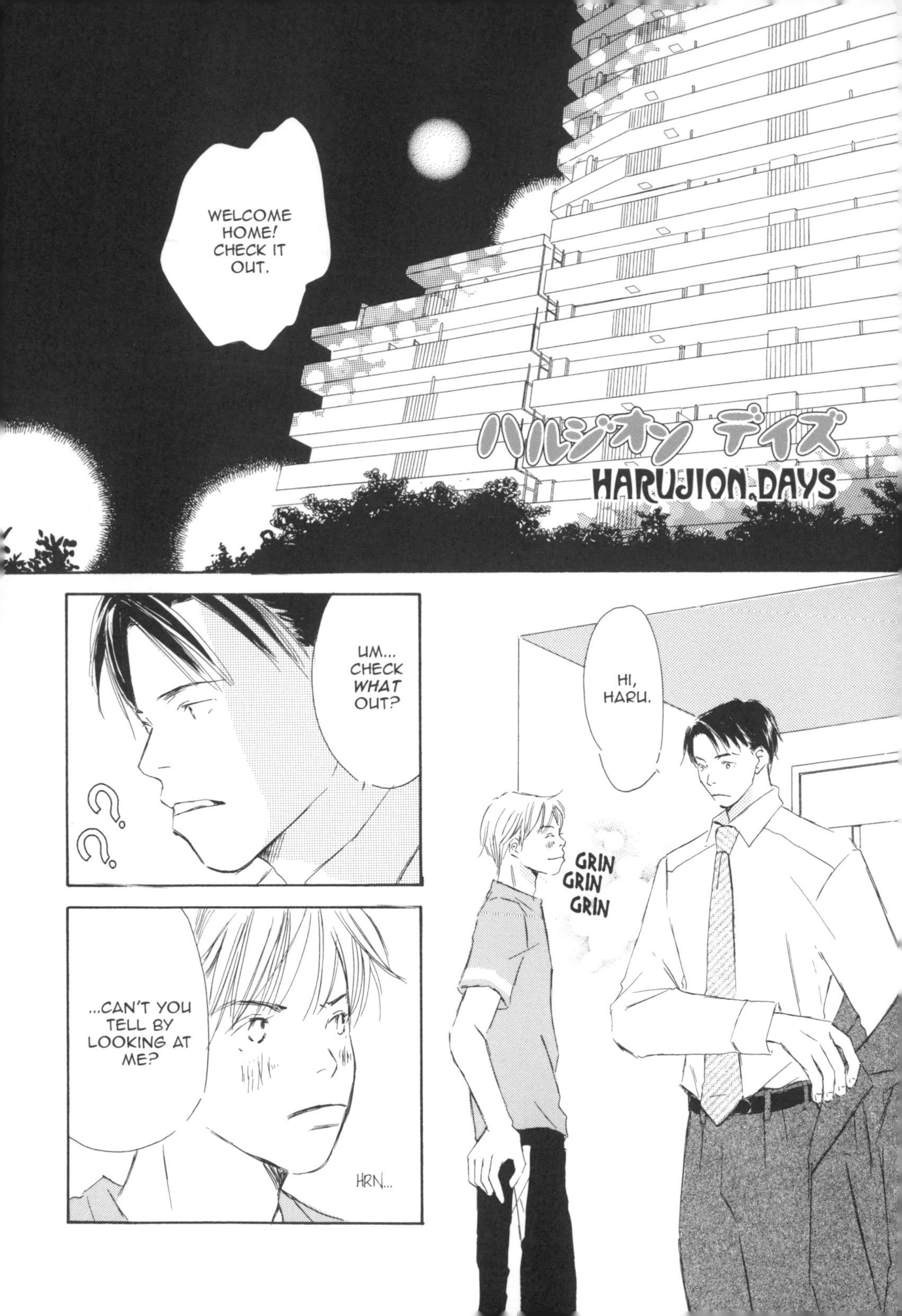
WELCOME HOME! CHECK IT OUT.
ハルジオン デイズ
HARUJION DAYS
HI, HARU.
GRIN GRIN GRIN
UM... CHECK *WHAT* OUT?
...CAN'T YOU TELL BY LOOKING AT ME?
HRN...

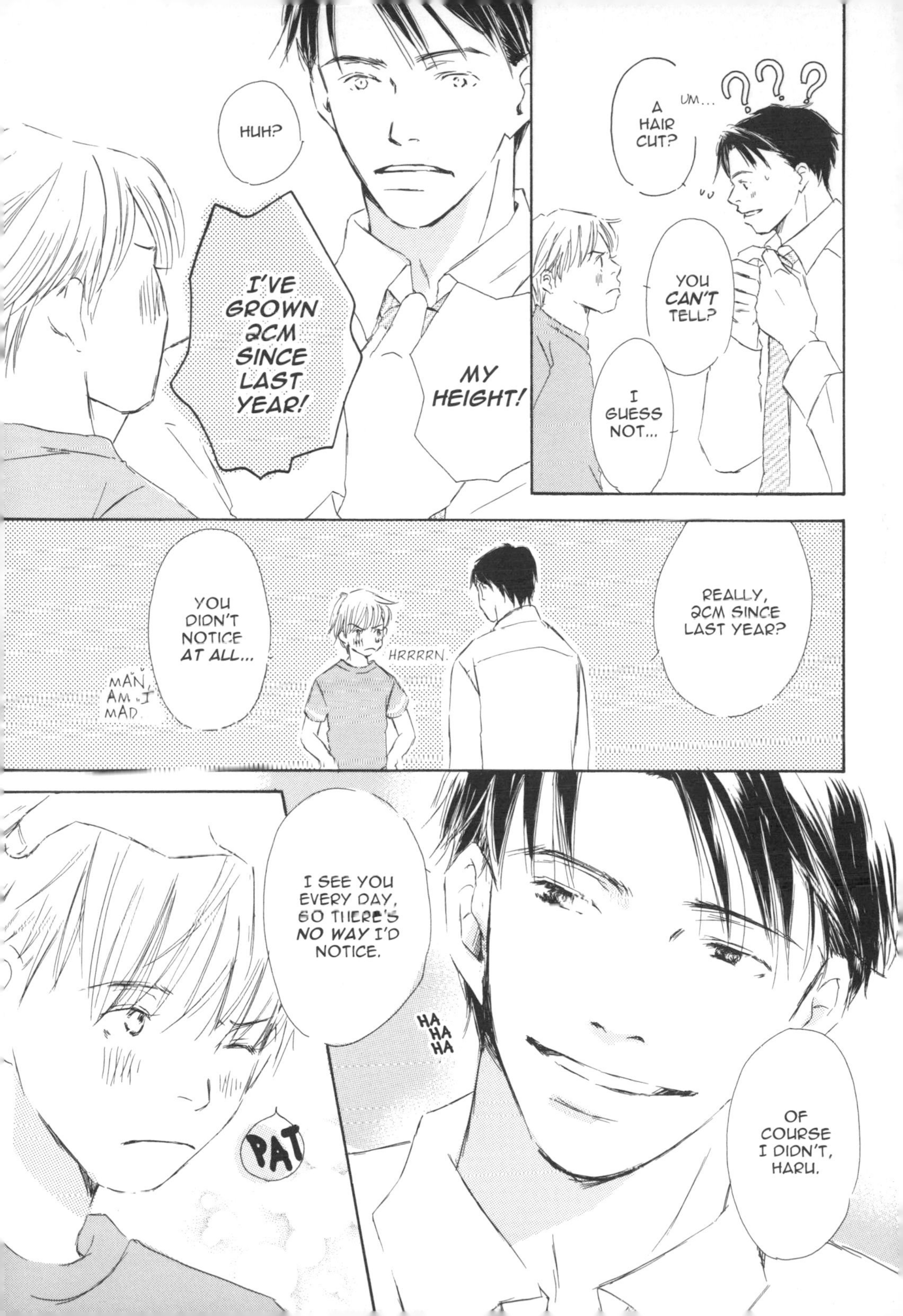

UM...
A HAIR CUT?
YOU CAN'T TELL?
I GUESS NOT...
HUH?
MY HEIGHT!
I'VE GROWN 2CM SINCE LAST YEAR!
REALLY, 2CM SINCE LAST YEAR?
HRRRRN.
YOU DIDN'T NOTICE AT ALL...
MAN, AM I MAD.
I SEE YOU EVERY DAY, SO THERE'S NO WAY I'D NOTICE.
HA HA HA
OF COURSE I DIDN'T, HARU.
PAT

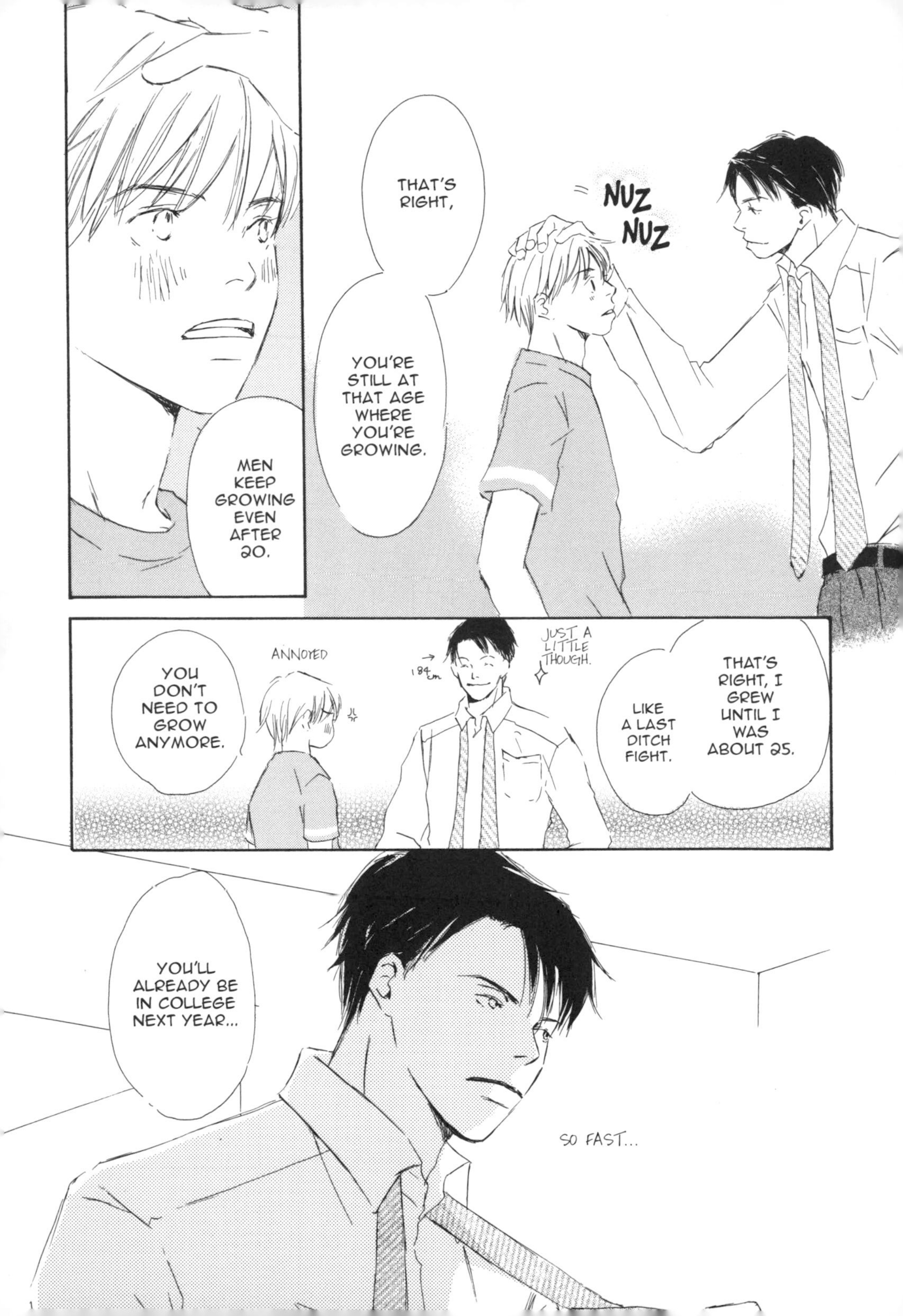
NUZ NUZ
THAT'S RIGHT,
YOU'RE STILL AT THAT AGE WHERE YOU'RE GROWING.
MEN KEEP GROWING EVEN AFTER 20.
THAT'S RIGHT, I GREW UNTIL I WAS ABOUT 25.
LIKE A LAST DITCH FIGHT.
JUST A LITTLE THOUGH.
184 cm
ANNOYED
YOU DON'T NEED TO GROW ANYMORE.
YOU'LL ALREADY BE IN COLLEGE NEXT YEAR...
SO FAST...

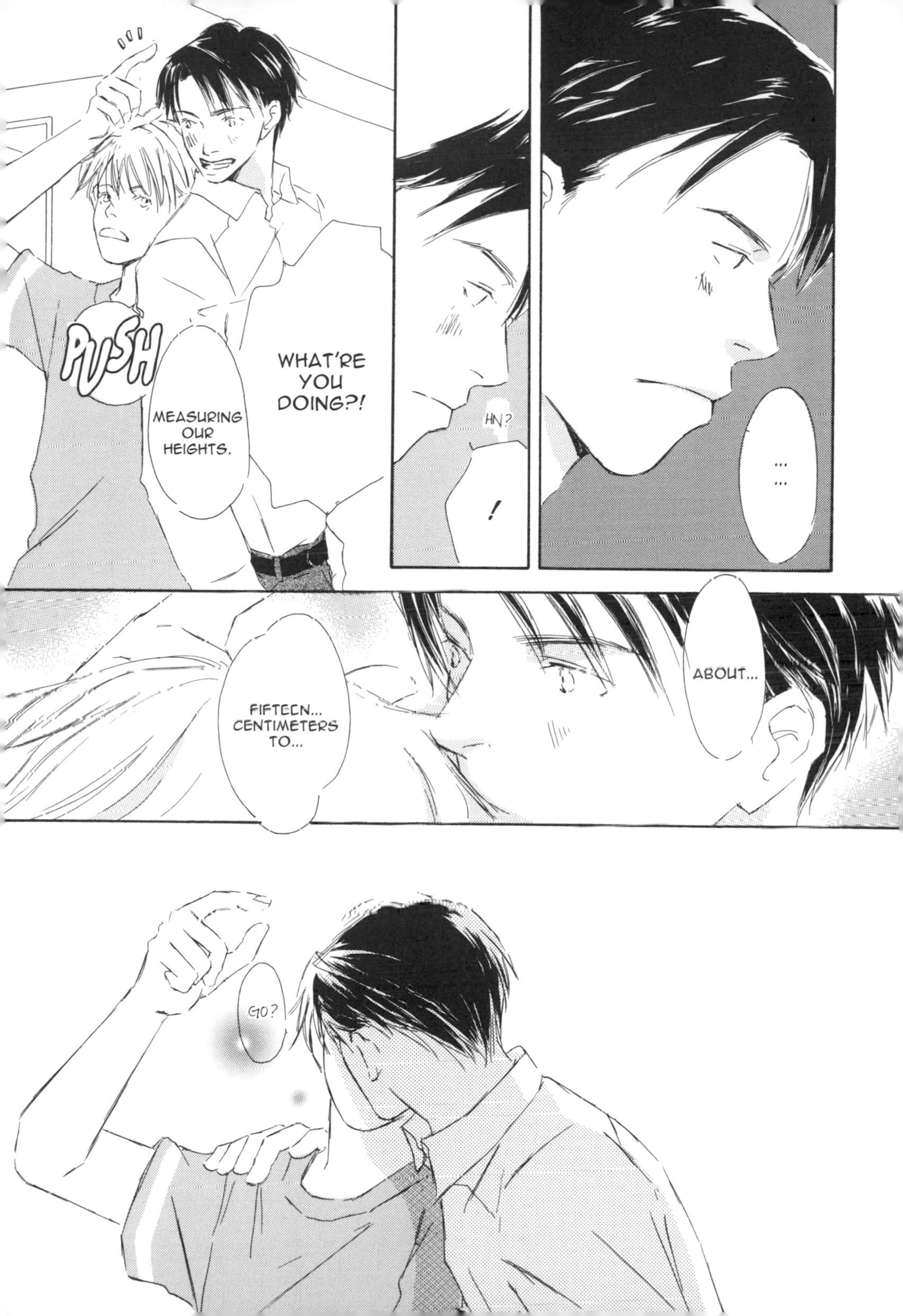
...
...
HN?
!
WHAT'RE YOU DOING?!
PUSH
MEASURING OUR HEIGHTS.
ABOUT...
FIFTEEN... CENTIMETERS TO...
GO?

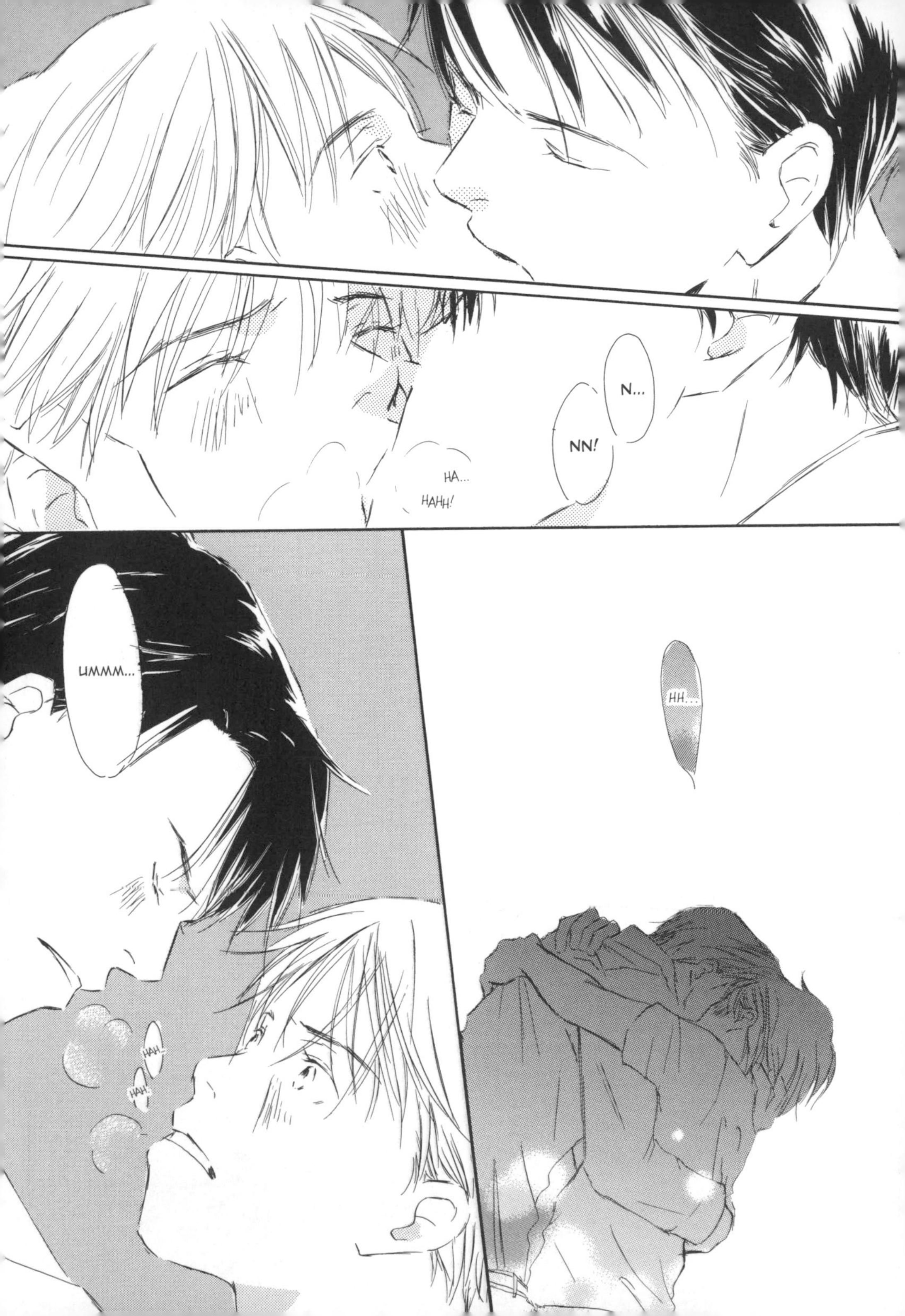
N...
NN!
HA...
HAHH!
HH...
UMMM...
HAH...
HAH.

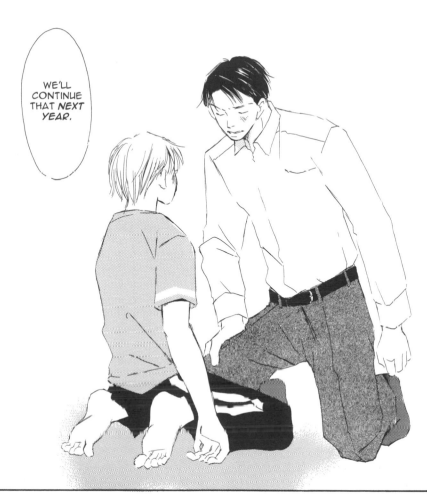

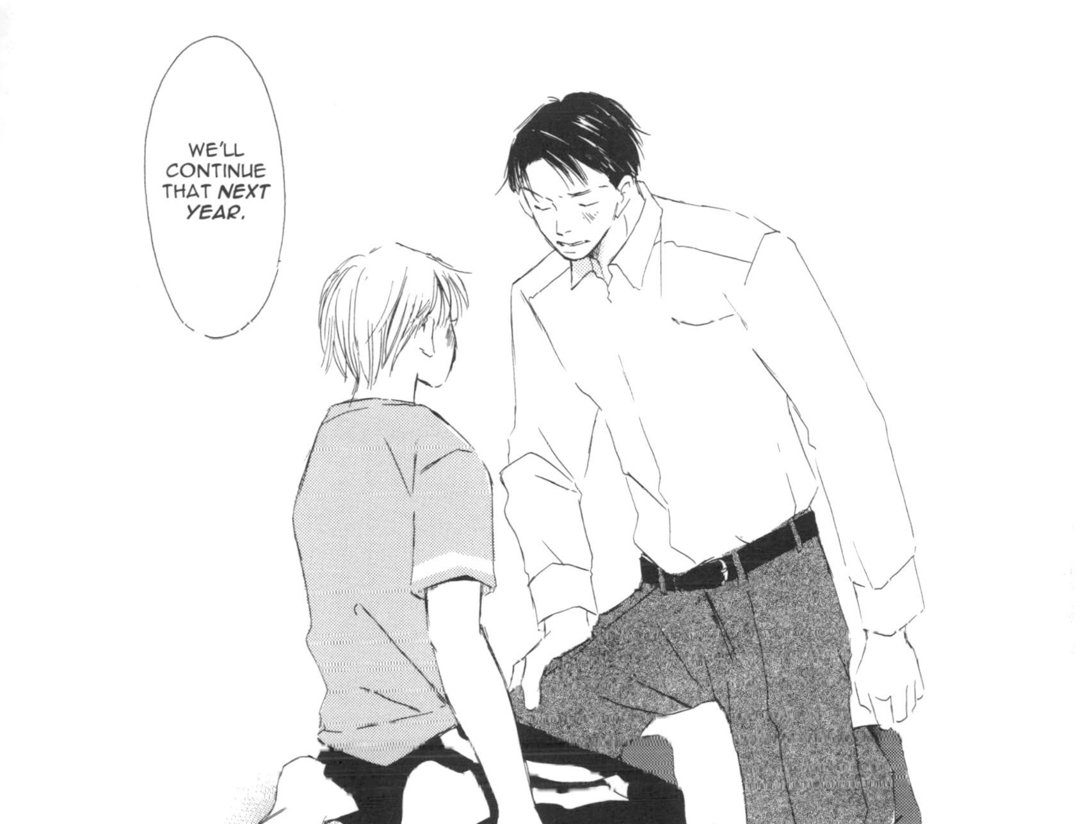
WE'LL CONTINUE THAT ***NEXT YEAR.***

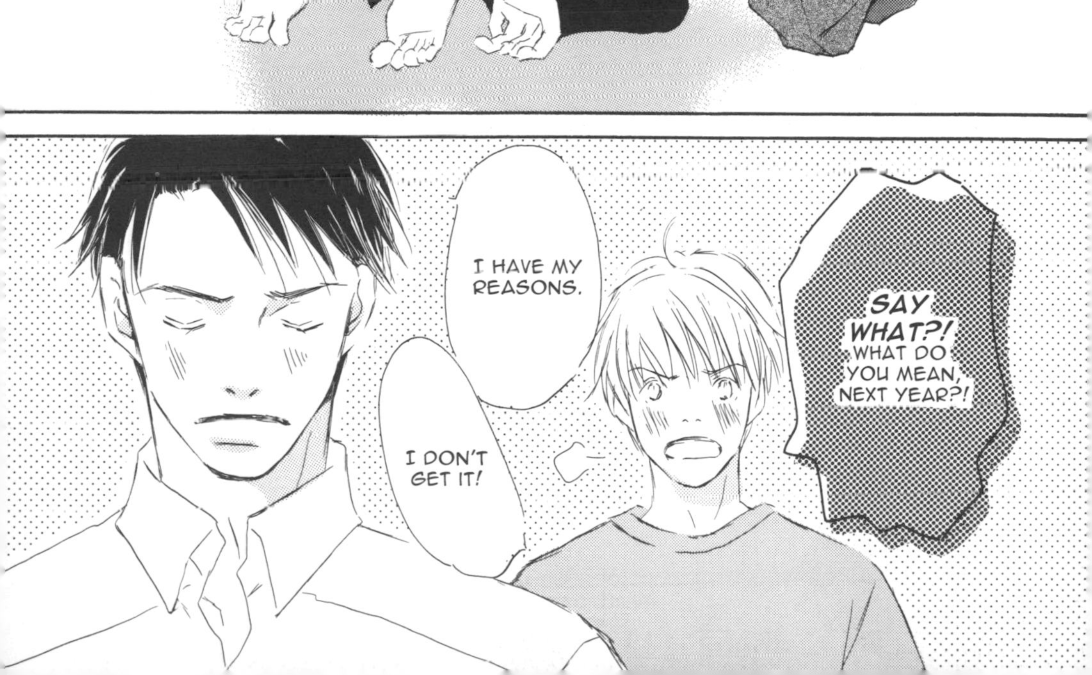
SAY WHAT?! WHAT DO YOU MEAN, NEXT YEAR?!
I HAVE MY REASONS.
I DON'T GET IT!

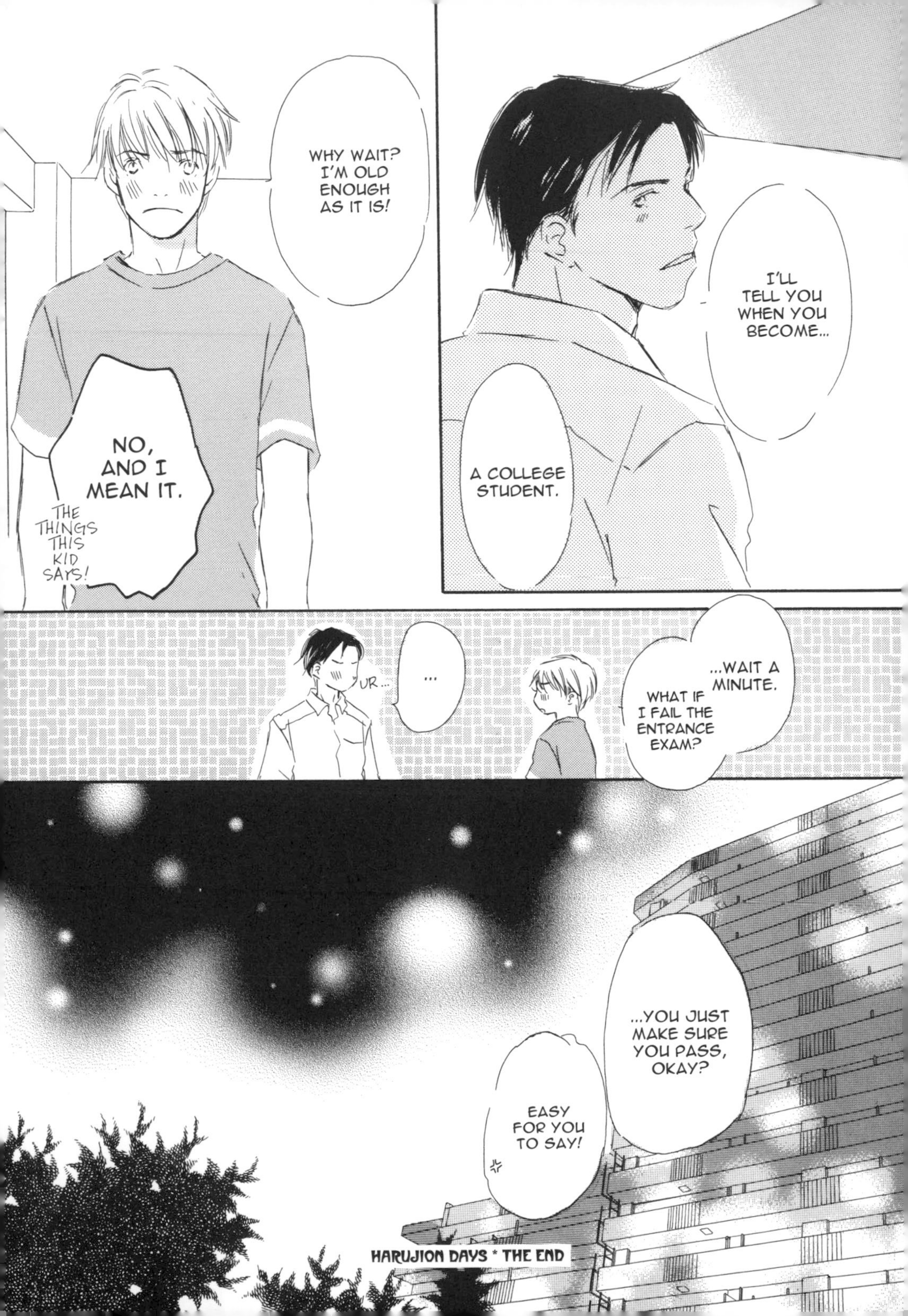
I'LL TELL YOU WHEN YOU BECOME...
A COLLEGE STUDENT.
WHY WAIT? I'M OLD ENOUGH AS IT IS!
NO, AND I MEAN IT.
THE THINGS THIS KID SAYS!
...WAIT A MINUTE.
WHAT IF I FAIL THE ENTRANCE EXAM?
...
UR...
...YOU JUST MAKE SURE YOU PASS, OKAY?
EASY FOR YOU TO SAY!

HARUJION DAYS * THE END

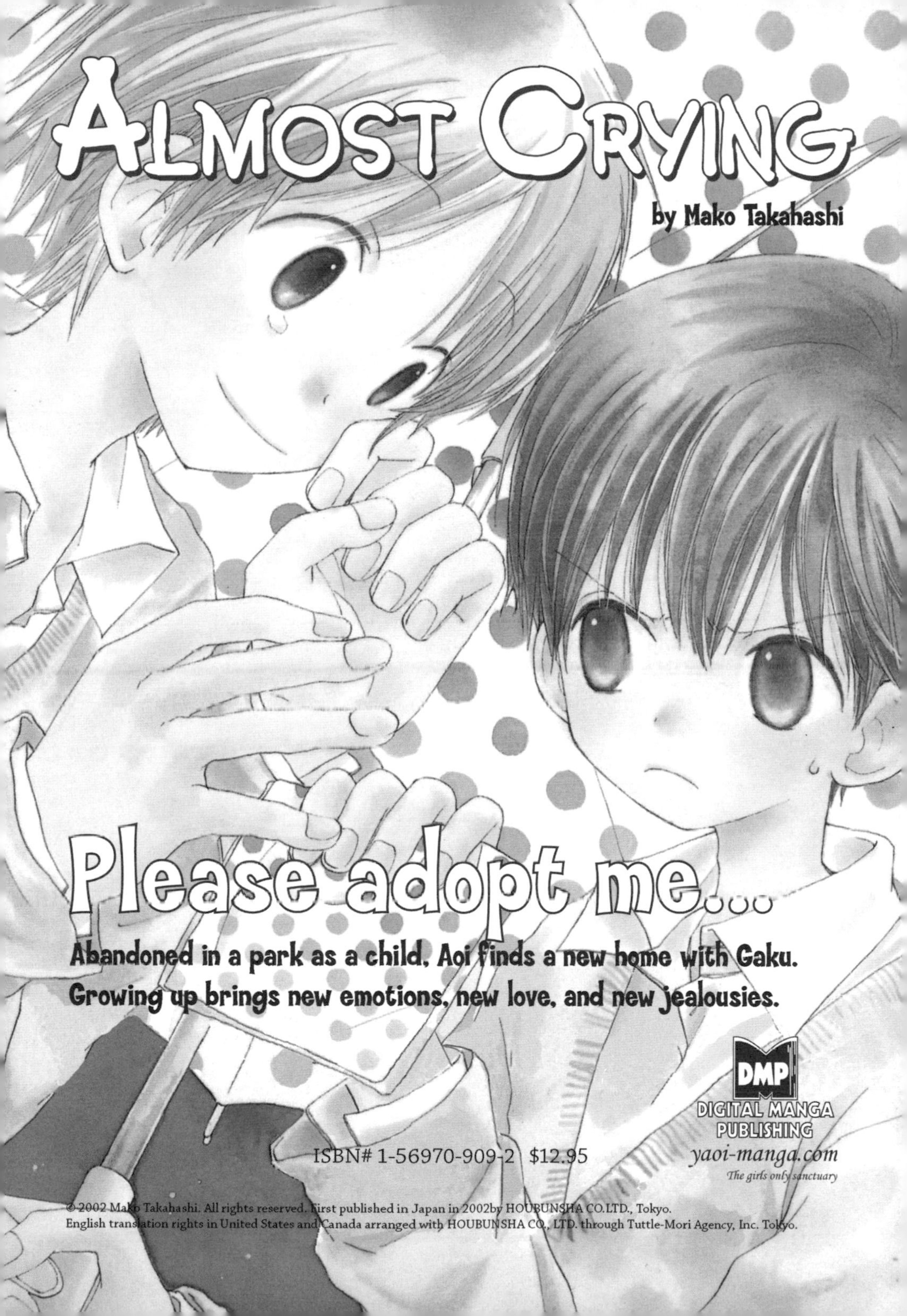
ALMOST CRYING
by Mako Takahashi
Please adopt me...
Abandoned in a park as a child, Aoi finds a new home with Gaku.
Growing up brings new emotions, new love, and new jealousies.
DMP
DIGITAL MANGA PUBLISHING
ISBN# 1-56970-909-2 $12.95
yaoi-manga.com
The girls only sanctuary
© 2002 Mako Takahashi. All rights reserved. First published in Japan in 2002by HOUBUNSHA CO.LTD., Tokyo.
English translation rights in United States and Canada arranged with HOUBUNSHA CO., LTD. through Tuttle-Mori Agency, Inc. Tokyo.

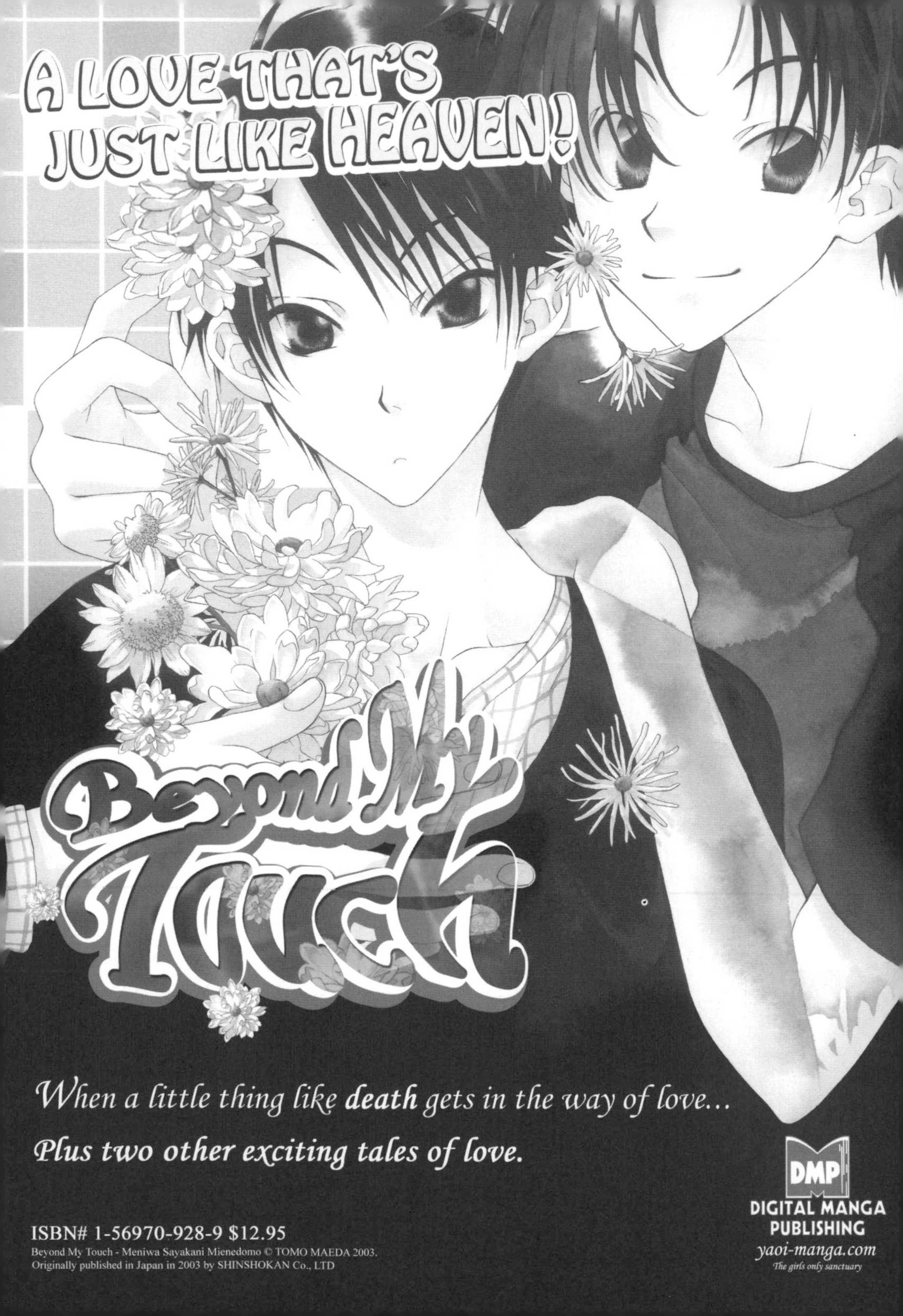
A LOVE THAT'S JUST LIKE HEAVEN!
Beyond My Touch
When a little thing like **death** gets in the way of love...
Plus two other exciting tales of love.
ISBN# 1-56970-928-9 $12.95
Beyond My Touch - Meniwa Sayakani Mienedomo © TOMO MAEDA 2003.
Originally published in Japan in 2003 by SHINSHOKAN Co., LTD
DMP
DIGITAL MANGA PUBLISHING
yaoi-manga.com
The girls only sanctuary

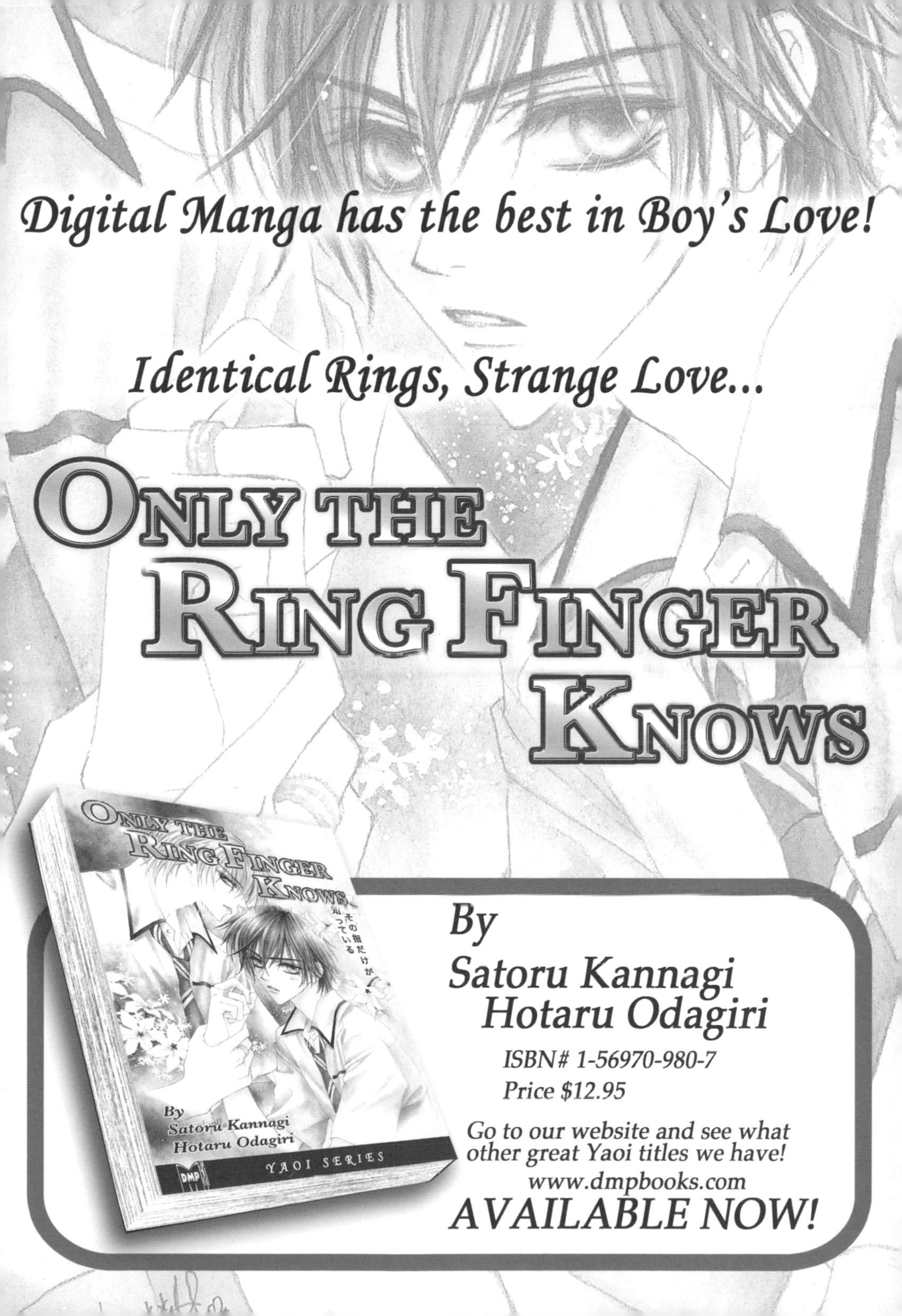
Digital Manga has the best in Boy's Love!
Identical Rings, Strange Love...
ONLY THE RING FINGER KNOWS
ONLY THE RING FINGER KNOWS
その指だけが知っている
By
Satoru Kannagi
Hotaru Odagiri
DMP
YAOI SERIES
By
Satoru Kannagi
Hotaru Odagiri
ISBN# 1-56970-980-7
Price $12.95
Go to our website and see what other great Yaoi titles we have!
www.dmpbooks.com
AVAILABLE NOW!

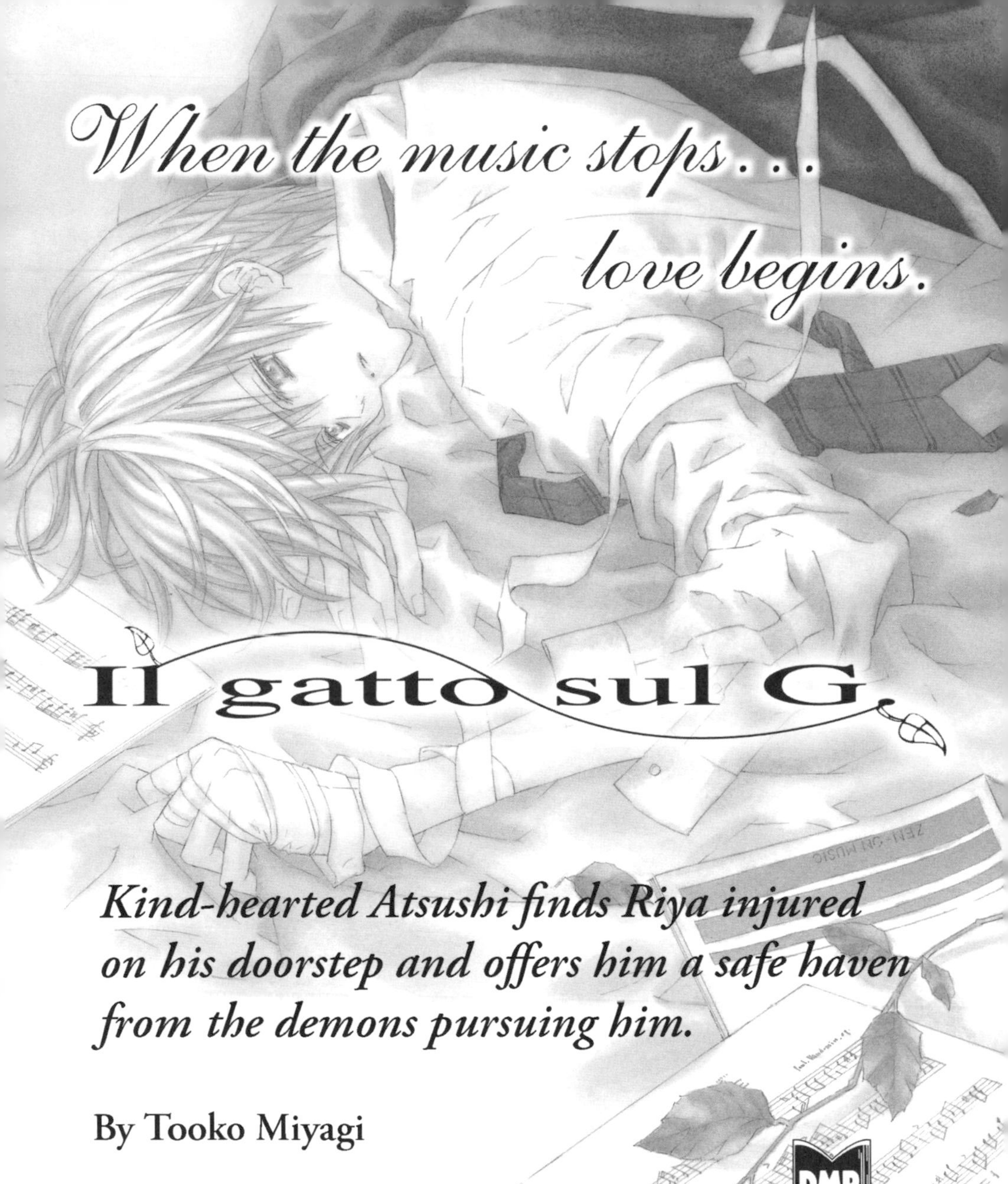
When the music stops . . .
. . . love begins.
Il gatto sul G
ZEN-ON MUSIC
Kind-hearted Atsushi finds Riya injured on his doorstep and offers him a safe haven from the demons pursuing him.
DMP
DIGITAL MANGA PUBLISHING

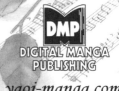

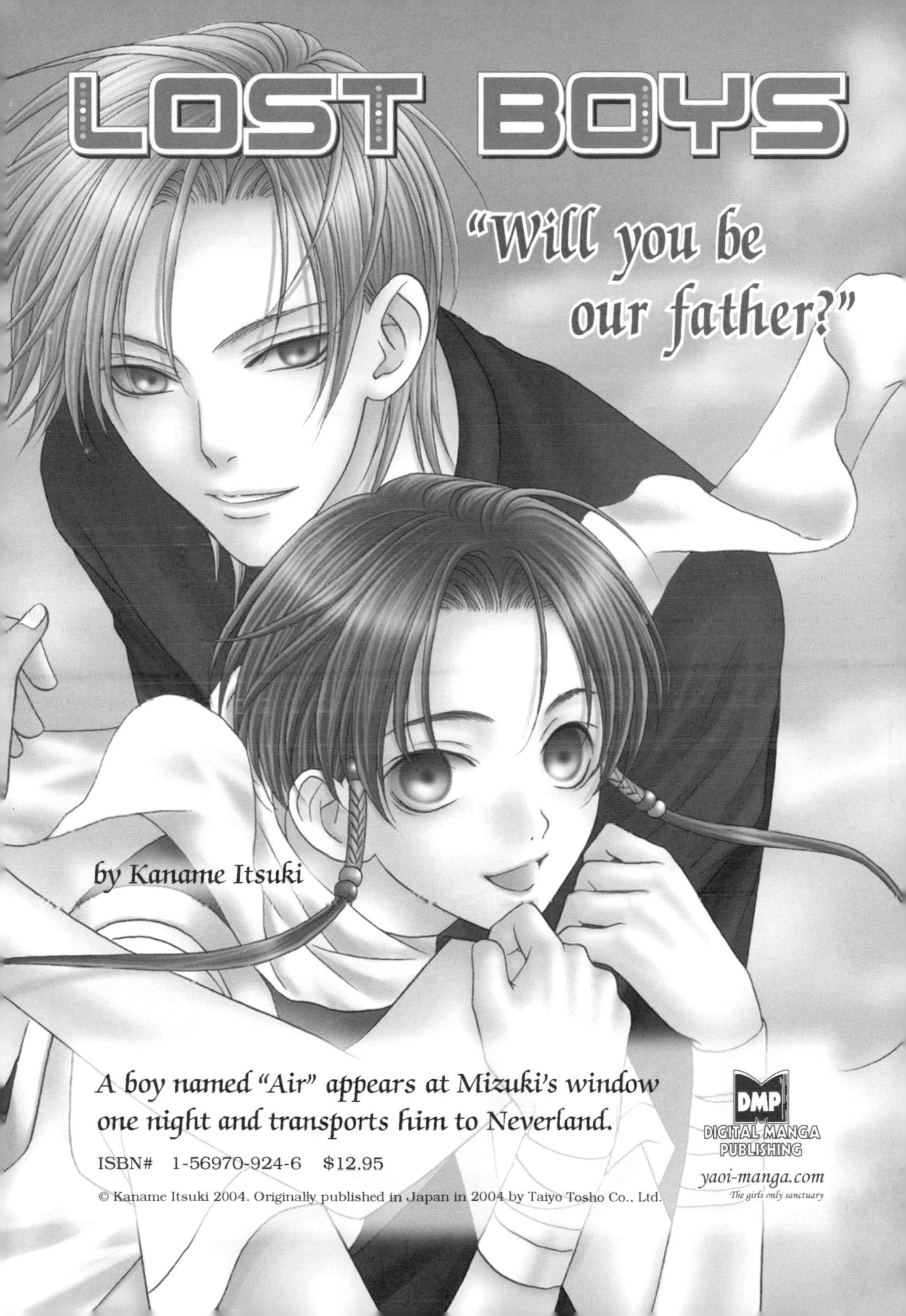
LOST BOYS
"Will you be our father?"
by Kaname Itsuki
A boy named "Air" appears at Mizuki's window one night and transports him to Neverland.
ISBN# 1-56970-924-6 $12.95
© Kaname Itsuki 2004. Originally published in Japan in 2004 by Taiyo Tosho Co., Ltd.
DMP
DIGITAL MANGA PUBLISHING
yaoi-manga.com
The girls only sanctuary

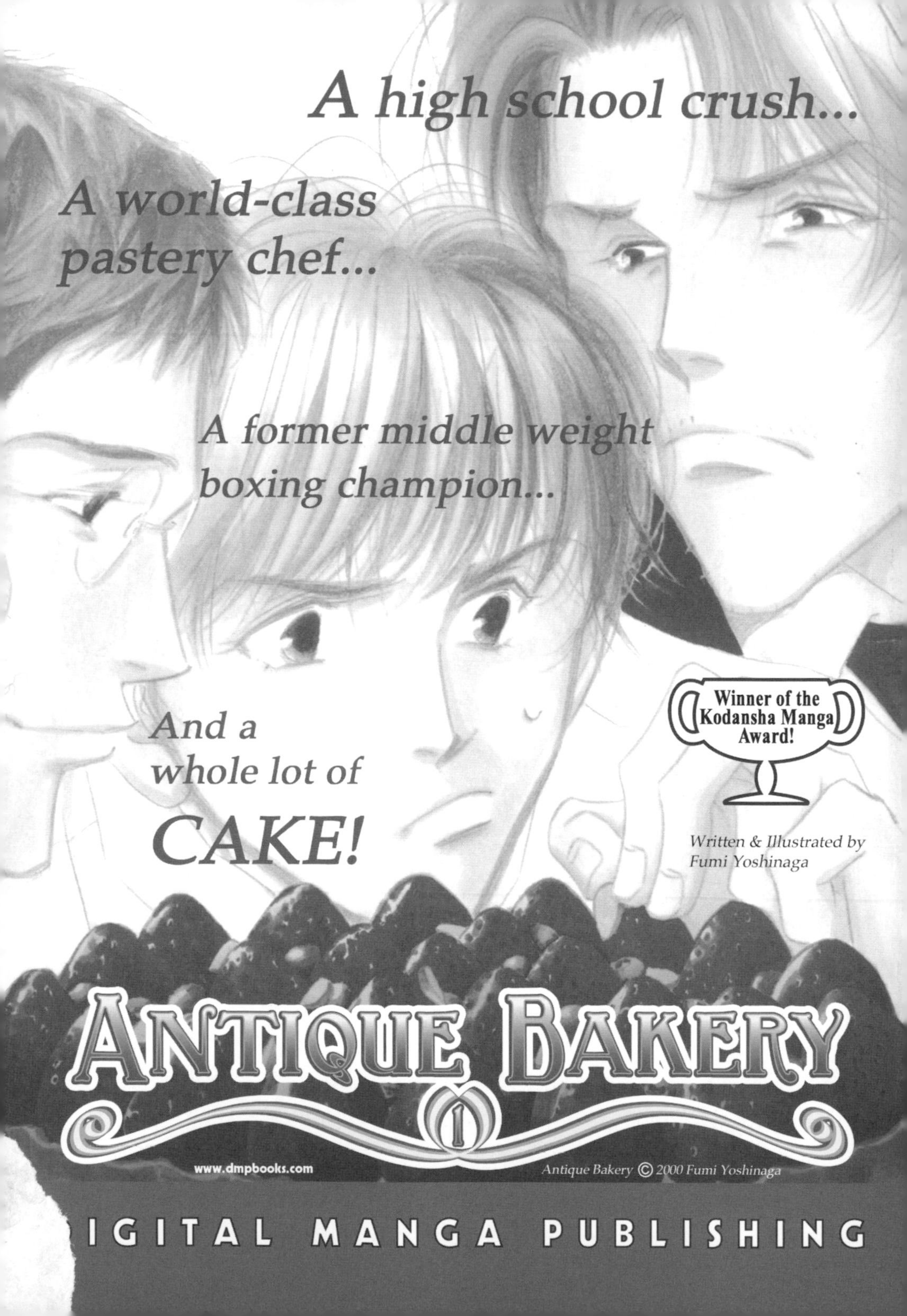
A high school crush...
A world-class pastery chef...
A former middle weight boxing champion...
And a whole lot of CAKE!
Winner of the Kodansha Manga Award!
Written & Illustrated by Fumi Yoshinaga
ANTIQUE BAKERY
1
www.dmpbooks.com
Antique Bakery © 2000 Fumi Yoshinaga
IGITAL MANGA PUBLISHING